HARVARD HISTORICAL STUDIES 195

Published under the auspices of the Department of History

From the income of the
Paul Revere Frothingham Bequest
Robert Louis Stroock Fund
Henry Warren Torrey Fund

THE DISCOVERY OF OTTOMAN GREECE

Knowledge, Encounter, and Belief
in the Mediterranean World of Martin Crusius

Richard Calis

HARVARD UNIVERSITY PRESS
CAMBRIDGE, MASSACHUSETTS
LONDON, ENGLAND
2025

Copyright © 2025 by the President and Fellows of Harvard College

All rights reserved

Printed in the United States of America

First printing

LIBRARY OF CONGRESS CATALOGING-IN-PUBLICATION DATA

Names: Calis, Richard, author.
Title: The discovery of Ottoman Greece : knowledge, encounter, and belief in the Mediterranean world of Martin Crusius / Richard Calis.
Other titles: Harvard historical studies ; v. 195.
Description: First. | Cambridge, Massachusetts ; London, England : Harvard University Press, 2025. | Series: Harvard historical studies ; 195 | Includes bibliographical references and index.
Identifiers: LCCN 2024010627 | ISBN 9780674292734 (cloth)
Subjects: LCSH: Crusius, Martin, 1526–1607. | Orthodoxos Ekklēsia tēs Hellados—History—16th century. | Lutheran Church—Relations—Orthodoxos Ekklēsia tēs Hellados. | Ethnology—Greece—History—16th century. | Europeans—Attitudes—History. | Greeks—Public opinion—History. | Greece—Historiography. | Greece—History—1453-1821.
Classification: LCC DF755 .C35 2025 | DDC 909/.048—dc23/eng/20240405
LC record available at https://lccn.loc.gov/2024010627

For Aniek

Contents

	Introduction	1
1	Christian Purity	22
2	A Lutheran Philhellene	44
3	Wandering Greeks	76
4	Household Conversations	106
5	Communities of Experts	141
6	Travel in the Mind's Eye	177
7	Visions of Ottoman Greece	201
	Conclusion	231
	ABBREVIATIONS	245
	NOTES	247
	ACKNOWLEDGMENTS	291
	INDEX	295

THE DISCOVERY OF OTTOMAN GREECE

INTRODUCTION

Tübingen, a small university town just south of Stuttgart, in the duchy of Württemberg, in the southwestern corner of the Holy Roman Empire, played host to one of the sixteenth century's most unlikely journeys of discovery. In this era of prolonged religious turmoil, dramatic globalization, and all the upheaval and uncertainty that these events caused, a now unknown professor of Greek by the name of Martin Crusius (1526–1607) compiled the period's richest record of Greek life under Ottoman rule.

From the comfort of his scholarly home, and without ever traveling, this deeply pious Lutheran dedicated his life to finding out everything there was to find out about the Greeks. The first Western scholar since antiquity to call himself a philhellene, Crusius collected numerous books of Ottoman and Greek history and enriched their margins with layers of penetrating commentary. He amassed one of the largest collections of vernacular Greek imprints north of the Alps through Lutheran contacts and Greek connections in different parts of the Mediterranean. Together with his students and lodgers, he made exact copies of the Greek manuscripts that passed through his hands and searched their pages and bindings for clues to reconstruct their provenance and the original context in which they had been used. On behalf of a group of Lutherans, he drew none other than the Greek Orthodox patriarch himself into a lengthy correspondence about Christian doctrine. And over the course of forty years, Crusius welcomed into his Tübingen home dozens of Greek Orthodox Christians, who traveled through European Christendom in search of alms to ransom captured family members. He systematically interviewed them about their culture, language, and religion. The evidence he thereby accumulated yielded one of the period's finest portraits of the Ottoman Greek world, full of color and perspective, rich in details and experiences. It was a body of knowledge that, although now largely forgotten, was unparalleled in his day and would remain so for centuries to come; Edward Gibbon cited Crusius's seminal publication on the Ottoman Greeks, the *Turcograecia,* in his own great historical works.

This book tells the story of this quixotic sixteenth-century Lutheran professor and his remarkable investigation into Ottoman Greek life. Through an extraordinary well-preserved set of sources—Crusius's nine-volume diary and hundreds of items from his personal library—I reconstruct the confluence of circumstances that made his learned endeavor possible. What motivations shaped his inquiry? What questions drove his actions and what stood in their way? Who were his informants? How did he collect and assess the evidence he collected? And how did he ultimately present his findings in his publications? The answers to these questions about Crusius and his work also shed light more broadly on how early modern Europeans studied cultures and religions that were not their own. This book, in other words, is a contextualized study focused on a series of episodes in what we could call the social and cultural life of knowledge. Yet it zooms out as much as it zooms in: Crusius offers us a unique case for understanding how three early modern phenomena now often studied separately—the Lutheran Reformation and its global dimensions, cultural and religious difference in the Mediterranean, and the burgeoning of European ethnography, spurred by new forms of encounter—were once a single arena of experience and investigation, and one that it behooves contemporary historians to observe once again through a single lens.

I came to Crusius as a historian with a background in classics, expecting to write about his teaching of Greek and his near-proverbial philhellenism. But, as I worked my way through his immense archive in Tübingen, I found an altogether different story that took me in all sorts of unexpected directions. My own journey of discovery revealed to me a world, now largely lost from view, in which religion furthered scholarship, and unknown forms of Mediterranean mobility turned a deeply gendered professorial home into a site of transnational and cross-cultural encounter, bookish, social, and otherwise. From Crusius's learned Tübingen household, once shown in close-up, arose deep questions about what it meant to be scholar and husband, teacher and author, Lutheran and Christian; what it meant to belong to a family, a learned society, and a religious community; what it meant to live through a period of intense religious reform and dramatic globalization. Crusius's archive made visible to me interactions and exchanges that early modern historians have tended to associate more exclusively with the Mediterranean and the long history of empire but that in this case took place under unusual circumstances in a corner of the Holy Roman Empire. From these sources emerged not the familiar world of Renaissance humanism and classical philology but one of encounter and religious exchange, scholarship and mobility, family and learned sociability. A story presented itself that revealed the imbrication of orientalism and philhellenism in sixteenth-century Europe, and one that showed the deep sense of decline that shaped European engagement with postclassical Greece. Crusius's complex life, I gradually discovered, defies historiographical patterns and types at the ready, and resists containment within the narrow bounds of our current disciplinary subfields.

The goal of this book, then, is not solely or even principally a detailed account of Crusius as a scholar. It rather paints a portrait of a person, a place, and a period—one that allows us to forge new connections across geographies and historiographies and see some of the period's greatest transformations anew. Crusius's story is one that requires us to think both globally and locally and, indeed, encourages us to interrogate the very parameters of these divergent scales of analysis. To understand what the Mediterranean had to do with Tübingen, why Greek Orthodox Christianity mattered to the history of Lutheranism, and how Crusius came to study Ottoman Greek culture, we must examine how historical actors like him experienced these relationships. Focusing our observations on the life and household of this early modern professor thus significantly widens our view.

A LUTHERAN PROFESSOR OF GREEK

Who was Crusius? Nothing in his early life suggested he would be anything more than a humble Lutheran preacher, let alone an eminent professor of Greek and celebrated expert on Ottoman Greek affairs. Born in 1526 in Grebern near Bamberg, in present-day Bavaria, to Maria Magdalena Trummer and Martin Kraus, Crusius was of humble origins.[1] His father was from a family of tailors and beer brewers while his mother's family consisted of tradesmen and artisans, and, as far as Crusius could trace back his own maternal family line, none of them had ever obtained a university degree.[2] He came of age in a divided world: his father, a minister who had embraced Lutheranism after hearing Luther speak in Wittenberg, was compelled to relocate his family often during the unsettling early decades of the Reformation. The family eventually set up home in Württemberg, after Duke Ulrich had officially introduced the evangelical movement there.

There Crusius's fortunes took a turn: several scholarships enabled him to enroll at the local grammar school in Ulm, a free imperial city, and later at the famous Protestant gymnasium of Johannes Sturm in Strasbourg, where he received a cutting-edge humanist education and excelled in the study of Greek. His parents, though, suffered severely at the hands of Catholic Spanish soldiers and nearly lost their lives in the Schmalkaldic War (1546–1547), which erupted shortly after Crusius had moved to Strasbourg. Not long thereafter, unwilling to accept the 1548 Augsburg Interim and unable to be openly Lutheran, his parents left for Nuremberg while Crusius finished his education.

No longer an adolescent, and eager to put his newfound learning to good use, Crusius began to make a career for himself as a pedagogue. He initially worked as a private tutor and teacher at Sturm's gymnasium and from 1554 onward was employed in Memmingen, where he had accepted the vacant position of rector at the local Latin school, partially to provide for his mother who had recently been widowed.[3] The first fruits of his scholarly labor, a set of Latin and Greek grammars that would be adopted by schools all over Württemberg, brought him great renown and eventually, in 1559, a position at the University of Tübingen. He was hired to teach Cicero's orations and Melanchthon's rhetoric but quickly became responsible for Greek classes as well.[4] He would stay in Tübingen for the rest of his life.

This corner of the Holy Roman Empire offered pious young Lutherans like Crusius—who had no university degree but eagerly sought for a way to place his scholarship in the service of scripture—just the right kind of ecosystem to organize a life of the mind. Tübingen's university, founded in 1477, had attracted some of the most prominent scholars of previous generations, including Philip Melanchthon and his great-uncle Johannes Reuchlin, the celebrated specialist in Greek and Hebrew, whose impassioned defense of the study of the latter language had caused quite the stir in the early sixteenth century. By the second half of the century, the *Tübinger Stift*—the renowned seminary for the education of Lutheran pastors, whose illustrious alumni would include Kepler, Hölderlin, and Hegel—and the university's recently reformed theology faculty had turned Tübingen into a Lutheran stronghold. Few places in the Holy Roman Empire, with perhaps the exception of Wittenberg, could compete with Tübingen for the title of true heir to Luther's legacy. Crusius participated fully in Tübingen's intellectual and religious life, attending sermons in the local Collegiate Church, the so-called *Stiftskirche,* and serving eight times as dean of the faculty and more often in other administrative positions. He initially combined his professorship in the Faculty of Arts with the position of head of the Collegium Illustre. This academy, founded in 1559 by Duke Christoph of Württemberg as an extension of the extensive educational and religious reforms of his father, prepared young men, who boarded with the head of the academy and received a scholarship, for state service. Becoming the academy's first head allowed Crusius—who married three times and had fifteen children—to create the kind of scholarly and pious household that professors of the period increasingly often chose to shape their public persona and improve their social standing.

Greece was Crusius's lifelong obsession. He taught Greek grammar and poetry for nearly fifty years and with tremendous success: his explications of Homer were so popular that the university had to break down a wall of the lecture room to accommodate all enrolled students. Crusius also innovated: by his own account, he was the first to teach the Greek vernacular in the Latin West. His library, of which nearly seven hundred items have survived, contained texts from all periods in Greek history: from ancient tragedies to Byzantine histories, from the writings of the Greek Church Fathers to medieval saints' lives. Every bit of news about the Eastern Mediterranean that reached Tübingen was recorded in his diary, as were the receipts of objects from those regions, including coins, paintings, and other gifts. Crusius exchanged dozens of letters with high-ranking Greek Orthodox ecclesiastics living in Venice and Istanbul. And he cherished these interactions with an affection that was all his own: his daughter Theodora was named after one of the Greeks with whom Crusius corresponded at length, and he once wrote that he "could rightly be said to be drunk with love for Greek affairs."[5]

Crusius's inquiry was calibrated by what was considered at the time to be one of the most dramatic events in world history: the 1453 Fall of Constantinople, which he commemorated despite being unsure in which year it had occurred, and the subsequent arrival of the Ottomans on the political scene.[6] By the late sixteenth century, the Ottomans' rapid advancements into Hungary and Austria had provoked a strong sense of anxiety throughout Western Christendom, and especially in Italy and the Germanic lands of the Holy Roman Empire. In sermons, broadsheets, single-leaf pamphlets, and numerous other treatises concerning the "Turkish menace" (*Türkengefahr*), early modern authors reported on the perceived threat that the Ottomans posed to the Christian way of life. This trope led to the construction of a powerful discourse of alterity that cast the Ottomans as a natural enemy to the Christian world—and one that had lasting consequences: to this very day the idea of a so-called Clash of Civilizations continues to engage the popular imagination.[7] It was in this world that Crusius looked to document what had remained of Greek civilization.

Yet Crusius never ventured to travel to the place he so zealously studied. Existential fears about the Ottomans may have deterred him. But the more mundane reality was that his teaching load at the university and his responsibilities as the head of a learned household prevented him from leaving Tübingen to set eyes on his beloved Greece. His philhellenism was in that sense markedly different from those nineteenth-century authors such as Lord Byron, who made travel and later even participation in the Greek War of Independence so central to their Romantic Hellenism. And yet those well-studied luminaries, as we shall see, shared with their forgotten ancestor a distinct way of envisioning Greece as a projection of their own sentiments and beliefs.

Crusius was a prolific writer, who believed his scholarship to be God's work but who was also, like many aspiring authors of the period, unrealistic about the prospective sales of his books. His seminal publication on the Ottoman Greek world, the *Turcograecia*, appeared in Basel in 1584 and was read by such eminent scholars as Joseph Justus Scaliger and later Edward Gibbon for the unique information it contained about this ill-documented period in Greek history. But it sold poorly. It was followed in 1585 by the *Germanograecia*, a sample of the fruits that Greek studies, according to Crusius, had borne in Germany. In specialist circles, and among regional historians in particular, Crusius is also known today for the *Annales Suevici* (1595–1596), a massive history of Swabia, in three parts, that continues to be one of the main sources for the sixteenth-century history of this region, but for which Crusius struggled to find a printer. He considered the sermons he collected in the *Corona Anni* (1602–1603) his main contribution to the world of print, but it is unclear if they ever reached their intended audience (Greek Orthodox Christians living in the Mediterranean). He dedicated many years of his life to writing a commentary on the entirety of Homer, whom he truly believed he had explicated as no other before him had done. Yet only his notes to the first two books of the *Iliad* made it into print, and posthumously; about two-thirds of the print run remained unsold. The grammar books he wrote for pupils in the 1550s did become a commercial success, and they brought him his Tübingen job. As he felt death approaching, he continued to pray that his latest works would find a readership: "Lord, let me live long enough," he sighted, "so that I can complete" this work of mine "which I want to begin in your name. You can take me away peacefully after that."[8]

Crusius died in 1607. His grave in Tübingen's *Stiftskirche* is marked by the epitaph that he composed for himself and which serves to this very day as a testament to his love of Greece and his Lutheran sympathies: "Here I lie, Martin Crusius, who taught Greek in Tübingen and believed only in you, Christ." This is exactly how Crusius came to be remembered by his colleagues and contemporaries: the funeral oration that Veit Müller delivered, and that was subsequently published by Tübingen's printer Georg Gruppenbach, reproduced the epitaph and portrayed Crusius as a paragon of Greek learning and as a staunch defender of the Lutheran faith.[9]

Crusius enjoys great renown in specialist circles. The success of his Greek teaching, his self-professed philhellenism, and the correspondence he and other Lutherans from Tübingen maintained with the Greek Orthodox patriarch have attracted the attention of Byzantinists, theologians, and historians working on intellectual life in early modern Germany.[10] His enormous diary—parts of which were meticulously edited and published in four volumes in the early twentieth century—has been often hailed as a historical treasure trove.[11] Yet surprisingly for someone with such a reputation, no original biography has been written about him since Müller's oration. No in-depth studies exist that take Crusius and his scholarship as their subject. The following seven chapters, then, situate Crusius and his scholarship in the context of the larger transformations that defined Europe in this period and in the early modern intellectual culture to which he belonged.

Each chapter seeks to illuminate one aspect of Crusius's "discovery" of the Ottoman Greek world. All speak to multiple historiographies that sometimes overlap, but that have more often developed in isolation. In this sense, the book extends conversations in three areas of early modern history—all of which, once examined through the lens of Crusius's Tübingen, prove far more interwoven than we have so far realized.

Mediterranean History from Afar

In the early modern period, Europeans encountered cultural and religious difference on an unprecedented scale and with far-reaching consequences. Travelers roamed the world, often as part of Europe's colonial expansion, and described the people that they encountered on their journeys, ranking civilizations and peoples in long-lasting hierarchies of civility and savagery, the racial legacies of which continue to haunt society today. Back in Europe these complex accounts circulated more widely than ever before both through print and via different forms of scribal publication. Knowledge of different Islamic dynasties invited comparisons and inspired inquiries into the Islamic world, aided in no small part by the ever-expanding number of Arabic and other "oriental" manuscripts in libraries all over Europe. Christian scholars across the confessional divide studied Judaism and a great number of Hebrew documents—from rabbinic commentaries to the Babylonian Talmud—in greater depth than ever before, and at times by talking or claiming to talk to Jewish informants. Documentary records from places as far away from Europe—both in reality and in the early modern mind—as China and the Americas unleashed epistemic crises and led to the erosion and eventual breakdown of old structures of knowledge and the creation of new ones, even as scholars strenuously sought to uphold revealed religion.

The early modern Mediterranean has long been seen as a fertile site for such cross-cultural inquiry. Home to the great ancient empires—from the Assyrians to the Romans—and the cradle of the three Abrahamic religions, the Middle Sea has attracted much critical attention from scholars interested in the long history of encounter and exchange. Variously studied as a contact zone, a shared world, a site of hybridity, and a paradigm of connectivity and the circulation of peoples, ideas, and commodities, the early modern Mediterranean has reemerged in recent years as a boundless space in which individuals of various cultural, ethnic, linguistic, and religious backgrounds interacted.[12]

Ottoman Greece has somewhat surprisingly not figured prominently in this new literature as a site of cultural contact. Specialists have recognized how mobility, fluidity, and cultural and religious diversity marked Greek life under Ottoman rule. Yet the Greek element in Ottoman-European encounters has not frequently been the center of attention.[13] This omission has partly been the result of disciplinary partitions: modern scholarship on early modern orientalists has focused attention on European scholars' engagement with Arabic, Persian, and Turkish materials and the different peoples from the Islamic world. It has left humanist interests in Greek—a language frequently studied by early modern orientalists to complement their inquiries into the Muslim world—to historians of Renaissance intellectual culture. Historians of humanism, in turn, have rarely focused their attention on the world of Greek learning in the Ottoman Empire. Ottomanists, for their part, and especially those working on the Ottoman state and on government sources in archives in Istanbul, have not often engaged with the specialist literature on the Ottoman Greek world produced by Greek scholars.

Yet this oversight has far deeper roots: already in the early modern period, Greeks proved difficult to categorize. European but part of the Ottoman Empire, Christian but belonging to an Eastern Christian tradition, oriental in the eyes of their Catholic and Protestant brothers but not quite as oriental as Muslims were, revered for centuries for their ancient history but by the sixteenth century a people that did not have a state or home of their own, the Greeks were the quintessential insider-outsider in the imagination of the rest of the contemporary Christian world. Interestingly, then, and somewhat paradoxically, the early modern Greek world has been overlooked, *because* it inhabited precisely the kind of liminal "in-between" position that recent work in the field of Mediterranean studies has recovered to such great effect.

Tracing the particulars of Crusius's inquiry enables us to explain how Greece came to occupy this liminal place in the Western imagination. His records reveal how his Greek informants—consisting of an eclectic group of mobile Greeks as well as elite Greek Orthodox clerics—communicated complicated notions of cultural difference that directly influenced the way Lutherans like him thought about the various people living in the Ottoman

Empire: "Greece," Crusius concluded in his *Turcograecia,* had been "turkified," and the Greeks had erred and fallen into superstitious ways. These responses have, at first, the look of stereotypes, based on assumptions rather than evidence. But appearances deceive: such statements should be seen not only as tendentious and partial depictions but also as informed—if by our standards erroneous—interpretations that call for closer analysis. Crusius's sense of cultural and religious superiority was not reflective of a timeless disdain for the "East." It was a misguided but by no means inevitable outcome of his lifelong engagement with that world: in his *Turcograecia,* and indeed throughout his notebooks, Crusius reproduced not only visual and textual evidence regarding the development of the Greek Orthodox Church but also numerous firsthand testimonies about the oppression that Greeks claimed to suffer at the hands of the Ottomans.

Focusing attention on the role of Greek Orthodox Christians in the creation of these tropes shows that they themselves contributed to an East–West binary that does not adequately describe the complexity of their lives. Greeks presented experiences that, although historically real, were also constructed in such a way that they met Crusius's expectations about the cruelty of Greek life under Ottoman rule. In other words: the categories by which some Greeks understood themselves fundamentally framed the ones Crusius used. And such Greek self-understandings would shape how the Ottoman period in Greece was remembered for centuries: the *tourkokratia* was long thought to be a period of suppression and enslavement in which Greeks suffered severely at the hands of the Ottoman Turks. Crusius's engagement with Ottoman Greek life thus affords new insight into a paradox central to much writing about cultural and religious difference: scholars like Crusius may have been biased, but they were certainly not uninformed. The ideas and stereotypes that Westerners used to describe other peoples could be based on the experiences of the peoples they purported to describe.

Crusius's inquiry into the Ottoman Greek world should in that sense not be mistaken for cultural openness, even though he always insisted on his good intentions. The intense observation of a system of beliefs that was all but unknown to Crusius brought him no sense of distance vis-à-vis his own religious sympathies. On the contrary: it only reified confessional boundaries. Carina Johnson has argued that in the second half of the sixteenth century, and in a world riven by confessional division, "adherence to correct religious doctrine became not just the crowning but the pre-eminent and necessary evaluative category of a culture or people." Religious relativism, and "categories of inclusion," she shows, gradually gave way to the formulation of distinct cultural hierarchies, as confessional lines were redrawn and hardened.[14] Crusius's opinion of the Greek world remained in the end ambivalent as well. He expressed his seemingly abiding love for all things Greek on many occasions, only to bemoan Greek Orthodox religious practices and underline the weaknesses and defects of Greek culture on others. But Crusius's penetrating vision of the Ottoman Greek world was not simply clouded by his Lutheran convictions. It was also enriched by them.[15] In the end, his religious sympathies did encourage him to take his inquiry in all kinds of unexpected directions: *because* he believed his beloved Greece was becoming "turkified" and *because* the Greek Orthodox Church had strayed, in his opinion, from the one true path, he felt the need to document that transitional moment in all its facets.

It is through the efforts of a Tübingen scholar, then, whose passions mirror our own fascination with the Mediterranean as a site of encounter and mediation, that we can answer the call of Mediterranean historians to shift emphasis back to this geographical unit "as a template for early modern discourses of cultural difference."[16] His records allow us to open up the field of Mediterranean studies to experiences that may have occurred beyond its shores and coastlines but were nevertheless an inextricable part of it. It is the view from afar, a moment in which the encounter came into the scholarly home, that helps us chart what the French historian Fernand Braudel once considered the "Mediterranean of the historian" and the full diversity of what Peregrine Horden and Nicholas Purcell recently called the Mediterranean's "extended hinterlands."[17] The French philosopher René Descartes, in a swipe against humanist learning, famously declared that one did not need history because one could travel and experience the book of the world. Crusius, in contrast, did not need physical travel, because the tools of humanist historical scholarship facilitated that experience for him.

Ethnography and the History of Cultural Encounter

Crusius was an ethnographer in all but name, and his story belongs to the longer history of early modern European ethnography that historians have so painstakingly put together in the last three decades.[18] Like other ethnographers of the period, Crusius tried to make sense of a culture and religion that were not his own. His work depicted and classified human diversity, offering powerful and enduring representations of Greek life under Ottoman rule that are not so different from other early modern ethnographies. Just as early historians of Amerindian civilizations had recorded the vibrant cultural and religious life that they encountered there—sometimes with amazement, sometimes with a misguided sense of cultural superiority—so Crusius, surprised about the survival of the Greek Orthodox Church, disappointed about its superstitious ways, and wretched at the devastation of ancient Greek cities, sought to assemble a full profile of Ottoman Greek society. Just as Jesuit missionaries studied local Chinese traditions in support of a proselytizing agenda, so the Lutheran in Crusius dreamed that his scholarship would someday bring Greek Orthodox Christians into the Lutheran fold. And like other places across the globe, the Ottoman Greek world was believed to be uncharted—but very promising—territory.

Crusius's "Mediterranean" encounters, then, mirrored those between Europeans and peoples living in other parts of the early modern globe. There were differences, to be sure, but they should be seen in terms of scale and not in kind. His interactions with Greek Orthodox Christians and with Greek Orthodox documents took place on the tiny stage of his Tübingen home. They occurred not in one singular, dramatic moment—this was not your typical "first encounter"—but over a prolonged period. Of all the ethnographies that have survived from this period, his was certainly not the most dramatic. Others, who did travel, experienced cultural difference and the shock of "discovery" in a more immediate way. But unlike these encounters and the scholarship they generated, in Crusius's case many of the raw materials in his workshop survive to illuminate the origins of his finished books. His records offer a glimpse behind the curtain that few of those of his contemporaries can. Not only did he obsessively document the particulars of his scholarly project, but his inquiry was by comparison also relatively open-ended and indiscriminate: as we will see, he had limited control over the kind of information that his informants brought him, and he therefore treasured and recorded every snippet. It is precisely this unfiltered accumulation of evidence that explains why his manuscripts are so full of material of a variegated nature. Even his *Turcograecia*—for which Crusius *had* filtered his information—is not systematic and often resists neat categorization.

One of the consequences is that Crusius's was not a finished ethnography; his project was always evolving and therefore all the more revealing for historians today. Following Elizabeth Horodowich's suggestion that we "better understand European responses to the first age of globalization if we attempt to understand them in their variety and specificity," I take Crusius's "discovery" of the Ottoman Greek world not as a historical given but as a highly contingent project that emerged from and belonged to a specific scholarly culture and a particular moment in the history of the Reformation.[19] My focus is not only on the results of Crusius's intellectual work but also on the processes through which his ideas took shape, an approach that shifts "emphasis from what is studied to how it is studied."[20] My examination of Crusius at work—writing letters, reading books, copying manuscripts, interviewing informants, and organizing his data in his notebooks and printed works—identifies the tools and methods that early modern scholars deployed when studying other cultures. It demonstrates how early modern ethnography, a quintessentially human pursuit, was one among many period forms of knowledge making in which tropes and techniques from several fields and disciplines came together fruitfully. I do not mean to suggest, however, that Crusius was sui generis in pulling together evidence from various traditions, nor that the specific set of skills he wielded was emblematic of early modern ethnography. Rather, the case of Crusius illustrates how early modern scholars often created their own versions of ethnography—making the practice appear less as a single discipline and more as a clutch of pursuits, a malleable genre appropriated and assembled as scholars saw fit.

Here my examination goes some way toward upending received wisdom in the history of ethnography and encounter. Others who pursued the kind of inquiry that Crusius pursued have frequently been identified as armchair travelers—an amorphous category usually deployed to dismiss those scholars who allegedly spun fictitious stories about human diversity from the comfort of their study and thus without the kind of impartial empirical knowledge that their traveling colleagues obtained. Their "ethnographies" were believed to be little more than projections of their own fantasies and texts based on other texts. Crusius, however, though he never traveled, resists such a clear-cut categorization. Indeed, numerous early modern scholars knew that this dichotomy—which subsequent generations have deployed to cut off the bookish humanities from the empirical sciences—was to some extent a fallacy: even those who championed the primacy of eyewitnessing and firsthand observation often relied on texts, while scholars who took information from books and manuscripts, such as Johann Buxtorf and John Selden—both of whom wrote influential treatises on Judaism and early modern Jewry—often claimed to be in conversation with people as well. But instead of repeating the platitude that mixed forms existed, and that books and conversation were never mutually exclusive, focusing our attention on Crusius's inquiry can help us determine how such a "hybrid hermeneutics," to borrow the words of Lorraine Daston, actually played out in practice.[21] The question, then, is not so much whether books or people were the most reliable sources—although that was one deeply important early modern debate—but how you could make them reveal their secrets, and how you could reconcile one with the other. Our answers to these questions depend largely on where we look: each situation required its own combination of methods and sources. But the point remains that combinations came in many shapes: Crusius shows us one such way in which a scholar learned from both books and conversations, from bookish as well as personal encounters.

What makes connecting Crusius to the longer history of ethnography and encounter so rewarding is thus precisely that his journey of discovery, despite its idiosyncrasies, is representative of larger mechanisms. It was a Lutheran household that for decades became the site of interaction, a place where different worldviews intersected, opportunities for cultural exchange arose, and notions of cultural difference found new forms. Distance really mattered here: the impact of "discovering" what was going on in the Ottoman Empire was in many ways comparable to the shock waves that radiated from the Americas and Asia and that would break on European shores, washing over people of all professional and confessional stripes. To appreciate the full magnitude of Crusius's encounter with the Ottoman Greek world, it is necessary for historians today, then, to understand just how much this place, seen from Lutheran Tübingen, was still a world away.

In that sense, Crusius's journey of discovery really was a journey of discovery. Much of what he found out was new, unexpected, and even shocking. Viewed from Lutheran Tübingen, Ottoman Greece was uncharted territory—not in the literal sense, of course, as in the case of the "New World," this was a world home to numerous ancient and modern civilizations where there was technically nothing to "discover" for Europeans. But Ottoman Greece was also a blank spot on the mind map of individuals like Crusius, whose visions of that part of the globe were calibrated by a deep sense of decline and degeneration. So little was known in sixteenth-century Europe about the postclassical development of Greece that in the learned circles to which Crusius belonged it was all too easy to cast the Greeks as a cultural and religious "Other," a group at once familiar and foreign. Learning about their plight under the Ottoman rule—so different from ancient Greek life—was as shocking to Crusius and his colleagues as any other early modern European "discovery" of other parts of the globe.

Global Lutheranism

Reconstructing Crusius's ambitions and his life as a Lutheran affords fresh new insights into the history of sixteenth-century Lutheranism. One of the great but still largely untold stories about the Lutheran Reformation concerns its relationship with Eastern Christianity. Historians of scholarship have shown how knowledge of Eastern Christian traditions became a matter of utmost urgency in the fierce early modern debates about the nature and direction of the Church, and the controversies over its present state and history. Catholics as well as Protestants began to publish editions of the Greek Fathers of the Church—Eusebius, Basil the Great, and Chrysostom among luminaries now lesser known—and to marshal these authorities in their biblical scholarship and their polemical histories of the Church.[22] But their bitter religious division also made them—and later Calvinists as well as Anglicans—look at the contemporary Greek Orthodox Church with a newfound curiosity. The arrival of the Ottomans as permanent players in the Mediterranean political arena had permitted Western Christians to see their Greek Orthodox brothers, the living heirs of those venerable Greek Fathers, no longer solely as schismatics, as was common throughout the higher Middle Ages, but also as victims of a common Christian foe. As religious division created deeper ruptures in Latin Christendom, the patriarchate of Constantinople, known as a venerable and ancient institution, was increasingly seen as a bulwark not only against the Ottomans but against other Christian denominations as well. Catholics and Protestants claimed continuity with the community of the early Church and turned to the Greek Orthodox Church to find these claims confirmed by historical evidence. In a world, then, that was fractured along religious lines, and at a time when the break between Catholics and Protestants began to look increasingly decisive, it paradoxically became possible to envision the Greeks as part of the *Corpus Christianum* in a new way.

Yet this moment of interconfessional possibility, and the willingness to listen to the Greeks, passed as quickly as it appeared. Once Crusius and others realized that Greek Orthodox Christians did not share their vision of the Christian life, it was critical to convince the patriarch and other Greeks of the Lutheran truth. This was true for Tridentine Rome as well: in this very period, and for the first time since the failed attempts at establishing a church union at the Council of Ferrara-Florence (1431–1449), the Roman Curia sent several official missions to the Eastern Mediterranean. To further their endeavor to spread Catholicism across all corners of the early modern globe, and to thwart Lutheran efforts to connect to Greek Orthodox ecclesiastics, Pope Gregory XIII repeatedly tried to convince the patriarch and representatives of other Eastern Christian Churches to adopt his calendar reforms and be in communion. To understand Lutheran-Catholic rivalries, then, is to recognize that the Greek Orthodox world had become both a testing ground for establishing which Christian tradition embodied the one true church and a prime site for proselytization.

For the Tridentine Church, whose global reach in this period has become a subject of particular attention, this is to some extent a familiar story. But turning our attention to Tübingen reveals scholarly projects and missionary activities that rivaled those of Rome. They, too, began to proselytize in the Eastern Mediterranean. The manpower that Rome marshaled in pursuit of its goals completely eclipsed what the Lutherans in Tübingen managed to bring together. But once these pursuits are studied in tandem, late sixteenth-century Lutheranism and the global Catholicism of the period begin to look more alike than scholars have acknowledged. Placing Tübingen next to Rome thus unsettles some deeply ingrained convictions about the Holy Roman Empire. It suggests that the Old Reich and the German hometown—an urban setting made famous in Mack Walker's foundational and still important study—were less provincial and isolated than previous generations of scholars have claimed.[23] Here my examination underlines with new evidence a point to which historians of the Protestant Reformation and its global dimensions have recently called attention: even though Protestant efforts at proselytization were ultimately less successful than those of their Catholic adversaries, this did not mean that the Germanic lands of the Holy Roman Empire somehow lagged.[24] On the contrary: the material examined here demonstrates that the sixteenth-century creation of distinct religious identities was not restricted to the heartlands of the Reformation but a drama played out on a much broader geographical scale—something that cannot be captured through a success-failure paradigm.

The ambitions of Crusius and other Lutherans from Tübingen to connect with the Greek Orthodox patriarch also adumbrate the organized missionary work that Lutherans developed in the eighteenth century. Not only in that later world, where the Pietist movement advocated for spiritual reform and active missionary efforts, but also in the decades after Luther's death, proselytization was high on the Lutheran agenda. In those troubling decades, deeply pious Lutherans like Crusius looked inward as much as they looked outward to ensure that their movement would root. The kind of Lutheranism that Crusius's story reveals to us is neither passive nor stationary but outward facing and vibrant, and in its ambitions to spread the faith not that different from Tridentine Rome.

The preservation of the rituals and practices of a German university town and a professorial household thus illuminate an unwritten chapter in what we could call the global history of Lutheranism. But Crusius's engagement with the Greek Orthodox world also reminds us that global lives of the kind that historians are now tracing need not be lived on a global scale.[25] The value of studying "local" individuals such as Crusius, who were deeply rooted in their communities, is that they allow us to see how some of early modernity's most transformative changes permeated all layers of society and in the process fundamentally expanded the horizons of those experiencing them: to travel, the case of Crusius suggests, one need not traverse vast distances.

An Exceptional Archive

My reconstruction of a single scholar and his immediate milieu thus aims to provide new interpretive leverage on how we write our histories of this global age. It shows us that to go deep into a single society or to examine the life of a single individual is to see how the actions of individuals and groups are embedded in larger, global processes and to see how these processes, in turn, inhabited them and shaped their lives. One of the methodological contributions of this book thus involves the relationship between the global and the local—between the general and the particular—in the entangled histories of the Mediterranean, global Lutheranism, and scholarship and ethnography. It is my hope that such a newfound attention on the local, which I share with recent practitioners of what is now increasingly often called "global microhistory," will become a model for historical writing once more.[26] For at its core, this book echoes Giovanni Levi's interpretation of history as a "science that generates questions" with "a general relevance" but for which there is an infinite number of "local answers."[27]

Such a methodological move is possible in no small part because of the survival of an extraordinary archive. In an age that saw no shortage of great diarists, Crusius ranked among the most compulsive, exhibiting the same energy that characterized other branches of his written activity: many of the nearly seven hundred books that have survived from his private library are coated with thick layers of marginal annotation. His manuscripts and notebooks, some of which are hundreds of pages long, record his scholarly practices and reveal how embodied his scholarship was: a skillful scribe, Crusius often copied manuscripts with a single quill, early in the morning before classes started and while standing up. The richest of his surviving documents takes the form of an immense diary. Divided into nine thick volumes, begun as a letter book, and kept for the twenty-eight years of his life, this largely untapped historical source opens a door to Crusius's world and to everyday life in sixteenth-century Tübingen. From observations of the weather to entries about Crusius's household expenditures; from lists of the Greek Orthodox Christians who showed up on his doorstep to drawings of the seating arrangements at dinner parties and weddings to which he was invited; from notes about the wine bought, sold, and received as part of his salary to summaries of the dreams that came to him at night and which he recorded at dawn; from descriptions of the books he read to notes about the texts he taught; from records of his incoming and outgoing correspondences to complaints about the endless stream of student papers he had to mark—Crusius's diary details it all. "Relaxing," he once intimated with no irony, "is something I cannot do."[28]

Many of Crusius's contemporaries also left long and winding paper trails. Historians have followed these, sometimes over decades and from archive to archive, to explain how early modern individuals made sense of the world around them as well as the past, the present, and the future.[29] Not often, though, do we get the chance to untangle scholars' printed and manuscript works through papers that document the social-cultural world to which they belonged as well as their day-to-day life as individuals, family members, and active agents in their hometown and religious community. Crusius's *Nachlass* allows for such an exploration. And it is precisely because the personal and the professional merge in his archive that we can narrate a story that is at once local and global, distinct and representative, specific and universal.

This brings us to a fundamental issue not yet addressed explicitly but which has been on my mind since I first made my way to Tübingen in the summer of 2016—and one that has prompted a question that I have been asked repeatedly: How distinctive was Crusius? It is undeniable that he was by most accounts idiosyncratic. His self-professed love of Greece was exceptional for his time: Did any of his contemporaries fill up nineteen thick volumes with Greek summaries of thousands of sermons that they heard in their local churches? Did any of his contemporaries correspond with the Greek Orthodox patriarch? Did any of his contemporaries subject dozens of Greek Orthodox Christians to lengthy interviews and leave extensive records of them? Only time will tell. But in his own estimation, Crusius "loved and admired the Greek language and the Greek people like none of his countrymen."[30]

Yet statements such as these, taken out of context and given a place of prominence in our accounts of the historical process, often obscure more mundane realities. In many ways, Crusius saw himself as an ordinary scholar trying to sustain himself and his family and serving God through his scholarship. By comparing Crusius with other scholars of the period, and by adducing evidence from related cases, I want to substantiate exactly that claim: that as a scholar, Crusius was anything but unusual. Few of his contemporaries were as consumed by Greece as he was, but the traditions on which his investigation rested flowered in many corners of the early modern learned world and were practiced by numerous men and occasionally women like him. Examining Crusius is thus seeing normal science at work. Crusius was no

Scaliger; no Casaubon; no Harvey—to name but a few of the usual suspects in the history of scholarship. Nor was he another Luther or Melanchthon. Neither did he live the life of Matteo Ricci or Bernardino de Sahagún—two of the most studied and celebrated early modern European "ethnographers." But their worlds were his; his concerns theirs; all were part of the great turning of their time. Crusius may not have exchanged letters with the high and mighty of the learned community; he may not have directly determined the course of Lutheranism; and he may not have traversed the globe to win souls for Christ. But the dreams that Crusius cherished for his God-given work were no less lofty than those of other missionaries of the period; he inhabited Lutheran circles and they inhabited him; and he had his own local Republic of Letters, whose lesser-known members are no less useful to think with when we write histories of the early modern period. Extraordinary in some regards, less so in others, Crusius's life and work—mapped against those of his peers and colleagues—transcend the specifics of a single case.

In focusing on one richly documented life, I also want to put the human moment back into the history of knowledge. This is a story about knowledge making that is populated not by ideas but by people. I offer yet another narrative of early modern connections, but one that prioritizes the experiences of those involved over the negotiations and publications that this form of connectedness produces. If we confine our examination of early modern intellectual culture to a clash or exchange of ideas, we risk overlooking the fundamentally human nature of such work. Here my historical reconstruction echoes other efforts to insert emotions into our histories of cultural encounter and empire and to recover the individual in our histories of knowledge.[31] When we do so, we can better gauge how scholars' "mental furniture," their cultural and religious baggage, shaped the contours of their inquiries.[32] Modern scholarship has shown how early modern descriptions of cultural difference often derived their form and framework from classical (and medieval) prototypes: "the classical past," in the words of Sabine MacCormack, "as studied by the humanists became the mirror that drew attention to the peculiarities and uniqueness not just of Europeans, but in due course also of non-European societies."[33] Classical Greece, as we will see throughout this book, did indeed play a hugely influential role in how Crusius came to view the Ottoman Greek world. But so did Crusius's own inner world, shaped as much by his Lutheran upbringing as his humanist education, his place within a community of learned scholars, and his position at the head of a gendered household.

Crusius's story unfolds across seven chapters. The first two chapters illustrate the confessional nature of his journey of discovery. Chapter 1 explores an unlikely and ultimately unsuccessful exchange of letters between theologians from Tübingen, the stronghold of Lutheran Orthodoxy, and the Greek Orthodox Patriarch Jeremias II. It shows how Crusius and his colleagues turned to the Greek Orthodox Church to find their Lutheran principles confirmed and to spread Lutheranism across the Greek Orthodox world. Chapter 2 turns to the history of reading, and to Crusius's own account of his Lutheran upbringing, to show that no confrontation with radically new facts, no matter how jarring, shook the foundations of Crusius's religious beliefs.

The next three chapters situate Crusius's inquiry within the larger history of cross-cultural encounters. Chapter 3 reconstructs the adverse circumstances that brought an otherwise undocumented group of Greek Orthodox alms collectors to Crusius's Tübingen home, showing how individuals like him decided to trust strangers from distant lands. Chapter 4 traces how Crusius's Greek guests became his informants and reveals how such processes relied on the particularly gendered organization of the early modern professorial home. The story then moves from the household to the university town, tracing what other skills and expertise Crusius's project demanded. Chapter 5 demonstrates that it was the symbiosis of scholarship and sociability in the early modern university town that offered scholars like Crusius the resources and manpower needed to develop their ideas.

The last two chapters dissect Crusius's seminal publication on the Ottoman Greek world and reconstruct his vision of Ottoman Greece. In the *Turcograecia,* which was full of original Greek sources, Crusius painted the period's richest portrait of Greek life under Ottoman rule, as Chapter 6 reveals. Yet Crusius ultimately narrated a story of decline, decrying the Greeks' degradation, ignorance, and superstition. Somewhat surprisingly, and paradoxically, as we will see in Chapter 7, elite Greeks themselves contributed to this narrative of decline and decadence—a trope that would come to dominate writing on early modern Greece for centuries to come.

1

CHRISTIAN PURITY

In the spring of 1576 an extraordinary, if ultimately unacceptable, proposition was put to a group of Lutherans from Tübingen. It came from none other than the Greek Orthodox Patriarch Jeremias II Tranos (c. 1530–1595).[1] The proposition itself was already something of a triumph: for the last three years this group of Lutherans, led by Martin Crusius, had repeatedly tried to contact members of the Greek Orthodox Church in Istanbul. One of their missives had included a Greek version of the Augsburg Confession, the single most important expression of their Lutheran principles. Now, in this long-awaited response, the patriarch finally pronounced his judgment on the Lutheran creed. Despite the various doctrinal divergences from Greek Orthodoxy that the patriarch indicated in the evangelical creed, he did not immediately break off contact. On the contrary, he welcomed the Lutherans with arms wide open:

> If, then, most learned German men and beloved children of our mediocrity, you wish to join our most holy Church, we, as loving fathers, will readily accept your love and kindness, provided that you are willing to follow the apostolic and synodal decrees in harmonious agreement with us, and to submit to them. Then you will truly be our consorts; and having, as it were, openly submitted to our holy and catholic Church of Christ, you will be praised by all prudent men. In this way the two churches will become one by the grace of God, we shall live together hereafter, and we will exist together in a God-pleasing way until we attain the heavenly kingdom.[2]

This statement, as historians of this episode have made clear, was unprecedented. For the first time, the head of the Greek Orthodox Church, which prided itself in embodying the principles of the Apostolic Church, professed in writing the basic tenets of the Greek Orthodox faith to representatives of a burgeoning evangelical movement that claimed a similar link with the early Christian past.[3]

This letter and the many others that Crusius and Tübingen's Lutheran theologians exchanged with representatives of the Greek Orthodox Church between 1573 and 1581 form the subject of this chapter. This unlikely and ultimately unsuccessful correspondence is by far the most-studied episode in Crusius's life. Several generations of scholars have explored the theological issues at stake, explained the various points of convergence and divergence, and reflected on how the representatives of these two Christian denominations exchanged ideas about their beliefs. By and large, they have considered this outreach made by Crusius and his colleagues as an ecumenical rapprochement, in which Lutheran Tübingen sought some form of doctrinal unification with the Greek Orthodox Church.[4] Yet Tübingen's ambitions were always more far-reaching than this framework allows. When Crusius composed his first letter to the Greek Orthodox patriarch, he had high hopes for what might come of any exchange with the head of what was seen at the time as one of Christianity's most ancient and venerable institutions: Crusius and his colleagues turned to the Greek Orthodox Church, which they believed followed particularly ancient rituals, predominantly to find their Lutheran principles confirmed. But when the patriarch's last letter found its way to Tübingen, such expectations of common ground gave way to a sense of disdain for Greek Orthodox Christianity and confirmed Lutherans in their belief that they needed to proselytize among Christians living in the Ottoman Empire.

This correspondence illustrates just how much and in what ways Crusius's religious convictions inspired his investigation into Greek life under Ottoman rule. In 1573, fearing that Greek learning had declined under the Ottomans, he decided, without any prior contact, to address a letter to the Greek Orthodox patriarch to learn whether Greeks still possessed "any culture" and to express his relief that a remnant of the Greek Orthodox Church had survived into their times, something he until recently thought impossible.[5] Yet those same beliefs also prevented Crusius from entering the exchange with an open mind: despite his innate curiosity and his eagerness to learn about the Greeks, their language, culture, and religion, the encounter with Greek Orthodox Christianity brought him no new perspective on his own beliefs. It only confirmed him in his conviction that Lutheranism offered the one and only acceptable Christian way of life. Early modern encounters such as this one were thus grounded in a degree of open-mindedness but also in the entrenchment of religious conviction.

The chapter begins with the circumstances that initially connected Tübingen with Istanbul, at a moment when Crusius and his colleagues seemed to be aiming for something like concord between Lutherans and Greek Orthodox Christians. It took a concerted effort on the part of Crusius and his fellow Lutherans to engage the Greek Orthodox Church in conversation. Yet the content of this correspondence, once initiated, shows that each side had a very different idea about where to locate doctrine. Spurred by the patriarch's response in 1576, their correspondence would soon become part of a broader program of Lutheran efforts—spearheaded at Tübingen—to convince other Christians of their truth.

Connecting Tübingen with Istanbul

In the beginning of the 1570s, nobody in Tübingen could have foreseen that for the next ten years they would be eagerly awaiting letters from the Greek Orthodox patriarch himself. In many ways, however, this story finds its origins not in Lutheran Tübingen but at the Habsburg court of Maximilian II. In 1572 the emperor, nominally Catholic but not unsympathetic to the reform movement, dispatched a Protestant aristocrat called David Ungnad von Sonnegg as his envoy to the Sublime Porte. One of Ungnad's main tasks was to reinforce Habsburg-Ottoman ceasefire agreements and thereby prevent any hostilities from erupting along its borders. Looking to recruit a chaplain to oversee his personnel's spiritual well-being, the future envoy wrote to Jacob Andreae, the chancellor of the University of Tübingen. This was not an arbitrary choice: the University of Tübingen was known at the time as a Lutheran stronghold, and Andreae was its leading Lutheran theologian.

Ungnad's letter specified that he was looking for a chaplain to preach Lutheran principles as laid out in the Augsburg Confession, a point repeated in the official letter from the imperial chancellery that was attached to his request. It was clear that not just anyone would do. The ideal candidate, according to Ungnad, had to be fluent in ancient as well as vernacular Greek to draw "erudite Greeks" into conversations about "the differences between the Eastern and the Western Churches" and inform Ungnad about them. Other tasks included offering spiritual support to Christian slaves living in the Ottoman capital. But under no circumstance were they to proselytize among the Christians there. It was essential that any form of unrest be avoided at all costs.[6]

Tübingen saw this post as a great opportunity. In a letter to Duke Louis III of Württemberg, who resided in Stuttgart and had to give official permission for any such appointment, Andreae expressed genuine sympathy for Ungnad's request: a chaplain from Tübingen would not only bestow great honor on the duchy but also bring Lutheran salvation to Christian captives. It was "a wonder," he emphasized, that they and not the Zwinglians could send a preacher to the Ottoman capital and spread "the pure word of God, which in Germany was being torn apart" among Christians living there.[7] He recommended for appointment a recent graduate from the University of Tübingen called Stephan Gerlach who was continuing his studies at the theological seminary, the famous *Tübinger Stift*. The plea had the desired effect: on April 9, 1573, having received official permission from both the university and the duke, and having been ordained by Andreae, Gerlach left Tübingen for Vienna, from where he traveled onward to the Ottoman capital.[8] Gerlach carried with him two letters addressed to the Greek Orthodox patriarch. One was the aforementioned letter by Crusius in which he asked the patriarch whether Greeks possessed "any culture." The other was by Andreae, who, after recommending Gerlach to the patriarch in the appropriate manner, stressed how Lutherans and Greek Orthodox Christians both believed in Christ as Savior and in salvation through Christ's death on the cross.[9]

These letters reflected a specific moment in the history of Lutheranism. In the generation after Luther's death, various Lutheran theologians, instead of fighting Catholicism as a unity, found themselves locked in debate over the nature and direction of their movement. Theological disagreements—mostly over the role of human will in salvation, the value of good works, what constituted as *adiaphora,* and the burning issue of whether Christ was substantially present in the Eucharist—had by the end of the sixteenth century created a deep rift between two opposing factions. The Philippists, based largely at Wittenberg and following the teachings of Philip Melanchthon, seriously considered the possibility of uniting with other reformed churches against the Catholics. In the eyes of their adversaries, the Gnesio-Lutherans, this meant adopting a too flexible interpretation of Luther's legacy. Led by Matthias Flacius Illyricus, the Gnesio-Lutherans claimed to uphold the one and only true form of Lutheranism, devoid of any outside influences be they Catholic or Calvinist.

Only toward the end of the 1570s did both parties manage to resolve their internal disagreements. Though this has been hailed as the work of a great number of important Lutheran theologians, historians of the episode have often singled out Andreae, a staunch defender of the Gnesio-Lutheran cause, as the resolution's chief architect, with his conciliatory *Six Sermons on the Division among Theologians of the Augsburg Confession* of 1573 setting off a series of publications that ultimately restored Lutheran unity. The single most important of these was the 1577 Formula of Concord (the *Konkordienformel*). In that year an eminent group of Lutheran theologians, including Andreae, met to craft earlier conciliatory attempts into a definitive formulation of Lutheran doctrine. Once circulated, the formula was accepted by an overwhelming majority of electoral princes, imperials cities, dukes, barons, theologians, and pastors in the Germanic lands of the Holy Roman Empire. The document was also included, after further revision, in the *Book of Concord* (or *Concordia*), a compendium of key Lutheran documents, which was printed in 1580 to mark the thirtieth anniversary of the Augsburg Confession.[10] Some dissent remained, as the declaration's final articulation was not so much a compromise as a precise articulation of Gnesio-Lutheran theology and an outright rejection of the Philippists' standpoint. But the Formula of Concord effectively put an end to the controversies that had beset Lutheranism for decades.

It was amid these attempts to end their turmoil that Andreae and Crusius turned their attention to the Greek Orthodox Church. Their ambitions to spread Lutheranism as far as the eastern shores of the Mediterranean thus originated in a world where it was far from a foregone conclusion that Lutheranism would survive, and if it did in what form exactly and where. Indeed, no one at the time could have foreseen—or would have wanted to know—that after 1733, merely a century after Crusius's death, Württemberg would be once again ruled by a Catholic duke. Yet Andreae's jubilation over the possibility of spreading the Lutheran word in the eastern Mediterranean ultimately reflected the absolute confidence that he and other Lutherans had in the truth of their beliefs.

On August 6, 1573, Ungnad's embassy was received in Istanbul with the customary dignity and protocols. His official audience with the sultan, where he handed over the Habsburg tribute, followed ten days later. Meanwhile, Gerlach occupied himself with his many tasks, setting up a social network and educating himself about the customs of the peoples living in the Ottoman Empire. On October 15, 1573, about two months after his arrival in Istanbul, he set out to meet the Greek Orthodox patriarch and deliver Crusius's and Andreae's letters. He had to comply with the strict protocols that governed such occasions: he was first asked to wait in an antechamber until the patriarch and his entourage had taken their seats. Then, upon entering the room, he had to approach Jeremias and give him the customary hand kiss. Two interpreters, Joannes Zygomalas and an Italian doctor, explained that the patriarch gave him a friendly and courteous welcome. It was then Gerlach's turn to hand the letters over to the patriarch. Before all formalities were completed, the chaplain kissed Jeremias's hand for a second time and was invited to join the patriarch for the evening prayer that he would be saying in a local church.[11]

Initially, then, all seemed to go as planned. But no sooner had the audience been concluded than Gerlach received a set of letters that must have filled him with consternation: one of the sermons that Crusius had appended to his letter had struck the wrong chord. The sermon in question, delivered by Andreae at Gerlach's ordination and translated by Crusius into Greek during its delivery, concerned a pericope in John about the Good Shepherd. It had been attached, according to Crusius, as "a specimen of our faith and of my Greek studies."[12] But what was done with the best intentions in one context appeared offensive in another: the patriarch, as Gerlach soon and Crusius not long thereafter discovered, had become disconcerted, taking the inclusion of the sermon as a suggestion that because of his lethargy he was no longer performing his pastoral duties adequately. Even though Zygomalas tried to convince the patriarch that Crusius had meant to suggest no such thing, a request to clarify the whole situation was sent to Gerlach.[13] Had it not been for his diplomatic skills—he explicitly made it clear that this was not an insult directed at Jeremias—the correspondence might never have taken off. But immediately thereafter, Gerlach had to face another unexpected turn of events. The patriarch, notwithstanding the promise of a quick reply, left Istanbul to conduct an episcopal visitation of his territories and would not return for nine months.

Gerlach, meanwhile, made the most of his time in the Ottoman capital observing the world of Greek Orthodoxy. He saw little cause for optimism: in one of his letters, he noted that there were no proper Greek schools beyond the most elementary level. Orthodox church officials were unlearned men with an insufficient command of the Greek language. Some of them scorned ancient Greek. If priests celebrated mass at all, which hardly any did, only a few listeners were able to understand what they were saying. "In terms of honesty in life," Gerlach lamented, "they were little better than Turks." In terms of doctrine, they had fallen into superstitious ways. "The status of the Greek Church," he concluded, "should be pitied." He did mention, however, that Greek Orthodox Christians were not on friendly terms with the pope and rejected some of the key doctrines of Catholicism. Similarly, the office and person of the patriarch, who cared little for splendor and was a humane man, did inspire in Gerlach a profound reverence, even if his overall assessment was critical.[14]

Greek Orthodox views on the Lutheran movement were hardly more constructive. Gerlach discovered that Greeks said Lutherans were "innovators," people who "departed from the canons of the apostles and the decrees of the [seven] ecumenical synods," and as such differed little from Rome. Lutherans, in the eyes of Greek Orthodox Christians, endeavored to detract from the cult of the saints and from saying sermons in honor of the dead. Their position on the *filioque* controversy—that is, the ancient question whether the Holy Spirit proceeds from the father or from the father *and the son*—was indistinguishable from the Catholic one. Lutherans used unleavened bread (*azymus*) in their liturgy, a choice Greek Orthodox Christians strongly opposed and a major point of contention in the fifteenth-century discussions about reunion at the Council of Ferrara-Florence. Greek Orthodox Christians also objected to the ways in which "Lutherans had stripped their mass of ancient rites [and] their churches of images against the decrees of the seven [ecumenical] councils." In sum, not only "Greek people" but also "Italians, and Armenians are utterly convinced that Lutherans do not believe in God, nor in Christ; that they lack baptism and all the sacraments; and that they were beyond doubt a godless people."[15] This was hardly an encouraging basis for a debate on church doctrine.

Gerlach managed to uncover so much because upon arrival he was drawn into a vibrant world of European-Ottoman sociability, not unlike the many other merchants and diplomats in service of European powers that had business in and beyond Istanbul throughout the early modern period.[16] In fulfilling his tasks as chaplain, and in facilitating the correspondence with the patriarch, Gerlach encountered hundreds of Ottoman subjects and other foreigners, many of whom are mentioned by name in the journal that he kept of his sojourn.[17] But such face-to-face interactions were never uncomplicated. Setting up and maintaining a network of informants required resources and inventiveness. Most of the relationships that Gerlach established with officials high up in the church hierarchy came at a price. Not only did Gerlach complain perpetually about the Greeks' avarice—"Greeks do nothing free of charge"—he also frequently shared his frustrations about having to bribe them: Joannes Zygomalas, for instance, would allegedly scorn any sum less than twenty *thalers* and had to be sent gifts all the time to win him over.[18] Gerlach even suspected that Zygomalas did not fully trust him and tried to limit his influence on the patriarch.[19] Zygomalas, in turn, once confided in Gerlach that on account of his interactions with the chaplain, other Greeks accused him of being a Lutheran.

As Gerlach's efforts to integrate into Ottoman society demonstrate, connecting Tübingen and Istanbul took serious work. Beneath the civilized veneer of European-Ottoman sociability, commonly rehearsed in early modern travelogues, there evidently lurked a world rife with enmity and suspicion. And delivering letters across vast distances and across imperial, cultural, linguistic, and confessional boundaries was by no means a straightforward endeavor. Indeed, the kind of tasks that Gerlach had to execute required resources—money, connections, diplomacy—as well as resourcefulness in the religious landscape of sixteenth-century Ottoman Istanbul.

Doctrinal Debates in the Ottoman Capital

Communication did eventually begin. Between 1573 and 1578, when Gerlach left Istanbul, he sent an estimated eighty-six letters back to Tübingen, twenty of which were written by Jeremias and other members of the patriarchate. In the following three years, Salomon Schweigger, Gerlach's successor, forwarded significantly fewer letters, but he still made sure that Tübingen's missives reached their intended destination. Three of these exchanges are particularly important to our story: the sending of the Augsburg Confession (September 1574) and the patriarch's first official reply (May 1576); the Lutheran response to this letter (June 1577) followed by a second official exposition from the patriarch (May 1579); and a second Lutheran response (June 1580) followed by the third comment from the patriarch and his team that formally ended the exchange (June 1581). One last letter from Tübingen, sent in December 1581, did not elicit a reply.

After Gerlach had delivered Crusius's and Andreae's letters to the patriarch in October 1573, they had generated little enthusiasm. A second set of letters in March 1574, to which Crusius had again appended a sermon, did not elicit the desired reaction either. In their third attempt, from September 1574, the Lutherans changed tactics. This time they had attached not another sermon but the Augsburg Confession. "That way," as Crusius and his colleagues wrote in hopeful terms,

> Your Holiness may see what our religion is and whether we agree with the teaching of the churches under the jurisdiction of Your Holiness; or whether perhaps, there might be something that is not in agreement (which I would not desire). I earnestly ask Your Holiness to ... kindly express your most favorable judgment concerning these articles, if God would grant that we think alike in Christ.[20]

This attempt did bear fruit: Jeremias apologized for the delay in responding and commented on the sermons that the Lutherans had sent. He spoke not a single word, however, about the Augsburg Confession or their request to assess its articles. Thus, in their next dispatch the Lutherans thanked the patriarch extensively for his erudite observations on the sermons, but nevertheless implored him to pronounce his "wise and most pious judgment" on the Augsburg Confession as well.[21]

This he did in May 1576, when he sent to Tübingen that extraordinary but ultimately unacceptable proposition with which this chapter opened. It consisted of two parts: a short and formal letter and a lengthy exposition of the main points of agreement and disagreement between the Lutheran and Orthodox positions. One by one, Jeremias responded to the Augsburg Confession's articles—not, he cared to emphasize, by offering his own views but by drawing extensively from the seven holy ecumenical synods and the opinions of the Fathers of the Church. No forms of innovation, he stressed, were to be found in his remarks on the trinity, original sin, the office of the ministry, the sacraments, confession, penance, faith and good works, the cult of saints, monastic vows, the article of justification, baptism, and the other doctrinal issues that passed in review. He was speaking in accordance with scripture, which they had received "in common accord."[22]

Jeremias's judgment was lengthy but critical. He admitted that some articles in the Augsburg Confession reflected the position of the Greek Orthodox Church. But the Lutherans wrongly contended that remission of sins is granted by faith alone. They were also wrong about the importance of good works and about the sacraments, all seven of which the Greek Orthodox Church deemed necessary. Lutherans had unjustly denounced the value of taking monastic vows, which was an honorable deed, and rejected the cult of saints, whose remembrance Greek Orthodox Christians considered profitable. The Lutherans' choice to administer unleavened bread (*azymus*) at the Eucharist, based on their contention that the bread consumed at the Last Supper had been unleavened, violated scripture. Lutherans had unnecessarily eliminated ceremonies, feasts, fixed fasts, and other occasions that could inspire Christians to good works. In that sense, only when the Lutherans were willing to conform to the ecumenical councils and "follow the canons of the apostles" could any lasting accord be reached. Otherwise, Jeremias posited, "what communion would one, who rejects the aforementioned canons and opposes the apostles and shamelessly turns himself against the holy apostles, have with us?"[23]

This was not the response the Lutherans were hoping for. One of their initial letters to the patriarch explicitly mentioned that they "were in no way innovating on the main articles concerning salvation" and that they "had embraced and preserved the faith that had been handed down by the holy apostles and Prophets, by the Fathers and Patriarchs who had been inspired by the Holy Spirit, and by the seven ecumenical synods that were founded upon the God-given Scriptures."[24] But the patriarch was now, without saying as much, accusing them of doing exactly that: innovating.

This was an incredibly serious allegation. Much of the ecclesiastical scholarship that emerged in the wake of the Reformation centered around exactly that issue: Which Christian tradition was uncorrupted and who had brought innovations into worship? Even though Lutherans were convinced that their beliefs had a scriptural basis, Catholics undermined these claims by pointing to the novelty of Protestantism versus the antiquity of Catholicism. Where, they asked, had the Lutheran Church been before Luther? Protestants, in turn, argued that the medieval church had erred from correct belief by introducing different innovations. It was in early Christianity, a period everybody agreed had been uncorrupted, that both Protestants and Catholics looked for historical precedent for their respective positions. Thus, when the patriarch, as the head of a venerable and ancient church, hurled the accusation of innovation at the Lutherans, it hit where it hurt most.

But however disappointing Jeremias's answer was, it was not completely unexpected. One of Gerlach's earlier reports on the Greek Orthodox faith had had a devastating impact in Tübingen. Crusius, who had been burning with desire to read it, was left disillusioned: "Oh! On how many points do the Greeks (a people I dearly love because of their language) err? I do not know how many." The only good thing to come out of this exchange was that the Greeks "now know from our confession of faith that we, despite the malicious charges of the Catholics, are not godless but have a truth that they cannot contradict."[25] In that sense, the patriarch's proposition to be in full communion with them, which arrived shortly after Crusius read Gerlach's letter, was a nonevent: How could they accept the patriarch's invitation to follow the apostolic and synodal decrees if they were already doing just that? How could they be innovators if they were anything but that? Jeremias's letter, then, however shocking, did not shake the foundations of their faith. On the contrary, the inevitable conclusion at which Crusius arrived was that everybody at the patriarchate could now see that Lutherans possessed an uncontestable truth.

This position echoed Gerlach's assessment. The chaplain doubted that "a consensus could be achieved," but it was still essential to send further materials to Istanbul to convince the patriarch of their beliefs. The Augsburg Confession had not sufficed in that respect: "I am not sure it is worth printing more copies because it does not seem to treat all of our religious principles and neither does it do so accurately." Gerlach thought that something more akin to a "compendium of [our] whole religion" was needed. His hope was to have such a text printed and bound together with the patriarch's letter. Once sent to Istanbul, such a book could be circulated in Greek Orthodox circles to "spread [the Lutheran] religion in the whole of Greece." A translation into vernacular Greek could then be commissioned. Such a document, since forming an accord was no longer a viable option, would at least open the eyes of Greek Orthodox Christians to the light of Lutheranism.[26] Later on, having heard even more Greek Orthodox Christians talk about the Lutherans as innovators and even as heretics, Gerlach further qualified what seemed possible: "I do not hope for a union in faith . . . but maybe it is possible through corresponding to come together in a friendship (if in light of religious differences friendship is possible) so that they do not slander [us] as the Papists do."[27]

In this moment a subtle but important change in the way the Lutherans conceptualized their exchange with the patriarch is discernible. Up until the spring of 1576, something like an agreement with the Greek Church, if not a union, was on the Lutherans' minds. In the spring of 1575, for instance, Crusius still envisioned the correspondence ending in concord (*concordia*) between Lutherans and Greek Orthodox Christians.[28] But the patriarch's response completely shattered that dream: any form of concord between Lutherans and Greek Orthodox Christians would be difficult, not because of their differences but because the Greek Orthodox Church, in their view, had strayed from the one true path. In the eyes of the Lutherans, this was no longer that venerable ancient church but a corrupted tradition. The Greek Orthodox Church, in Gerlach's assessment, suffered from a "deplorable disease" and had to be "healed" by Lutheran medicine.[29] To convince Greek Orthodox Christians of the correctness of the Lutheran creed thus became of paramount importance. This sudden shift in emphasis made explicit what earlier letters had already implied: that the Lutherans, through engagement with the Greek Orthodox Church, hoped to find their own confessional beliefs confirmed more than they were looking to heal the body of Christ.

The Lutherans' next letter was long in coming. Andreae was away from Tübingen working on what would ultimately become the Formula of Concord. Other theologians who had become involved in the correspondence expressed uncertainty about the next steps. Only Gerlach and Crusius kept urging all involved to formulate an official answer. It had to be done quickly as well: Gerlach feared that his own successor might be a Catholic, and he knew that the patriarch was getting impatient. In the end, the duke intervened and decided, upon Gerlach's recommendation, to send gifts to the patriarchate and other Greek ecclesiastics.[30] He ordered three expensive clocks to be made, knowing full well that European watches and clocks were highly regarded in the Ottoman capital and that such inventions could gain one the favor of court officials and others in authority.[31] Lucas Osiander, who together with Jacob Heerbrand would later produce the first Latin translation of the Formula of Concord, was made responsible for writing the response, which had to include, again upon Gerlach's recommendation, specific references to the Greek Church Fathers.

Osiander worked swiftly. On May 5 and 6, 1577, everybody involved met in the neighboring monastery of Bebenhausen to proofread the answer he had formulated. Once revisions were done, a copy was sent to Andreae while Crusius diligently applied himself to translating all the materials into Greek.[32] In an interesting turn of events, on the day that the documents were signed (June 16, 1577), another dispatch from Gerlach arrived. Not knowing an answer had been formulated, the chaplain not only urged Tübingen to craft a response but also intimated that Jeremias was interested in having a Greek translation of Heerbrand's *Compendium Theologiae*. Published in Tübingen in 1573, this massive work treated more Lutheran principles in more depth than the Augsburg Confession had. Seeing an opportunity to circulate further Lutheran materials among Eastern Christians, Crusius volunteered to translate Heerbrand's hefty tome into Greek. Three months later—he had not been able to work faster because of his many teaching obligations—the translation was done.[33] It had required diligent research because Crusius could not bear "making a mistake" and had had to check many passages against the writings of the Greek Church Fathers and the Septuagint—in case the latter "was mistaken," he had followed "the sense of our Latin Bible."[34]

The work was sent to Istanbul in October 1577 so that, as the cover letter made clear, the patriarch would now have a document in which all Lutheran principles were collected.[35] Yet by then there was serious noise on the line connecting Tübingen with Istanbul. The earlier response that Osiander had written had not yet arrived in Istanbul, giving Gerlach the impression that nobody in Tübingen was putting in enough time and energy. Seeing Jeremias grow ever more impatient—it had been fifteen months since the patriarch had sent his response to Tübingen—Gerlach feared the patriarch might think the Lutherans incapable of answering or, worse still, that they did not deem his letter worthy of a reply. He stressed how in Greek Orthodox circles Lutherans were believed to be not just innovators but heretics. The situation had become so painful that the chaplain did not dare show his face at the patriarchate anymore.[36]

It was only at the end of the year that Osiander's reply, Crusius's translation of the *Compendium Theologiae*, the clocks, and the cover letters arrived in Istanbul. Ironically, just two days after this, the patriarch left Istanbul to carry out another visitation. Gerlach was nevertheless able to deliver some materials to other members of the patriarchate and seemingly with the desired results: Theodosius Zygomalas, another one of Gerlach's connections, read Osiander's response and, though he was afraid to admit it in public, had in private conversation, according to Gerlach, condemned "the austerity of fasting, the cult of images, and other superstitions."[37] Michael Cantacuzenus, a wealthy Greek magnate with enormous political influence, had been similarly impressed with the Augsburg Confession; he now wanted a copy of Heerbrand's *Compendium* and Osiander's response as well.[38] Even in the patriarch's absence Gerlach saw room for optimism: through his travels the Lutheran creed "would be known in all the major churches of Greece."[39]

Circumstances in Istanbul were nevertheless becoming more tenuous. Gerlach's stay in Istanbul was winding to an end, and his successor would have to be instructed about "the prudence with which one should deal with the Greeks; about what one should ask; and about what one should elaborate on."[40] Jeremias's position also appeared more precarious by the day. Cantacuzenus, one of his most ardent supporters, had recently been strangled to death. "Now that he has been removed," Gerlach intimated, "there is the danger that Jeremias will be deposed and his (predecessor) reinstated." Should this come about, the translation of Heerbrand's *Compendium* had to be taken back from Jeremias and offered together with a copy of Osiander's letter to Metrophanes III who would take over from Jeremias as patriarch. But this was risky too: the exact position and authority of this man were not so easy to gauge since Gerlach knew that he had been excommunicated in the past for trying to negotiate a union with Rome. The chaplain closed his letter by emphasizing that he would soon know what the future had in store for both these ecclesiastics.[41]

Even considering these events, Gerlach's missives continue to convey a strong sense of optimism about the outcome of the exchange. In part, this was because he, together with Crusius and Andreae, saw in the exchange God's hand at work.[42] But developments over the next few months would prove just how tenuous the whole enterprise had become. In July 1578 Gerlach's final dispatch from Istanbul arrived. It contained no fewer than five letters from Jeremias: one to Andreae, Heerbrand, Osiander, and Crusius collectively; and one to each of these men individually. The patriarch thanked the Lutherans for the materials and gifts and promised to send an evaluation back to Tübingen via Schweigger.[43] But by April 1579 Crusius had much to his own frustration not yet received a single letter from the new chaplain. It was only in May of that year, just after the Lutherans had sent further materials to Istanbul—including, intriguingly, portraits of Luther—that Jeremias's second, long-awaited response finally arrived in Tübingen.

This document was as unequivocal as Jeremias's first answer. It essentially offered a point-for-point refutation of the same Lutheran articles that Jeremias's first answer had tried to refute: the procession of the Holy Spirit, the question of justification and good works, the number and function of the sacraments, the cult of saints, and the importance of the monastic life. This time, however, the patriarch had not just epitomized the position of the Greek Orthodox Church by drawing on tradition. Instead, he cited in extenso the opinions of different Fathers of the Church in support of his claims. In Tübingen the letter fell on stony ground: the text, whose composition was considered makeshift, was considered nothing more than a "hodgepodge" of poorly cited passages from the synods and the Church Fathers.[44]

This reading of Jeremias's booklet alludes to another tension that permeated the exchange: the relationship between tradition and scripture. Greek Orthodox doctrine, as the Lutherans in Tübingen discovered in the patriarch's responses, was deeply grounded in the theology of the Church Fathers and the seven holy synods. For them tradition was a cornerstone of their creed. Lutherans, by contrast, as is well known, emphasized that only scripture (*sola scriptura*) can grant authority in matters of doctrine. The Formula of Concord stated it thus: scripture is "the only rule or guideline by which all teachers and doctrines are to be judged."[45] The Fathers were witnesses to the gospel, but they could only be read in conjunction with scripture. One of their letters to Istanbul specified that theirs was indeed a small canon: only those texts that were in agreement with scripture could be part of tradition. The Greek Orthodox Church simply relied too much on the Fathers of Church and too little on scripture.[46] Crusius, too, wondered why tradition and not scripture appeared to have been the Greek Orthodox Church's primary point of reference. His objection to this position was a familiar one and went back to Luther's objections against Catholicism: the Fathers were fallible; scripture was not. According to Crusius the fact that they did not know Hebrew and relied on the faulty Septuagint translation testified to that.[47] The problem with Jeremias's responses was thus not so much that the Fathers of the Church appeared in them repeatedly but that scripture did not. For those reasons the Lutherans made a point of emphasizing in their next letter—their response to Jeremias's second answer—that their position "was structured on the foundations of the Holy Scripture."[48]

Getting this letter delivered took some doing. Toward the end of 1579 Jeremias was indeed deposed and Metrophanes III indeed reinstated. When Crusius and the others convened at the monastery of Bebenhausen in the beginning of May 1580, they wondered whether to send their response to Jeremias or to his successor. In the end it was decided to send to Theodosius Zygomalas one copy addressed to Jeremias and one to Metrophanes.[49] Their reliance on this Greek was greater than ever at this point because Schweigger had not been "the second Gerlach" they had hoped he would be: in the more than two years that he spent in Istanbul, Gerlach's successor directed only three letters directly to Crusius.[50] Indeed, Crusius had to hear through other channels that Jeremias was deposed. Schweigger's letters confirming this tragic course of events only arrived after the Lutherans had sent their second response to Istanbul. Later, Crusius learned that the arrest of a courier had put the life of the imperial ambassador at risk and that considering the threatening situation, Schweigger desperately wanted to leave the Ottoman capital.[51] In the beginning of the 1580s, then, things were not looking up for the Lutherans.

But for the Lutherans the vagaries of communication were no reason to give up. Their last letter to Jeremias continued to convey a strong sense of confidence about their position. They had countered the plethora of citations from the Church Fathers with a history lesson about how to use tradition. Your Holiness, they wrote, "knows very well after all that the opinions of all men"—including the testimonies of the Fathers of the Church—

"should be subjected to the judgment of the scriptures of the Prophets and Apostles, because they are a lamp unto our feet." This was, after all, exactly what the Fathers, "those luminaries and heroes of the Church," had done themselves: "they did not hesitate to subject their writings to the judgment of all, as long as they judged these writings in accordance with the salubrious fountains of Scripture."[52] Now, the letter insinuated, who would they be if they did not follow the Fathers in their practice of grounding doctrine in scripture?

Not unexpectedly, this letter did not sway Jeremias. His final answer, which arrived in Tübingen in September 1581, turned the Lutherans' argument against them. His cover letter had been remarkably irenic: "above all, we promise one gift of grace: that we will always publicly declare a steadfast sincerity, love, and inclination to you."[53] But the actual response was nothing less than a full-scale refutation of everything the Lutherans had argued. Jeremias acknowledged the importance of scripture, but the problem was that the Lutherans had manipulated it: "you have quite plainly altered Holy Scripture as well as the interpretation of the . . . holy men according to your own will."[54] The patriarch emphasized that not a single Father of the Church, inspired by the Holy Spirit, had interpreted certain parts of scripture the way the Lutherans had. "Have you," he asked, "considered your own writings better and preferable to those that have survived of the true Theologians?"[55] Neither had the patriarch forgotten their remarks about the alleged flaws of the Septuagint and the lack of Hebrew knowledge among the Fathers: the Greek Orthodox Church, he stressed, was not in communion with the Jews. In fact, contempt for icons and holy relics found its origins in the Hebrew tradition and the Lutherans were now reviving those "schisms" that "lead to more evil and which grow worse by the day."[56] His conclusion was inescapable: the Lutherans were the real heretics. The patriarch closed his letter by stressing the incommensurability of their respective positions, a point that all involved seemed to have blissfully ignored for years:

> Therefore, we request that from henceforth you do not cause us more grief, nor write to us on the same subject or send us any writings if you wish to treat these luminaries and theologians of the Church in a different manner. You honor and exalt them in words, but you reject them in deeds. For you try to prove our weapons which are

their holy and divine discourses as unsuitable. And it is with these documents that we would have to write and contradict you. Thus, as for you, please release us from these cares. So going about your ways, write no longer about dogma, but only for friendship's sake.[57]

Even this wholesale rejection did not undermine the Lutherans' confidence. In a letter to Andreae, Crusius wrote that he was not alarmed that "the Greeks no longer want to be advised by us about religion" because "we have sowed the seeds that God in many years will awaken in them." His letter to the duke expressed a similar sentiment.[58] Osiander also believed that the patriarch had not overturned the Lutheran creed, because he had relied on tradition and not on scripture.[59] Crusius's choice of words is telling: note how the Lutherans are now "advising" the patriarch on Christian doctrine. His interest was evidently not in finding common confessional ground but in telling the members of this other Christian denomination what he knew to be right.

Global Lutheranism

And so hopes continued to be high in Tübingen. In fact, several similarly ambitious projects show that this attempt at spreading Lutheranism far beyond the borders of the Holy Roman Empire was by no means an anomaly. In March 1583, less than two years after Jeremias had ended the exchange, a lengthy letter arrived in Tübingen that prompted a similar attempt at spreading Lutheran principles among Eastern Christians. Johannes Thalius, a physician from Thuringia, wrote Crusius about his desire to learn Arabic, his frustrations over the lack of available Arabic books, and his failed plan to send an acquaintance of his to Fez to learn Arabic. Thalius wondered whether Crusius, when he next wrote to Istanbul, could perhaps ask if his Greek contacts could provide "any Arabic books."[60] Realizing the opportunities that sending somebody to Fez would offer, Crusius showed the letter to Andreae, who forwarded it to Stuttgart with a recommendation for Georg Weigenmaier, Tübingen's professor of Hebrew. Andreae's letter emphasized that the Ethiopian Church was not in communion with Rome and bore strong similarities with Lutheranism: their clergy married; they did not say Mass for the dead; they celebrated communion under both kinds; and they did

40 THE DISCOVERY OF OTTOMAN GREECE

not include confirmation and the anointing of the sick among the sacraments. In a separate letter to the duke's secretary, Crusius made it clear that learning languages was essential in the battle for Christian souls. The Jesuits, who were "extremely diligent at learning languages" and whose order Crusius believed had been founded to curb the diffusion of Lutheranism, had already "spread to America and India and propagated Papism as much as they could." Moreover, "in Rome Pope Gregory XIII had founded colleges for foreign languages to crush what [Catholics] considered heresies."[61] Echoing arguments made by Andreae for sending Gerlach to Istanbul, Crusius further emphasized that a mission to Fez would bring great honor to the duchy: "God seems to have opened a window for the dissemination of His word."[62] In the end, though, nothing came of this extraordinary idea: Weigenmaier ultimately preferred to stay with his pregnant wife in Tübingen, having seen two of their children die in infancy.[63]

Two book projects further illustrate just how strong the Lutherans' urge to spread their beliefs continued to be throughout the 1580s. On June 3, 1579, more than 150 Georgian captives, including two rulers who were brothers, arrived in Istanbul. The younger brother and his retinue immediately converted to Islam. The older brother, Quarquare Hodobag, did not. For a while this man visited Joachim von Sinzendorf, the new Habsburg ambassador, in his residence in Pera. At one point, to strengthen Hodobag in the faith, the ambassador asked Schweigger to commission Theodosius Zygomalas to make a manuscript copy of the Greek Augsburg Confession. The book, enriched by a personal dedication in Greek by von Sinzendorf, greatly impressed his Georgian guest, who arranged for translations to be made into vernacular Greek as well as Georgian.[64] In 1585, having returned from Istanbul a few years earlier, Schweigger had an Italian translation of Luther's small catechism printed in Tübingen. The treatise, paid for by the duke, was meant to be distributed among the many Christian slaves that Schweigger had encountered during his sojourn in the Ottoman Empire. It is unknown who read it—if it was read at all—but it is clear that motivations underlying this translation project as well as the encounter with Hodobag were not so different from those that spurred Crusius and Andreae to engage the patriarch in conversation or to send Weigenmaier to Fez: if only Eastern Christians could be exposed to Lutheran principles, by reading Lutheran treatises in their own languages, they would see how the Lutherans were the genuine custodians of Christian orthodoxy.[65]

Three interrelated points emerge from these Lutheran efforts to spread the faith. First, the involvement of the duke illustrates that this was as much a story of Tübingen as it was of early modern Württemberg and thus of the Reformation more broadly. The ambition to spread Lutheranism among Christians living throughout the Mediterranean evidently mattered not only to Andreae and Crusius but to a great number of other Lutherans. Second, all agreed that the book could act as an effective agent of religious change: it was their unshakable faith in the written word that encouraged them to invest time and money in translating Lutheran materials into Greek and bring them to the attention of Greek Orthodox Christians. In no small part, as Crusius and Gerlach made repeatedly clear, these aspirations were fueled by their conflict with Rome: Gerlach observed that Dominicans living in Istanbul, in what was evidently a form of inquisition, threatened anyone in possession of a Lutheran book with excommunication. Time and again the Lutherans urged the patriarch not to believe the malicious rumors that the Jesuits spread about them. Crusius feared that the very purpose of the pope's colleges in Rome was repressing Lutheranism.[66] Third, the ambitions and endeavors examined here adumbrate the organized missionary work that Lutherans developed throughout the eighteenth century. Proselytization was already high up on the Lutheran agenda in the decades after Luther's death, long before the eighteenth-century Pietist movement advocated for spiritual reform and active missionary efforts. In those troubling decades, deeply pious Lutherans like Andreae, Crusius, Gerlach, and Schweigger looked inward as much as they looked outward to ensure that their movement would take root outside of the Holy Roman Empire.

The exchanges between these Lutherans and the Greek Orthodox patriarch thus underscore a point to which historians of the Protestant Reformation have recently called attention: although Protestant efforts at proselytization were ultimately less successful than those of their Catholic adversaries, this did not mean that the Germanic lands of the Holy Roman Empire lagged. On the contrary, tracing how Crusius and his colleagues sought to spread their religious convictions demonstrates once more that the Old Reich was less isolated than previous generations of scholars have claimed.[67] The reformations that Catholics and Protestants set in motion refracted across Protestant and Catholic worlds perhaps not in equal degree but certainly in similar ways.[68]

Conclusion

Gerlach's appointment as chaplain enabled Crusius and members of the Faculty of Theology at Tübingen to begin an extraordinary exchange of letters with the Greek Orthodox patriarch and other representatives of the Greek Church. It is undeniable that this correspondence, in the beginning, was meant to negotiate some sort of lasting accord. Motivations in Tübingen appear to have been more complex, however, and as more and more letters reached their destination, they gradually took on less conciliatory overtones. No longer was this outreach only about establishing Christian unity. The stakes had changed dramatically: reading the correspondence between Tübingen and Istanbul vis-à-vis the new confessional landscape that began to take shape in this period strongly suggests that the allegedly uncorrupted tradition of the Greek Orthodox Church became a touchstone for Lutherans like Crusius to determine who was the genuine custodian of Christian orthodoxy. Of course, any concord that could follow from an exchange with the patriarch was a particularly welcome front against the Catholics: Crusius knew full well that your enemy's enemy is your friend. But Tübingen turned to the Greek Orthodox Church not to find common confessional ground but predominantly to have its own religious convictions confirmed.

This was exactly the reason why these exchanges ultimately failed. Openly Lutheran Tübingen and the patriarchate of Constantinople may have spoken of being in full communion with each other and of celebrating Christian holy days together; however, each side just hoped to find confirmation for their own beliefs. These exchanges, then, operated much like other intercultural exchanges during this period: they assumed "much of what its users set out to prove."[69] Convinced of their own truth, Lutherans dismissed as superstitious anything that did not conform to what they believed. Nobody was willing to yield an inch. And how could they? There was simply too much at stake: to admit that they were wrong—in the very moment when the Formula of Concord was being drafted—would have meant admitting that their entire reform movement was wrong, that Luther had been wrong. It would have meant questioning the whole set of beliefs on which Lutheranism rested. "Searching for unity," as Nicholas Terpstra has reminded us, "was no guarantee of finding it, particularly when for many a parallel search for purity of faith and worship took precedence."[70]

In one of his letters, Crusius had mentioned that the vast distance separating the Lutherans from the Greek Orthodox Church could have—but hopefully had not—resulted in a divergence in confessional practices.[71] In some sense, what Crusius feared had indeed happened: the geographical distances that separated different Christian denominations had led to cultural and religious ones as well. Attempts to convince the Greek Orthodox patriarch of the Lutheran truth did nothing to break through these barriers. They only reinforced them. Religious motivations had prompted the Lutherans to initiate an exchange about church doctrine—and to bridge these distances—but in the end their confession also prevented them from entering it with an open mind.

Yet for Crusius this was only the beginning. Nothing in this episode in his life suggests he lost faith in his beliefs. The Greek Orthodox Church may have been an ancient and venerable institution, but once it dawned on him and others that Lutherans and Greek Orthodox Christians were not perfectly alike in Christ, it was easy to dismiss the Greeks' position as misguided and marred by superstitions. When we turn from this exchange of letters to the privacy of Crusius's diaries and annotated books, we can see just how much the encounter with Greek Orthodox Christianity only reified his religious convictions. Never again would the Tübingen theologians embark on such a lengthy and costly endeavor to spread their beliefs. But Crusius's documents show how, in other contexts, he continued to entertain high hopes of convincing Greeks of his Lutheran truth.

2

A LUTHERAN PHILHELLENE

The correspondence with the patriarch did not shake Crusius's abiding faith in his Lutheran truth. Neither had it wrecked his hope that Lutheranism would one day be preached in the Eastern Mediterranean. Nowhere, though, did his unshakable faith manifest itself more emphatically than in the intimacy of his study. From the 1560s onward, right before and during the exchange with the patriarch, Crusius coated numerous books and manuscripts about the Greeks and their religion with comment after comment, each more disparaging than the last. Focusing our attention on these impassioned notes reveals that no confrontation with radically new facts, no matter how jarring, shook the foundations of Crusius's religious beliefs. On the contrary, learning more about contemporary Greek Orthodox Christianity only confirmed Crusius in his belief that Lutherans alone embodied the one true church. Reading for Crusius was a deeply religious practice, a devotional exercise, that left little room for the accommodation of other religious convictions.

To understand how reading became such an act of piety, it is necessary to examine his affective reading habits against his upbringing as a Lutheran. His parents were among the first to embrace Luther's new vision of Christian life, and they suffered severely for that choice in the tumultuous early decades of the Reformation: they nearly lost their lives in the Schmalkaldic War (1546–1547). This ordeal had a tremendous impact on Crusius and shaped the ways in which he performed his Lutheranism later in life. His religious beliefs, the trauma that his parents' suffering had instilled in him, and his emotional attachment to books and learning converged in ways that were not easily dislodged, not even through prolonged study of Greek Orthodox Christianity—a denomination that, like Lutheranism, took pride in adhering to ancient rituals. It is ultimately his coming of age, at a time when religious war wreaked havoc in the heartlands of the Holy Roman Empire, that explains how the encounter between German Lutheranism and Greek Orthodox Christianity—two different belief systems, two different Christian traditions, two different worlds—played out in his Tübingen home.

Of course, many factors other than Crusius's upbringing may have—and probably had—shaped his engagement with Greek Orthodox Christianity. Yet historians working in different fields have shown how examining people's inner lives and the way they expressed their thoughts and emotions can illuminate complex personalities and shed light on intricate historical processes.[1] In reconstructing the circumstances of Crusius's upbringing and the powerful emotions that reading awakened in him, I aim to paint his inner landscape without reducing him and his actions to mere patterns. What becomes apparent through both this personal history and his study of Greek texts is rather his ambivalence toward Greece. Crusius expressed his abiding love for all things ancient Greek on many occasions, only to bemoan Greek Orthodox religious practices and underline the weaknesses and defects of contemporary Greek culture on others. His records thus allow us to paint a detailed portrait of the complex role that his religious persona played in these cultural and religious encounters.

In this sense, Crusius's story can also deepen our understanding of the broader history of encounter. His encounter mirrored those of other early modern scholars for whom culture was not relative but absolute, and its comparison made distinct cultural hierarchies visible and reinforced ideas of cultural and religious superiority. In other cases, historians have reconstructed how encounters contributed to the erosion and eventual breakdown of established religious and intellectual structures of thought. Non-Europeans changed Europeans, and vice versa.[2] The Jesuit Matteo Ricci, for instance, who famously dressed as a "Chinaman," sought to proselytize and win the esteem of his hosts not only by studying their beliefs but also by participating in local Chinese learned culture, in accordance with the notorious Jesuit policy of accommodation.[3] Of course, such forms of cultural and religious accommodation were out of the question in Tübingen, the epicenter of attempts to restore Lutheran unity. In this university town, one's beliefs and patterns of behavior—interiorized and externalized conceptions of religion—were subjected to intense scrutiny. Transformations of the kind that Matteo Ricci underwent perhaps speak, in that sense, to differences between confessions, differences between Rome and Tübingen. Yet even more so, they reveal how performing one's beliefs in the center and the periphery required different types of behavior.

READING AS RELIGIOUS PRACTICE

Crusius's self-professed love of all things Greek is easily discernible in his many writings. The first person since antiquity to call himself a "philhellene" (φιλέλλην), Crusius often noted that all good things came from the Greeks and that "everything Greek delighted" him "as toys delight children."[4] It is no exaggeration to say that Crusius was obsessed by the Greek language. Throughout his long life, he eagerly studied textual materials from all periods of Greek history, from antiquity to Byzantine times, and from the patristic era all the way to the Ottoman period. These documents made visible the numerous developments that the Greek language had undergone, all of which could help him understand ancient Greek better: "I would like to connect the knowledge of this modern version of Greek," he confessed at one point, "with the ancient and genuine Greek, because it does not appear proper to me to know the old, more or less, but not to know what is right in front of my feet."[5]

What is less often noted, however, is that Crusius's studies of the Greek language converged with his interest in Greek Orthodox Christianity. In his manuscript copy of the Byzantine chronicler Constantine Manasses, for instance, Crusius wrote that "this historian was worth knowing for his wise brevity, the history and other ideas, his lavish adjectives, the many beautiful and wise *exempla*, his proverbs . . . his prosopographies and other beautiful descriptions, [and] for better understanding the Greek language."[6] In the rich sets of glosses that Crusius left in its margins, he commented on the seven ecumenical councils, Greek Orthodox bishops, Greek Orthodox views on fasting, the cult of saints, and the many doctrinal issues on which Catholics and Greek Orthodox Christians differed.[7]

Examining such notes reveals how reading about Greek Orthodoxy was an occasion for Crusius to perform his religious sympathies. Indeed, much of what he discovered about the religion of the Greeks was not to his liking. The irenic tone and the reverence that permeate the correspondence with the patriarch contrast sharply with the cries of outrage about what he deemed doctrinal lapses that we discover in his private documents. In the layers and layers of annotations that he left in his books and manuscripts, Crusius protested primarily at passages where Greek Orthodox views differed from the core components of the Lutheran creed, differences that he and others had discussed with the patriarch: the alleged efficacy of good works, the emphasis on faith alone, and, of course, the article of justification. Yet his notes also show how it was possible for Crusius to both praise and blame the Greeks by changing the way he read.

Nothing irritated Crusius more than the Greek adherence to the cult of saints and the Marian devotion that flowered among Greek Orthodox Christians. In his annotated books and manuscripts, Crusius voiced his strong disapproval of this practice. One of his manuscripts, for instance, contained some sort of "chant . . . or rule" that could very well be a paraphrase from the Gospel of Luke and the prophecies mentioned there. But "this idolatrous fragment" invoked Mary and thus misdirected praise that "belonged to Christ alone."[8] Comments left elsewhere in the manuscript were equally unequivocal: "Only through Christ, not through Mary we can be reconciled with God. He alone," Crusius noted while paraphrasing the prophet Isaiah, "has trodden the winepress."[9] In the next section of the hymn, he repeated that not Mary but Christ was "the immovable tower of the Church." He was humankind's sole "liberator."[10] Only months later, when he found the same fragment in a Greek *Horologion*—a type of book of hours used for daily services in the Greek Orthodox Church—did Crusius realize that it was a hymn to Mary.[11] No wonder that in the back of one of his copies of this *Horologion* he grouped together passages from the book in which Mary was praised with references to other "idolatries."[12] Few documents, Crusius's indexing seems to say, rendered the Greek adherence to the cult of saints, a tissue of superstitious errors according to Lutheran theology, more visible than these books of hours.

Precisely because Marian devotion, and the cult of saints more generally, was deemed so abject, documents that testified to this practice merited intense scrutiny. Perhaps Crusius knew that elsewhere in Germany different forms of Marian veneration had persisted.[13] But he believed that every doctrinal lapse had to be marked. Next to the very last sentence of a short Greek treatise that Crusius called "an idolatrous booklet on the invocation of the Saints" he commented dryly but vindictively: "Why don't you invoke Christ, you idolater?"[14] Medieval saints' lives stirred up similar emotions. Crusius was extremely eager to study such *vitae* to better understand "the Greek language . . . and because of the various saints and fathers: and not least because of the places and cities." But these lives, which are so typical of office-books in Greek Orthodox Christianity, also helped him to see "the deep-seated errors of the Greeks in the pursuit of monasticism, their faith in good works, the invocation of the Saints etc." Greeks, Crusius concluded, "do not understand the article of Justification."[15] One of his manuscript copies of these saints' lives, which stretches to nearly one thousand pages, brims with indignation: parts of one sermon were "against holy scripture" and reeked of Anabaptism, while the invocation of a saint in another section "belonged to Christ."[16] Yet another part was nothing but "poetic fiction."[17] Where in these hagiographies, Crusius wondered, would he find any evidence of "faith in Christ"?[18]

Notes such as these capture vividly how for Crusius reading was no passive act. It was a clash of religious beliefs, a fierce battle with an author whose heterodox religious beliefs he answered with withering scorn and written reprimand. It is not always easy to reconstruct the sources of Crusius's discontent. One of his surviving books shows, however, that long before he had considered any possible contact with a representative of the Greek Orthodox Church, Crusius emphasized the importance of having faith in Christ alone. In 1553, while still a teacher in Memmingen, he had marked his way through the 1544 Basel edition of Italian reformed theologian Pietro Martyre Vermigli's exposition of the Apostles' Creed that served as a standard by which to measure the author's beliefs. Crusius's annotations, appropriately in Italian, expressed agreement with this Italian reformed theologian that "Christ is the head of the Church, not the pope" and that "the Church only has one head."[19]

Crusius was not alone in berating the Greeks for their belief in the intercessory power of saints and martyrs. Numerous Protestants of the period shared an obsession with idolatry.[20] David Chytraeus, a Lutheran theologian from Rostock with whom Crusius corresponded, is a case in point. A serious Greek scholar in his own right and the author of a brief exposition of the Greek Orthodox Church, Chytraeus also owned a copy of the *Horologion* and concluded from his reading of this book that the "superstitious cult of the Holy Mary" still flourished in Greece.[21] Schweigger had regarded the way Greeks interacted with icons as idolatrous as well, and, keen observer that he was, even noticed that churchgoers kissed the image of Mary before they venerated the one of baby Jesus. Gerlach had shared similar experiences: when urged by Theodosius Zygomalas to bow in front of an icon, Gerlach refused point-blank.[22] Intercessory prayer to saints detracted from the central role of Christ in the eyes of Crusius and these other Lutherans, because such a negation of the primacy of Christ had no justification in the Bible.[23]

Crusius did believe, like many other Protestants, that reading saints' lives could be a meaningful exercise. Lutheran theologians, starting with Luther himself, protested the veneration of the saints while also commending the study of the saints as "God's chosen witnesses" for personal devotion in every station of life.[24] Luther adopted a "balanced stance toward the fathers of the Church" and used them selectively in his theology. Yet he "treated them not just as dead authorities but also as human beings and living believers."[25] Crusius's position was similar: the excessive forms of asceticism that monastics performed and the way "they beat their bodies"—practices with which "they wanted to deserve heaven," according to Crusius—repelled him, as did their eagerness to be martyred.[26] But he agreed that holy men and women, who were the shining lights that had led the early church by their virtue, did merit attention from the faithful as models for living a pious life. Crusius seems to have had a particular interest in female exempla: in a collection of prayers and saints' lives that he was given in 1597, the only part that contains annotation is the vita of Euphrosyne of Alexandria, who, to avoid an arranged marriage, assumed the identity of a man and joined a monastic community. Crusius filled up the incredibly narrow margins of this text with notes tracing the plot of her story.[27] Another manuscript contained the legend of Theoctista, a ninth-century saint from Lesbos, which, although "pitiful," Crusius considered to be "most pleasant because of its sentiment."[28]

Crusius believed that the Church Fathers merited specific attention. Their lives could tell early modern readers about the heresies that had beset the Early Church, and their works offered details of how Christianity had triumphed over paganism in a period in which ideas about what constituted Christian orthodoxy were staged and tested, spread and evaluated. In the work of Eusebius, for instance, Crusius found confirmation for the belief that Christ had been the only true miracle worker of his time. In the early fourth century, Eusebius had penned a passionate response to the late Roman aristocrat Sossianus Hierocles, who, to discredit Christianity and to urge emperor Diocletian to persecute Christians systematically, had compared the life of Jesus of Nazareth rather unfavorably with the Pythagorean philosopher and teacher Apollonius of Tyana. Hierocles's work had not survived. But another Late Antique novel, written in the beginning of the third century AD by the Greek sophist Philostratus, also narrated the life of Apollonius and his travels from Spain to India and from the Levant to Africa. Crusius owned a copy of this work, which had strong apologetic dimensions and portrayed Apollonius as a man with divine powers, able to work miracles, and a champion of classical oratorical culture. Eusebius's treatise defended the superior position of Christ and ridiculed the fanciful, and most probably fictitious, travels of Apollonius and this man's so-called miracles. According to Crusius, the "Bishop of Caesarea did well to write his refutation against Hierocles," because "all learned men agree that Philostratus is a great fabulist," and readers, persuaded by his storytelling, could thus easily mistake diabolical magic for genuine and prodigious miracles. Echoing critiques that other early modern scholars had voiced, Crusius alleged "that the Devil had wanted to cast Christ and Christianity entirely into the shadows through this Apollonius and thus keep the idolatry of the pagans intact." Tellingly, despite the evil depiction of Apollonius that he found in Philostratus's work, Crusius still expressed his admiration for this Late Antique writer, who "in all other regards" wrote elegant Greek and "has many beautiful things."[29]

Crusius's confessional beliefs also did not prevent him from reading historically. Consider his personal copy of Chrysostom's *On the Priesthood*, whose densely annotated pages reveal high levels of readerly interaction. In the margin, Crusius paraphrased the Suda lexicon's entry on Chrysostom, in which the Church Father's treatise on the priesthood was praised for its "sublimity, phrasing, smoothness, and beauty of words."[30] Yet the Suda lexicon, a recently printed tenth-century Byzantine encyclopedia, omitted basic biographical details. For such information, Crusius and others had to turn to hagiography: "the life of Chrysostom," which he found in another collection of Greek saints' lives, had "pleased" him "more than the other" lives that had drawn his attention and was "useful and beautiful."[31] Documents of this kind showed Crusius how the authors of the books in his library had been historical actors themselves, and in some ways exemplary ones, whose lives further contextualized of their writings.

Sometimes Crusius made the evidence serve his confessional agenda through selective reading practices. His oration on the life of the Cappadocian Church Father Basil the Great, given in 1559, is a case in point. Most accounts of this man's life—including the ones Crusius used, namely those of Eusebius, Nicephorus, Zonaras, and the Suda lexicon—begin with Basil's studies in Athens before turning to his travels to Palestine, Egypt, and Syria to study ascetic practices. They almost all mention Basil's interest in the ascetic and the monastic life and describe the monastic settlement that he founded on his family's estate near Annesi. Crusius's sources describe how Basil became deacon in Caesarea in 362 and was later anointed presbyter in 365 and eventually, following the death of his predecessor Eusebius, bishop in 370. In this capacity, so the authors of his vita narrate, Basil vigorously combated Arianism, which was prevalent in this part of the empire, while also serving his congregation constantly. Crusius's vita differs in one hugely important respect: Basil's interest in an ascetic life, and his founding of the monastic community near Annesi, is not mentioned at all. Nor does he specifically mention the Church Father's writings on the monastic life, so extremely influential in both Eastern and Western Christian traditions. Crusius instead stayed on an abstract plane: "even today many distinguished books of Basil are extant. From these, one can recognize the excellence of his piety, erudition, and eloquence."[32] The rest of Crusius's vita focuses almost exclusively on Basil's defense of the church doctrine against the Arians. Crusius thus filtered out information from his sources to make Basil conform his own ideas about what this early Christian Father ought to represent.

Crusius's approach was also guided by period questions of chronology and authority. Which Christian writers still embodied the beliefs of the original Church and who had strayed from the path? Which authors could he safely read and learn from? Matthias Flacius Illyricus's *Catalogus Testium Veritatis* served as one of the most important touchstones by which card-carrying Lutherans like Crusius determined who in Christianity's long history had been witnesses to the truth. The book argued that sometime around the year 300 the "seeds of errors and certain abuses had gradually begun to be scattered in the Church." Before 600, however, these doctrinal lapses "were not so pernicious" and could be excused: for "whoever reads the writers and Father of that period . . . will easily notice that their opinion on many articles agreed with our doctrine." These men were, in that sense, connected by one large unbroken chain of orthodoxy. Anything written after 600, however, "as the rule of the Papacy grew," was suspect according to Flacius.[33] The temporal proximity of the Fathers to the Apostolic Church, that ideal Christian community to which many Lutherans aspired, gave them a privileged status among early modern readers of the patristic past.[34] Denouncing Basil the Great's sympathies for monasticism—and thus effectively detracting from the overall authority of one of the most important Fathers of the Church—was therefore much harder for Crusius than pointing out doctrinal errors in a book of hours or a medieval saint's life.

Yet Crusius must have known about other solutions to the problem of Basil's monasticism as well. The entry on Basil in Flacius's *Catalogus Testium Veritatis*, with which Crusius was intimately familiar, described how both the Church and Eusebius had been critical of Basil's communal monasticism.[35] "From there," Flacius was eager to point out, "one can see how already in those days many condemned monasticism and those new sorts of piety."[36] Flacius thus used Eusebius to highlight one of Basil's less pernicious errors. Crusius, by contrast, as he prepared his oration on Basil, had chosen to manipulate his sources and sacrifice historical veracity for the sake of salvaging the faith. Brushing over Basil's monasticism, he seems to have realized, was more productive than mentioning and denouncing it. Narrating the lives of the Father was evidently a delicate balancing act and one with problems that could be solved in more than one way.

Here Crusius's case is emblematic of the ways in which early Christian literature was read in an age in which the relationship between tradition and scripture had come under enormous pressure. Different members of the Church of England, for instance, mobilized philology and an array of scholarly technologies to root the Anglican *via media* in the teaching of the Fathers and the veneration of early Christianity.[37] Readers and editors of Augustine used the African Father of the Church similarly "to support particularly different, even contrasting theological arguments" while "often pointing to the same texts to draw opposite conclusions."[38] Erasmus, for instance, caused a stir when he pointed out that Augustine had in fact never called himself a monk.³⁹ Elsewhere in his writings the Dutch humanist also played down Jerome's asceticism and commitment to the monastic life.⁴⁰ This creative treatment of the evidence gained even more currency in the often-apologetic Church histories that mushroomed after 1517 and that aimed to reveal the errors of their opponents by revealing how they had mishandled their sources. These techniques ranged from censoring and excising to filtering out material; to leaving out crucial evidence that contradicted one's thesis and quoting a Church Father in a Latin translation rather than the original Greek. No wonder that, as controversy spread, different guides on how best to read patristic literature began to circulate and efforts to create one uniform patristic tradition—in which all Church Fathers, as authorities, reached consensus—multiplied.⁴¹

One of the most fascinating books to have survived from Crusius's library, a densely annotated copy of Paul Eber's *Calendarium Historicum*, shows just how deeply ingrained the saints and the Church Fathers were in Crusius's life.⁴² Essentially the Lutheran equivalent of the *Martyrologium Romanum*, this so-called recording or writing calendar presented a distinctly Lutheran vision of ordering time. Eber had eliminated most of the saints that had populated earlier Christian calendars and filled its pages, each of which was dedicated to one day of the year, with references to the major historical events that had taken place on those days since Creation. The book's organization and *mise-en-page* invited an active form of reading: readers were supposed to customize and update Eber's list of historical episodes by filling each page's ample blank space with comments on current affairs.⁴³ Calendars such as this one thus encouraged readers to reflect, as one historian has described, on "God's administration of history" and to collect further evidence of His hand at work in the world—a habit that could offer "daily reassurances of God's continuing presence in human affairs."⁴⁴ Users of such books, in other words, were encouraged to turn it into an archive of personal religiosity and an expression of their undying devotion, not unlike contemporary Catholic readers of books of hours.⁴⁵

Crusius perused his copy of Eber's *Calendarium* in multiple ways. He inserted information from the prologue, which contained a magnificent exposition of how different cultures organize time, in a miscellaneous notebook in which he also recorded how the Greeks in ancient Athens had counted the months, a subject of great interest in humanist circles.⁴⁶ The

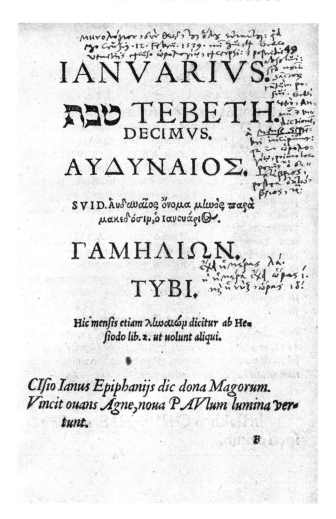

2.1 Crusius's annotated copy of Paul Eber's *Calendarium*. On the top of the page is a lengthy gloss in Crusius's hand describing how he had copied into this Lutheran calendar details about Greek saints and how the Greek year did not start in January but in September.
Credit: Universitätsbibliothek Tübingen Fb 18, p. 49.

rest of the book he enriched not only with notes about his private life, as many readers of such books did, but also, interestingly, with systematic references to the feast days of Greek saints: on the top of every other page, Crusius recorded which specific saint or martyr was venerated on that day in the Greek Orthodox Church. Their inclusion, as one of his notes reveals, had been prompted by his reading of a collection of Greek saints' lives in his *Horologion* and by the realization that Eber's calendar could essentially perform a similar function: the very first annotation on the frontispiece even identified Eber's work as a *menologion*, the technical term used in Greek liturgy for such collections of saints' lives.[47] Ironically, then, for his studies of how the Greek organized the years, Crusius turned Eber's calendar back into a record of saints and martyrs—exactly what Eber had endeavored to eradicate. As long as the holy men and women of the past were not venerated but studied, they merited inclusion in Crusius's life.

For Crusius, then, reading about the Fathers and the Greek Orthodox Church involved a process of engaging—and often strongly rebutting—their religious beliefs from his position as a Lutheran. Crusius dismissed doctrinal errors in Byzantine saints' lives without blinking an eye, while he merely removed any mention of Basil's monasticism in his oration. He could do without the latter but needed the former. Different kinds of reading also allowed for different kinds of responses: when he was reading historically, he could allow for more flexibility than when he was reading theologically. And characteristically, Crusius often combined critical remarks about Greek Orthodox writers' beliefs with praise for the beauty of their Greek.

Rome against Tübingen

One set of marginalia can help us further contextualize Crusius's demeanor as a confessional reader. Crusius flourished his Lutheran beliefs not only while reading about Greek Orthodox Christianity but also when Tübingen faced a severe backlash for its involvement with Jeremias II. In 1582 part of the Lutheran authorities' correspondence with the patriarch was published by Stanislav Socolovius, a Catholic theologian at the court of the Transylvanian prince Stephen Báthory. In the bitter controversy that subsequently arose, Crusius became the target of especially fierce criticism from various Catholic writings. The affective responses he penned in the margins of their books demonstrate once more how for Crusius reading was a performance of his Lutheran sympathies. And they reveal, in graphic detail, that he did not reserve his indignation for Greek Orthodox texts. Catholic attacks stirred up outright animosity. Here, too, Crusius turned the margins of his books into sites of confessional rivalry.

It began with Socolovius's 1582 *Censura Orientalis Ecclesiae*, a pirated edition of the correspondence with the patriarch, which he published "so that" the Lutherans "feel ashamed of their innovations."[48] Reprinted at least three times in the next few years, the book was a bombshell.[49] The Lutherans had proceeded with extreme caution in their outreach to the Greek Orthodox patriarch, which they were eager to keep secret. In Tübingen, of course, many knew about the correspondence and the letters circulated among members of the Theology faculty. But Andreae had implored Crusius to take care "that neither the translation nor the Greek version of the patriarch would fall in the hands of others." Keeping the correspondence secret was critical, Andreae continued, because it "could create new calumnies and impede our pious and sacred project or plan for which I labor until death."[50] If details about the exchange of letters circulated, it could seriously jeopardize Andreae's effort to reconcile the different Lutheran factions. Notwithstanding Andreae's admonition, Crusius frequently mentioned the correspondence with the patriarch in letters to his acquaintances. He even sent copies of some of the patriarch's letters to Chytraeus, who printed them together with his oration on the various Eastern Churches. But while Crusius considered Chytraeus a pious advocate of the evangelical movement, Socolovius's publication was entirely adversarial and malicious.

Other critics quickly joined Socolovius's ranks. In 1583, after having learned of the *Censura* at the Imperial Diet of Augsburg, Johann Baptist Fickler, a jurist from Salzburg who had worked at the Council of Trent and studied under the future Pope Gregory XIII, translated the work into German and published it in Ingolstadt.[51] That same year Willem Lindanus, the Bishop of Roermond, used the Lutheran correspondence with the patriarch as ammunition for his vicious attack on the Lutherans' *Book of Concord*.[52] The Viennese Jesuit Georg Scherer also put in his two cents by publishing, first, a small booklet, in the format of a news pamphlet, that pointed to the patriarch's rejection of the Augsburg Confession. He later followed up with two other works that similarly demonstrated just how wrong the Lutherans were.[53]

It had taken the Lutherans years and tremendous effort to get their letters delivered to the patriarch, but once published by Socolovius, knowledge of the correspondence spread like wildfire: from Lviv to Augsburg, from Roermond to Salzburg, and further on to Jesuit circles. Soon the Lutherans' turn to the Greek Orthodox Church was known in every corner of Catholic Europe. This was in no small part because these works were printed in the most important Catholic cities in the Holy Roman Empire: Scherer and Fickler published their works in Ingolstadt and Mainz; Lindanus in Cologne. Ironically, it had been much harder to connect Tübingen with Istanbul than it was, eventually, to produce versions of those discussions that traveled across Europe.

Lutheran Tübingen had no option but to tell their side of the story. Debate and discussions of this kind often took place through the circulation of books and manuscripts. The citation of primary sources was a well-established and crucial tradition in such ecclesiastical controversy: Luther and Eck famously disagreed in their respective work about the scriptural basis of the former's propositions. In the deeply divided confessional landscape of the sixteenth century, publishing the sources, and publishing them correctly and with the appropriate apparatus, was thus ever more pressing: only by showing the evidence could you prove you were right and counter the slander of your adversaries. So in two separate pamphlets, published in Tübingen in 1583 and 1584, Heerbrand and Osiander rallied to defend the Lutherans against Scherer's attack.[54] In the meantime, Crusius was tasked with translating every single Greek letter into Latin and preparing the material for publication. Eventually published in Wittenberg in 1584 as the *Acta et Scripta Theologorum Wirtembergensium, et Patriarchae Constantinopolitani D. Hieremiae,* the Lutheran version of the exchange, which included the Greek originals, aimed to refute the "lies and charges of that Polish man" and to "demonstrate the virtue of their cause and provide a testament of their innocence." Socolovius, whom they tried to discredit with all their means, was just a parasite and a sycophant, whose "biting, hateful, false, deceitful, and poisonous preface to Pope Gregory XIII was full of sophistry and misrepresentations."[55]

Point by point, the edition denounced the accusations Socolovius had leveled against the Lutherans. The accusation of heresy was not only "heinous and intolerable" but had no scriptural basis: "We have so far not been convicted of any heresy by a legitimate judgment from the Holy Scripture."[56] Neither did they, having turned their backs on the Western Church, seek "to be in communion with the Eastern Church" or want the patriarch to be their new head of Church. On the contrary, fair-minded readers would find in the *Acta* ample evidence that the Lutherans had wanted to let Greek Orthodox Christians "know about the pure doctrine of their religion" and had hoped that "by the grace of God and the working of the Holy Spirit the eyes of the blind would be opened in this way"—that is, by sending the Augsburg Confession—"to recognize the truth."[57] Relying on a very biblical metaphor, the Lutherans claimed they were simply spreading the gospel.

If they hoped that the publication of the exchange would nip further criticism in the bud, they were gravely mistaken. Their fiery preface only added fuel to the flames. Socolovius and Fickler, whose attack had received a similar treatment, gladly took up the gauntlet that the Lutherans had dropped with so much enmity. Fickler translated the patriarch's second and third response, as printed in the *Acta,* into German, published them and penned a relentless invective, the *Spongia,* in which he called the Augsburg Confession the Lutherans' Koran and Luther himself a new Mohammed. At one point, he addressed the Lutherans directly: "You arrogant pigs," he cried out, "who do not want to be tamed or corrected; and who do not want to listen to the words of the Catholic truth."[58] Socolovius was hardly less spiteful. Just months after the *Acta*'s publication, he put out a "short response," followed by a full-blown attack called the *Antidotus,* to which his publisher, Thomas Sunobig, appended a litigious preface.[59] Crusius bound his copy of the *Antidotus* with another reaction to the *Acta* that had directly critiqued him: Jacob Gorski's *Animadversio sive Crusius: in theologos Wirtembergenses* of 1586.[60] Published in Cologne, this treatise by Socolovius's teacher blatantly told Crusius that he had placed his philological acumen, however admirable, in the service of the wrong people.

No official Lutheran response followed. It is not immediately apparent why. Perhaps Tübingen believed that having all the evidence in print was justification enough—to the extent that their actions required any justification—because anyone could now access their version of the truth. Such reasoning had, after all, also encouraged the Lutherans to send Greek translations of the Augsburg Confession and Heerbrand's *Compendium* to Istanbul. But perhaps the Lutherans realized that ignoring their critics was the best way of silencing them. Or did they fear that responding would draw even more attention to what had been an unsuccessful exchange? For they clearly experienced the risk—and irony—of circulating their version of the story: once published, it not only laid them open to brutal criticism but also gave others ammunition against them.

Whatever motivated the Lutherans at this point, their silence stands in sharp contrast to the cries of outrage that Crusius voiced in his own copies of his critics' works. Thick layers of annotation not only expressed his disapproval of Catholic beliefs but also ranted at what he deemed were deliberate misrepresentations of the facts. Nothing but "a lie," he responded to a passage in Sunobig's preface where the publisher had called the Lutherans "miserable weak men," who out of despair had "fled to the patriarch as if to a sacred anchor," suggesting they revered him as a saint.[61] It is "a lie," Crusius repeated when Sunobig told the Lutherans that they had called the patriarch "a most saintly leader."[62] Nothing but lies, Crusius snorted, when Sunobig professed that even to him it was remarkable that the Lutherans called the patriarch's hands "saintly."[63] Again and again, Crusius expressed his outrage, often in Greek, at what he was reading. Evidently the matter had become personal.

It was not just doctrine at stake here. The issue was also fundamentally philological. The problem that Crusius encountered, as he pored over his adversaries' works, was that they distorted the evidence. This was as true for Sunobig's preface as for Socolovius's *Antidotus,* a work that contained "much waggery" according to Crusius.[64] The *Antidotus* had a simple structure and one commonly used in polemical writing: a passage from the *Acta* was followed by a detailed exposition of individual parts of the citation. Yet already on the very first page of the *Antidotus* Crusius expressed his displeasure: "Certain things here are wrongly attributed to us. We did not write everything in this way."[65] "This is not the translation of Crusius nor is it the composition of Osiander," he clarified elsewhere, "but of that papist, and one that does not always correctly translate the proper Greek version of Crusius."[66] Socolovius, in other words, did not cite the official sanctioned translation of the *Acta* but his own rendition, which distorted the Lutherans' motivations. In every new exposition of a passage from the correspondence, Crusius encountered gross misrepresentations: "a false gloss" based on "a false interpretation of the Greek text," "a wrong translation," "a bad rendering," "a false exposition," "a gloss based on a wrong version," "a misrepresentation," and "a gross misrepresentation" are only a few of the philological complaints that he registered in his copy of the *Antidotus.*[67]

Crusius dwelled on matters of accuracy and citation because these misrepresentations questioned his integrity as a translator, which for early modern scholars was as harrowing as being called a bad Christian. He also realized that his deviations from textual precision could lead to major problems in interpretation. In their reaction to the patriarch's third official response, for instance, the Lutherans, according to the *Acta,* thanked God for helping the patriarch be restored to the throne. But the translation in the *Antidotus* had the Lutherans congratulate the patriarch that God allowed the Greeks to follow the ancient customs of the Church—that is, the seat of Andrew, the first patriarch of Constantinople. Similarly, in his initial assault, Socolovius had seized upon a single word used by the theologians— κρίσιν, which he considered to mean "judgment"—to argue that the Lutherans had reached out to the patriarch for approval. Yet according to the Lutherans, they only meant to ask for the patriarch's "opinion," since approval implied that they were looking for a new head of Church, which they decidedly were not.[68] To some extent this "exchange" had also degenerated into an ordinary quarrel about who was telling the truth: "You're lying," Crusius responded tellingly when the text accused the Lutherans of lying.[69]

The last text in the bundle, Gorski's *Animadversio sive Crusius,* struck a particularly powerful chord. It was not so overtly critical of the *Acta* as the first two texts in the convolute, but it was hardly less contentious. Socolovius and Sunobig had sought a polemic by lambasting the *Acta,* line for line, word for word, letter for letter. Gorski, by contrast, took aim at the Lutherans and their beliefs by refuting their doctrines one at a time. And while Socolovius's critique had been aimed at the Lutherans in general, Gorski's diatribe singled out Crusius alone as its main target. He attacked repeatedly and, as Crusius's marginal notes reveal, accurately: throughout the work, Crusius fulminated at Gorski and at what he deemed were his duplicitous ways. Gorski had begun his account, for instance, by praising Crusius: "The best and most learned of men (not just yours, but also Catholics) strongly approve and admire the diligence and faithful rendering [that you showed] in editing [the *Acta*] and in translating it into Latin." High praise indeed, but Crusius would have none of it: "Praise the Devil, Gorski, not me," he jibed cynically in the margin.[70] When Gorski attempted to flatter Crusius by remarking that he had poured out the Greek light on the world of learning, Crusius quipped: "Thank your Devil, you mocker."[71] Unsurprisingly, on the frontispiece of Gorski's treatise, the page that other early modern scholars reserved for a succinct summary of the text, Crusius dismissed his adversary as "a poisonous declamator."[72]

Crusius also suspected that Gorski only praised his fidelity as a translator and scholar of Greek to put certain words in his mouth. When Socolovius's teacher noted, for instance, that Crusius had made his translations from the Greek into the Latin "bona fide"—translations that showed how "Greeks in defending the Catholic Faith agree with the institutes of the Father and the decrees of the Synods"—Crusius responded with indignation: "I did not write this." He did not, as Gorski implied, agree with the content of a document simply because he edited and translated it.[73] "None of this," Crusius fumed after reading a similar passage in which Gorski alleged that Lutherans adhered to the pope's ecclesiastical jurisdiction: "I merely translated an account, like a faithful interpreter. I did not add that I believe all these things, or that I approve of them."[74] When Gorski accused the Lutherans of having forsaken that pure virgin, the Catholic Church, Crusius corrected him but went along with this ancient metaphor: the Church was not a pure virgin with no wrinkles but "an impure liar."[75] Translations, in other words, were not endorsements. Crusius was just a faithful interpreter, a *fidus interpres*, who, as this old set phrase indicated, created a literal rendering of a text, neither manipulating nor otherwise altering the original.[76]

Humanist methods for organizing information enabled Crusius to expose his adversaries' distortions and misrepresentations. He repeatedly turned to blank flyleaves and pastedowns to draw up lists of problematic passages found in these books. While the one detailing the "errors in Sunobig's version" was short and contained no more than eight entries, the one-page list drawn up in the back of Gorski's *Animadversio* included detailed references to passages on which Lutherans and Catholics were divided.[77] The latter included not only polemical passages—such as the one where Gorski alleged that the Lutherans "had been damned by the Greeks" and those where he had mocked or desecrated the *Acta*—but also ones that offered Crusius ammunition: using his favorite rebuttal, he pointed out that the notion that in Rome there were no idols, which Gorski put forth toward the end of his book, was ludicrous and nothing but "a lie."[78] These lists, which mirrored those that he compiled when he read Greek Orthodox treatises, facilitated consultation and made bits of the book more easily retrievable. Together with the layers of notes that Crusius left in the margins, they also turned the book into a record of Catholic deceit and a testament to the Lutheran truth.

Crusius's religious sensitivities, then, guided his interpretations and became the dominant intellectual force driving his reading. Of course, disputes such as this one were hardly ever dispassionate in his world. Especially in the ecclesiastical scholarship of the period, heated debates about who the best reader was—which is essentially what this altercation boiled down to—inspired countless investigations into the Christian, Jewish, and pagan pasts. From Flacius to Baronio to Casaubon, scholars across the confessional divide directed their energies at their opponents' learned volumes and dissected them with microscopic precision.[79] Often such confessional controversies were pursued with all the resources of rhetoric and supported by arguments that were as much or more ad hominem as ad rem. Reading, in that sense, quickly became a performance of one's confessional identity. Obviously, much was at stake: here, as in the correspondence with the patriarch, to admit defeat would have had disastrous consequences for Crusius and, by proxy, the Lutheran movement.

In some ways, though, Crusius's impatience with the bad scholarship of his Catholic adversaries also shows how personal this readerly debate had become. Crusius had been singled out, not only for being wrong but also for placing his extraordinary command of Greek in the service of the wrong kind of Christianity. To ignore such allegations was impossible for one who hoped that his writings would one day bring forth "a fruit well pleasing to God, if He allows it."[80] In Crusius's case, reading was not an exchange but a clash of ideas, one that urged him to reveal his Lutheran identity. To examine him as a reader is to see that philology and religiosity, reading and believing, were inextricable in his mind. The latter inspired the former, and the former guided the latter.

Growing Up Lutheran

One final set of sources affords insight into why Crusius read the way he did, and thus why the encounter with Greek Orthodox Christianity changed him so little. To understand his attitude as a reader and the impassioned responses he penned in his books, we need to turn to his experience growing up Lutheran in an age of division, and specifically to the ways in which he remembered his parents' suffering for their faith.

Crusius came from a relatively humble background.[81] His paternal grandfather, Peter Kraus, had been a tailor and beer brewer in present-day Bavaria. A citizen of Pottenstein, Peter Kraus served for thirty years as one of the city's senators. His wife, Margarete Schaller, bore him eight children, two girls and six boys, one of whom, Martin Kraus, was Crusius's father. Born around 1490 and educated at different schools in and around Bamberg, Kraus matriculated in Leipzig in 1509, as did his brother Johann Kraus, Crusius's uncle. A year later he obtained the bachelor's degree and in 1511 was awarded the grade of magister. In 1512 Kraus became a teacher in Halle and served as cantor in the local Ulrich Church. The next three years were spent in Berlin, where he was a teacher and cantor at the Nicolai Church. Just before Christmas 1515 he was ordained as acolyte in Ziesar, fifty kilometers north of Magdeburg. He was ordained subdeacon and deacon the year after. An outbreak of the plague forced him to move southward, to Wittenberg, where, on March 22, 1516, he joined the priesthood, having been ordained by none other than Albert of Brandenburg, the future cardinal and adversary of Luther. For the next five years, he served as a minister in several towns in and around Bamberg.

In this period Kraus married Maria Magdalena Trummer, Crusius's mother, who came from Klein-Gesee, a village not more than twenty kilometers from Walkersbrunn. Her family mostly consisted of tradesman and artisans, and none of them had ever obtained a university degree. Her grandfather Johan, Crusius's great-grandfather, had been a woodworker and innkeeper in Klein-Gesee. His son, Haintz, was also a tradesman but had married well: his first wife and Crusius's grandmother, Anna Laucher, was a descendant of the Dandorff family, a noble lineage. Their only son continued the craft of his father and grandfather, while their two daughters seem to have married above their station. The same was true for Haintz's children from a second marriage.[82] Nothing is known of Maria Magdalena Trummer's childhood and education.

The Reformation and all the change and turmoil that it brought marked the lives of Crusius's parents in decisive ways. Crusius told his parents' story in different places, but most elaborately in a family history that he would gift to the university's Faculty of Arts. It depicted his father as an early follower of Luther: around twenty-seven years old at the time, Kraus "completed a change" after having heard the Augustinian friar lecture in Wittenberg in 1516.[83] Luther's preaching and teaching did indeed electrify and persuaded many to adopt his ideas about redemption, salvation, and justification, as did his charisma and affable personality and the wave of his pamphlets and other books that flooded the book market during the 1520s and 1530s.[84] But it is by now also a commonplace among historians of religious change that conversion in the early modern period was a prolonged and complex process.[85] Crusius's portrayal of his father's religious awakening as a singular moment—articulated years after the fact, and possibly clouded by what happened in between—may therefore have been modeled on those "conversions" of other Christians, including Paul, Augustine, and Luther himself, whose moment of illumination, sometimes known as the *Turmerlebnis*, brought him a new understanding of Paul's epistles to the Romans.[86]

In Crusius's narration, his father appears not only as an early adopter of this new vision of Christianity—note how his father's "conversion" occurred in 1516, before the formulation of Luther's famous ninety-five theses—but also as an extremely zealous one. In the next few years, spent in and around Nuremberg, his father struggled, according to Crusius, to align his own beliefs with his job as a minister and eventually requested to be relocated to "a friendlier place . . . away from the wilderness . . . where he was in imminent danger because of his love for the gospel."[87] "Irreligious" parishioners, like those about whom Kraus complained, were indeed no aberration in this period of transition. Since Gerald Strauss's pathbreaking study, scholars have debated how far Luther's message actually sank in and noted that older forms of devotion often continued to exist.[88] Nuremberg, for instance, formally adopted Lutheranism in 1525, but from the diary of the city's most famous daughter, Caritas Pirckheimer, we know that this prioress of the convent of St. Clare's successfully petitioned against the dissolution of her community.[89] Andrew Pettegree has similarly emphasized how the choice to accept Luther's message "ended friendships, caused division between neighbors and kin," and risked incarceration and even death because of the continuation of older structures of worship.[90] In this period, Crusius's uncle, a Lutheran minister like his brother, would be arrested and incarcerated for two months "because of his evangelical doctrine."[91] The "wilderness" and "danger" of which Kraus spoke thus evidently reflected the divisions and transformations that grew out of the creation of Luther's new religious order.

Not until 1527, when Kraus moved to Bruck, did he leave the "wilderness." His family, which included newborn Martin, spent the next seven years in this town just north of Nuremberg. In 1536, after a brief stay in St. Jobst, just east of Nuremberg, the family left the region altogether: on May 13 of that year Crusius's father was examined in Stuttgart, where he "gave a specimen of his doctrine by preaching." Having passed, he took up a position in

Steinenberg, not too far from Schorndorf, just east of Stuttgart, lured there by the prospects of expressing his religious beliefs freely.[92] Just two years earlier, Duke Ulrich had returned from exile and begun reforming his duchy along the new evangelical doctrines: monasteries were closed; Catholic churches stripped; new educational institutions founded; and existing ones reorganized. The most eminent university in the duchy—the University of Tübingen, established in 1477—became the first existing university in the Holy Roman Empire after Wittenberg that saw a far-reaching reformation of its educational curriculum. The duke had also converted the city's former Augustinian monastery into the *Tübinger Stift*—the seminary for the preparation of Protestant ministers.[93]

Here Crusius and his parents parted ways. Crusius enrolled at the local grammar school of Gregor Leonhard in Ulm, a free imperial city, in February 1540 while his parents moved to Lehr, which was just north of the city, where his father took up the position of preacher. A year later they successfully petitioned the senate of Ulm to grant their son a scholarship.[94] It was in Ulm that Crusius started learning Greek. He initially received private instruction, after formal classes had ended, because unlike his peers he had no knowledge of the language. Looking back at this period as an almost seventy-year-old reputable professor, Crusius intimated that, although passionate about the subject, he was not diligent enough in studying grammar. Rather than going over the rules of Greek, Crusius secretly attended the lectures on Greek literature. But when his language instructor once called on him to answer a grammatical question and found Crusius unable to answer it, he called him "an old shoe" (*caligula*) to the general amusement of the other students. This "reprimand" hit where it hurt most: *An old shoe?* Crusius thought. *Never!* The next time, Crusius answered every single question "about syntax and the meaning of prepositions," even though he had not yet officially studied this topic with his teacher, "while the others, who had heard more Greek, were silent."[95] Crusius's parents, meanwhile, moved to Luizhausen, just a few miles north of Lehr, in part because his father would earn a higher salary there, but also, as Crusius's account suggests, because of the Anabaptists living around Lehr.[96]

In 1545 Crusius was sent to Strasbourg, where he enrolled, again on a scholarship, at the famous Protestant gymnasium of Johannes Sturm. This institution offered a cutting-edge secondary education and became a model for many other reformed schools of the period.[97] Crusius was initially placed in the *secunda,* the second-highest form at the gymnasium, where he—in his own estimation—was quickly writing Greek "flawlessly."[98] Two years later Crusius came top of his class and was promoted to attending the public lectures, the next level in the curriculum. He received a monetary prize as well as the honor of giving a public oration—the kind of public performance and symbolic ritual from which the Holy Roman Empire and its cities derived their meaning and coherence.[99] Crusius gave the oration not only in Latin, as was customary, but also, in the presence of some of the most acclaimed professors, in Greek, which no other before him had done. Even if we take Crusius's own account of his remarkable progress with a grain of salt—although there is no real reason why we should—Strasbourg evidently offered him an environment in which he thrived.[100]

For his parents, by contrast, this was one of the most traumatic periods in their lives. Between 1546 and 1547, just months after Luther's death, the forces of Emperor Charles V, resolved to restore religious unity, clashed with the Schmalkaldic League, an alliance of Lutheran princes that had pledged to defend each other in case of an attack on their territories. Brief but intense moments of violence erupted. In no time, Spanish troops reached the hills outside the city walls of Ulm. Unsure what to do, given that Crusius's father was a minister, his mother went into the city to inquire. She "only barely made it," Crusius wrote, and once back home, "urged my father to leave." Hastily they collected their belongings, hid them in the local church, and quickly made their way to Geislingen, just a few miles north. With the help of local preachers, "they sustained themselves for" the almost biblical number of "forty-two days." In what was undoubtedly a considerable and hazardous undertaking, his mother "made sure that some of their belongings were brought to Ulm and Geislingen." Not long thereafter, hoping the danger was over, his parents returned to Lech, only to be forced to flee for a second time.[101]

Ulm surrendered to Charles V early in 1547. It was agreed that nothing would be taken from the people, although some food would have to be distributed among the soldiers, and preachers would have to persuade their congregation to collect money because of the costs of the war.[102] The citizens of Ulm, including Crusius's parents, quickly discovered that these were empty promises:

On Tuesday, after the first Sunday of Epiphany, fifteen soldiers of the emperor's first band came to Luizhausen. Together with their prostitutes they spent their time at my parents' place. Even though my father served them food and wine in abundance, they still threatened him with a noose to wrench some money out of him. Their pretext was a sermon on the gospel (i.e. that the emperor had not left this to the inhabitants of Ulm, and moreover that the city had been given to the soldiers to loot). In the middle of the night, one of them, from the area of Lake Constance, wanted to pierce an awl through my father's genitals to obtain forty guilders. But he was forced to abandon his attempt because his friends were drunk, and my mother intervened.[103]

Not long thereafter, when another group of soldiers had knocked on their door, Crusius's father was forced to hide in their dovecote. It was only when the soldiers started searching for food that he managed to escape to the house of a fellow minister. Later Kraus's wife reached her husband "with great trepidation": Spanish soldiers had stopped her twice on her way over and forced her to hand over her possessions. Through her cunning—"she feigned an illness" and wore an unclean headscarf—she "tried to keep herself safe from the impudence" of the soldiers.[104]

Their predicament continued, however. Crusius described how they had to hide in the ossuary of the local cemetery and later heard the screaming of a group of women who were being raped.[105] When they were back in Ulm, his father was assaulted by a group of Spanish soldiers and only managed to escape—bruised, without his belongings, and with his clothes torn—because he spoke Latin. Still later, when a soldier threatened to strangle his mother, "God offered help": a dog that was lying close by bit the attacker in the leg, which allowed his mother to escape. (Crusius noted that his parents adopted the dog.[106]) Yet his staging of this moment of divine intervention also gives the whole narrative the aura of a martyr story (*passio*), in which his parents, although not paying the ultimate price, were tested and rewarded for adhering to Luther's new vision of Christian life.

Crusius emphasized that these calamities scarred his parents deeply. "Three times my mother saw my father cry," he noted, "first, because of Martin Luther's death; second, because he lost his books, which for a large part had been written in his hand, in small letters, and closely packed together; and, finally, because not long thereafter he had heard that the Elector of Saxony, Johann Frederic, had been captured."[107] More than once Crusius emphasized just how "much his parents had suffered in Christ's name" and "in particular in Ulm during the war with Charles V for professing the gospel."[108]

It bears noting that, while his parents had to endure these hardships around Ulm, Crusius was still a young man of twenty studying the intricacies of Greek grammar in Strasbourg. This is more than just a rhetorical coupling: one of his father's letters from this period not only told Crusius about these experiences following the outbreak of the war but also castigated him for not being studious enough.[109] Here the story brings us back to reading. Of course, narrating his parent's misfortune years after the fact served to cultivate a sense of religious belonging in a period when professing one's confessional stripes mattered greatly. But I believe these connections ran deeper.

As in the best Lutheran households, Crusius had initially learned the rudiments of how to read and write from his father.[110] Yet this form of domestic instruction had not ended after Crusius went off to school: later in life, father and son continued to read books together and exchange notes. In what was evidently a reversal of roles, his father at one point even excerpted the annotations Crusius had made in his classes in Ulm on one of the plays of the Lutheran dramaturgist Thomas Naogeorgus.[111] The play in question denounced Catholicism and, although Crusius left no record of such a conversation, it is not difficult to imagine father and son sharing notes about—and perhaps even bonding over—what they considered heretical beliefs.

This kind of communal reading also continued when Crusius inherited his father's books, after the latter's death in 1554. Crusius read these books repeatedly, explicitly marked them as his father's, and even turned them into tributes to his father's reading habits.[112] He made an effort to record for every future reader how arduous it had been for his father to peruse his books: on the frontispiece of Luther's German translation of the Bible, Crusius noted how his father had "annotated it throughout" while "he could only see with his right eye, having earlier lost vision in his left [eye] due to an illness."[113] Yet Crusius also knew that it had been worth his father's while to customize his books so assiduously: commonplacing, excerpting, and annotating the gospels and other such texts was exactly, as Crusius detailed repeatedly, how Martin Kraus prepared to preach.[114] That is what made losing

2.2 Martin Kraus's annotated copy of Luther's translation of the New Testament. All notes are in Crusius's father's hands, except the note on the bottom, in which Crusius indicates that he himself had read this book in 1554, 1586, and 1595, while his father, when the book was still his, had read it in 1523 and 1530. *Credit: Universitätsbibliothek Tübingen Ga LIII 43, title page.*

a part of them in the Schmalkaldic War so incredibly traumatic: these had been his father's working copies, documents that he had placed in the service of the faith, carriers of a theological truth that could ensure that the Lutheran faith would root in the "wilderness."

It is not only relevant that Crusius knew what direct religious motives his father's reading practices served; where and how he recorded that information is equally illuminating. One of his students had prepared a neat copy of Crusius's family history but, characteristically, even when it was done, Crusius felt the need to insert more information about his father's reading and preaching practices. These notes told the reader that in 1520 Kraus "had collected a *monotessaron*"—the technical term for a continuous narrative about Christ's passion prepared from a collation of the four gospels—while a few years later he had "drawn up annotations on the whole Gospel of Matthew and preached them in Grebern and in Bruck." One set of Crusius's notes specified when his father had summarized "the arguments of the individual chapters of the Old Testament" and excerpted Philip Melanchthon's 1521 *Loci communes rerum theologicarum,* the first systematic treatment of Lutheran thought organized around eleven commonplaces, and according to Luther the most important Lutheran book after scripture. Another annotated page spoke of the "descriptions" Kraus had made of the Gospel of John. Yet another of Crusius's notes indicated that "Kraus had drawn up many sermons from Paul's epistles and delivered them in public."[115] Crusius's marginalia thus reveal how closely connected reading and preaching had been for his father. He found in his father's books a form of reading aimed at mastering the gospels and spreading the truth of scripture.

Crusius also inherited from his father an absolute confidence in the sermon as a conduit for spreading the faith. This was, of course, no idiosyncrasy. Preaching had been a cornerstone of Christianity practically since its origin. In the early modern period, an overwhelmingly oral society, preachers across the confessional divide took to the pulpit to inculcate their beliefs and rebuke those ideas they deemed heretical.[116] Harnessing one's skills on this front was thus of paramount importance, as Crusius knew his father had done for years: Crusius's summary of the aforementioned copy of Chrysostom's *On the Priesthood* specified how "in this book is written against those who heedlessly, without having considered the magnitude of the task of preaching, jump to the pulpit," often merely to sustain themselves, "because they do not know how to feed themselves."[117] His father, as Crusius knew from experience but also learned in the richly annotated books that he inherited, had been the antithesis of such cunning preachers.

Some documents reveal just how neatly Crusius's interests in sermons as conduits of the faith overlapped with those of his father. For almost fifty years, sitting on his knees, Crusius made running summaries—extemporaneously and in ancient Greek—of nearly 7000 sermons that he heard the theologians deliver from the pulpit in the *Stiftskirche*. Why did he do this? Recording these sermons—one during the week and two on Sundays—would aid the retention of the "many pious matters" that local theologians treated "with the greatest wisdom" and confirm his students, instructed to copy the sermons as well, in this "excellent practice." Crusius also felt that as a professor of Greek, he ought to be fluent in the language he was teaching. And he admitted that, had he not taken such notes, "the Devil would have made my thoughts wander."[118] Crusius was extremely proud that, when Chrysostom's homilies could not be found, the duchy adopted one of his own sermon collections for the edification of the youth.[119] Clearly, Crusius's attendance in Church, his sermon collections, his pedagogy, and his unshakable faith in Lutheranism converged in intricate ways.[120]

Over time, Crusius saw how these summaries could serve as a vehicle for proselytizing Greek Orthodox Christians. Toward the end of his life, some of them were printed in the four volumes of his *Corona Anni* of 1602–1603.[121] Crusius was almost eighty by the time this work, which he considered his most important contribution to the world of print, was published. But he still had high hopes for this collection of 516 sermons in ancient Greek with a facing Latin translation: he wondered if a few copies could be sent to the king of Denmark, who could then forward them to Moscow and to "the princes of those regions." Surely, Crusius continued, a Greek could be found there, given that the Russians resembled the Greeks in their version of Christianity. From Moscow, these copies could then be sent to the Ottoman Empire. The plan was optimistic, to say the least. Yet he pursued more ambitious aims: by having the book read by Orthodox Greek Christians, God would allow "the pure gospel" to be poured over the population there.[122] No wonder that Crusius made a point of emphasizing how the loss of his father's annotated books had made his father cry. As a vehicle for proselytization, and a means of moral and religious instruction, the sermon was an unsurpassed tool. Anything that threatened a Lutheran's effort at preaching was therefore a dangerous and despicable affair.[123]

Reading all these documents next to one another reveals the imbrication of several important themes: reading, preaching, proselytization, and persecution. It is the sermon that runs through the lives of Crusius and his father as Ariadne's thread. The examination of one of Kraus's sermons got him a job in Württemberg; Crusius, as we saw in Chapter 1, had appended a sermon to his letter to the patriarch, which caused so much confusion, "as a sample of my faith"; through a collection of sermons, printed toward the end of his life, Crusius hoped to convince Greek Orthodox Christians of the Lutheran truth; his father had excerpted and summarized the gospels for sermons meant to inculcate Lutheran beliefs in the "wilderness." Kraus thus appears to have instilled in his son a deep sense of religious belonging and imparted to Crusius that typical Lutheran belief in the efficacy of the written word. Hence it was his parents' traumatic experiences in the Schmalkaldic War, and the way they suffered for their faith, that fundamentally shaped their son's ideas of what it meant to be Lutheran. And it was the dynamic religious climate in which he grew up as an adolescent, and all the turmoil that occurred in those troubling early decades of the Reformation, that influenced how Crusius came to view and evaluate Greek Orthodox Christianity vis-à-vis his own beliefs.

Conclusion

On January 4, 1604, at the formidable age of seventy-eight, shortly after the *Corona Anni* had been published, Crusius recorded one of the dreams that had come to him at night:

> Dream. I stood alone on the western flank of the Österberg. I saw my head, beautiful and white as snow with the hairs of an old man, on the top of the mountain. The back of my head was facing me [but] my face was truly facing the oriental gate of the world: where Greece is. In all ease it floated in the air without any support.[124]

There and then, according to one historian, Crusius dreamed of being the apostle of the Orient.[125] One might say that such an interpretation reads too much into this otherwise rather unremarkable dream. Yet it is compelling to think of Crusius in exactly this way: the dream captures emphatically what was on Crusius's mind when he was asleep and what kept him awake during the day. Greece was his chosen obsession and the world toward which he directed his gaze. Indeed, just two months after recording the dream, Crusius decided to write a chronology of Lutheranism "from the moment Luther began to rise up against the pope." He intended to print it together with his *Panhaeresium,* a work that has not survived but in which he hoped that "false ways were refuted." These were Crusius's last works—"I do not know what to write anymore," he told an acquaintance at the time—and he hoped that God would "direct it" toward the Greeks, like the sermons collected in the *Corona Anni,* "in which the true path to heaven is shown."[126] As a true apostle, he believed that everyone would embrace Lutheranism once they read Lutheran materials in their own language.

Yet Crusius must also have known just how much hinged on one's reading of such materials. Herein lies the irony of this story: although Lutherans insisted that on matters as delicate and potentially incendiary as religious doctrine it was necessary to publish the evidence for all to peruse—and that it was crucial, therefore, to ensure the evidence was indisputable—reading confounded these principles. Evidence could be distorted, texts misread, citations manipulated. Only by being more accomplished at these tasks than one's adversaries could one mold the truth to one's will. And even then, once texts had entered the public domain or had fallen in the hands of an uncharitable reader, interpretations were difficult to control, as Crusius and the Tübingen theologians discovered. Ironically, Crusius's own behavior as a reader—his heated reactions to the accusations of his antagonists and the "superstitions" that he found in Greek Orthodox texts—could have told him plainly that reading was hardly ever impartial. In a divided confessional landscape, and in a period of intense confessional rivalry, being the best reader—or at least being the better reader—was what mattered.

Reconstructing historical reading practices thus enables a more intimate view of Crusius than has been possible in the past. Reading Crusius's marginalia next to his family history reveals the nexus between remembering, reading, preaching, and belonging that shaped his inner life and the ways in which he encountered religious diversity. Crusius's remarkably well-documented case also offers insights into how a whole generation of Lutherans performed their religious beliefs and the broader history of encounter. It is tempting to state that Europeans, when engaging with other beliefs and other peoples, simply wanted to confirm their own superiority. But probing into the cultural-religious climate in which such people came of age shows that deeper forces were at work as well. As Crusius's case shows, so much was at stake for those first-generation Lutherans whose parents had suffered for embracing Luther's message. For other early modern Europeans, whose books have not survived, whose inner lives have escaped our attention, and whose upbringing cannot be reconstructed in such granular detail, the same might be the case: whether Catholic or Protestant, growing up in a divided world left little room for critically engaging with one's own belief system when encountering other religions, cultures, and peoples.

Crusius's reading practices ultimately encourage us to embrace the inconsistencies that made him human. He spent years, and with great success, teaching Homer as a fountain of rhetorical and ethical knowledge. But when he turned his attention to Eusebius's *Preparation for the Gospel*—the Church Father's celebrated attempt to demonstrate the superiority of Christianity over paganism—he summarized nearly five hundred pages of dense apologetic exegesis in a single note on the work's title page: "Amongst the Greeks there is nothing sound for the salvation of the souls, neither in theology, nor in philosophy. So with good reason did we cross over from paganism to Christianity."[127] The irenic tone of the correspondence with the patriarch stands in sharp contrast to the adversarial notes Crusius left in his books and manuscripts. Only reconstructing Crusius as a reader renders this ambivalent but deeply human aspect of his engagement with Greek Orthodox Christianity visible.

It would be too easy to explain these discrepancies only in terms of the medium—the "public" correspondence versus the (semi)private setting of his study—or to reduce them to an expression of Crusius's confessional beliefs. Crusius was, after all, not just a staunch Lutheran or a devout philhellene. To attempt to reconcile these extremes, creating order and uniformity out of the thicket of notes that Crusius jotted in the margins, would be to miss the essence of what makes his engagement with the Greek world so distinctive—namely, that he could be inconsistent and often took seemingly conflicting positions. It is more fruitful, as historians of reading have repeatedly proven, to resist the urge to reduce all the evidence into a single narrative: Crusius's complete disdain for Greek Orthodox Christianity did not discourage him from welcoming waves of Greek Orthodox Christians into his Tübingen home and subjecting these men and women to lengthy interviews about their life and culture, their language and religion. This is the story that Chapters 3 and 4 narrate.

3

WANDERING GREEKS

On August 31, 1587, at five in the afternoon, Crusius and his wife Catharina Vetscher went for a walk. They left their house close to the city walls and passed through the Lustnauer gate, continuing their journey eastward to their garden on the Österberg, the 1400-foot-high hill that loomed over the landscape outside the city walls of Tübingen. But just when they were about to climb to the top, their maid Barbara Hagelloch called out to them: Gabriel I, the Greek Orthodox archbishop of Ohrid, was about to arrive, accompanied by twelve Greek Orthodox ecclesiastics. Crusius was to go down and greet them. And this he did: he immediately made his way back, following the wide road that overlooked the Neckar, the river that ran south of the city, and told the mayor of the arrival of what no doubt was an extremely distinguished party for a German university town the size of Tübingen. Crusius then went to a local hotel, the Lamb's Inn, where he instructed the innkeeper to prepare a set of rooms. By the time he returned to the gate to greet and accompany the visitors formally, a crowd of spectators had gathered. In a solemn but no less intimate moment, Crusius approached the archbishop with care, saluted him, and, as custom dictated, kissed his right hand.

Crusius then escorted the party into the city. The Greeks, wearing traditional ecclesiastical dress, traveled with no fewer than three carriages and twelve horses. Held up high and erect in one of the carriages was the archbishop's long scepter (πατερίτζα). Crusius later noted that the staff's heptagon-shaped core was divided by three silver knobs and made of brown sandalwood, while its silver head bore the image of a serpent. When the procession arrived at the Lamb's Inn, Crusius invited the Greeks to sit in one of

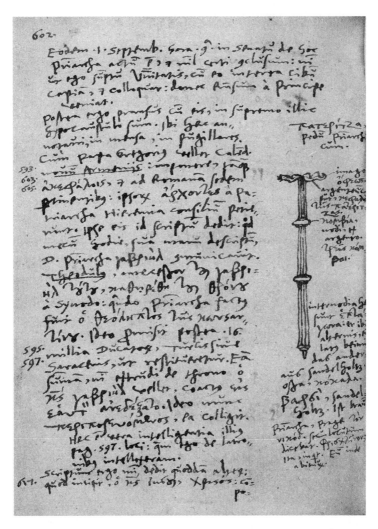

3.1 The archbishop of Ohrid's scepter (πατερίτζα). In his explanatory note, Crusius reveals that it was made of sandalwood and bone with a silver head and silver nobs. Credit: Universitätsbibliothek Tübingen Mh 466, vol. 3, fol. 602.

the back rooms. There the archbishop handed him a large piece of parchment that detailed, in Greek, the woeful reasons that had prompted the man to leave his diocese: a group of thieves had robbed the archbishop of the astronomical sum of sixteen thousand ducats. The document, which had been signed by numerous Greek Orthodox ecclesiastics, called on all of Christianity to support the archbishop on his journey in search of alms. Not long after Crusius finished reading the letter, he was invited by the archbishop to join them for dinner, a meal that consisted of fish, crabs, soup, and greens because "those three Greek ecclesiastics and others," as Crusius noted in his diary, "never eat meat."[1]

Over dinner the men made conversation. Crusius asked where they came from and where they had been. They informed him about the current name of Sparta and the Greek churches of Sofia and Athens. They also mentioned Pope Gregory XIII's intention to introduce his calendar among the Armenian Christians, an innovation this group vehemently opposed. The next day Crusius and the Greeks continued their conversation over lunch. This time they talked not only about what the Greeks considered the intrusions of the pope but also about the beginning of the Greek Orthodox year (the *indiction*), which coincided with the very day they were talking. Later that night, again at dinner, conversation turned to the various archbishops in the Greek Orthodox world and the number of Greeks living in these lands. For the next four days many more thoughts about religion were exchanged over lunch and dinner, until, on September 5, 1587, the Greeks left the Lamb's Inn to continue their journey to Ulm and Augsburg, and from there to Venice. Seated in his carriage, the archbishop wished Crusius well and asked to write him in the future. "And so," he noted in his diary, "they took off from here. Good luck to them."[2]

Encounters such as this one do not generally appear in our accounts of the Holy Roman Empire. Yet the archbishop and his party were by no means an anomaly. Between 1579 and 1606, just a year before Crusius's death, over sixty Greek men and women ended up on his doorstep and informed him in all sorts of ways about the Greek world. What bonds of trust made these interactions work? How could travelers such as the archbishop of Ohrid convince people of the need to support them? How did Crusius know that what he was told was true? In short: What where the terms of exchange? Examining these questions not only affords us deep insights into how cross-cultural encounters worked on the most fundamental level. It also tells us something about Crusius's ambitions as a Lutheran looking to proselytize as well as about the kind of work ethnographers like him undertook to assess the reliability of their informants. And, last, these questions help us capture the varied experiences of a group of Greek itinerants, who offered essential contributions to the ways in which Europeans like Crusius came to see the Greeks but who have so far been all but forgotten.

Encounters in Crusius's home were effective, as we will see, for the simple reason that both parties decided they needed to be. Though Crusius suspected at some point that his guests might not all have been honest about their intentions and lied about who they were, he nevertheless decided it was worth listening to their stories and remunerating them for the invaluable intelligence they brought from the Eastern Mediterranean. He decided to trust them where he felt it did not pay off for them to deceive. Crusius's interlocutors, by contrast, knew the value of amplifying their hardships and of infusing their life stories with elements that met European expectations about Greek life under Ottoman rule. They were not passive respondents but tried to guess what would gain them what they wanted and shaped their narratives accordingly. Such storytelling was not without risks: Crusius's guests presented a version of the truth that capitalized on a shared dislike of the Ottomans, but in so doing they unintentionally contributed to the negative stereotypes about wandering Eastern Christians and the Greek experience under Ottoman rule that in this very period began to capture the imagination of Christians all over western Europe.

To get what they wanted, then, Crusius's guests had to tell a story that was just right for the circumstances. That is not to say, though, that they were necessarily forced to spin a new narrative everywhere they went. Rather, like all great storytellers, they always had more than one way of telling their story and could creatively adapt elements of the narrative to suit different purposes. Crusius's interlocutors had to narrate a story that was true enough to convey a sense of the real and to persuade their hosts to remunerate them.[3] Such storytelling could involve forms of dissimulation, self-fashioning, and improvisation. The stories that Crusius's interlocutors told are therefore best seen not as altogether fictitious nor as historically real but rather as a set of evaluations, some of them calculative, others more makeshift, meant to convince a given audience of the integrity of their arguments. They were, in the words of Giovanni Levi, "the result of an individual's constant negotiation, manipulation, choices and decisions in the face of a normative reality which, though pervasive, nevertheless offers many possibilities for personal interpretations and freedoms."[4]

My goal in what follows, then, is not to pass judgment on the validity of these testimonies. There is simply no evidence to argue conclusively whether they were true or false, or something in between. Instead, I want to weigh the currency that the stories of strangers enjoyed in a world rife with duplicity and deceit. Rather than resolving the inherent ambiguity surrounding these cross-cultural encounters, our task is to measure what degrees of trust were needed to make them work.

Greek Orthodox Christians in Sixteenth-Century Europe

The general circumstances that brought Greek Orthodox Christians like the archbishop of Ohrid into contact with Crusius were not exceptional. In recent years the study of early modern mobility, exile, and migration has brought renewed attention to the great number of lives lived on the road and the various forms of displacement and dispersion that distinguished Europe in this period. Though reliable data and solid long-term quantitative analyses are still unavailable, even the most conservative estimates paint a picture of near unprecedented forms of mobility.[5] The movements of Eastern Christians, previously known only to a handful of specialists, have become a subject of growing interest within this new paradigm. Historians have not only brought to light the great number of Eastern Christians on the road but also afforded penetrating insights into their experiences as they crossed vast distances, from Aleppo all the way to the Spanish colonies in South America.[6]

The direct impetus for the movements of Crusius's guests came from a very distinct practice of the Greek Orthodox Church: the *ziteia* (ζητεία). In accordance with this custom, monks, ecclesiastics, and even laypeople—armed with a letter of recommendation from the Patriarch, a bishop, an abbot, or the local authorities—left their homes to collect alms in support of their communities. Even though the exact origins and developments of the *ziteia* are still poorly understood, it has been suggested that especially after the 1569 *fetva* by Sultan Selim II, which decreed that all monastic and Church properties be confiscated, this custom became one of the Greek Orthodox Church's main sources of income for repurchasing confiscated estates.[7] It is indeed not unlikely that this practice evolved at least partially in tandem with the geopolitical changes that followed the arrival of the Ottomans in the Eastern Mediterranean: by the sixteenth century, the *ziteia* was no longer just a local affair in which Greek Orthodox Christians traveled within their own dioceses and to neighboring communities but a broader phenomenon that prompted Greeks of all walks of life to traverse the whole of Christendom in search of alms. Tübingen was thus not the final or even the primary destination of the Greeks whom Crusius would come to meet. It was but one stop on a much lengthier journey that brought them to numerous German towns and to places all over Christian Europe, from England to Spain, and from France to Russia.

Yet there is no set of documents that details the existence of this group of itinerant Greek Orthodox Christians in as much detail as Crusius's notebooks. Between 1579 and 1606 Crusius met over sixty Greek Orthodox Christians whose lives and travels are not documented in any other surviving records.[8] His notes reveal how he fed these travelers, offered them beds for the night, supported them financially, and subjected them to lengthy interviews about their life and family, religion and culture. Their stories eventually filled hundreds of pages in one of his quarto-sized manuscript notebooks.[9] Each entry includes the day, date, and time of arrival. It usually offers a description of his guests' place of origin, their family situation, and their appearance. Crusius's introductory notes also cover the letters of recommendation that his visitors were carrying, the places they had visited before they stepped on his doorstep, and whatever other special information he had obtained through conversation. This could be a topographical description of the Greek archipelago, a catalog of Greek books, or an almost verbatim recording of a conversation about the Greek Orthodox Church. Most often, though, Crusius made long lists of the vernacular Greek words that his guests taught him. He usually also recorded the misfortune that had driven these Greeks on the road: on one occasion, he was told that North African corsairs had carried in captivity a family member of one of his guests. On another, he learned that local Ottoman authorities had unjustly arrested a certain Greek and convicted the person of supposedly illegal activities. In some cases, it appeared that his interlocutors had themselves been enslaved or condemned to the galleys. Yet all stories emphasized one crucial point: significant sums of money had to be raised to ransom those taken captive.

The Greeks who visited Crusius formed a varied group of individuals from different social strata. Stamatius Donatus, the first Greek whom Crusius met in Tübingen in 1579, and Alexandro Trucello, whom Crusius interviewed three years later, had both been farmers. Gabriel Calonas and Joannes Tholoitis were priests. In captivity the latter had also worked as a beekeeper. Andreas

Darmarius was a learned scribe who knew more than one language and hoped to sell some of his Greek books and manuscripts while in Tübingen. Some were monks. In 1585 Daniel Palaeologus claimed to be connected to the Byzantine imperial house; Petrus Phokas made a similar claim in 1590. They hailed from places all over mainland Greece as well as the islands. Some of them, like the archbishop of Ohrid, arrived in groups; others traveled in pairs; still others came alone. Nearly all of them were men. Occasionally, though, they were accompanied by their wives or daughters. Once a woman from Philippopolis called Antonia made an extraordinary impression on Crusius by composing a Greek song for him.[10]

The story that Crusius's first Greek Orthodox visitor in Tübingen recounted can be taken as a typical one. In 1579 Donatus told Crusius that he hoped to collect 250 Venetian golden ducats to ransom his mother, Frankoula, and his two brothers, Dimitri and Andria. They had been captured by the Ottomans in the 1570 siege of Nicosia, one of the campaigns that initiated years of hostilities between the Republic of Venice and the Ottoman Empire. For the last seven years, a man Donatus knew as Mehmet Celebi had been holding his family members captive in Istanbul. To set them free, Donatus had traveled from parish to parish, across the Low Countries and all the way up to Poland, before arriving in Tübingen, collecting alms in all the places he visited. The letter of recommendation he had obtained from the Patriarch before his departure sanctioned his travels. In Rome he had exchanged that precious document for an equally valuable letter from Pope Gregory XIII. But fortune, Donatus intimated to Crusius, had not been on his side: it had been impossible to collect money in Italy because he had been banned from entering cities following an outbreak of the plague. In Poland, where he went next, Donatus said that he had only received a few guilders from the king of Poland. "Peasants there," he explained, "are poor and the nobility treat them like slaves." The distance between cities had been vast as well, and there was nothing but fields and destitution between them. But the worst was yet to come: in the Low Countries soldiers had torn his papal letter of recommendation into shreds, leaving him with just a piece of the pope's lead seal. "Such a document," they declared while adding insult to injury, "was not worth anything." In Tübingen Donatus could thus only give Crusius a fragment of what had once been an authoritative document and a story of why he was unable to offer any further evidence that could vouch for his good intentions.[11]

Nearly all aspects of this story were standard. Crusius's guests spoke almost without exception of the long periods that they had spent on the road. Lukas and Andreas Argyrus, who visited Tübingen in January 1581, mentioned that they had been forced to flee their hometown on Santorini when Ottoman corsairs raided one of its castles in 1577. From Crete they had moved on to Zakynthos in the Ionian Sea. Their subsequent travels brought them to Ancona, Rome, and eventually Venice. They continued westward to France. But since Paris experienced a major outbreak of the plague, they were forced back on the road. Their next stops were Trier, Mainz, and Würzburg. Augsburg came after that, followed by Regensburg, Passau, and Salzburg. Turning around, they traveled to Munich and all the way to Konstanz before heading north to Rottenburg am Neccar. On January 23, 1581, almost four years after they fled Santorini, they arrived in Tübingen, where Crusius recorded their itinerary as well as their plans: they intended to visit Aurach next, then Strasbourg, Ghent, and France again.[12] In 1582 Gabriel Calonas, a priest from northern Greece, told Crusius that he had wandered through Italy and Poland for two years before spending another six months passing through different German towns. Although he was unsure where to continue his journey after Tübingen, Calonas hoped God would allow him to reach Augsburg for a meeting with the emperor and other local German rulers at the 1582 Reichstag.[13]

Often these Greeks emphasized the great losses they had suffered. Raising enough money, they stressed, could literally be the difference between life and death, and between liberty and captivity, as is borne out by Calonas's tragic testimony. The sole purpose of his travels was to raise enough money to set his brother free. Back in Greece Calonas had helped a group of Italian fugitives by sheltering them from the Ottomans. The authorities got wind of this, arrested him, and brought him to Serres, a town in northern Greece and the seat of the local metropolitan. There he was detained for six months, until his brother Antonius, to whom he had sent word of his misfortunes, agreed to act as guarantor. This arrangement meant that his brother was imprisoned, while Calonas had to collect the hefty sums of money that had been set as bail. The first three hundred pieces he had paid off immediately, he said, by selling all his belongings. In Italy he had managed to gather another two hundred, which he had already sent back to his brother through a merchant from Venice. The remainder, Crusius was told, still had to be settled.[14]

Many stories focused on the grueling hardships that Crusius's interlocutors claimed to have endured. Let us consider the case of Joannes Constantinus Paraskeva, a man so old and fragile that he arrived in Tübingen, accompanied by his cousin Andreas, on a donkey's back—a circumstance that may have reminded any Lutheran as pious as Crusius of Jesus's arrival in Jerusalem and the prophecy it fulfilled in the book of Zechariah. Paraskeva had been arrested in Istanbul for reasons that remain unclear in Crusius's notes. Somehow, though, he managed to escape and liberate twenty-four of his fellow prisoners. They fled to Thessaloniki, but before reaching the city, they were again apprehended. This time Paraskeva was subjected to brutal torture and severe corporal punishment: the authorities, he told Crusius, had subjected him to the *strappado,* the cord by which prisoners, hands tied behind their backs, were pulled up to the ceiling and then allowed to fall. They had also stuffed ash and vinegar into his nose and dislocated or otherwise mutilated his left arm. He almost lost his eyesight and would have been burned at the stake, had not someone intervened on his behalf: instead of capital punishment Paraskeva was sentenced to pay seven hundred golden ducats. Crusius learned that four hundred of these had already been paid off and that Paraskeva hoped to collect the remainder on his travels through the Christian world: from the Low Countries to Poland and to Spain, and from there to Tübingen. But before he had been granted permission to leave, he had to put two of his sons and another cousin in pledge.[15] For Paraskeva, as for Calonas, alms collecting was his only chance of ever seeing his loved ones again.

One story captures the trials and tribulations that Crusius's Greek visitors claimed to have endured more than any of the others. During the 1570 siege of Nicosia, the Ottomans had captured Alexandro Trucello and his family. Not long thereafter, this farmer took part—probably as an Ottoman galley slave and certainly against his will—in the Battle of Lepanto. But "through the grace of the Lord Christ the Christian armada prevailed," as Trucello declared to show Crusius his true colors.[16] In the aftermath of that siege, while still enslaved, Trucello recovered from an illness that he contracted on one of the prison ships. Crusius learned that he was subsequently brought to Istanbul, before being shipped to Naupaktos to be sold as a slave to the highest bidder. His buyer—whom Trucello calls his "master," ἀφένδης, or *efendi*—brought him to a small village close to present-day Lamia in central Greece, close to the Malian Gulf. He stayed there for three months until his owner died and the widow sold him to another man, who lived in Arta, north of Lefkada. It is unclear how, but Trucello managed to escape to Preveza, a town just west of Arta, reaching the island of Lefkada a little later. Fleeing from one place to another, Trucello eventually managed to find a boat that took him to Corfu, then under Venetian rule, and thus what seemed to be his ticket to freedom.[17]

But Trucello's sorrows were not over yet. He told Crusius of his travels to Venice, where he stayed for six months, not knowing what had happened to his family until a Cypriot merchant sailing from the Ottoman capital eventually broke the tragic news to Trucello that his father had passed away and that his mother, two brothers, and one sister had died in captivity.[18] One other brother and one other sister were still alive, though, and the Ottoman trader who held them captive was willing to sell them. Trucello immediately wrote the Venetian *bailo*, imploring him to intervene on his behalf by offering to pay the trader part of the ransom price. He also beseeched Giovanni Trevisano, the Patriarch of Venice and a former Benedictine abbot, to write him a letter of recommendation. Armed with this permission to travel, Trucello set out to raise the money that would guarantee his brother's and sister's release. He initially failed to obtain a letter of recommendation from the pope in Rome but eventually acquired one through the intercession of a cardinal. Trucello then crossed large parts of northern Italy, stopping in Siena, Florence, Bologna, Padua, Treviso, Vicenza, Verona, Brescia, Bergamo, Milan, Turin, Genoa, and Parma. He eventually boarded a ship in Mantua and sailed up the Po to Venice, from where he continued his journey north to Innsbruck, Munich, Regensburg, Passau, Salzburg, Augsburg, and Ulm, before reaching Tübingen in 1582.[19]

The intensity of such human suffering was not lost on Crusius, who was often instrumental in raising the sums of money that Trucello and others took away from Tübingen. He always tried to obtain permission for them to beg at a local church. Donatus managed to collect "more than a few guilders" by waiting for the local congregation to leave the *Stiftskirche* after mass. Trucello collected about four guilders by begging at the same church doors after the congregation had been encouraged to support the Greek piously on their way out. Crusius also mobilized his social and professional connections. As dean of the arts faculty, he ensured that his colleagues, including the rector, remunerated Trucello while Donatus had profited from Crusius's position at the university in similar ways. Crusius had brought Donatus to his Greek classes and to his lectures on Cicero, where the students gave him a little money.[20] Even Crusius's boarders, some of whom came from affluent aristocratic families, were willing to support these alms collectors, as happened in February 1585, when Andreas Argyrus and Joannes Tholoitis were in Tübingen.[21]

Given their aim—remuneration—it is hardly surprising that these Greek Orthodox Christians went to such great lengths to communicate the extreme precariousness of their positions. It is no surprise either that in this specific context their testimonies began to look awfully similar: the only reason they were allowed to travel in the first place was to collect alms. In no other circumstances would these men and women have set out on such lengthy journeys or have traveled to Tübingen and other such remote places. In that sense, it seems that the only story that Crusius could have heard was one of hardship and captivity. This is not to cast doubt about the veracity of their tales. It was of course always possible that these men and women had been taken captive. Indeed, behind these narratives was the grim reality of the Mediterranean slave trade. A recent estimate is that between 1500 and 1800 around two and a half million slaves lived in Christian Europe and another four to six million in the Ottoman Empire.[22] Even though many of these were brought north by slave traders from East and West Africa, the roughly one million enslaved Christians living in the Ottoman Empire and another 850,000 captives in places along the North African coast—nominally under Ottoman suzerainty, but in reality fairly autonomous—caused great anxiety among communities all over Europe. The numerous Christians, for instance, who had died and the thousands of others who had been enslaved at the Battle of Lepanto, had had a profound impact on Crusius.[23] In his view, such could easily have been the fate of his interlocutors.

But the stories of these Greek Orthodox Christians also catered to the increasingly established conventions of a genre. Throughout the early modern period captivity narratives, which appeared in great numbers and enjoyed widespread popularity in print, described in lurid detail the experiences of those taken captive by pirates, corsairs, and privateers from all over the globe.[24] Those lucky enough to be redeemed brought back chilling tales of captivity that had little good to say of those that enslaved them. One-time captives often invoked deep-rooted stereotypes—Muslims, for instance, were often portrayed as libidinous and violent—and emphasized that they had tried everything to preserve their honor and faith while in captivity. Such narratives also appeared to corroborate ideas about the Ottoman Turks that began to circulate in Western Europe after the Fall of Constantinople: in texts of various kinds—from poems to invectives, from university orations to humanist histories—Europeans commented on the atrocities committed by the Ottomans and the cruel fate that befell the Greeks as well as Greek learning. Thus, when Donatus, Paraskeva, and Trucello told such tales of captivity, highlighted their adherence to the Christian faith, or emphasized the hardships they had suffered at the hands of the Ottomans, they drew from a particular type of storytelling with which Crusius and his contemporaries were all too familiar.

Crusius's guests sometimes also seem to have told him what they thought he wanted to hear. In 1585, for instance, one of Crusius's guests professed to know Theodosius Zygomalas and told his host that this man's wife, Maria, had died six months earlier. This confused Crusius: he knew her name to be Irene and he had heard nothing of her death in Zygomalas's last letter, which had been delivered just a few months earlier.[25] Why, then, would his guest make such a claim? It is possible, of course, that this Greek was simply mistaken. He may have misremembered. But it is also possible that this Greek sought to interest Crusius by pretending to know more than he did: playing up to Crusius was one way of creating a sense of familiarity that would make it more likely to leave Tübingen with his pockets filled. Andreas Argyrus once claimed that he could bring to Tübingen age-old manuscripts from Venice.[26] Perhaps he could have. But tempting Crusius in this way could also have been another tactic to encourage his host to support him financially. Darmarius told Crusius that Jeremias II would not accept the calendar reform that the pope proposed. Even though we now know this to be true, at the time it was not clear in Tübingen where Jeremias's alliances lay. Darmarius may very well have sensed that capitalizing on a shared dislike of the pope's innovations helped him sell some of his manuscripts.[27] Darmarius also mentioned that Calonas had been collecting alms by fraud. This may have been true—Crusius, as we will see in more detail, also had his suspicions—but speaking ill of an earlier alms collector could also bolster one's own credibility. In straddling multiple cultural contexts, Crusius's Greek visitors evidently knew all too well the value of saying the right thing at the right time.

What, then, are we to make of these Greeks? Evidently it was worth their while to meet the expectations that people like Crusius had about the Ottoman Turks. Crusius expected that Greeks experienced cruelty at the hands of the Ottomans, and thus emphasizing or even amplifying the hardships that they had suffered made sense to his Greek interlocutors. Yet to simply dismiss these stories as fictitious because they were generic or perhaps exaggerated would distort the past in important ways. The revisionist historiography that has appeared in recent years on the Greek experience under Ottoman rule has shown that Greek accounts of slavery and captivity were on a whole exaggerated. Greeks, we now know, also enjoyed great opportunities for social mobility under Ottoman rule, and Greek merchants profited in various ways from the international commercial order that developed in the sixteenth- and seventeenth-century Mediterranean.[28] But we also know that early modern individuals did suffer real traumas from their captivities. Telling their stories in whatever way they chose may thus have seriously empowered Greeks and one-time captives and given them again control over their lives.[29] On an individual level, then, the stories that Crusius was told may have given voice to very real and incredibly traumatic experiences.

Converting Greeks

In the summer of 1587 Joannes Dondis and Cosmas Papadatos stayed in Tübingen for no fewer than fifty-four days, making theirs by far the longest visit of all. Papadatos, upon his arrival, presented Crusius an extraordinary letter that detailed his tragic life story: he had been enslaved by the Ottomans and through coercion had been "forced to be a Turk." Now that he was free again Papadatos wished to be baptized "by Lutherans rather than Papists"—a choice that must have been music to the ears of a staunch Lutheran like Crusius. We have seen how Crusius tried to spread Lutheran beliefs by corresponding with the Greek Orthodox Patriarch, but at one point he had also entertained the idea of having Greeks come to Tübingen to learn about Lutheranism.[30] Now he was unexpectedly given the opportunity to do in person exactly what he was unable to do in writing. This was his chance to put words into action. His interactions with Papadatos illustrate how throughout his life Crusius continued to entertain high hopes for bringing Greeks into the Lutheran fold. Yet in this case, too, his ambitions were frustrated, not in the least because Papadatos crafted his story to match the expectations of a pious Lutheran like Crusius.

Initially, the theologians in Tübingen did not want to approve Papadatos for baptism because they were unsure whether this Greek knew the tenets of the Lutheran faith.[31] Yet the fears underlying their decision may have been broader. In the second half of the sixteenth century, baptisms of adult men were considered dangerous in Lutheran circles because they could be mistaken for a form of Anabaptism: if Papadatos had already been baptized, which was possible since he was born a Greek Orthodox Christian, baptizing him again would seriously violate Lutheran doctrine. The fears of Nicodemism—believing one set of doctrines but outwardly practicing another—which spread through the Christian world in this period, could also have influenced the theologians' decision: What if Papadatos was not whom he claimed to be? What if nothing in this captivity narrative was true? What if he just wanted to collect alms as long as possible? Papadatos's request to be baptized was therefore as perilous as it was propitious for Crusius and other Lutherans in Tübingen.

To avoid any missteps on their part, Crusius decided to confer with the authorities in Stuttgart, who could pass judgment on such delicate matters. The exact correspondence has not survived among Crusius's documents, but from his diary we can surmise that Stuttgart granted Crusius permission to instruct Papadatos and prepare him for baptism. Crusius then took it upon himself to ensure that this Greek would know the intricacies of Lutheranism, including the Sunday Sermon and the Lord's Prayer, by heart. He also wrote an epitome of Lutheranism in Greek and made Dondis, who had agreed to help, swear to read this catechism of sorts repeatedly with Papadatos, who was illiterate. The two men were also ordered to come to Crusius's house twice a day for further instruction: at six in the morning and at noon, before and after lecture hours.[32] Crusius even arranged for them to attend service in the local church, seemingly—given that these Greeks knew no Latin or German—to have them *see* rather than *hear* how Lutherans performed mass. This religious instruction would go on for weeks, if not always completely to Crusius's satisfaction: at some point he realized that Papadatos, probably because of his illiteracy, had not yet learned half of what he was supposed to know, even though Crusius had broken the rudiments of the Lutheran faith down into small, digestible units.[33] "How unfortunate," he intimated in his diary, "that Papadatos cannot read!"[34] And thus, nearly a month after Crusius had first formulated this Greek catechism, he still found himself going over several of the articles of faith with Papadatos.[35]

The frustrations that Crusius voiced in this case reflect not only his commitment to this cause—translating all the relevant documentation must have taken up a lot of his time, to say nothing of their daily meetings—but also the deeply Lutheran context of this exchange. Instructing Papadatos may have been a difficult task, but it was in Crusius's view an act of piety and charity that belonged to the good works that Christians were supposed to do in life.[36] His motivations also mirrored those that had prompted him to send Lutheran materials to the Patriarch and other Eastern Christians: if only Papadatos would read about Lutheran doctrine in his mother tongue, he would surely become convinced of its truth. Catechisms such as the one that Crusius made were, moreover, one of the few nonbiblical traditions that Lutherans kept for instruction of the faithful: "The catechism," according to Luther, "is the layman's Bible. It contains the whole of what every Christian must know of Christian doctrine to be saved."[37] Meant primarily to encourage memorization rather than explication, the catechism was the cornerstone of Lutheranism and supplemented preaching in planting God's word in the hearts of the faithful. Luther's own catechism became hugely popular and eventually acquired canonical status when it was included in the *Book of Concord*. Thus, when Crusius put together the tenets of the Lutheran faith in his Greek epitome and used it to teach Papadatos, he followed a common Lutheran tradition of instruction.

Crusius's efforts eventually did bear fruit. On August 20, 1587, more than a month after the Greeks' arrival in Tübingen, Jacob Heerbrand baptized Papadatos in the local church. The great number of people who had gathered inside and outside the church to witness the event testified to the consequence and perhaps also the unconventionality of this baptism in the eyes of Tübingen's inhabitants. How often, after all, would the local population see a stranger from distant lands join their flock?[38] Or was the great interest in Papadatos's conversion perhaps also indicative of a certain level of mistrust toward this Greek's intentions?[39] It is for that reason even more unfortunate that the documents only tell Crusius's side of the story. What specific devotional, personal, or practical reasons influenced Papadatos's decision to be baptized in Tübingen? In what part of the Christian world did he envision living his further life as a Lutheran? Not in Italy, he intimated to Crusius, because they would burn him for being a Lutheran.[40] What did Dondis, himself a Greek Orthodox Christian, think of Papadatos's decision to convert to a Christian creed that many in the Orthodox world frowned upon? While Crusius's motivations are relatively transparent, those of his traveling interlocutors are lost in the fog of history: shortly after his baptism Papadatos left Tübingen, never, it appears, to have returned.

Information that Crusius was given four years later may therefore have come as quite a surprise. In 1591 an "illustrious" man by the name of Thomas Palaeologus revealed to Crusius that Papadatos "had been baptized in Mantua" and that Dondis was "a very cunning man," effectively suggesting that the "baptism" in Tübingen had been feigned.[41] Though there is no direct evidence to evaluate Papadatos's intentions, it is possible that they were not entirely virtuous. The baptism had been worth his while after all: Crusius and Heerbrand wrote him a set of official letters confirming the baptism, which he could show to those whom he met on his future travels as evidence of his sincerity, and they gave him some money.[42] But, again, it is also possible that Palaeologus exposed and vilified their motivations so that he would appear more trustworthy in the eyes of his host and others whom he met in and beyond Tübingen. Crusius's notes did not provide his perspective on the matter: characteristically, he focused on recording the details of his guests' testimonies instead of revealing which of his Greek interlocutors he decided to believe.

Problems of Credibility

The possibility that some of Crusius's visitors sought to tarnish the reputation of others by accusing them of duplicity reflects a concern of much broader proportions: How could one trust a stranger from a distant land? In Crusius's world, the motives of his guests were never above suspicion. His reputed friend Gerlach, for instance, reckoned that these men and women might not be completely honest about their intentions. In March 1579, only weeks after Donatus had been in Tübingen, he told Crusius that only when in possession of a letter of recommendation from the Patriarch could such alms collectors be trusted. Gerlach later intimated that there were impostors in Istanbul claiming to be related to the Byzantine imperial family. It was not that it was a priori impossible that these Greeks were really who they claimed to be: in one of their many conversations Gerlach had also mentioned that beggars, mostly women, lived on the streets of Istanbul.[43] Rather, the great number of Greeks traveling through Europe made suspicions about their intentions grow stronger. As Crusius recorded in his diary,

> because nowadays Greeks come to us more frequently, it seems likely to me and to Stephan Gerlach that they are sent out by the Patriarch or the bishops under the pretext of a captivity—which they perhaps feign—in order to collect alms from the Germans by stealth.[44]

The travels of Crusius's Greek guests provoked a similar reaction among his colleagues and acquaintances as well. Chytraeus had written a letter for another Greek, Philippus Mauricius, in which he noted that, although he did not contest anything in his story, he did find the frequency of these Greeks' visits unprecedented: "Within a timespan of eight days, three [alms collectors] came to me with letters from the Patriarch, avowing that they came from Greece."[45] In January 1583, about half a year after Calonas's visit to Tübingen, Bruno Seidel, a physician from Erfurt, confided his suspicions to Crusius in a similar vein: "I thought that he feigned his captivity." Seidel added that Calonas had "collected more than thirty-four guilders in Erfurt" and "talked about Elisabeth [the mother of John the Baptist] who is worshipped in the Patriarchal Monastery in Constantinople." Yet, he wondered, how is this man "still doing miracles"?[46]

Such concerns reflected a more general apprehension. Throughout the early modern period, there was a widespread sense among Europeans that individuals were possibly not who they claimed to be. Judicial records have revealed that identity theft was, although perhaps not the order of the day, certainly not uncommon and often extremely disruptive within specific communities. Even though authorities sought to stamp out any form of dissimulation among their subjects, they had little success: vagabonds claiming to be the deserving poor burdened authorities; rogues in all walks of life assumed false identities and violated sumptuary laws by wearing different sets of clothes; dissemblers feigned sanctity or even claimed to be the Messiah himself; tricksters masqueraded as clerics, healers, or princes from faraway lands. Travel and diplomacy provided plenty of opportunity for developing new identities: exiles reinvented themselves as experts; false ambassadors courted royals under false pretenses; genuine ambassadors acted as double agents; royal pretenders traversed the world to press their claims. Impostors, in short, were everywhere.[47] Indeed, the early modern period witnessed the rise of a distinct body of scholarship on the topic: treatises and manuals on dissimulation, which appeared in all major European vernaculars, taught their readers with unparalleled precision "the shadowy art of dissimulation."[48]

Different forms of religious dissimulation and insincerity came to be seen as a particularly vexing problem.[49] Nicodemism, although denounced by all Christian denominations, nonetheless occurred on all sides of the confessional divide. In part, this reflected a changing religious landscape: in the wake of those unsettling first decades of the Reformation, religious nonconformists were forced to conceal their beliefs in many parts of the Christian world. Newsletters frequently reported that throughout the Mediterranean Christians had "turned Turk" and continued to live their lives as Muslims. In the Iberian Peninsula, where Muslims and Jews were forcefully encouraged to become New Christians, conversions had completely changed the face of individual communities and entire societies. Yet one need only look at the activities of the Spanish Inquisition, which made exposing dissimulation and rooting out superstitions one of its special occupations, to see widespread anxiety that these new Christians were Christians in name only. The fear of crypto-Jews led people to accuse their neighbors of Judaizing activities. Similar anxieties about the insincerity of converts from Islam triggered the Spanish Crown to decree the expulsion of these so-called Moriscos in 1609.

The religious wars waged by Protestants and Catholics and their attempts to vilify one another's beliefs further aggravated the situation. Conflicting interpretations of religious objects made Christians across the confessional divide more attuned to the possibility of fraud and deception. Protestants zealously denounced the cult of relics, which reeked of idolatry, and labored to expose all relics as counterfeits. In Catholic circles these same objects emanated a mystical salvific power and provided uncontestable evidence of God's work in the world as well as protection and intercession from the saints. In the witch craze that peaked in this period, problems of assessing what was true or false, and what was illusory and what was real, were a matter of life and death. Even the simplest day-to-day activities of one's neighbor could reveal that they worshipped the Satan or had fallen victim to diabolic possession. It is not only the astounding numbers of witchcraft accusations that illustrates the obsession with duplicity and insincerity but also the widespread sense and lingering fear that literally anybody could have made a secret pact with the Devil.[50]

The specific situation that Crusius found himself in reflected many of these issues. The fact that his guests were thought to be strangers from distant lands made their testimonies hard to evaluate and potentially suspect. Although scholars of the period firmly believed travel and autopsy to be powerful ways to gain accurate knowledge, travelers were thought to maintain a vexed relationship with established standards of truth and were often suspected of being liars.[51] Similarly, however pious the intentions of his Greek guests may have been, many contemporary critics considered them to be ordinary beggars. And such sturdy beggars—unlike the deserving poor for whom early modern government institutions and religious fraternities frequently made provisions—were thought to display deviant behavior and were stereotyped as being poor because of their laziness.[52] The distinction between the deserving poor and charlatans also led early modern cities to monitor the movements of beggars closely and issue specific instructions to refuse them entry to the city.[53] Indeed, when Mauricius arrived in Tübingen in 1585, one of the city's porters made him wait at the gate and sent word to Crusius. Even after he had talked to the porter—and had presumably vouched for Mauricius's good intentions—the Greek was only allowed in after he had sworn that he had not been in places where the plague had recently erupted.[54] Such had been the grim reality of some of Crusius's other Greek guests as well: the deputy bishop of Florence had refused to provide Trucello with a license to beg, while Donatus had been banned from entering certain other cities following an outbreak of the plague and had not been able to obtain permission to collect alms in Stuttgart.[55]

Some of Crusius's notes reveal just how complicated and disruptive the presence of his Greek guests could be. Mauricius, for instance, did in the end receive some money in Tübingen: from Crusius, with whom he lodged; from the Faculty of Arts; and from Gerlach. But outside this close-knit group of individuals—who all knew Crusius and, presumably, accepted his judgment—Mauricius's status met with more skepticism. On the third day of his stay, Crusius asked the prefect of the *Stiftskirche* to grant Mauricius permission to collect alms after service had ended, as other Greeks before him had done. Much to Crusius's surprise, however, the request was denied. No fewer than six reasons were given: the Church authorities held that there were already too many poor people in the area and poor relief would only aggravate the situation. The city's treasury was also nearly empty. Worse still, the authorities feared that allowing Mauricius to beg at the church doors would set a precedent for future pilgrims: "At other times many pilgrims come hither to seek alms" and "soon we shall see that others will come." Neither had Mauricius been allowed to beg at the Church doors in Stuttgart. The patriarchal letter that he carried was also suspected to be a counterfeit taken or copied from somebody else: the theologian Theodor Schnepf had "recently said that [Patriarch] Jeremias had been deposed before this patriarchal letter [was written]." For all these reasons the prefect warned Crusius to stop intervening on behalf of these pilgrims if he wanted to avoid enmity within the community.[56] Mauricius's stay evidently set social relations in Tübingen on edge.

By contemporary standards, moreover, individuals like Mauricius presented dubious personal credentials. At an early age he had been selected by the Ottoman authorities for an elite education as preparation for state service. Like the countless other Greek boys that this child levy, known as *devşirme*, turned into apostates, Mauricius was ultimately recruited into the Janissary corps, the elite guards of the Ottoman sultan, and joined the *Sipahi*, the fief-based Ottoman provincial cavalry corps, at a later stage. Those who wanted to question Mauricius's sincere belief in Christianity could find further incriminating evidence in his marriage to a Turkish woman and the child that she had borne him. Only his flight to Venice, albeit under unclear circumstances, and his subsequent baptism by the Greek Orthodox metropolitan of Philadelphia could account for his current position as a Christian alms collector.[57] Mauricius, in other words, was one of those apostates who—like so many intermediaries, captives, go-betweens, and renegades—were often subjected to rigorous scrutiny by inquisitors and neighbors alike, especially when they sought readmittance in their former religious community.[58] Apostasy, although an effective means of self-preservation and social mobility in the early modern world, was believed to warrant severe punishment if the accused was unable to provide evidence of mitigating circumstances, such as coercion or fear for one's life.[59] In the case of itinerant individuals like Mauricius, fear of religious dissimulation loomed large in the public mind.

Confessionalization also influenced how these Greeks were received. Crusius himself, as we have seen, thought Greeks were superstitious and erred in their beliefs. So did his colleague Lucas Osiander: "I bemoan their poverty and their misery, but I do not approve of their religion, nor of their habits."[60] This is not to say, of course, that all Greek Orthodox alms collectors had to defend themselves against such stereotypes when encountering Crusius and others in Tübingen. That a trope is available does not mean it is always deployed. But it is undeniable that the Greeks had been the subject of numerous negative stereotypes over the centuries, all of which could have influenced the ways in which Crusius and his contemporaries responded to Greek Orthodox Christians.

In some of the stories that Crusius recorded, he also found details that just seemed off. Donatus had told him in 1579, for instance, that he hailed from Cyprus. His hometown was a place called Sithuni and was located on the southwestern part of the island. It was a city bigger than Tübingen and comprised about nine thousand households. But when Crusius checked this information with Trucello, his other informant from Cyprus, he was told that no such place existed on the island. Trucello did know of a place with that name, but it was located on the Greek mainland. This prompted Crusius to return to his notes on Donatus: he first corrected what he had written down about Donatus's provenance, and then added, in a different color of ink, that Sithuni was a city in Thessaly, not a place on Cyprus.[61] Three years later Donatus's identity became even more suspect: in May 1586 a priest by the name of Michael made his way to Tübingen. Accompanying him was an interpreter called Stamatius who, intriguingly, claimed his hometown to be Sithuni. This could hardly be a coincidence: Crusius, although not entirely sure, strongly suspected that this interpreter was the same man who had lodged with him in 1579. The facial features of this Stamatius even resembled those of the other one.[62] But his guest gave no sign of recognition. Neither did his identity come up in conversation. Not a word was uttered about the location of Sithuni, nor about the 1579 visit of that other Stamatius. In this case Crusius, somewhat curiously, seems not to have brought up his suspicions in conversation but to have confided them to his notebooks alone. If Crusius discovered anything at all by talking to the man, it was that this interpreter could *not* be the same Stamatius who visited him in 1579: that man had told Crusius how he and his family had been held captive in Istanbul. This Stamatius claimed never to have been in the Ottoman capital.[63]

How, then, could Crusius assess the reliability of what he was told? He was willing to support these Greeks in no small part because they could offer him, as we will see in more detail in Chapter 4, a unique inside perspective on the Ottoman Greek world. But if they were lying to him about their identities, if they were collecting money through fraud, how could he really know that what they said about their culture and religion was true?

Establishing *Fides*

In this world teeming with identity fraud, rife with various forms of dissimulation and deceit, and populated by impostors and dissemblers, there was always more than one way of knowing who people were. Early modern ideas about which sources constituted incontrovertible proof, and about what kind of truth was in operation in any given situation, were extremely diverse.[64] Jurists, travelers, newsmongers, merchants, brokers, diplomats, historians, naturalists, antiquaries, doctors, churchmen, notaries, courtiers, and generals all knew, in their respective ways, how to weigh the evidence that was relevant to their assorted tasks. Coercive methods and public interrogation were the primary tools that some of them sharpened. Others plied their trade mostly through intelligence gathering or selecting classical exempla. Still others preferred travel and empirical observation. Documents that held up in court were not necessarily authoritative on the marketplace, in the library, or on the battlefield. Testimonies given in public appealed to different standards of validity than those uttered in private or reproduced in print. Even within a single profession or discipline, entire wars were sometimes waged about what constituted reliable evidence. This happened in the most varied fields but famously in the ecclesiastical scholarship that emerged in the wake of the Reformation.[65]

The one point, however, that early modern individuals of many professional and confessional stripes seemingly agreed on was that *fides*, or credibility, was essential in weighing testimonies, be they oral or written, ancient or modern. Establishing the *fides* of a text or an individual was a hermeneutical practice with roots in Roman oratory. Ancient rhetorical standards held that both the medium and the message of a testimony needed to be credible and reliable for it to be valid. In the case of epideictic speeches, for instance, the branch of rhetoric concerned with praise and blame, Roman oratory emphasized the importance of portraying a life. It was necessary, according to Cicero, Quintilian, the *Rhetorica ad Herennium*, and many of their early modern commentators, to introduce in the beginning of a speech the subject's external circumstances (e.g., family, education, wealth), their physical attributes (e.g., strength, beauty, health), and their qualities of character (e.g., wisdom, courage, justice). These "topics for persons" (*loci personarum*) not only aided orators in faithfully depicting individuals but also allowed people to draw inferences about an individual's credibility. One's birth, one's name, and one's country of origin, sex, age, education, bodily disposition, fortune, occupation, temperament, physical condition, and family all contained invaluable clues about one's virtue. One's virtue, in turn, determined one's credibility.[66]

In keeping with this ancient practice, familiar to Crusius through his studies and teaching of classical rhetoric, he assumed that testimonies were best evaluated by assessing the reliability of the persons who gave them. Whenever visitors arrived on his doorstep, he always sought to establish their capabilities and credentials, and did so, in the first instance, by focusing on their genealogy. At the most basic level, then, establishing the *fides* of a witness meant subjecting nearly all visitors to a careful investigation of their place of origin, their family situation, and the direct itinerary that had brought them to Tübingen. Crusius's inquiry also included questions about other family members who had been taken captive. Genealogy and origins mattered so much to Crusius that he would check with one visitor the background of another.[67] Even Johann Friedrich Weidner, the interpreter who accompanied Lukas and Andreas Argyrus, was asked to provide details about his lineage: Crusius remarked that Weidner's father had been a professor, and he made sure to highlight the passage in the margin of his note for future reference.[68]

Appearance was another criterion. In his notebook entries, Crusius also documented the finer details of his visitors' appearance. He noted the color and variety of his guests' clothing, their beards, if they had any, and even the various objects that his guests carried: Donatus showed Crusius a booklet in which he recorded the alms he had collected.[69] Other visitors carried sacks and weapons. Not a single entry is more illustrative of how Crusius "read" his guests than his prosopography—to be taken in the literal sense here—of Gabriel Calonas: this man wore a "long black habit with long sleeves . . . down to his ankles." It had faded so much that it appeared to be dark blue and resembled the garb of a Greek priest or layman. Underneath he wore "another black tunic" and a vest. "He had covered his head with a *sokalimaukho*," a "small travelers' cap that he had bought in Leipzig," and a *skufia*, the brimless cap adorned with a cross that Greek clergy wear. "His chestnut brown beard," Crusius continued, "was long and pointed," and "unlike most young laymen, he had [muttonchops] on both sides of his face." Calonas wore boots and was carrying a walking stick.[70] Such a strong focus on the physiognomy and costume of his visitors could tell Crusius more about what a genuine Greek Orthodox Christian was supposed to look like, and, by extension, how reliable their testimony was.

This means of identification and verification was widely practiced in premodern Europe. Throughout the fifteenth and sixteenth centuries, seals, passports, letters of safe conduct, coats of arms, badges, and banners as well as birthmarks, names, tattoos, skin, and linguistic competence served as signs of identity. Identity papers were not faithful portraits from life of the people that carried them but descriptions of their appearance, their height, and especially their dress. In that sense they represented an individual in words and provided a double of the person described.[71] The importance of appearance in early modern societies, in which sumptuary legislation confirmed social hierarchies, explains in part why individuals expended vast amounts of money on their clothing. One's perception of selfhood was intrinsically bound up with what one wore: garments immediately revealed the social group one belonged to or the status one enjoyed within a particular community. In the early modern period, in other words, tailors made men and women, as well as communities and societies.[72]

But processes of identification were never as straightforward as simply reading people's appearances or establishing their genealogy. Looks could be deceiving, as Crusius knew all too well. In November 1566 his second wife, Catharina Vogler, had died of the plague. The situation in Tübingen was so threatening that for the time being the university was relocated to

Esslingen, a town some twenty miles away. The university also thought it would be better for Crusius to take a leave of absence. He thus found himself leaving for Basel to work with Johannes Oporinus, the famous humanist printer who had published Crusius's Greek grammar booklets a few years earlier.[73] Once in Basel, and having arrived at the print shop, Crusius announced himself. But much to his own astonishment Oporinus did not recognize him at first, declaring that the last time he had seen Crusius, the scholar had not boasted such a long beard. Neither was the real Crusius as tall as the man who was now standing before him. Crusius insisted: he was the man whom Oporinus was describing. But even a letter in the hand of an acquaintance of theirs—Crusius had not brought other written evidence with him—could not completely sway the printer. Only after a former student recognized Crusius on the street did Oporinus seem convinced that the man who had come to visit him was indeed his friend from Tübingen: "Do you see," Crusius teased Oporinus, "that I am Crusius?" But however comical Crusius believed the confusion to be, the episode demonstrates how even in situations where one could provide evidence of one's identity, duplicity was always on other people's minds—in this case especially so because Oporinus, as Crusius would later learn, had been recently deceived in exactly this way.[74]

Later in life Crusius found himself at the other end of the table: in 1587 a group of Greeks arrived including an interpreter who claimed he had been in Tübingen three years before. Yet the man's name was unfamiliar. Crusius, unsure what to make of this, simply assumed that either the man had given another name back then or that he was lying now. His third wife, Catharina Vetscher, whom he has asked about the man, remembered him rather well and confirmed that the interpreter had indeed been in Tübingen before, but she also told her husband that this man had used a different name then. He had also come here with a different Greek than the one Crusius supposed.[75] Unfortunately, Crusius's notes stop at this point, leaving us to guess what kind of conclusions he drew from this conversation. Yet it is evident that processes of identification were extremely complex: what was correct according to one person's statement could appear false in another one's memory.

Arguably the most important evidence that could document the reliability and ethical quality of a person appeared in written form: Crusius agreed with Gerlach that letters of recommendation, which doubled as passports or letters of safe conduct, were essential. Throughout the early modern period, travelers were supposed to carry this type of documentation.[76] Alms collectors were particularly well advised to have written evidence that could vouch for their intentions and confirmed their status as itinerants. Crusius considered them a sine qua non. At one point, Crusius gave one of his guests an extraordinary invitation encouraging other Greeks to come to Tübingen on the condition that they bring him vernacular Greek books and letters of recommendation:

> Exhortations to Greeks: a) Nobody should come to Tübingen to Martin Crusius unless he is a good man and in possession of proper testimonies or recommendations. It is after all necessary that he is credible lest he be in danger. b) Nobody should come to said Crusius unless he brings him a book (preferably a work of history) in the vernacular, either printed or in manuscript. And when it is a precious book I shall offer compensation for it, and assist in other ways. Otherwise, I will not. c) Nobody should do anything bad in Germany, because one bad person hurts many good ones.[77]

In Crusius's household, letters of recommendation not only contributed to a safe passage but also helped establish credibility.

Nearly all Crusius's visitors came with such documentation. "It is true that nobody from Greece comes to these regions without a testimony," he reminisced at some point.[78] Crusius always copied out the letters that his guests presented and told those without such papers to write down their misfortunes.[79] Over time, more and more visitors came with several recommendations. Mauricius, for instance, managed to present Crusius with no fewer than fourteen such testimonies, beginning with a Greek letter bearing the elaborate signature and seal of Jeremias II. The Frankfurter theologian Jacob Coler had also written an account of Mauricius's itinerary in his German letter of recommendation. In Prague, Mauricius had obtained a multitude of letters, including one from the city council. In Niepołomice, close to Cracow, no less a distinguished figure as Cardinal Andrew Báthory wrote Mauricius another testimonial. He even secured a letter signed by Anna Jagiellon, the queen of Poland. At his departure from Tübingen, Crusius wrote him one as well. For itinerant individuals like Mauricius the only proof that their intentions and testimonies were sincere, and their itineraries justified, could be found in the letters of support that they carried with them—evidence that in Mauricius's case had paradoxically marked him as an apostate in the first place. Traveling evidently meant venturing onto thin ice.

But quantity was not necessarily prioritized over quality. Documentation from ecclesiastical authorities ranked as particularly authoritative in Crusius's eyes. He could use a letter from the Patriarch to confirm details mentioned in another letter, as happened in the case of Mauricius. In general, an ecclesiastical stamp of approval verified, or at least mentioned, the woeful fates of the individuals in question and their relatives, while also vouching for their good intentions and endorsing their reasons for collecting alms. Notes from scholars that Crusius knew personally or corresponded with could also confirm a traveler's bona fides. On more than one occasion, Hugo Blotius, the head librarian of Maximilian II's imperial library, sent Greeks to Tübingen after providing each of them with a signed letter of recommendation.[80] The circulation of testimonials from learned friends, whom Crusius deemed reliable, enabled him to pass judgment on issues of credibility more than a multitude of letters from unknown individuals could.

This exchange of letters of recommendation was part of what could be called an early modern economy of trust. Establishing credibility at a distance or in people from faraway lands was a particularly vexing problem in this period. Merchants trading in the Mediterranean and places farther away from home notoriously confronted this issue in their business correspondences. These merchants not only relied on a highly utilitarian language of affection but also exchanged letters of recommendation to establish bonds of reciprocity and assess whether someone in a distant place made for a reliable business partner.[81] The monetary economy more generally also operated on social credit and cultural capital.[82] In that sense, the process of establishing *fides* did not differ much from other period ways of establishing factual knowledge: Steven Shapin has suggested that "scientific truth" in the early modern period was often the realm of "gentlemanly conversations." The "conventions, codes, and values" of male scholars often dictated what was considered true or deemed credible. "Knowledge," he summarizes, was "a collective good."[83] Trust was evidently the product of a similarly collective agreement. In this case, however, the codes and conventions manifested themselves not just in the clothing and demeanor of Crusius's visitors but also in the letters of recommendation they carried.

But this early modern economy of trust operated at times in unexpected ways. In 1599 two Greek ecclesiastics arrived in Tübingen: Athanasius, the successor of Gabriel as archbishop of Ohrid, and a certain Hieremias, who had also accompanied Gabriel on his 1587 visit to Tübingen. Instead of the patriarchal letter of recommendation that Crusius's other guests carried, these two men could only show an Ottoman letter of safe conduct that came directly, so they said, from the sultan. The materiality of the document impressed Crusius greatly: this "long piece of paper, written in a beautiful Arabic script, carried the sultan's seal . . . it was like a Turkish bond or hat with underneath a cross, almost like a dagger."[84] In talking to these men, Crusius also discovered a great deal about Greek Orthodoxy. It was thus evidently worth his while to share his meals with these men. But it proved much harder to establish whether they were actually in the financial need they claimed to be: although the rector and the senate of the university decided to support them, they also advised Crusius "to not believe [them] too much, because they did not have any letters of recommendation." Crusius was initially skeptical for the same reasons as well—letters of recommendation were after all a sine qua non—but in the end he was inclined to give them the benefit of the doubt: "I too thought [that they could not be trusted], but because Hieremias, as a truthful and honest man, was here eleven and a half years earlier with Gabriel, the archbishop of Ohrid, I now do not question their credibility."[85] Familiarity, then, did not always breed contempt: Crusius could come to his judgment of someone's credibility on the basis of a short encounter some eleven-odd years earlier.

This last scene captures not only the complexity of establishing credibility in a general sense but also the flexibility that specific situations demanded. Crusius cast a wide net to find methods for assessing witnesses and their testimonies. But familiarity and even intuition could sometimes establish bonds of trust that proved more enduring and more powerful than letters of recommendation. Perhaps that was the reason why he was so confused when Oporinus did not recognize him in Basel: Were they not tied by bonds of friendship? Reversely, even in cases where his interlocutors did bring such documents, Crusius could harbor considerable doubt about the captivity stories that they told him, in part perhaps because he knew that counterfeits circulated.[86] It appears, in that sense, that to some extent Crusius also decided to believe what he was told, when it suited him or simply where he felt like it: however insincere the direct motives of his interlocutors may have appeared, and even when a letter may have been a fake, Crusius was able to separate the account from the person that gave it. These encounters, just as cross-cultural trade of the period, were thus not governed by a complete sense of trust but required a willing suspension of disbelief: lying about one thing would not automatically disqualify a person in Crusius's eyes from being informative about another.

CONCLUSION

On the very last page of the thick manuscript notebook that Crusius kept for recording Greek testimonials, we find four short notes about the last Greek Orthodox Christians who visited him in Tübingen. On July 13, 1599, three illiterate Greeks had lunch with Crusius and asked him for money. Two years later an old merchant from Mytilene by the name of Staurikos Rhalis came by to collect alms. Two brothers from Thessaloniki, the third note revealed, were on a similar mission when they met Crusius in 1605. The last note—written in the small, more compressed, and occasionally blotted handwriting characteristic of Crusius in his old age—makes mention of a noble Greek who stayed for a few days in a local inn to collect alms. For reasons otherwise unspecified, Crusius believed it was not necessary to reward him abundantly.[87] Though he was a septuagenarian by the time these men arrived in Tübingen, his enthusiasm for documenting their movements was far from fading. While these notes are far less extensive than those he took on his first set of visitors, their seventeen concise sentences still give us a glimpse—if only a brief one—of the lives and journeys of a group of itinerant men who for a fleeting moment became part of Crusius's world.

It is worthwhile to construe the motivations and conditions that enabled these moments of contact to take place. It was evidently in the interest of both Crusius and his Greek interlocutors to accept the stakes of these encounters and find creative ways to make them work. Crusius was willing to accept that his guests may have amplified some of their hardships, as it allowed him to draw them into ever-lengthier discussions: the longer their stay in Tübingen, the more he could make these men and women serve his scholarly needs. In moments when he doubted the sincerity of their motives, he could rely on a wide range of evidence to expose different forms of dissimulation and to determine whether somebody told the truth or not. His guests, by contrast, realized perhaps that they could only count on Crusius's generous hospitality and support as long as they gave him what he wanted. They thus painted an image of Ottoman–Greek interactions that is completely black and white—much like the authors of captivity narratives—but one that nevertheless captured the imagination of Crusius and his colleagues in powerful ways. I contend that their success depended in no small part on whether they, as Eastern Christians, could capitalize on their status as familiar strangers, by casting Ottoman characters into a negative light, and by describing the dire predicament in which they found themselves.

Such storytelling, however profitable, was not without consequences, though. It has been argued that in this very period the stereotype of the wandering Eastern Christian who fled Muslim persecution crystallized into a stock character.[88] As we have seen, the very people that these stereotypes purport to describe in this case were to some extent complicit in their creation and circulation. In recounting the drama that had unfolded in their lives and in emphasizing their dire straits, Crusius's Greek visitors, a varied group, simultaneously exaggerated and downplayed notions of cultural difference: they themselves appeared again and again as poor wandering Christians whose lives had been disrupted by undeserved misfortune, while they cast Ottoman Turks as perpetual enemies, whose rage and greed had led to the enslavement of numerous innocent Christians. Recounting this narrative of captivity and hardship, of servitude and ransom, thus made a seemingly stereotypical story seem very real.

4

HOUSEHOLD CONVERSATIONS

Conversation was one of Crusius's most important means of understanding the language, religion, and culture of the Greeks. He welcomed Greek Orthodox visitors into his home and listened to their stories, recording their firsthand knowledge and thereby preserving voices otherwise lost. But making knowledge out of conversation was never self-evident. Ethnography in Crusius's home required multiple modes of engagement and involved different degrees of improvisation. Some of the conversations with his Greek guests mirrored those of early modern antiquaries with their informants. Other situations bore resemblances to the classroom or the port city. For still other exchanges, Crusius acted like an inquisitor. Conversation could be a textual process but was also marked by the use of gestures, sign language, and reading aloud. Knowledge in Crusius's world was made over books and other objects; through moments of collaborative reading; through listening carefully and hearing attentively; and through observation and other forms of visualization. His was a hybrid hermeneutics: in his method, practices of reading and observing and firsthand and secondhand experiences merged.[1] He may have been a classicist by profession, but he was an ocularcentrist by conviction and one who valued highly trained ears and an exceptional degree of proficiency in what I call "aural literacy."

Following recent work in the history of science that has called attention to the domestic space as a site of scientific inquiry, I situate Crusius's particular type of knowledge making firmly within the setting of his household.[2] In drawing an eclectic group of informants into ever-lengthier conversations about their culture and their beliefs, Crusius essentially turned his Tübingen home into a site of encounter and ethnography. Opening his house to strangers from distant lands evidently offered him the opportunity to obtain unique evidence about the full richness of Ottoman Greek life in a way that reading alone or corresponding from afar could not. But showing such hospitality was possible only because of the particularly gendered organization of Crusius's scholarly home: it was the labor of its female members that enabled Crusius to receive so many informants for so long and to reap the fruit of their conversations.

The conversations that Crusius had with his Greek guests were far from unique, as ethnographers throughout the early modern world engaged in similar conversations and ones that yielded analogous results. The scenes analyzed in this chapter were as complex and vivid as those painted by historians of European contact with non-European peoples—and they suggest that long-standing dichotomies of stay-at-home ethnographers and those who did do fieldwork obscure more than they illuminate in an early modern world, where mediation operated in multiple directions. Numerous other stay-at-home scholars, such as Nicolás Monardes and Pietro Martire d'Anghiera, relied on the testimonies of travelers to inform themselves about other cultures.[3] In the course of the sixteenth century, Ethiopian scholars introduced their European colleagues to a hitherto unknown tradition of Eastern Christianity in a similar vein.[4] Christian Hebraists surveying the customs and religion of their Jewish acquaintances discovered a whole new world of rituals through compilation as well as conversation.[5] The same is true for those who did not stay at home: celebrated and lesser-known ethnographers studying Amerindian and Asian civilizations and languages at best relied on indigenous populations, and at worst appropriated their expertise to disastrous effect. But in all these cases mediation and conversation between indigenous people and European ethnographers shaped what learned Europe "discovered" about other people.

My aims in this chapter are to illuminate the complexity of such early modern mediation.[6] Crusius was not exceptional because of the singularity of his interactions with information brokers. What did make him an exception, to some extent, is that he deemed it worthwhile to record how he arrived at his conclusions and to document how mediation worked in all its complexity. Few ethnographers of the period—whether they stayed at home or went into the field—afford us a glimpse behind the curtain that is as penetrating and illuminating as this one. Even a passing glance at Crusius's materials reveals how, from many points of view, his ethnographic practice was as complex as it was straightforward, as makeshift as it was systematic, as oral as it was aural, as sensory as it was material, and as bookish as it was full of life. Boundaries between textual scholarship and first-person encounter blurred as knowledge took shape in ever-expanding trains of thought—as happened in so many other contexts that are less well-documented.

CONVERSATION AS KNOWLEDGE MAKING

Early modern scholars saw conversation as an effective way of exchanging information and as central to different types of scholarly inquiries. In museums, laboratories, anatomy theaters, botanical gardens, and print shops, in the lecture hall and in the classroom, in the marketplace and on the piazza, in apothecaries' shops and in coffeehouses, men and women traded expertise through conversation.[7] Historians have shown how the period even witnessed the rise of a distinct body of literature on the art of conversation: from Renaissance Italy to France's *Grand Siècle* to eighteenth-century England, conversation was nothing less than a form of art. In humanist circles, but also in academies, and across the Republic of Letters, polite conversation, as well as letter writing, offered those who mastered its subtleties a means to cultivate all fields of learning, to pursue lofty ideals of civility, to demarcate scholarly communities, to show off their erudition, and to charm their interlocutors with their wit. Civil conversations, treatises on this topic taught its students, were part and parcel of the good manners and courtly behavior that educated men and women were expected to embody. One was supposed to be able to shift between different registers, to use polished phrasing, to avoid barbarisms, to not speak about oneself all the time, and, importantly, to know when to speak and when to remain silent.[8]

Emphasizing the importance of conversation in the pursuit of knowledge may, however, run the risk of turning conversation into a nebulous concept that obscures more than it clarifies. After all, keeping up polite conversation at faculty dinners was one thing; it was quite another to extract information about another culture from a group of strangers. Reasoned debate in the French salon was not identical to formalized disputations in the world of the university. Yet, given how little attention conversation as a scholarly method has enjoyed from historians, it is worth underlining not only how very different these types of conversations were but also how they converged in one hugely important way: in any of these situations—and not exclusively in the highest echelons of the learned world—Crusius and his contemporaries would have had to develop not only a set of conversational skills but also a high degree of proficiency in what I call aural literacy: the art of listening. How, we may wonder, did early modern people learn to listen to others? How would Crusius and others have honed their auditory skills? Is it possible to reconstruct something like a period ear for those scholars who embraced conversation as a way of knowledge making?[9]

For questions of such magnitude, there is of course no single answer. Scholars interested in pedagogy might emphasize that in the world of the university, students learned how to listen by engaging in disputations with colleagues and professors about practical or theoretical problems.[10] Historians of music might point to the importance of musical education for training the ear.[11] Hearing sermons and attending other religious services, as scholars of religion could rightly acknowledge, would have made early modern individuals more attuned to taking in information by ear and following complex oral narratives.[12] The education of the ear, in short, was a complex and prolonged process.

Yet in Crusius's case overwhelming evidence shows that precisely these three overlapping spheres of life made him the extraordinary listener that he was. He had an ear for music: in a diary entry from 1595, he proudly listed the dozens of songs and hymns that he knew by heart. Throughout his life he also owned various instruments, including a virginal, a guitar, and the two lutes that he played for many years. In 1582, at the respectable age of fifty-seven, Crusius even engaged an organist to give him lessons.[13] His musical education had started, as for so many of his contemporaries, in the home, where his father taught him music. In his formative years at school Crusius continued his musical training. It is telling that Crusius later in life began to study Greek musical annotation.[14] Tübingen was a world resounding with music as well: many of the Duke's stipend holders were trained as singers. Choral singing, in addition to praying and reciting the catechism, was an integral part of Tübingen's and Württemberg's educational system.[15] Major celebrations, such as the centennial jubilee of the University of Tübingen in

1577 as well as more everyday events were musical occasions in which singers and other musicians took part. But Crusius mostly learned by listening. It is my contention that his habit of recording in ancient Greek the sermons that were delivered in the *Stiftskirche* taught him precisely what he needed to know to draw Greeks into conversation: how to listen carefully, how to switch between languages, and how to take detailed notes about complex (theological) matters at the same time. Merely recording the sermons in his native tongue would have sharpened Crusius's skills as a listener: but what better way to prepare somebody for drawing a group of Greek Orthodox Christians into ever-lengthier conversations about their religions, society, and culture than to translate sermons into Greek?

But although Crusius could—and would—put his prowess as a listener to effective use when over the years different types of Greek Orthodox Christians arrived in Tübingen, in talking to this group he had to practice one final set of skills. The ensuing discussion emphasizes the fraught power dynamics lying behind the kind of ethnographic field work that Crusius practiced. In his case, as in those of so many other early modern ethnographers, conversation could sometimes become mutually beneficial, but it was never on an equal footing. It was "the product of a peculiar, utterly unbalanced interrelationship," in which Crusius and others had to mount an inquiry that consisted of a series of suggestive questions and answers, designed to elicit certain truths and meant to uncover beliefs and customs that were fundamentally alien to them.[16] In that sense, the exchanges discussed here also resemble what Mary Louise Pratt termed the contact zone, a social space where different cultures "meet, clash, and grapple with each other, often in highly asymmetrical relations of domination and subordination."[17] In the end, though, the powerful techniques that Crusius employed in the pursuit of knowledge—asking sharp questions and listening attentively to the answers—were two sides of the same coin: one reinforced the other and being adept at both was crucial for discovering yet more about the Ottoman Greek world.

Voices from the Ottoman Greek World

The conversations for which Crusius left the most extensive records took place by and large in the 1580s and 1590s, thus roughly around the time the correspondence with the representatives of the Greek Orthodox Church came to an end. But, at least initially, doctrine was not the main topic of conversation. It certainly came up, especially when Crusius met learned clergymen, but it appears that these encounters in the first place served his interest in reconstructing what we could call the social life of the Greek language, or a linguistic history of Greek from antiquity to the Ottoman period.

Crusius would come to classify the Greek language into three categories: "classical," "vernacular," and "ecclesiastical"—with "vernacular" including both spoken Greek and the deviations from the classical norm that he found in his Byzantine book. Leaving aside the thorny question of how exactly these three versions differed from one another—Crusius is not always consistent on this point—it is worth emphasizing just how much this classification implied a story of decline. Even though Crusius was passionate about learning the Greek vernacular, and proudly asserted that he was the first to teach it at a German university, he saw the vernacular as essentially a corrupted version of a pure ancient form—a viewpoint borne out in the vocabulary that he used for the vernacular ("barbaroGraeca").

Understanding this "corrupted" Greek was no mean feat. Crusius had compiled one of the largest and most important collections of vernacular Greek books and manuscripts north of the Alps. It was after the Battle of Lepanto in 1571, where so many Christians lost their lives, that he first attempted to read these Greek chapbooks. Initially, though, he made little progress: the specific meaning of the words escaped him, leaving us to guess what he made of the texts themselves.[18] Since in Crusius's time no lexica existed for those interested in the Greek vernacular, he thus turned to his Mediterranean contacts: Stephan Gerlach and Salomon Schweigger as well as Zygomalas and Gabriel Severus, the metropolitan of Philadelphia residing in Venice, received requests from Crusius for dictionaries and translations of vernacular Greek word lists. None of their responses helped Crusius make serious headway, though.[19] How, then, could a sixteenth-century classics professor in a German university town begin to think about mastering the Greek vernacular?

One solution presented itself serendipitously on February 21, 1579, in the form of an individual from Cyprus by the name of Stamatius Donatus, whom we met in Chapter 3. Crusius invited him into his home and for the seven days that this Greek stayed in Tübingen, Crusius used him as his own living lexicon.[20] Day after day Crusius asked Donatus to explain more and more vernacular Greek words, eventually filling up forty-seven pages of his notebook with his guest's explications of the Greek vernacular. This did not just happen through conversation in the traditional sense. Together the two men marked their way through precisely these vernacular Greek books that had baffled Crusius earlier: they read his copy of the 1546 vernacular Greek edition of the *Flower of Virtue,* originally a widely read fourteenth-century Italian anthology of vices and virtues; the 1564 edition of the *Apolonios,* a hugely popular folk epic that recounts the trials and adventures of Apollonius, prince of Tyre; the 1526 vernacular Greek paraphrase of the *Iliad*; and the *Tale of Belisarius,* a medieval text on the celebrated general of Emperor Justinian.[21] It took Crusius years to have the word lists that he sent to the Ottoman capital translated. Now, in a week, Crusius took down an impressive total of more than twenty-six hundred vernacular Greek words and phrases.[22] Donatus was exactly what Crusius was looking for.

Little did Crusius know, however, that Donatus was only the first of a string of Greek Orthodox Christians who would help him read his Greek books. Nearly every one of Crusius's visitors explicated words from the Greek books in his collection: in January 1581, for example, Andreas Argyrus guided Crusius through at least four modern Greek chapbooks; in April 1582 Trucello helped Crusius understand another book in his library. In June that year Crusius read no less than ten books and some manuscript letters with Calonas. Darmarius explicated words from another four of Crusius's vernacular Greek books. With Tholoitis from Thessaloniki, Crusius pored over another three works in 1585. Later that year Mauricius glossed at least four of Crusius's books.[23] One of Crusius's guests even gave him an outline of a vernacular Greek romance he had heard of but did not yet own.[24] Crusius's encounters with these Greeks were thus erected on multiple collaborative reading sessions.

The margins of some of his books reveal immense determination in the pursuit of knowledge. Let us consider the 1546 edition of the *Flower of Virtue,* in which Crusius discovered the mysterious Greek word τὸ ναέλην. A first investigation of its meaning paid no dividends: "None of the Greeks who was with me in 1582 knew this [word]," Crusius noted sourly in the margin. Four years later Donatus, who had come back after his first visit, told him it referred to a stork. A year after that, in 1587, Gabriel Severus suggested it was some sort of grayish bird. Finally, in 1589, another one of Crusius's guests, Damatius Larissaeus, suggested yet another rendering: eagle.[25] This was knowledge making as practiced in Crusius's household: over seven years

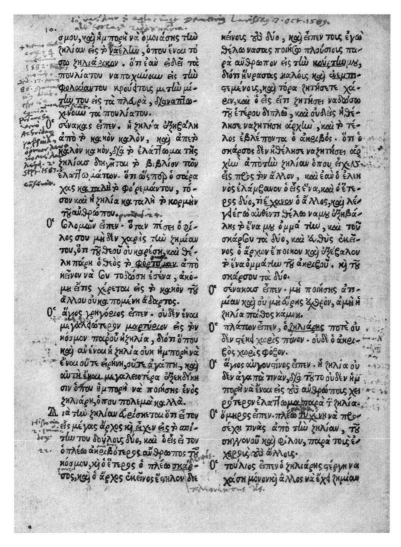

4.1 Crusius records the different translations that his Greek guests gave him over seven years for the mysterious Greek word τὸ ναέλην, which refers to some sort of bird. *Credit: Universitätsbibliothek Tübingen Dk I 6.4°, fol. 10.*

Crusius approached a single page, even a single word, again and again with the same purpose in mind, always hoping that a new, yet similar, reading of the same text with another glossator might unlock its lexicographical mysteries. Sadly, which translation Crusius decided to accept cannot be inferred from the marginal notes. He compiled explanations with concentration and determination, but often without further comment.

114   THE DISCOVERY OF OTTOMAN GREECE

The bookish nature of these interactions should not obscure the fact that this was a deeply oral process. Donatus, as Crusius noted in his description of his guest, could not read or write and knew only a few words of German. His illiteracy meant that he and Crusius had to interpret texts through a motley mix of languages, including Italian, Latin, and German, rather than translating from one language into the other. Crusius noted that Donatus would often use "gestures, his hands, and paraphrases" to elucidate specific words and sentences.[26] Similarly, the nearly three hundred words that Andreas Argyrus explained to Crusius in January 1581 came from the texts he and Crusius read together, and their explication often involved "examining the context" in which they occurred.[27] On this occasion, more than one language and form of communication was used as well: if they did not talk in Italian, Crusius spoke ancient Greek, Andreas a Greek vernacular. That this was not opportune is suggested by the presence of an interpreter who occasionally greased the wheels of communication. This young man from Leipzig spoke Italian with the Greeks and then turned to Latin or German when he spoke to Crusius, trying to ensure that nothing was lost in translation.[28]

Sometimes these collaborative reading sessions went far beyond the material book. Any object in Crusius's house could be brought to bear on his interests in the social history of the Greek language: the lyre that stood in his study set off at one point a conversation about musical terminology; at another, Crusius took Donatus by the hand, guided him through the house, and recorded the vernacular Greek names of parts of the house and of the individual domestic items that Donatus translated, including the stables, a chandelier, a flour cabinet, an oven, and a grater.[29] Crusius learned thousands of Greek words and phrases through these collaborative reading and question-and-answer sessions. Topics of conversation ranged from orthodox theology to household items, from dress to topography, from subjects that made his guests blush to stock phrases about the amount of attention women paid to their appearance. His knowledge of the Greek vernacular was thus incredibly extensive, perhaps unparalleled for the period. But it was also serendipitous and by no means comprehensive: Crusius had to make do with what his guests told him.

Just how important mastering the Greek vernacular was to Crusius is also indicated by the way he recorded what he was told. He not only took down these words in the margins of his vernacular Greek chapbooks and in two separate manuscripts—his diary and a notebook that he specifically kept for recording Greek testimonies—but at some point also organized that material in the margins of his copy of Aldus Manutius's 1496 *Thesaurus cornu copiae,* itself a great lexicographical work.[30] Beginning in April 1579, a few months after the first Greek had visited Crusius in Tübingen, he arranged the very same words that he had copied down in conversation in four neat alphabetical lists of vernacular Greek words, and kept updating this record as time passed by. Crusius thus enriched his copy of Manutius's *Thesaurus* with nearly eighteen thousand vernacular Greek words and phrases.[31]

It was not just the sheer quantity of words that mattered to Crusius. Engaging his guests in conversation could also illustrate the heterogeneity of Greek. Crusius usually wrote down words and phrases precisely as he heard them being pronounced and thus gained insight into the Greek language in ways that simply listing words could not. Hearing Donatus speak in 1579 and Trucello in 1582 made him realize, for instance, that these Greeks "pronounced the theta as a phi in the Cypriot way."[32] Probably on Crusius's request Donatus also elaborated on "the great variety of the Greek language" and many other languages spoken on the island: Greek, Albanian, Turkish, Italian, and Armenian were all spoken there and influenced one another. The Cretan language, he was told, was difficult to understand even for other Greeks—not, Crusius realized, unlike Flemish for Germans.[33] In rural areas, Donatus explained, farmers added unusual prefixes and suffixes (containing the phoneme -τζ-) to common nouns and spoke what Crusius called "a more corrupt" language.[34] In other cases, Crusius labeled specific words as Turkish loanwords or showed that he knew that some Greeks called their language "romaika."[35] Ever the meticulous observer, Crusius thus connected language and geography. Yet he did not believe that a necessary correlation between the two would establish how much trust his informants deserved as authoritative witnesses. Unlike Jean Bodin, the famous French political philosopher of the period, Crusius did not see geography as a key to personal character and intellect.[36] Rather, through oral interactions with Greeks from all over the Mediterranean, Crusius became aware of his informants' exact position within a web of languages and dialects, with contemporary Greek at its center.

It is evident that Crusius could acquire this type of information only through conversation. Not only did his guests bring to life books that would otherwise have remained mute but they also, by virtue of being native speakers, testified to the diversity of vernacular Greek spoken in the Ottoman Greek Mediterranean. Perhaps aware of the inability of print to communicate the sound of the Greek vernacular, and of language in general, Crusius hung on his guests' every word.[37] True, he never arrived at a comprehensive view of the vernacular Greek language. His knowledge was piecemeal, and more than once even his Greek guests had to admit their difficulty with specific Greek dialects. But, taken together, his notes do bespeak a growing awareness of the different Greek dialects and different regional pronunciations. It nevertheless does not appear that Crusius actually spoke vernacular Greek, and if he did, to what degree of fluency. Although he has often been hailed as one of the first Western scholars proficient in a type of modern Greek, no evidence in the surviving documentation shows him speaking vernacular Greek with his guests in any substantial way.

Crusius's situation is instead typical of various types of communication across languages. His lack of fluency in vernacular Greek is in some ways emblematic of patterns of communication in the early modern Mediterranean. In this complex linguistic ecosystem most individuals had not mastered languages to perfection but bridged linguistic differences well enough to ensure effective communication.[38] In another way, Crusius's situation was emblematic of how many individuals in the early modern period learned foreign languages, a process as conversational as it was textual, as oral as it was aural.[39] In the early modern classroom, students learned Latin and ancient Greek by listening to their teacher explicate texts, by taking notes, and by asking questions about the books that were prescribed as course materials. Such explications of books, though supposed to be done all in Latin, often switched into the vernacular for part or all of a sentence and then switched back. Third, Crusius's linguistic encounters mirrored those of other early modern ethnographers. They often started their inquiries by mastering a language in the way Crusius had: Jesuit missionaries to China, such as Michele Ruggieri and Matteo Ricci, attempted to acquire fluency in the Chinese language by listening attentively as their Chinese teachers explained basic grammar and vocabulary from the schoolbooks and language primers they had acquired.[40] The Franciscan friar Bernardino de Sahagún similarly recruited a group of knowledgeable Nahua elders to explain Aztec pictorial form of writing to him and to educate him about their culture and history.[41] But perhaps most comparable to the case of Crusius and his Greek guests were those Moriscos who, after their expulsion from the Iberian Peninsula, taught Arabic to learned scholars throughout early modern Europe—a particularly well-documented case being Aḥmad ibn Qāsim al-Ḥajarī, who taught Thomas Erpenius some Arabic by reading a set of books with him.[42] Yet, more than any of these situations, Crusius's household conversations show us how aural and oral these encounters were, how textual and material, and how these categories shifted as conversation moved from text to object and back.

One final snippet of evidence illustrates how his Greek guests offered Crusius penetrating insights into the Ottoman Greek linguistic world. In 1593 a Greek Orthodox woman by the name of Antonia arrived in Tübingen with her husband Andreas and composed a Greek lament—in political verses and addressed to Crusius—about the many hardships she had suffered in her life. While accompanying herself "skillfully and pleasantly," this Greek woman passionately performed the song twice, even though she had spent three years in captivity, where "her teeth had been beaten out of her mouth." Such lives showed Crusius very vividly the type of violence that enslaved individuals like Antonia were subjected to in captivity, something he made a point of mentioning in his publication.[43] Her performance also brought the contemporary Greek world to life in a way that hearing his other Greek guests speak could not. On other occasions, Crusius talked about Greece's musical traditions with his guests and learned that in some places women engaged in singing competitions. He was interested, in other words, in folk songs long before they became a common way to learn about a people and a culture.[44] Songs like Antonia's brought this musical world, this snippet of Greek culture, directly into his home. Her performance afforded a rare opportunity to hear in Tübingen some of the sounds and rhythms that characterized everyday life in Greece. Antonia, then, made audible what Crusius could otherwise only know through oral inquiry. It is telling that he reproduced the song in full in one of his publications.

Virtual Witnessing

Given the nature of Crusius's encounters and the nature of language learning in this period, it is hardly surprising that listening attentively was perhaps his single most important tool for expanding his understanding of the Greek language. But conversation revolved not exclusively around language. Over the years his guests informed him about other aspects of the Ottoman Greek world as well. Conversation could quickly turn from explications of the Greek vernacular to discussions about Greek Orthodoxy, the Greek archipelago, or the demographics and religious landscape of specific islands and certain cities. For these topics, too, as we shall see, Crusius harnessed his skills as a listener, but in an altogether different way: even though he learned of their world through conversation as well, his guests went to great lengths to help him visualize the early modern Greek world. In answering the questions Crusius put to them, they directed the mind's eye to the Hellenic world he was so profoundly interested in but never visited. For all their glitches and complexities, these exchanges enabled Crusius to see the Ottoman Greek world, as it were, through the eyes of his guests.

Such knowledge making processes often started with a book as well. One of the most complex vernacular Greek texts in Crusius's collection was "a nautical book that contained the roads and distances between [different Mediterranean] ports."[45] This portolanos, as it was called, had been printed in Venice in 1573 and had been acquired by Crusius on September 6, 1580, through an acquaintance of his named Hieronymus Vischer, whom we will meet again in Chapter 5.[46] This short booklet was essentially an encyclopedic list of Mediterranean ports and their surroundings, a kind of *vademecum* for navigators. It was also a remarkably complex text, written in an idiom that was both technical and idiosyncratic. Crusius could not understand it when he first read it. Neither was his contact in Venice of much help in this respect: Crusius wrote to Vischer, requesting more vernacular Greek books, and—not unlike the other vocabulary lists that he earlier had sent to Gerlach and Schweigger—he attached a list of words from the Portolanos "that some Greek [in Venice] should interpret." But even if the response that Crusius received may not have been unexpected, it was certainly disappointing: Vischer told Crusius that not even Gabriel Severus, the aforementioned patriarch of Alexandria, could understand the text. In fact, as Vischer specified, the "dialect of this Portolanos is only known to sailors."[47] How, then, would Crusius ever be able to peruse this book?

The solution came once again in the form of an individual. In the summer of 1587, a man from Chania named Dondis stayed in Tübingen for no fewer than fifty-four days. This was the same Dondis who helped Crusius instruct

Papadatos for the latter's baptism. Interestingly, as Crusius noted, Dondis "had been a sailor for years"—he even showed him the wounds he had suffered at the Battle of Lepanto—and thus offered exactly the type of expertise that the portolanos required.[48] This man would indeed make the book speak to Crusius in ways he could not have imagined: Dondis informed Crusius, as they pored over the book, about several Venetian islands including Zakynthos and Corfu. The inhabitants of Astypalaia, in the Dodecanese archipelago, were, according to Dondis, "all Greek but ruled by a Turkish prefect."[49] In explaining what he knew, Dondis often appealed to the standard of direct observation: as they went over the entry on the Gallipoli peninsula, he told Crusius he had seen the Dardanelles Strait with his own eyes.[50] Crusius also recorded that Dondis himself had been in Tripoli and on the island of Djerba, off the coast of Tunisia, where he had been held captive. Unsurprisingly, Dondis had few positive things to say about Djerba: the water was not good, there were no mountains, and the people were barbaric.[51]

In different parts of the book these conversations appear in strikingly visual form. There is a map of Crete on one page and a drawing of the port of Lisbon on another, while Crusius enriched the description of one of Menorca's ports, with an image of the port's three capes and towers that Dondis had presumably used to explicate the phrase.[52] None of these are very elaborate drawings, but in their simple form they did make intelligible a text that was linguistically complex and in its orthography heavily influenced by the contemporary pronunciation of Greek. Dondis also gave Crusius an aid to visualize the distances between different places and to understand their internal connections: on the first page of the book Crusius copied out a compass, which, he noted, "is called a *bousoula*" in Greek and without which "it is impossible to navigate far." It was "[made of] paper [that had been] enclosed in glass."[53] On the final page of the book Crusius reproduced Dondis's explanation of the units of measurements that were current in the Greek-speaking world. The Greeks used the so-called *podaria*, Crusius noted, which equals the length one gets when "the nails of two extended thumbs touch each other."[54]

Dondis's attempts at communicating what he knew about the geography of the Mediterranean, straightforward though they may seem, offered Crusius an invaluable tool to unravel the intricacies of a book. It also enriched his knowledge of the Greek vernacular and made visible to him different parts of the Mediterranean's rich topography. Other conversations were

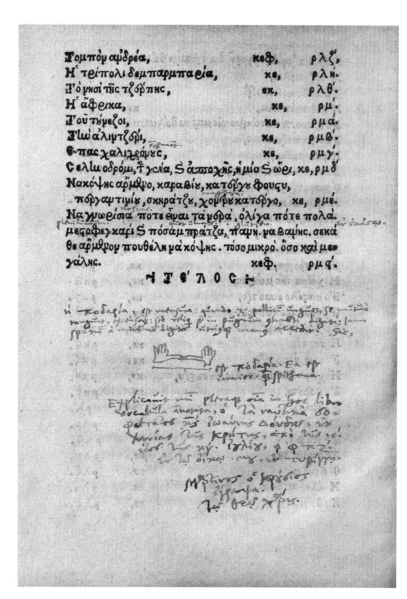

4.2 Note in Crusius's hand on the *podaria*, a Greek unit of measurement. Crusius records not only what his informant, Dondis, told him but also how this Greek showed him that a *podaria* equals the length you get when "the nails of two extended thumbs touch each other." Credit: Universitätsbibliothek Tübingen Fa 16a, final unpaginated page.

aimed at acquiring similar information about the geopolitical and religious landscape of the Mediterranean and involved similar forms of visualization. From Donatus, Crusius learned that "in the whole of Cyprus there are fifteen thousand cities and villages," that the capital is Nicosia and its second city Famagusta.[55] He also described to Crusius what was left of ancient Troy: "[Donatus] says he has even seen the ruins of Troy which is [a] white land, close to the sea. Not far away is the island Tenedos. There are still many walls. But the rest has been destroyed. Constantinople is a bigger city. Not far from Troy and Tenedos is a small island called Archistrategos."[56] What Donatus was doing here, was guiding Crusius through the remnants of ancient Troy, not unlike an early modern travel writer, comparing it with better-known places (Constantinople) while also offering his audience specific clues (Tenedos, Archistrategos) to locate this ancient city on the map of the Greek world.

Individual guests could offer different details about the places they knew. Andreas and Lukas Argyrus, for instance, gave Crusius the names of the twelve islands around Santorini and also mentioned the castles and cities that adorned these places.[57] On the island of Paros, for instance, in the city of Parikia, there was an episcopacy, while the island of Mykonos had "one castle and many small villas."[58] Andreas Argyrus could tell Crusius that "Chania, Rethymno, Heraklion and Sitia" were the four principal cities of Crete.[59] Some of his other guests also described places they knew firsthand. Alexandro Trucello intimated that there were four bishoprics on the island of Cyprus: "Nicosia, Paphos, Famagusta, and Lefkara."[60] Calonas told Crusius, quite curiously, that "on Athos no male animal is admitted because sodomy is feared."[61]

Not surprisingly, as a professor of Latin and Greek, Crusius seems to have been particularly eager to hear what his Greek guests knew about contemporary Athens: he asked nearly all his visitors for details of the city's schools and churches, its inhabitants and physical contours. In 1582 Trucello told Crusius "he had seen Athens and that the lower city had been destroyed. The upper city, however, was around three times the size of Tübingen."[62] Two years later the Greek copyist Andreas Darmarius shared (on Crusius's instigation) what he knew about Athens as well as Corinth, Sparta, and other Greek cities and places.[63] After yet another two years, in May 1586, a priest named Michael had made his way to Tübingen and described to Crusius some of the cities that he knew: Athens was "a city bigger than Augsburg"; Thessaloniki, "big, like Paris"; and Corinth, "about the same size as Augsburg" with "many olive gardens."[64] Still later, when the archbishop of Ohrid and his party stayed in Tübingen, Crusius learned that Athens "was still a big city" with several churches.[65] It is striking how often Crusius's informants also tried to make this form of visualization easier by comparing Greek cities to places he knew or may have known better: Trucello compared Athens to Tübingen; Michael compared it to Augsburg. Through comparisons such as these, however elemental, Crusius could better comprehend the sizes of places he had never witnessed firsthand.

These conversations reflected the kind of inquiries that early modern antiquaries and cartographers conducted. Cristoforo Buondelmonti, for instance, sailed the Mediterranean seas and offered detailed descriptions of the Greek ports and islands that he visited, illustrating many of them with celebrated sets of drawings. Fra Mauro relied on the testimonies of a host of Italian sailors and merchants for his monumental map of the world. Peter Gillis, whose descriptions of Istanbul and the Bosporus Crusius owned and read, became a model of this type of quantitative interests in cities and places. Nicolas-Claude Fabri de Peiresc, famously, mobilized a whole network of merchants, ship captains, and other informants to send him exact measurements of Mediterranean port cities, shipping patterns, and much more.[66] Obtaining exact measurements, then, through conversation or firsthand observation, was evidently one hugely important way in which Crusius and his colleagues sought to understand far-off places. Such examinations had deep roots: Strabo and Ptolemy, whose works Crusius annotated with great care, had advocated the art of describing the world's many regions. But it was in the late medieval and early modern periods, influenced by the rapid rise of antiquarian studies, that the scholarly engagement with landscapes and places, and their past and present lives, really started to flourish.[67] Crusius could thus build himself a mental image, one piece at the time, of the Greek Mediterranean and of Athens in particular, not unlike what his traveling colleagues did for other places in and beyond the Mediterranean.

It is important to acknowledge, however, that such forms of knowledge making were not solely the product of Crusius's prowess as a listener or the result of his almost inquisitorial line of questioning. For the descriptions that Crusius's guests provided were often much more than just descriptions. They were attempts at making visible something that lay beyond what was directly discernible for Crusius and could be considered what has been called "virtual witnessing" for a different context: the images that Crusius's interlocutors painted of places in the Mediterranean Greek world enabled him to create a sort of mental image of these places although he had not directly witnessed them.[68] The very precise terminology that Crusius used to record his interactions suggests that his guests indeed went to great lengths to actually visualize the cities that they were describing: sometimes he noted that his guests "painted" (*depinxit*) the cities they were talking about—as Joannes Tholoitis did for Thessaloniki and Platamon and Mauricius for Corinth and Athens.[69] No actual drawings of these places survive in Crusius's records. Instead, it seems that Crusius's specific choice of words reflects the vividness (*enargeia*) with which his guests verbally described these places: they created what ancient rhetorical standards would have considered verbal paintings. In theory such images were so powerful that they re-created these Greek places in words, almost as if Crusius saw them with his own eyes.[70]

In at least one case actual drawings and maps played an important role in the conversations between Crusius and his informants. In September 1585 Crusius diligently subjected Daniel Palaeologus to his customary interrogation: Palaeologus, Crusius learned, was originally from Athens, where his father worked as a merchant. In time, he had become a monk at the Iviron monastery on Mount Athos, the single most important site of Greek Orthodox monasticism. On Crusius's instigation, Palaeologus clarified a few dozen vernacular Greek words from the books in his study.[71] Crusius also asked his guest for a description of Athens. Even though the monk initially confessed to "hardly being able to write his own name" and thus certainty incapable of "painting" (*depingere*) his hometown, he eventually agreed to do so.[72] Athens, Palaeologus revealed, had a citadel and a city around it. It had "many good springs" and was surrounded by olive trees. The Ottomans held its castle. Greek Orthodox churches defined the skyline of the city, including, close to the ancient marketplace, "the big church of Saint Anne." There were fifteen female monasteries but no male monasteries—male monastics lived "outside the city in the wilderness." Many powerful and rich Byzantine families had moved to Athens after the fall of Constantinople, including the Palaeologi and the Comneni, who could both claim an impressive imperial lineage. Local Ottoman magistrates feared some of these families according to Paleaologus, even though Greeks and Ottoman Turks lived largely in separate parts of the city. Some Greek inhabitants, Palaeologus went on, had become rich through commerce. The circumference of the ancient city was "eighteen Italian miles." The current city, however, was almost five times as small and there were no walls anymore. The castle in the citadel—the Acropolis—was "three Italian miles away from the sea."[73]

It was this level of precision that allowed Crusius, once Palaeologus had finished talking, to draw a map of the city in his notebook with the help of an acquaintance of his called Simon Eisen.[74] It depicted nearly all locations mentioned by Palaeologus and paid close attention to the orientation of both the map and the buildings. Once Palaeologus started describing Athos, the process was repeated: he revealed that there were no fewer than twenty-one Greek Orthodox monasteries on the peninsula with a total of around twelve thousand monks living there, all of whom were men and all of whom followed the rule of Basil the Great. The monasteries themselves were well fortified and abbots were appointed as their head. The monks had to pay a tribute to the Ottoman government, but "not a single Turk" came to Athos. Even though the notes that Crusius took on Athos are not as elaborate as those about Athens, they did suffice to create a map of the peninsula. In this case, too, Crusius carefully located and numbered each and every monastery that Palaeologus talked about—a practice that mirrored the burgeoning urban cartographical work of antiquaries and mapmakers of the period who sought to compile ever more complex and detailed plans and measurements of cities and landscapes.[75] Perhaps Crusius even sought to document the religious landscape of the Greek Orthodox world, in a literal and figurative sense, to gauge where Lutheranism might spread, just as Catholic missionaries always sought to know the lay of the land for proselytizing purposes.[76]

Actual images of and from the Ottoman Greek world also became topic of conversation. In December 1578, shortly after his return from the Ottoman Empire, Gerlach had given Crusius pictures of the wide variety of people living in these regions.[77] Such visual collections derived from a stock set of images that foreigners like Gerlach could acquire in the Ottoman Empire and are found in numerous costume books that have survived from the period. The details of the various types of clothing intrigued Crusius greatly: when Donatus was in Tübingen, Crusius asked his guest to clarify and translate the names of the garments of these various individuals. In a series of notes as precise as they were elaborate, Donatus not only explained what individual pieces of clothing were called but also specified how they were worn and by

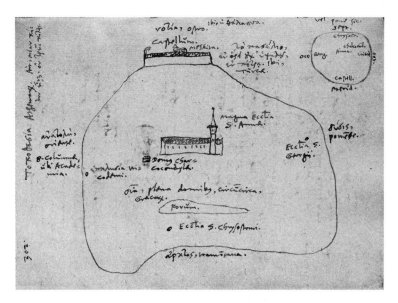

4.3 The map of Athens that Crusius drew based on Palaeologus's description. In the center, Crusius located a Greek church dedicated to St. Anne; towering over the city is the Acropolis, at the time still, as Crusius noted, a mosque (*meskita*). *Credit: Universitätsbibliothek Tübingen 466, vol. 3, fol. 302.*

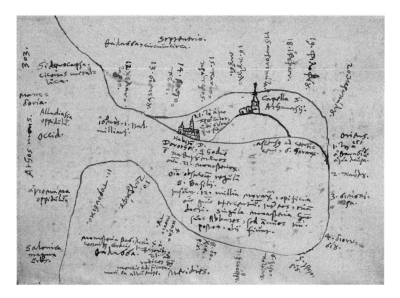

4.4 The map of Athos that Crusius drew from Palaeologus's description. Dotted all over the peninsula are various Greek Orthodox monasteries, still standing today, including the Iviron monastery (nr. 18), the Xeropotamou monastery (nr. 6), and, slightly too much toward the cape, the Simonopetra monastery (nr. 3). *Credit: Universitätsbibliothek Tübingen 466, vol. 3, fol. 303.*

whom: "The dress that Greeks wear in the city differed little or nothing from that of a Turk" apart from the color of their hats. The hoods that Greek monks used to cover their head were not attached to their habit. And Greek women, according to Donatus, had certain "golden ribbons" hanging down from their dresses and wore necklaces made of beads.[78]

Conversations such as these reveal exactly how in the early modern period images from costume books could be studied. These books not only portrayed the full diversity of the world's peoples as visible in their appearance but also advanced specific and complex classifications of the human race. Costume books were connected to the cartographic impulse to map the globe and exhibited that early modern preference for organizing knowledge in an encyclopedic way and offered certain ethnographic clues to character and culture.[79] Illustrations of clothing and individual appearance thus informed the way Crusius and his contemporaries understood the peoples portrayed, not unlike the ethnographic illustrations on maps and in travel books.[80] By carefully observing and considering these objects with Donatus, Crusius acquired valuable lexicographical details, but also ethnographic information about the appearance of Greek women, the attributes of the Byzantine patriarch, and the garments of a Turkish soldier.[81] In that sense, Crusius's Greek visitors, oftentimes clothed in traditional attire, offered another occasion for Crusius to see a world he never saw in person.

Whether Crusius was in conversation with his Greek interlocutors, perusing one of his many books or objects, or both at the same time, the eye served as an instrument of apprehension, even when this process was premised on Crusius's competency as a hearer. The forms of visualization that defined these encounters demonstrate how Crusius's Greek interlocutors helped him see their world through their eyes and how their descriptions offered Crusius replacements of the journeys that his interlocutors had undertaken. It is tempting to conclude that Crusius encouraged his guests to paint their homelands because he himself was homebound: as an armchair scholar, he had to develop methods to see the Greek Orthodox world without ever going there. But in other cases, too, when Europeans did do ethnography far away from home and saw the world with their own eyes, they often relied on indigenous people to read maps and decode images. They did not need virtual witnessing the way Crusius did, but their ethnographies were enriched by the vividness with which their informants guided them through their worlds and educated them on what meanings and valences buildings, rituals, plants, and other cultural expressions had. The kind of seeing that went on in Crusius's home was thus no anomaly. Neither was the hybrid nature of his ethnography: others, too, whether they stayed at home or went into the field, often mixed first- and secondhand observation, and combined oral and written testimony.

Embodied Encounters

Conversation in Crusius's home was makeshift, took place at unusual moments, and was often unexpected, as visitors could show up at his doorstep at any time. Crusius had to combine hospitality and inquiry with his day-to-day job as a professor, which made these encounters physically demanding. This was no less true for his Greek guests: Crusius's inquiries took place at unregular hours, were lengthy, and sometimes were incredibly intense. Understanding how mediation in this and other contexts worked thus encourages us to see it as a deeply embodied practice as well.

In the first place, time was always of the essence. Crusius had no way to predict when people might appear on his doorstep. Sometimes years separated the departure of one Greek from the arrival of another. Lukas and Andreas Argyrus, for instance, arrived nearly two years after Donatus, and it would take over a year before Trucello, the next pilgrim, knocked on Crusius's door. Most of his guests stayed in Tübingen for only a few days before they continued their journeys: in 1581 Lukas and Andreas Argyrus visited Tübingen for just two days, as did Alexandro Trucello in 1582, Daniel Palaeologus in 1584, and Jonas Taritzius in 1592. Joannes Tholoitis remained not much longer. Neither did Darmarius in 1584, even though Crusius begged this knowledgeable scribe to extend his stay.[82] Even the archbishop of Ohrid stayed for less than a week. Paraskeva would stay for just a single day. It is not always clear how these men and women divided their time in Tübingen, but we may very well assume that they dedicated much of it to collecting alms from the local population.

The full teaching load that kept Crusius occupied during term time limited time for conversation even further. In August 1589 Crusius could only give a Cypriot from Famagusta some money because, much to his own displeasure, his many occupations prevented him from talking to the man properly.[83] Crusius repeatedly complained about being up to his ears in work and about having to correct his students' many papers. Similarly, when the Greek copyist Andreas Darmarius was in Tübingen, Crusius had to set exams and attend the wedding of his godchild Barbara Hailand. Even though he brought Darmarius to the wedding and helped the scribe sell some of his books to the duke, he nevertheless complained that "many things prevented [him] from using [Darmarius] to explicate [his] vernacular Greek books" to satisfaction.[84]

Knowing that time was limited and that the flow of Greek visitors might stop, Crusius thus tried to make the most of their precious time together. His determination to hear them out really jumps off the pages of his notebooks. Crusius confessed that he had not given Donatus, who himself had been a very eager talker, a single moment of rest.[85] During the four-day visit of Calonas, "who spoke very fast" and "was lisping" in such a way that "he was incredibly hard to understand," Crusius got so carried away that his "head was full of Greek and was buzzing with it," while he had to admit that his interrogation had tired his guest considerably.[86] Even as Calonas was departing, Crusius would not leave the man alone. He followed him to the gates of the city, pen and paper in hand. As Calonas read the city, pointing out and translating individual objects, Crusius eagerly scribbled these items on his Greek word list.[87] In that respect, whether it was day or night, early morning or late evening, mattered less than the potential harvest that could be gathered: it was the dead of night when Crusius, together with Stephan Gerlach, had first sat down to record Calonas's tragic testimonies about his life and travels.

Even meals did not interrupt his interrogations but rather offered new topics of conversation. When Lukas and Andreas Argyrus had dinner with Crusius, they talked, appropriately, about tableware.[88] Next to a short note about some sort of Cypriot side dish of roasted meat with vinegar and saffron, mentioned by Donatus in 1579, Crusius recorded excitedly: "We had this for dinner!" Crusius also listed, with great precision, the vernacular Greek names of the individual ingredients of the dish—a powerful reminder that he even learned about the contemporary Greek world through taste.[89] But it was not only the food that appeared on the table that encouraged conversation. Sometimes what was *not* eaten was talked about as well. Many of the Greeks who shared Crusius's table were fasting. In February 1585, for instance, the visit of two Greeks coincided with the beginning of Lent, which prompted Crusius to make the following observation:

> Tomorrow on the 22nd of February, their Lent (Τεσσαρακοστή) begins, which is forty-eight days. On the Monday, Tuesday, and Wednesday of the first week and on the Thursday, Friday, and Saturday of the last week Greek ecclesiastics do not eat and drink anything for three whole days. In Church they sing and they read. For the entire fasting period they only eat bread and drink wine: nothing else. That is why these [two Greeks] took nothing but bread and wine when they sat at my table on February 22 and 23.[90]

In these cross-cultural conversations, then, whether Crusius was tasting Greek dishes and recording the vernacular names of their ingredients or whether he observed his guests' religious practices, the dinner table was as much a site of knowledge making as the study. This was not accidental. In Crusius's world, meals enacted highly symbolic and ritualized moments of sociability. In his diary, Crusius would always record, in considerable detail, not only the dinner parties to which scholars and other prominent citizens of the duchy invited him but also the specific place he was given at the table, highlighting those moments when he sat in "the honored corner." Occupying such places of honor carried great weight because they revealed one's social standing in the scholarly world of sixteenth-century Tübingen.[91]

Food was an important element of Crusius's scholarly identity in another way as well. Meals provided a formal as well as joyous occasion for Crusius to display his qualities as a table companion and impress his acquaintances with his ascetic disposition. Ideals of asceticism and practices of temperance were two important models by which learned individuals cultivated their self-image.[92] Attractive conduct at the dinner table could not only heighten a sense of community between scholars and deepen bonds of scholarly friendship but also establish one's reputation and convey "a social stance"—not unlike the epistolary exchanges on which contemporary ideals of the Republic of Letters rested.[93] Thus, when Crusius shared his meals with his Greek guests—and by extension invited them to attend weddings in town and classes at the university—he drew them deep into a richly ritualized world in which sociability and the pursuit of learning merged in fruitful ways.

Taken together, these small vignettes gesture at a broader truth: conversation in Crusius's home was a deeply embodied way of making knowledge. To ask how Crusius made knowledge out of encounter is to realize that knowledge was in many ways an interpersonal affair. It was the confined space of Crusius's home, combined with the limited amount of time for conversation, that made these encounters intellectually intense and physically demanding. Even though these Greek Orthodox Christians spent significant amounts of time collecting alms—and, admittedly, sometimes lodged not with Crusius but, like the archbishop of Ohrid and his party, in one of Tübingen's inns—they and Crusius nevertheless spent hours in each other's presence. The promise of the information that he might glean from his guests goes some way toward explaining the eagerness with which he subjected his visitors to systematic interviews. Opening his home to these Greeks and serving them a hot meal was evidently worth Crusius's while.

Women's Labor in the Scholarly Household

Showing hospitality to his Greek guests was possible, in no small part, because of the gendered organization of Crusius's scholarly household. Only with a supportive wife and a hospitable table could he have received so many Greek informants for so long. Only relatively recently had Crusius's household arrangement become a viable model for scholars. From the fifteenth century onward, marriage and maintaining a family became an increasingly attractive option for organizing a scholarly life. This refiguring of the scholarly habitus shaped the organization of the domestic space. While scholars' wives took charge of the household affairs, their husbands could dedicate their energies to activities that guaranteed social recognition and a salary.[94] Evidently this new division of the domestic sphere formed the bedrock of Crusius's scholarly practices. He married three times: to Sybilla Rhoner from 1558 to 1561; to Catharina Vogler from 1563 to 1566; and to Catharina Vetscher from 1567 to 1599.

Even the most passing glance at the surviving evidence reveals that each of these three women was vital to Crusius's success as a scholar. Marriage had, for instance, been instrumental in getting Crusius his job in Tübingen. When the university appointed Crusius as professor, he also became the first head of the newly founded Collegium Illustre, a school that offered young aristocratic men a scholarship to prepare them for state service—a kind of secular version of the evangelical *Stift* that Duke Ulrich had founded.[95] As head of the college Crusius received an additional salary, lived in Tübingen's former Franciscan monastery, and offered room and board to the scholarship holders. Crusius's exemplary knowledge of Greek may have gotten him a job at the university; it was his marriage to Sybilla Rhoner that enabled him to accept the directorship of the college and to take in large numbers of boarders. Marriage thus made it possible to create the extended male household in which sociability and scholarship merged.[96]

Yet taking lodgers could become an incredibly heavy burden for the female members of Crusius's household to shoulder. While their roles in the family cannot be simply reduced to domestic labor, boarders strained their physical energy to the limit. In Crusius's first two years in Tübingen, no fewer than sixteen students lived with him and his wife. When Sybilla Rhoner was pregnant with their second child, fourteen lodgers shared their home. Five left when she was in the final month of her pregnancy, suggesting their presence had overtaxed her strengths. Eight of the remaining nine students left within a week after she had died in childbirth.[97] It is telling that Crusius only started taking lodgers again after he had married Catharina Vogler. Of the five lodgers that lived with them when she died of the plague in November 1566, three of them left just two days after her death, the other two before the end of the year. In this case Crusius explicitly acknowledged that they had to leave "because of the death of the materfamilias."[98] His motivations for marrying a third time—"he wanted to enhance his status," to quote him directly, "both in teaching in the Academy and in educating the nobility's minors"—further illustrate how indispensable a female presence was for creating a scholarly household of the new kind.[99] It is again telling that in the last eight years of Crusius' life, after the death of his third wife, somebody was hired to take care of his domestic affairs.[100]

Marriage also helped Crusius integrate into Tübingen society, a community to which he was not native, and to gain recognition as a scholar there. Not unlike other scholars in the period, Crusius married locally—Catharina Vogler was the daughter of a grocer from Tübingen; Catharina Vetscher the daughter of a notary from neighboring Esslingen—because such marriages granted access to the social fabric of a place.[101] Hospitality, a highly ritualized set of practices usually entrusted to female members of the household,

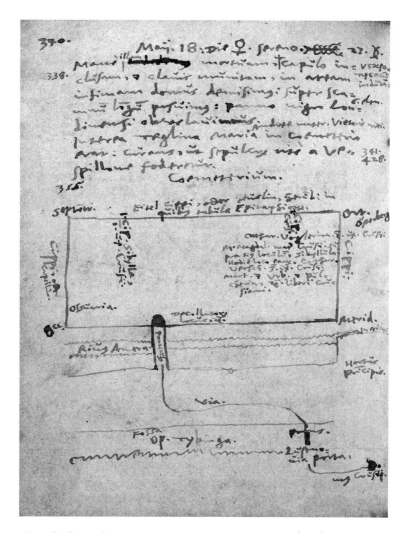

4.5 Drawing of Tübingen's cemetery. The vertical note on the left (nr. 1) identifies the grave of Crusius's first wife, Sybilla Rhoner, while the longer note on the right (nr. 2) seems to mark the family grave, where Crusius's other two wives and some of his children are buried. Credit: Universitätsbibliothek Tübingen Mh 466, vol. 7, fol. 340.

was one of the most important ways in which scholars could elevate their status within a given community. Throughout the early modern period, opening one's home and offering nourishment to guests was expected of great homes and households of common people alike.[102] Managing such a scholarly household and conforming to such ideals of hospitality was never easy, however, and always subject to experimentation. Its success depended in no small part on the ability of women to welcome visitors in the home—and run the household more generally—while ensuring that their husbands, fathers, or sons could dedicate themselves to their work. Only then could a scholar's household make a name for itself and attract enough patrons and financial support to be successful and to thrive.[103] In Crusius's case one important model for emulation may have been the household of Martin Luther and Katharina von Bora, in which many of the reformer's followers and students had jotted down the conversations that went on around the table and elsewhere.[104]

The running of this scholarly household was an extraordinarily complex endeavor. During his third marriage, to Catharina Vetscher, for which more evidence has survived than for his two previous marriages, Crusius owned a large house close to the Lustnauer gate—bought in 1576 for a substantial sum—as well as a granary, a wine cellar, a plot of land in the city, and a larger garden on the Österberg. Even if Catharina Vetscher was not solely responsible for looking after all of these properties—Crusius worked in his garden and hired help to attend to his trees—she did attend to most of the domestic affairs, sometimes with the aid of housemaids or one of her daughters, and was also involved in maintaining the household's financial health through a set of small-scale activities: she supplemented Crusius's salary, for instance, by selling wine and occasionally also by selling part of their livestock.[105]

The occasions, then, that the household and the dinner table offered Crusius for sociability and learning were made possible only through his wives and other female members of the household. One minute bit of evidence reveals just how vital a role Crusius's wife—in this instance, Catharina Vetscher—played in staging these conversations: when Lukas and Andreas Argyrus left Tübingen in January 1581 after just two days, Crusius noted that—despite his own hopes of a longer encounter—their departure was probably for the better, because his "wife was already most occupied with doing the laundry."[106] This is not merely an irrelevant detail. It was this kind of work that was vital for creating opportunities for company. Conversation, in that sense, and the considerable fame that Crusius and his household would enjoy in Greek Orthodox circles in the Ottoman Empire, was no more Crusius's work than it was the product of the often mundane and silent labor of his wives and the other often unnamed female members of his household.[107]

Crusius's scholarly world was, like those of numerous other early modern scholars, "not a world without women but a world *among* women," to stress a point made by Deborah Harkness.[108] It appears, though, that the women in Crusius's household did not participate in the kinds of intellectual exchange that historians have recently recovered for early modern women in other contexts. This was not the world that Sarah Gwyneth Ross has so vividly described, in which early modern women, sponsored or supported by the family patriarch, used the deeply patriarchal arrangement of the "intellectual household" to their advantage and carved out a literary space for themselves that went beyond then-current models of female authorship.[109] Nor did Crusius's household resemble those reconstructed by Elaine Leong, in which male and female members of the family collaborated in the creation of recipe books and medicinal knowledge.[110] Even more striking is the contrast between Crusius's household and other Protestant households of the period that embraced learned forms of sociability and in which collective reading sessions, including both men and women, and even madrigal singing took place on a regular basis.[111] In many ways, Crusius's household resonates most strongly with Lyndal Roper's work on the holy household, which has shown that some Lutheran divines came "to view women almost exclusively as wives, whose sphere it was to be subordinate to their husbands and instructed by their preachers."[112] Participation in a "holy household"—without sin, but structured by piety, discipline, and order as its defining characteristics—became their primary expression in the social world created by the reformations.

In this case, then, Crusius's household occupied one end of a spectrum of possibilities. Of course, the sources may not tell the whole story. Perhaps Crusius simply did not deem his wives' direct involvement in the pursuit of knowledge worthy of documenting. Occasionally, the available evidence does suggest departures from a structure in which the women focused on the domestic affairs and the men talked. Once, Crusius asked Catharina Vetscher to help identify one of the men who had showed up on their doorstep and seemed to be lying about his identity.[113] Some of the seating arrangements that Crusius recorded in his diary show that his wife and daughters also sat at the table when he entertained his Greek visitors. It was his wife, moreover, who usually brought the wine from the cellar, opened it, and served it to his guests, possibly at strategic moments in the conversation, possibly to reinvigorate an exchange after a brief lull. On special occasions, it was she who would bring one of the household's most precious cups from the cupboard to the table.[114] But even such scarce vignettes as these, which offer a glimpse of the participation of women in ritualized sociability, reveal frustratingly little about the intellectual lives of Sybilla Rhoner, Catharina Vogler, and Catharina Vetscher. In general, it appears more likely that Crusius's home reflected the more mundane, possibly more stereotypical, but certainly no less uncommon reality that women were fundamental in the creation of knowledge not in spite of gendered models of behavior but because of them.

Material Culture

Crusius's cross-cultural encounters were profoundly material. Books served as objects and subjects of conversation; images made visible a world Crusius never saw with his own eyes; the clothes worn by his guests satisfied his curiosity; and even the dinner table in all its copiousness inspired conversation. But material culture gave meaning especially to the departure of Crusius's guests: the gift giving that occurred when Crusius's visitors were leaving Tübingen reveals that all involved looked to objects of various kinds for providing these fleeting moments with a legacy.

Crusius's Greek guests received all sorts of gifts. Crusius and his wife gave Stamatius Donatus a few napkins and a shirt. In 1584 they gave Darmarius a set of gloves and a beautiful napkin, itself a gift from the wife of an acquaintance.[115] Books were the most common gift that Crusius gave his guests at their departure. For scholars throughout the early modern world, gifting books, both printed and in manuscript form, was an effective medium for self-promotion.[116] Throughout the early modern world, formalized gift transactions such as these also played a prominent role in forming social bonds and shaping interactions on a local and a global level. Crusius's home was no exception. Darmarius received not only a napkin but also three books that had been published in Tübingen, all of which bore handwritten inscriptions by Crusius: a catechism written by Augustin Brunn, a Greek grammar, and a copy of Crusius's own *Civitas Coelestis*, another bilingual sermon collection of his that was published in 1588 as a kind of catechism.[117] Crusius gave a copy of the *Iliad* and a copy of Isocrates's work to a man from Athens named Emmanuel.[118] Dondis was given a copy of Schweigger's Italian catechism, again perhaps to tempt this Greek to adopt Luther's vision of Christianity.[119] In return, his guests would give Crusius books as well: from Emmanuel Crusius received a Greek manuscript book.[120] From Andreas and Lukas Argyrus he received a manuscript of Epictetus that made a great impression on him: Crusius noted its elegant script and small letters, as well as the beautiful bookbinding that was adorned by the seal of the French king.[121] On his second visit to Tübingen in February 1585, Andreas Argyrus would again bring Crusius a copy of Damascenus's *Thesaurus*.[122]

Circulating a flattering portrait of oneself was an important mechanism for building one's intellectual reputation and for giving fleeting moments of conversation and short encounters a prolonged impact. Crusius did this on more than one occasion with a printed portrait, other copies of which he glued to the pastedowns of some of his books and manuscripts, sometimes accompanied by his family's coat of arms, to claim ownership over them.[123] The paper portrait in question depicted him in his capacity as a professor: book in hand and boasting the black robes (and broad ruff) that early modern scholars wore to indicate their rank.[124] The beard that Crusius had grown, like nearly all of his male peers, established his masculinity and asserted the authority that, as the Greek caption around the image made clear, befitted his respectable age and status as a university professor.[125] Often Crusius would also adorn this portrait of himself with personal inscriptions: the portrait that he gave to Donatus was enriched by a Greek paraphrase of Psalm 121, one of the songs of ascent traditionally associated with pilgrimage.[126] When Trucello departed, Crusius gave him not one but two portraits "so that if he loses one, he has another." One of them bore a similar paraphrase of Psalm 121, as well as a personal dedication to Trucello that stressed the friendship bonds between this Cypriot and Crusius.[127] In no small part, then, Crusius gave his guests these portraits so that they would have a visual keepsake of their stay in Tübingen.[128]

Crusius not only wrote his Greek guests personal inscriptions upon their departure; he also made them inscribe his manuscript notebooks "for the sake of memorializing."[129] Calonas, for example, left Crusius a personal note meant as a remembrance of their time together.[130] So did Andreas Argyrus in 1581 and again in 1585. Once Crusius even cut out the signature from a letter of one of his Greek correspondents and pasted it in his diary.[131] His interest in collecting signatures reflected the more common practice of writing

4.6 Crusius's 1578 portrait showing him in semi-profile, with a large beard and dressed in professional attire. He is seated, and holds a book in his right hand. *Credit: Universitätsbibliothek Tübingen Cd855, rear pastedown.*

in friendship books, so-called *alba amicorum*, which emerged in exactly this period. Throughout the early modern world learned men and women collected the signatures, witty aphorisms, and inscriptions of their friends and acquaintances. These *alba* became a means to foster a group identity, to establish or affirm scholarly networks, or a place to immortalize friendship bonds in writing.[132] Whatever the specific purpose of individual copies, they were all based on the premise that the inscription could, in a way, serve as a memorial stand-in for the individual that had left it on the page. Crusius inscribed many of these *alba,* leaving quick-witted notes in his friends' and students' paper books, as well as those of his Greek guests.[133] These inscriptions, not unlike the Greek signatures that Crusius collected in his notebook, represented the writer in writing. They preserved tangible traces of intimate connections. They, in short, immortalized friendships at a distance—in Crusius's case between Tübingen and a place he would never visit. And he seems to have succeeded in this goal: at some point he was told that a portrait of his adorned a house in Istanbul.[134]

The books, portraits, and other gifts exchanged in Crusius's home were meant as tokens of friendships, reminders of shared experiences, as much as they offered hopes for a safe onward journey and a way to develop bonds of friendship. But exchanges such as these were always performative as well, raising expectations and incurring obligations to reciprocate. Historians of gifting in premodern societies have not only pointed out its pervasiveness but also scrutinized the many ambivalences surrounding gift exchange.[135] Put simply: no gift was unconditional. What kind of expectations, one might ask, would Crusius have raised by enabling his guests to collect alms? What should one think of the many moments when Crusius urged—and his guests promised—to write him from their future destinations with further information or to send him vernacular Greek books?[136] What did his guests think of the deeply Lutheran booklets—Crusius's *Civitas Coelestis*; Schweigger's Italian catechism—that they received? To what extent, then, did these Greeks infer that they could count on Crusius's generous hospitality and unrelenting (financial) support only as long as they gave their Tübingen host what he wanted?

Conclusion

Cross-cultural conversations in sixteenth-century Tübingen took serious work, involved a great number of individuals, relied heavily on the labor of the household's female members, and were profoundly embodied and material experiences. Crusius informed himself by listening carefully and by visualizing places and distances; he tasted Greek food; heard Greek songs; guided his Greek guests through his house; got up early and only finished work once his head was full of Greek and his guest had grown tired. Conversation involved the exchange of books and other gifts, and was kept alive by hopes for a safe onward journey and the promise of new bonds of friendship.

It is important not to lose sight of the fraught power dynamics upon which these encounters were premised. It is tempting to see reflected in Crusius's hospitality his philhellenic nature. There is every reason to suppose that Crusius was genuinely interested in forging bonds of friendship with these Greeks—as the paraphrases of Psalm 121, the frequent prayers that this deeply pious Lutheran said for his guests' well-being on their onward journeys, the exchanges of books, the hospitality shown to these Greeks, and everything that went on in Crusius's home make abundantly clear.[137] Yet to consider these encounters solely in the context of Crusius's self-professed love of Greece would be to misread the situation in at least one important respect: he may have opened his home to them, but he did so on his own terms. Crusius longed for information and had a vested interest in supporting these Greeks financially and in encouraging them to keep in touch. In that sense, every object implied an obligation; every effort that Crusius expended to making these Greeks' visit to Tübingen worth their while operated on the premise of reciprocity; the success of every conversation was contingent upon their willingness, sometimes long after their departure, to act as his informants about the Ottoman Greek world.

Neither should Crusius's hospitality be mistaken for some sort of cultural cosmopolitanism. He could be fiercely critical of the religious views of his guests and express his disagreement in unequivocal language. In May 1599, Crusius and two Greek Orthodox archbishops—called Athanasius and Hieremias—exchanged details about their religion over dinner:

> Both Greeks dined with me. We talked about various things. With Athanasius I conferred about religion. We agreed on the following points: 1) We are all corrupt in our nature. 2) We have been elevated by the promise of our seed in Paradise. 3) This prediction is found in the Church Fathers. 4) Among the Hebrew people, who were elected specifically, there were types and shadows of Christ. 5) Now that Christ is revealed truth and light has come, and [the Hebrews] have been abolished. 6) We are justified and conserved by faith, that is by trust in Christ alone. 7) Fruits, that is good works and works of

charity, give and testify to faith. We disagreed about invocation. He wanted to invoke the Saints because all of their deeds were created in the image of God (and) because the Holy Spirit is pure and acts before the face of God. I responded that the invocation of the Saints does not follow from these arguments and that they ought not to be invoked because in the holy script no command or example for such activity exists; that it deprives God of his honor; Christ says "Come to me," not to Peter or Mary; he says the Lord's prayer; that in Psalm 50 (the Lord says) "invoke me" not somebody else; that in Isaiah is written: "Abraham does not know us"; that the saints are not almighty, that they are circumscribed and not everywhere. He was quiet. I said: "Remember these words."[138]

The condescending tone that Crusius adopted in his exchange with Athanasius and Hieremias is indicative of the uneven power that dynamics dictated this exchange.[139] It is therefore more unfortunate that we only have his side of the story.

Crusius's openness would dwindle even more rapidly when it came to adherents to other religions. Crusius studied Hebrew with comparable diligence and intellectual curiosity as Greek—albeit with less success. Yet when an Italian Jew was appointed at Stuttgart's court he quickly shared his concerns that "Jews and sorcerers would eventually take over the duchy."[140] Similarly, in his copy of Eusebius's *Ecclesiastical History,* he remarked that Pilatus and Emperor Caligula had inflicted many woes on the Jewish people, but he believed these punishments "to be correct because the Jews had nefariously killed Christ."[141] When it suited his purposes, he thus adopted that dangerous discourse of alterity, which for centuries had cast Jews in negative stereotypical roles and which led to the revival of ritual murder trials in the late fifteenth and sixteenth centuries and to the circulation of similar slander by Luther among others.[142] Crusius's worldview, in other words, could be as closed as that of many of his contemporaries—and this, too, was an important aspect of the conversations that took place in his Tübingen home.

5

COMMUNITIES OF EXPERTS

Interviewing Greek Orthodox Christians was part of a larger effort at accumulating evidence. Throughout his life, Crusius brought a specific type of bookish attention to material texts of all kinds, not only looking for clues to date the Greek manuscripts, books, and other paper objects that passed through his hands but also collecting traces about their provenance and the contexts in which they originated. For nearly forty years, he recorded rumors and reports on the Ottoman Turks, keeping close tabs on battles lost and won, the deaths of famous sultans, and the births of their Christian adversaries. Knowing full well that even the tiniest bits of evidence could carry great weight in the pursuit of knowledge, Crusius mobilized an extensive network of Lutheran contacts throughout the Holy Roman Empire and the Mediterranean in search of Greek books and manuscripts as well as information to contextualize these textual artifacts. The result was a tremendous amount of information, recorded in the margins of his many books and manuscripts, and scattered over the thousands of pages of his handwritten diary. Ethnography was for Crusius an act of recording and the product of years of compilation.

Crusius's collaborations with Greek informants illustrated how crucial the professorial household and learned sociability were for this type of ethnography. His guests offered expertise on Greek life under Ottoman rule that he was not able to develop on his own. The symbiosis of scholarship and sociability fostered by Tübingen offered him further resources and manpower—in the forms of friends and correspondents, but also students and amanuenses—needed to develop his ideas. Crusius's project evolved not only in the household and through conversations with Greek Orthodox Christians but also at faculty dinners, at receptions, and through personal exchanges in and around the local church. Participation in different kinds of learned communities and various epistolary networks offered Crusius new opportunities for intellectual exchange as well as access to knowledge and information markets otherwise closed off to him: Tübingen's university life connected him with scholars and especially alumni in other places, who either by training, through their profession, or by being at the right place at the right time, could further his research in ways that he could not on his own. Crusius may not have had a word for "expert," but he knew full well that his scholarship was rooted in the fruitful exchange of different forms of expertise.[1]

Situating Crusius not only in the learned household but also in the university town thus provides a clear view of how sociability, formal and informal, presented a way toward collaboration when one professor needed help from another, their students, amanuenses, and informants further afield. Crusius complemented what he learned through conversation with Greek Orthodox Christians in three distinct ways. The most elementary one was through carefully copying, collating, and studying Greek books and manuscripts, paying close attention to what the materiality of these documents—from penmanship to seals—could tell him about the Greek world. For this standard feature of early modern learned life, Crusius collaborated with his students. Collaboration more broadly was crucial for collecting information from afar: Crusius accumulated books, manuscripts, and other documentation through a network of Lutheran informants, many of whom were alumni of the University of Tübingen. In this sense, the reach of the university town stretched far beyond its physical borders: as alumni and associates traveled the Mediterranean, men like Gerlach and Schweigger and others became conduits for information that Crusius could never have acquired on his own. Finally, Crusius regularly deferred to the expertise of others in his community to evaluate the news about the movements of the Ottomans and to find confirmation of his conclusions. Crusius's Greek Orthodox guests were thus only one group of information brokers who furthered his scholarship.

The Early Modern University Town

Modern scholarship on the early modern university is incredibly wide-ranging. Traditional accounts have generally focused on its institutional and educational history, creating a *Bildungsgeschichte* that charted the curricula and its changes over time, examined university statutes and degrees, chronicled academic requirements such as matriculation and graduation, and reconstructed students' (rowdy) social life. Other scholars have provided an intellectual history of higher education, examining what was actually taught and discussed in the classroom. In more recent years, a vibrant historiography has developed on the cultural history of the early modern university, ranging from academic ceremonies to scholars' self-representations, their public image, and the social norms that granted membership to the scholarly community. The university that has emerged from these strands of research is one of ritualized social interaction and rigorous academic self-fashioning, in addition to being a place of instruction.[2]

Yet determining how scholarship and sociability reinforced one another has proved more difficult. Historians of scholarly personae have by and large focused their attention on understanding scholars as members of a distinct social group and on describing the different cultural templates adopted by or given to professors and other scholars. Historians of scholarship have traditionally examined the output of early modern scholars. The voluminous literature on the Republic of Letters, which has emphasized the friendship bonds, epistolary exchanges, and other forms of sociability on which this community was founded, has also been surprisingly silent about the specific organization of scholars' personal and professional lives. Even historians interested in learned practices, although increasingly receptive to the ways in which scholarly collaboration was connected to the household and scholars' professional lives as teachers, have not given a thick description of the early modern symbiosis of sociability and scholarship. In part, this has been a problem of the sources: even though more material surfaces, we often still have frustratingly little evidence to capture scholars' daily lives in the round.

Examining the situation in early modern Tübingen, which Crusius documented in incredible detail, can help harmonize these different strands. Crusius's Tübingen is a particularly compelling case study because it draws attention to one aspect of Crusius's social setting that to my knowledge has thus far not received much scrutiny as a category of historical analysis: it is not the university per se but the university town that emerges as a particularly rewarding category for thinking about sites of intellectual exchange. In places like Tübingen, university and town were part of an organic whole, creating an ecosystem that fostered conversation inside the classroom and beyond it, around the church and in the scholarly home. Scholars met scholars at lunch and dinner, after mass, and at important events such as the birthday of the duke or the centennial celebration of Tübingen's university in 1577. In this scholarly theater, human interaction, and the scholarship that it precipitated, was highly performative and often designed to impress other members of the community. It was through face-to-face interaction, and through different forms of sociability, that scholars like Crusius managed to acquire their expertise and earned their reputations. In that respect, Tübingen resembled that quintessentially German hometown where everybody knew everybody else.[3]

This enveloping of town and university manifested itself noticeably in Tübingen's built environment. In the Middle Ages, Tübingen had been a small tract of land enclosed by two rivers: the Ammer on the north side, the Neckar on the south side. The upper town, running along the Neckar, was dominated by a castle that originally belonged to the palsgraves of Tübingen and later to the dukes of Württemberg. The town had a regional market, one Franciscan and one Augustinian monastery, a church, and a pilgrims' chapel, as Tübingen lay on one of the routes to Santiago de Compostella. Through a single organized construction project—and one that would only find its equal in town-planning efforts of the nineteenth century—Eberhard I, duke of Württemberg, transformed this small market town into the flagship university of the duchy: beginning in 1466 and in a time span of not more than twenty-five years the University of Tübingen was erected in the very heart of the town. In the upper town, a cluster of educational and administrative buildings was developed: just east of the castle (*Schloss*), in what is now the Münzgasse, the university's main building, currently known as the *Alte Aula*, emerged. In that same street, which still connects the castle to the local parish church, a cluster of residential buildings, a faculty house, a prison, and a place for the papal chancellor, who acted as dean and was also the one who conferred degrees, were realized. In the street parallel to this one, along the river, the duke had a boarding school, known as the *Bursa*, built for students. (It is here that Melanchthon stayed when he was a student in Tübingen.) A new choir, which would also serve as one of the university's first lecture halls, was added to the Church of Saint George. This parish church also received the chapter of the county's collegiate church (which had hitherto been in nearby Sindelfingen) and has since then been known as the *Stiftskirche*. The *Pfleghof,* a sizable complex that served as the administrative center of the

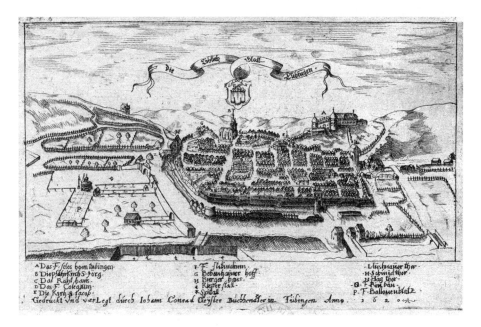

5.1 Early seventeenth-century view of Tübingen. In the top right is visible the Duke's castle, the *Schloss*; in the top left towering above the city is the Collegiate Church (*Stiftskirche*), where Crusius attended Lutheran services. Credit: *Universitätsbibliothek Tübingen Pa 4*.

neighboring monastery of Bebenhausen, emerged just east of the parish church, along the old city walls. The university's successful integration into the urban milieu, which has been praised as an outstanding piece of town planning and formed the basis of Tübingen's unsuccessful bid for UNESCO World Heritage status, can still be experienced by taking a stroll through its extraordinarily well-preserved *Altstadt*.[4]

In the second half of the sixteenth century, the area around the *Stiftskirche* and the *Schloss* was also the place where professors set up their extended scholarly households. In 1576 Crusius moved from the Collegium Illustre to his home next to the *Pfleghof*, close to the Lustnauer gate, in what is now the Pfleghofstraße. His next-door neighbors were Eusebius Stetter, rector of Tübingen's Latin school and professor of philosophy, and Johann Hochmann, a professor in the law faculty. Georg Hamberger, professor of medicine, lived close by as well.[5] The professors Georg Hitzler and Matthaeus Enzlin were neighbors.[6] Johan Halbritter, who joined Tübingen's law faculty in 1586, lived not far from Heerbrand.[7] Professors would often buy

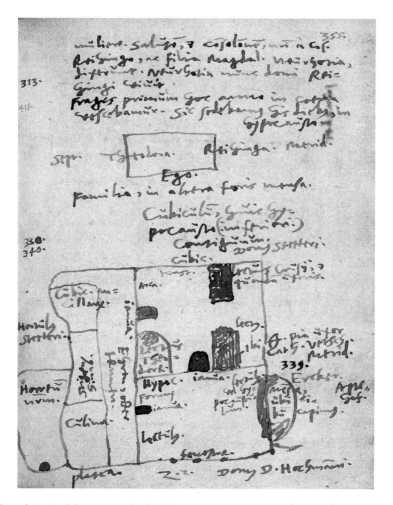

5.2 Plan of Crusius's house. On the far left we see the family barn (*horreum*); on the top right is the bedroom with the bed of Crusius's daughter Theodora (left), his own bed (top), and (right) the bed in which Crusius's third wife, Catharina Vetscher, died. Credit: *Universitätsbibliothek Tübingen Mh 466, vol. 7, fol. 355.*

other professors' houses: Halbritter bought Heerbrand's house after the latter's death in 1600, giving Sebastian Blossius the opportunity to acquire Halbritter's former home.[8] Throughout the early modern period professors also intermarried and, like Crusius, took in boarders. Many of Tübingen's colleges—in addition to the Collegium Illustre and the *Stift*, there were several others—were also located in the upper town, creating further opportunities for sociability.[9]

Even Tübingen's streets facilitated intellectual exchange. Walking was just as formal an affair as every other part of public performance and often a prized occasion for sociability. Crusius regularly walked together with others, often after mass, sometimes through Tübingen, sometimes on the meadow next to the Neckar.[10] The exact length of such walks is unknown, but they could easily take an hour out of Crusius's packed workday.[11] Occasionally these would be longer hikes (*expatationes*) to sites throughout Württemberg: together with Eusebius Stetter and two others Crusius once walked to nearby Reutlingen and contemplated the ruins of Achalm Castle.[12] Later Stetter and others joined Crusius on a hike to the famous Hohenstaufen Castle near Lorch, which had been destroyed in the German Peasants' War of 1524–1525, and where they sang songs, bemoaned the vicissitudes of time, and left their names on one of the surviving walls.[13] But especially within the city, "streets and squares acted as conduits for social transactions, arenas for the display of personal or civic honor, and settings for elaborate practices of sociability."[14] When leaving home to lecture, for instance, Crusius would first pass the *Pfleghof* that was a few houses away. He would then take a right and cross the square that unfolded south of the *Stiftskirche* before arriving at the university. On these and other walks, he must have met numerous acquaintances and struck up countless conversations. In most cases, what they exactly talked about is lost in the fog of history, but the occasional glimmer seeps through: Eusebius Stetter once read Crusius "under the Elms of the Neckar" a prognostication, while on another occasion Georg Weigenmaier told him and others about an "aurora" (*chasma*) he had seen two nights before.[15] Exchanges such as these were more than idle chitchat about the weather: reading the skies, as we will see, was crucial for understanding geopolitical affairs in the Ottoman Empire, which in turn was part of understanding the history of the Greeks.

The close relationship between the *Stiftskirche* and Tübingen's university, and its physical proximity, only heightened this sense of scholarly intimacy. The *Stift*, for instance, that celebrated seminary for preparation of Protestant ministers, was located next to the *Bursa* in a former Augustinian monastery, less than a five-minute walk from the university's main building. Professors attended mass regularly, where they exchanged departmental gossip and caught up on the latest news. The weddings that were officiated in the local Church, and the lunches and dinners that celebrated these unions, provided other opportunities for sociability and intellectual exchange. For Crusius, who took pride in his sobriety, these meals, much like the suppers he shared with his Greek guests, were important occasions to display his qualities as a table companion.[16] Church business could also be transacted at the university: when the German version of the Formula of Concord had to be signed by all the faculty members, it stayed at the university until all had done so. In moments such as these, sociability and expectations about one's personhood converged: in the act of signing, which was expected of faculty, Crusius and his colleagues publicly demonstrated their religious sensibilities and received membership to a community of likeminded believers. Not adding one's signature to the list could have had dramatic consequences: following the introduction of the Reformation in Tübingen, and throughout the sixteenth century, faculty members with other religious sympathies and those unwilling to submit to the Lutheran creed were ousted from the university.[17] No wonder that Crusius boasted that he was the first to have signed the Formula of Concord; all others signees would see his name tower above the rest.[18]

Understanding Material Culture

Making sense of materials produced in different scribal and pictorial cultures was among the greatest challenges that Crusius faced, and with him many other ethnographers who committed themselves to the study of civilizations past and present: whether it was a Greek manuscript, a Mesoamerican codex, Chinese documentary records, or Egyptian hieroglyphs, understanding the material culture of others was no mean feat.[19] Crusius nevertheless acquired an unusual fluency in deciphering Greek documents—so much so that people began to seek him out to do exactly that: Lucas Osiander, royal court chaplain to the duchy of Württemberg, once sent him a Greek letter, which he had found "unintelligible because of the *ductus* of the letters and the abbreviations," with the request to "transcribe it into legible script" and "to translate it into Latin."[20] Doing this kind of work for the duke, as Crusius had experienced on other occasions, was often handsomely compensated and would earn him the kind of recognition that scholars of his ilk often strived for. Though largely the result of his specific skill set and innate curiosity. This was also a process facilitated by forms of sociability in Tübingen. Where his Greek informants gave him valuable information about Greek language and vocabulary, his professorship gave him a community of students who helped him copy manuscripts and who, in return, acquired familiarity in deciphering Greek script.

Understanding Greek documents was more complex than the ubiquity of Greek in early modern scholarly circles might make us believe. In the first centuries of print, there was no standardized way to print Greek, and most books contained ligatures that were not always immediately apparent, even to a seasoned reader of Greek such as Crusius: once he complained that the dialect in which one of his Greek books was written was "difficult because it deviates a lot from the Greek language" and that the book itself contained "many ligatures without an apostrophe," which meant that "a lexicon was needed" to understand the work.[21] The Greek manuscripts and letters that passed through his hands posed similar problems, as they were written in different scripts and made of different kinds of materials and adorned by intricate signatures and complex dates. How did Crusius decode such complex material?

Crusius usually started his inquiries by examining and describing the document's form and material characteristics, from the binding to the paper and the parchment, and even the *mise-en-page* of the text. One quarto-sized manuscript, for instance, was "closed by a leather strap," which was "pinned together by a prong (like a belt)."[22] Two books that his agent in Venice had sent him were, according to Crusius, bound "in the Greek style" (*alla Greca*).[23] One of his letters was made of "regal paper with sides of uneven length," while the paper of another manuscript was "old and afflicted by moisture."[24] In glosses that adumbrated the great flourishing of codicological studies a century after his time, Crusius once observed that a manuscript containing Greek saints' lives was bound "in wooden boards and brown leather" that were held together by "two clasps." The handwriting was not as neat as that of another manuscript he had recently copied, but it was old.[25] From examining the parchment, which was very thick, Crusius concluded that the skin had to have come from a calf. It bothered him, though, "that in these manuscripts there was no name of the scribe, no date, no place to be found." This could only be evidence of "monastic humility."[26] Such notes bespeak a mixture of fascination for the antiquity of these documents, their provenance, and their aesthetic appeal. This is precisely what made these descriptions more than just descriptions: the simple fact that a book was bound *alla Greca* was an important indicator of its origins. The crosses that so often framed Greek letters told Crusius how the original letter had been folded up, and thus indicated how Greeks handled their papers.[27] Attending to a document's outer appearance revealed information that was inside.

Crusius also, and in the best of humanist traditions, turned to the script for evidence about a manuscript's antiquity and provenance. Through reading and excerpting, transcribing and copying, early modern scholars learned to distinguish between different kinds of hands and scripts.[28] Such comparisons made Crusius discover, for instance, the similarities of one manuscript containing some of Plato's dialogues with another that contained commentaries on the Bible.[29] His classical training also aided his inquiries: he once concluded that the writing in a codex had "faded so much through age" (*ob vetustatem* ἀμυδρωθείσῃ) that it had to be old.[30] His language here was based directly on a passage in Thucydides's *Histories*—a text Crusius enjoyed teaching—that mentioned a barely legible inscription (ἀμυδροῖς γράμμασι) that the statesman Pisistratus had dedicated to the office of his father Hippias, the sixth-century tyrant of Athens.[31] Elsewhere in his notebooks Crusius again borrowed Thucydides's expression to describe the seal attached to a letter of a certain Joasaph of Thessaloniki: it was made, Crusius noted, of white wax and the *ductus* of the letters had been "unclear" (ἀμυδροὶ).[32] An expression used once in an ancient Greek text to describe the material conditions of one tiny bit of evidence thus offered Crusius's the technical terminology he needed.

Orthography offered yet further clues about a document's origins. Crusius's engagement with Greek manuscript materials meant confronting the many vowel shifts that had occurred in nonclassical Greek. These corruptions, as Crusius would call them, attested to the "simplicity" of the Greeks and showed him which manuscripts were "faulty."[33] Rather than correcting these faults of which he disapproved, Crusius often copied these mistakes intentionally because they indicated the "ignorance and the negligence of those that transcribed" these manuscripts and thus made it possible to situate a document in time.[34] This basic philological principle had been established by Lorenzo Valla and Angelo Poliziano in the fifteenth century and was adopted by the best students of Greek glossaries: errors could reveal indispensable things about language developments and needed to be preserved and studied, whether one was working on manuscript transmission or on spelling.³⁵ Observations based on tiny details evidently allowed for sophisticated conclusions.

Other material traces yielded similar insights. In the margins of some liturgical manuscripts, Crusius discovered traces of wax. His conclusion, upon finishing his transcriptions, was that Greek saints' lives "were originally recited in Church by the Greeks, because on many pages drops of old white wax," which could only come from one of the many dripping candles that illuminated Greek Orthodox churches, "stick [to the paper] here and there."³⁶ Once he grasped the meaning of these remnants, Crusius applied his findings to another document and established its authenticity: it appeared to be an autograph used in Church because it contained exactly these wax stains.³⁷ Through a comparison, then, of the materiality of different manuscripts, Crusius managed to reconstruct their original purpose and to further inform himself about Greek Orthodox Christianity. Crusius could have been wrong here—these bits of wax could have come from any candle—but his conclusions were probable at the time because he knew from his informants that numerous candles lit Greek Orthodox churches.³⁸

One arresting bit of evidence attests to the meticulousness of Crusius's efforts at understanding the original context of his documents. In the spring of 1577, Crusius had been studying the homilies of Basil the Great in an old manuscript. This document, much like other manuscripts he examined, contained no discernible clues about its provenance. But a single annotation on a single page caught his attention: in the cropped margins, barely visible, one could read the letters "Μαρία Παλες." Crusius immediately wrote to Gerlach and asked him if any of his Greek informants in Istanbul could help decipher this curious annotation. The chaplain, however, was unable to help. This encouraged Crusius to draw his own conclusion, which he inserted in the back of the original manuscript, now in the Bayerische Staatsbibliothek in Munich:

> In the Greek manuscript of Basil the Great, in the margin of page 139, is written Μαρία Παλες. The parchment there is damaged so that the letter ς is not whole. I think it was an ο. So it seems that παλεολόγος or παλαιολογίνη was what was written, which means that the manuscript once belonged to a certain Maria Palaeologa, from the imperial family of that name.³⁹

Studying a single fragmentary note in the margin of a single damaged page could conjure up a whole world.

Seals, critical to giving any letter and legal document its authoritative status, also attracted Crusius's attention.[40] These bits of material evidence demanded sharp eyes and serious penmanship. For instance, one of the documents that Schweigger brought back from the Holy Land was a letter written by the patriarch of Jerusalem. Crusius made a careful copy of the man's signature and seal and included an extraordinary detailed description of its material characteristics and what was depicted on it: the original was made of red wax—and Crusius thus used red ink for his reproduction—and unlike some of the other seals that he had seen, this one was not pressed unto the paper, but presumably attached to it. The iconography, however, was intricate and difficult to make out. "On the seal," Crusius observed,

> there was someone bending over and offering, as it were, his hand to someone else, who was, as it were, sticking out of the ground up to his waist and who was stretching his hands from the surface in supplication (like Lazarus coming back to life). A rock, as it were, with vineyards on top towered above him. Behind the "Christ" figure there were, as it were, two disciples. Around this whole circular image there were capital Greek letters.[41]

This description, however precise, fails to identify the scene and serves as a reminder of the limitations of Crusius's capacities. He could do description, but not always iconography. That he still went to great lengths to describe what he saw illustrates how inseparable form and content really were for Crusius. To understand the meaning of a seal, and by extension the way in which it functioned, meant observing its meaning and its materiality through a single lens.

Once, Crusius's ambitions exceeded his competence in an even more striking way. When Schweigger showed him an Ottoman letter of safe conduct, Crusius's inability to read Turkish or Arabic did not discourage him from trying to copy the document and record its material idiosyncrasies in great, if unusual, detail. He accurately reproduced the fine Ottoman calligraphy of the seal (or *tughra*) of Sultan Murad III, but then scribbled underneath it a very loose impression of the rest of the document, fifteen lines of

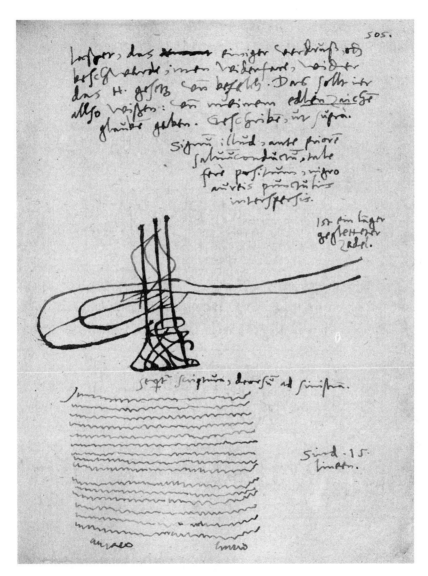

5.3 Crusius's attempt to reproduce a Turkish letter of safe conduct. His penmanship enabled him to copy the elaborate signature of the Ottoman sultan, the *tughra*, but his lack of knowledge of Ottoman Turkish meant the rest was reproduced as scribbles. *Credit: Universitätsbibliothek Tübingen Mh 466, vol. 2, fol. 505.*

Turkish in Arabic script. The point, however, was that replicating the form of the document mattered, as did explaining the hermeneutical mechanics. Crusius noted that there were fifteen lines and that you had to read this document from right to left if you were to understand it. In this case recording meant again preserving the layout of the original document even when such a graphic reproduction would not preserve the content of the document. The fact that he had also copied the German translation, and thus could access its content anyway, must have been reassuring.[42]

Documents in Arabic script, which Crusius could not read, posed similar problems, especially in situations when the expertise of others conflicted. One of the most remarkable documents to have survived from Crusius's collection is a small Arabic manuscript containing parts of the Koran. It has a curious history: Crusius received it in February 1576 from an otherwise unknown acquaintance of his, a certain Gailing, whose family members had kept the manuscript in their possession for twelve years. It had come to them when the brother of Gailing's wife was in Hungary bringing supplies to the army and found the book in the pocket of a deceased Turkish man.[43] Gerlach initially told Crusius that the document was written in Turkish and was probably a soothsaying book: "Every day," the chaplain explained, Ottoman Turks "open it in the morning and whatever page their eyes happen to rest on first, they fit their actions for the day to its content."[44] In 1583, however, Georg Weigenmaier, Tübingen's Hebraist, told Crusius that it was an Arabic document. He also explained where the book—part of which had been bound in the wrong order and upside down—was supposed to begin.[45] Only Weigenmaier's explanation enabled Crusius to understand how the manuscript was supposed to be read in the first place. But still, neither Gerlach nor Weigenmaier could make the content available for him, since both lacked knowledge of Arabic.

Signatures received more scrutiny from Crusius than any other formal feature. Lingering somewhere between the visual and the textual, between letter and image, signatures had by the sixteenth century become the preferred method of validating a document and imbuing it with authority.[46] Those adorning Greek letters were of a special kind: Greeks made their signatures with elaborate calligraphic strokes, complex ligatures, and distinctive abbreviations and contractions. These *monokondyla*, as they are known, were often written in one stroke, without the pen leaving the page, creating a visual language of their own. Crusius copied these signatures by the dozen: the first few pages of one of his notebooks contain almost thirty of them, while there are numerous others in his diary. Copying meant more than just transliterating. It meant making what we would call a facsimile. This was never a straightforward affair. Once, Crusius found two signatures that he could not decipher "because they had faded through age and wear."[47] Earlier he had asked Gerlach for help deciphering the Greek abbreviation around the seal of the patriarch that depicted an image of baby Jesus—adding, perhaps with a touch of resignation, that "I cannot know everything."[48]

Crusius even ventured to copy signatures in Arabic, despite not knowing the language. In November 1581, Schweigger brought home an album that was full of letters from high-ranking Greek ecclesiastics. Two letters, written by Michael VI, the then Greek Orthodox patriarch of Antioch, boasted an intricate set of signatures. Most Greek letters that passed through Crusius's hands were signed only in Greek. The patriarch of Antioch, however, had signed his name in Greek as well as Arabic, the other language used by the Greek Orthodox Church in that region. Crusius reproduced the Greek *monokondylon* as he did for other letters and tried to reproduce the Arabic signature, which although not completely correct, still approximated the original closely.[49]

Greek signatures made such an impression on Crusius that he—in what was evidently a form of self-fashioning—started signing his own name in this Greek way.[50] In an age when humanist pedagogues valued good penmanship and espoused good writing skills for the edification of students, Crusius's choice to change his signature was pregnant with significance: the signatures that early modern individuals penned in their book made "a statement about the intermingling of [these authors'] technical command . . . and their identity."[51] It was also an extreme expression of that more common custom among humanists across the confessional divide to Latinize and Hellenize their names.[52] The belief that one's name would lend further prestige to one's scholarship and scholarly persona had led Crusius in his younger days to sign his name as "Martinus Craus" and "Martinus Kraus."[53] It had also prompted him to come up with a rather fanciful Greek etymology of his own name: "Why should I not reasonably be called Crusius (Κρούσιος)," he reckoned at one point, "I, who have been sent far away from home, have knocked (ἔκρουσα) on closed doors. . . . and the Lord has appeared to him who knocked."[54]

Ego M. Martinus Crusius, professor Acad. Tybing. αὐτόχειρί fateor: me á Bibliotheca Augustana inclytæ Reipub. Græca, accepisse commodato, manuscr. Codice Græcū Eustathii ὑπομνὶς τῆ Ὁμήρου: necnon Græce, ἀσπλασμὸν τῆ ἀνεραστον, cum primum petero C. libro in optimā εὐν θεῶ, in brevi) nunc eum ἐκχρησίας huic tipographicis, sine cujusp[iam] impensa restitutum. – Tybingæ mense julio, anno salutis. 1584.

μ[αρ]τῖνο ὁ κρου:—

Ego M. Christophorus Neubergius, ad Minoritas Augustanos Parochus, pro Dno Mgro Martino Crusio Sponsor, hoc Chirographum manu subscripsi propria, eodem mense Iulio, eodemq[ue] anno Salutis M.D.XXCIV. ipso D. Jacobi festo.

Recepi ego M. Mart. Crusius 12. martij. 1585. libro didimū Augustanis restituto.

5.4 One of Crusius's own *monokondyla*. Credit: Universitätsbibliothek Tübingen Mb 36, fol. 339.

Connecting his name to the Greek verb "to knock," and referencing various passages from the gospel, Crusius believed his name to reflect his curiosity and confirm his piety. Crusius's adoption of the Greek *monokondylon* was thus a bold assertion of his capability in reproducing a foreign scribal practice and part of a longer search for a name that befitted his reputation as a scholar of all things Greek.

The diligence with which Crusius recorded autograph letters and studied signatures is certainly not unheard-of. In the early modern period, handwriting always added a special layer of meaning while autograph letters were deemed more valuable and more meaningful than versions in the hand of a third party.[55] Early modern scholars would sometimes cut owners' signatures off title pages and collect them as treasured objects. In the Lutheran circles to which Crusius belonged, some men and women even venerated signatures and pieces of handwriting as relics, believing these snippets of paper to be imbued with spiritual and religious efficacy.[56] Yet none of his correspondents expressed as much enthusiasm for signatures and seals as Crusius did. Nobody in his environment adopted Greek writing the way Crusius did. None of his direct colleagues in Tübingen sought to reproduce them with similar attention, so systematically, and with such pride. Neither did they wring knowledge out of handwriting in this fashion. Once, Crusius even requested that the wife of one of his Greek correspondents send him letters "so that [he] may have the handwriting of women."[57]

Crusius often hinted at the strenuous physical work that went into the process of copying. "I started transcribing this volume of George Pachymeres," he intimated in his copy of the works of this Byzantine historian, "on May 17 and finished it with great effort on August 14, 1578, in my study, standing the whole time, with my chest faced towards the higher table against the wall, using one and the same goose pen."[58] Emphasizing his use of only one pen, which he did repeatedly, was a way of drawing attention to his manual dexterity. Mentioning that he did this work standing up reflects the kind of physical endurance that male scholars deep into the nineteenth century claimed was needed for their work. It is also indicative of the kind of bodily disposition that Crusius adopted for doing work in a room—the study—that had only recently become a formal feature of scholarly homes.[59] Often Crusius also revealed the unlikely moments when he had time to transcribe: in order to copy one manuscript Crusius got up at four in the morning. In 1581 Crusius read and copied a total of twenty-two letters in one of the rooms of Faculty of Arts. At the very end of his transcription, he emphasized that "in many cases [he had] imitated the writing of the autographs." But he had only had time to do so "in between examining the master's students."[60] No doubt Crusius had to find time in his busy schedule for copying these texts. But given that other scholars of the period also intimated how early they rose to begin work, we can begin to see how Crusius contributed and conformed to a gendered persona of the scholar: a busy thinker, unaccustomed with domestic work, whose hard-won expertise rested on his ability to defy his bodily needs.[61]

Crusius was evidently willing to get his hands dirty—in the proverbial and the literal senses—but also relied heavily on his students and different amanuenses to do copying for him. Jakob Maier, for instance, facilitated Crusius's incoming and outgoing correspondences by transcribing letters for him.[62] Bernard Haus was asked to transcribe Greek letters from the patriarch and Zygomalas.[63] His boarders did similar tasks.[64] When he wanted a copy of Chalkokondyles's *Histories,* a massive and complex work, Crusius enlisted no fewer than thirteen of his students. Once the whole text had been transcribed, all sections were bound with other Byzantine Greek treatises in a single manuscript.[65] His students and amanuenses also aided him in collating, which was often done by a student and his teacher, one reading aloud and one entering the results.[66] In 1578 Crusius had his students copy a faulty manuscript of Athanasius that he later checked against the original with Jakob Maier.[67] Together with Hieronymus Megisser Crusius collated a Greek treatise on feeding and nursing hawks.[68] He had Michael Oesterlin copy the text of the *Alexiad* while he himself added marginalia and other paratextual material. Later, for no fewer than twelve days, they together compared the whole manuscript against the original.[69]

For his bookish inquiries Crusius thus relied heavily on the labor of others in Tübingen. It does not appear, though, that his amanuenses were involved in independent work such as acquiring or making synopses of books, as happened in other cases.[70] A case in point is Crusius's attempt to correct his materials when his own manuscript copy was faulty. On January 5, 1579, Crusius finished copying a manuscript of Constantine Manasses's world chronicle, brought from Istanbul by Gerlach. But not long thereafter Crusius used another copy of the same Byzantine work to correct his transcription.[71] No students or amanuenses seem to have been involved. This was no aberration: when Crusius repeated the exercise for another Byzantine chronicle—which he compared to a vernacular Greek version borrowed from the imperial library in Augsburg—he again worked alone.[72]

Crusius, then, like other scholars of the period, often delegated to students and amanuenses the kind of labor deemed mechanical, while reserving their own precious time for the creation of new creative works.[73] Yet such a hierarchy could have great pedagogical value: group work of the kind explored here often ensured the transmission of a valuable type of expertise, such as the ability to read and copy Greek handwriting.[74] Such apprenticeships also afforded students the opportunity to learn the skills necessary to become bookmen.[75] Through collating and copying, Crusius's students developed a familiarity with decoding Greek scripts, which was exactly the kind of expertise that others in Tübingen, and even those working for the duke in Stuttgart, were all too keen to recognize in their teacher. In a world in which there was little formal training in the study of Greek paleography and codicology, this kind of specialized and hands-on knowledge—which included manual dexterity, penmanship, and perhaps even the correct bodily disposition—would surely be much appreciated. Crusius, who had no university degree, had not had access to this kind of expertise when he was young. He had had to learn this through trial and error. But Crusius ensured that his students did have some training. Through a "system of personal apprenticeship and guidance" they were thus inducted "into the communities established by their elders" and could become recognized experts.[76]

Information Gathering

One important and obvious consequence of Crusius never leaving Tübingen was that for acquiring firsthand information he also had to rely on the expertise and assistance of others, with all the benefits and limitations that that involved. Conversation with his Greek guests opened up a world that lay beyond what was directly discernible. But Crusius mobilized other networks as well. Here we see precisely how Tübingen furthered Crusius's project by connecting him to information agents further afield: two of his most important informants were Gerlach and Schweigger—Tübingen alumni—whose day-to-day activities as chaplains in Istanbul granted them access to information markets not available in Tübingen. Not only in their reports, which teemed with precise observations about their experiences in the Ottoman Empire, but also when they themselves returned from their journeys, Gerlach and Schweigger made Crusius see a part of the world he would never directly see himself.

Even the most cursory glance at their correspondences reveals how much Crusius relied on Gerlach's and Schweigger's skills as observers. In 1578, when it was confirmed that Schweigger would replace Gerlach as chaplain to the imperial ambassador, Crusius had sent a lengthy letter imploring Schweigger to be "another Gerlach"—to be, in other words, the diligent and trustworthy intermediary that his predecessor had been. From Samuel Hailand, Tübingen's professor of ethics, Crusius had heard that Schweigger was an accomplished painter—a talent he shared with his father, Heinrich Schweigger—and he therefore hoped the chaplain could make a copy of "the images of the old emperors and their wives, the monument of emperor Alexius Comnenus, and other Greek things that have survived on the walls of the *prodromos* monastery and the patriarchal Church." Crusius also urged Schweigger to "transcribe inscriptions and other Greek antiquities."[77] In that way the chaplain, whom Crusius believed Providence had selected for this divine mission, would continue "what Gerlach had started so well" and bring greater "glory and praise to God's name."[78] Crusius thus hoped that Schweigger, like Gerlach, would be his eyes and ears in the Ottoman capital.

One of Crusius's letters captures in dizzying detail his complete reliance on Schweigger's competence as a painter and observer. "My requests," Crusius wrote,

> If you have any information, send it to your father . . . if you leave Byzantium for some other place (such as Thessaloniki, Athens, the islands, or Asia, write me letters from these places) . . . Please learn, if possible, the titles and the names of the bishops of Thessaloniki, Athens, and other places, and write them out. I already seem to fly to these places! Please send images of the following: the city of Constantinople itself, or at least a rough sketch, the most important places, buildings, churches, gates, both ancient and recent ones; the Church of Sophia, the patriarchate; and especially Athens. And please also send images of the emperors, and empresses, and other illustrious people [depicted] in the patriarchate and the Prodromos

Church, so that we can see the dress and ornamentation of the Greeks, because I have a history of them. Please also send images of Patriarch Jeremias and of both [Theodosius and Joannes] Zygomalas, and of the attire of Greek monks, brides, weddings, masses etc. In case you cannot do all of this at once, please send me images of the patriarch, Zygomalas, the old emperor and empress first. What are the names of the churches and the Greek monasteries from the Byzantine period? Please compare Greek musical notes with ours and write them down: and send a short song with notes. And why don't you invite Theodosius Zygomalas to your sermon, and to the celebration of the Lord's Supper, so that he can see our religion in some form?[79]

The sheer number of requests alone captures Crusius's hunger for knowledge as well as his desire to see the Ottoman Greek world through Schweigger's eyes. Yet even the most seasoned observer may have felt disheartened by the expectations that this letter raised. Did Schweigger want to be the expert Crusius wanted him to be? To what extent was Schweigger even able to comply with Crusius's requests, given that his main task was to provide for the spiritual well-being of the embassy's personnel?

Crusius wanted from Schweigger and Gerlach what he wanted from his Greek informants: information about cities, specifics of the topography of the Greek Orthodox world, further details about the Greek Orthodox Church, and anything else they might encounter and observe in and beyond Istanbul. Yet this was a slightly different context: Crusius extracted from his Greek informants predominantly what they knew about their own culture, language, and religion. What Gerlach and Schweigger divulged to Crusius is more akin to the ethnographies that Western travelers from the period published of their journeys to distant lands—books that Crusius devoured with as much appetite as he listened to Gerlach and Schweigger, as is borne out by his annotated copies of Ogier Ghiselin de Busbecq's account of his travels through the Ottoman Empire and Pierre Gilles's book on the topography of Constantinople. The information that Crusius received from Gerlach and Schweigger, in that sense, complemented what he learned by reading—and vice versa. The crucial difference was, of course, that through written encouragements Crusius hoped to control what aspects of life in Istanbul and the Ottoman Empire his informants set their eyes on.

Schweigger and Gerlach did not let Crusius down. The surviving material is, again, overwhelming. Schweigger once recounted vividly what he had seen while attending the wedding of Theodosius Zygomalas.[80] Appended to another one of Schweigger's letters was a very old bronze coin, on which, although it was rusted, Crusius could still make out the face and name of the ancient poet Homer.[81] Early in 1578 Schweigger had sent the duke, via Tübingen, a set of images that he had drawn of the different people living in the Ottoman Empire. Crusius had one of his amanuenses copy as many of them as possible before the package was forwarded to Stuttgart.[82] Gerlach had given Crusius a strikingly visual description of Greek women that stands out for its extraordinary amount of detail and sophistication: "It is almost unbelievable for [us] Germans," he wrote in one of his earliest letters to Tübingen, "how extravagant the attire of Greek women is. They veil their hair with the purest gold. They adorn their heads and ears with precious gems and sumptuous earrings. They wear collars around their necks and jewelry of the finest gold on their arms. Necklaces of gold and silver lie on their chests. And with their other ornaments they do not compete with our Empress. They leave her behind by miles."[83] This evocative set piece contained exactly the kind of information Crusius was after. Once it had come to his attention that the duke owned a costume book that he very much liked to see, he wrote to Osiander to ask if he could have the copy in question for a few days so that he could copy it.[84]

Gerlach and Schweigger also expanded on what they had written once they had returned to Tübingen. Gerlach told Crusius, for instance, right after his return, that "Greek women pronounce the Greek language very beautifully and eloquently" and that "learned Greeks spoke ancient Greek freely and quickly." He also mentioned that Theodosius Zygomalas and another Greek ecclesiastic had kissed a portrait that Schweigger had made of Andreae and Crusius in the same way as they kissed their icons. It must have pleased Crusius, though, that Joannes Zygomalas, according to Gerlach, aspired "to sail to Italy" and from there onward to Tübingen.[85] Other bits of information were simply shocking: "Egyptians," the chaplain explained, are "a thin people, feeble, peaceful, and scarcely dressed. Sailors and those living by the Nile are often completely naked and do not cover up their private parts. Women walk around with bare breasts. Egyptians drink only water and nothing else." Crusius could not hide his utter astonishment at what he heard: "I asked whether there are any really splendid homes there. He said there were none. Perhaps there were some like mine? Not even in the whole of Constantinople, he said. I showed him the bed on which he would sleep should he want to stay. He said that he had not seen a single bed in the whole of the East. I was astonished."[86] Here as elsewhere the shock of discovery could be tremendous indeed.

Conversations such as these often took place at the dinner table and in the presence of acquaintances and friends. Gerlach, for instance, talked extensively about Jeremias and other experiences he had had on his journey at a dinner where Crusius, Hailand, and others were also present.[87] Crusius even offered to put Gerlach up in case he had no better option.[88] The conversation about the Egyptians that astonished Crusius so profoundly took place over dinner, in this case in the presence of Hailand and Gerlach—and note how Crusius had also invited Schweigger to stay for the night. The arrival of missives, and their circulation in and around Tübingen, had often been a similarly social affair: on one occasion, Schweigger's father Heinrich showed Crusius the letters and images from his son, all of which offered a great amount of ethnographic detail, including careful descriptions of the sultan's meal, Istanbul's many monuments, and the appearances of the various nations living there.[89] On another occasion, he showed Crusius certain Turkish coins that his son had sent him. Heinrich also intimated that his son had shown to certain Greeks the portrait of Crusius that Heinrich had colored in and sent to Istanbul.[90] The reports that Gerlach sent back, and which Crusius copied or excerpted in his notebooks, circulated in similar ways among the various Tübingen theologians involved in the correspondence while Crusius sometimes excerpted letters while they were being recited.[91] In January 1576, Crusius even showed and "hastily interpreted" in his classes on Homer and Thucydides a Greek letter that Theodosius Zygomalas had addressed to the students of the University of Tübingen encouraging them in their study of Greek.[92] Gathering and transmitting information was evidently a communal affair and one in which sociability furthered the circulation of information coming to Tübingen.

But Gerlach and Schweigger, like so many others who had business in the Ottoman capital, deferred to the expertise of local agents as well. One of

Gerlach's documents was a report written by Theodosius Zygomalas about the journey through the Aegean that he had undertaken to collect a church tax.[93] Once it had come to Gerlach's attention that Zygomalas would make this trip, he asked him to take notes on the number of Christians living there, the Christian churches in those regions, and anything else that caught his attention. Gerlach also gave him a small sum of money for the purchase of books that Crusius had asked Gerlach to acquire. The report that Zygomalas gave to Gerlach included information of a variegated nature, from comments on the number of monks on Athos to lists of cities and succinct descriptions of the islands in the Aegean. Zygomalas also collected the signatures of different high-ranking ecclesiastics. The distribution of the information is somewhat uneven, which suggests that for some parts of the description Zygomalas, too, relied on secondary observation. So the report that Crusius copied in his Tübingen home was the product of a chain of observations that linked different individuals in different places and different times.

In addition to Gerlach and Schweigger, Crusius also mobilized others in his Tübingen network. He had quickly learned that Greek books were not readily available in Istanbul. In 1587, long after Gerlach and Schweigger had returned from their stays in the Ottoman Empire, Crusius received from Johann Friedrich Hofmann, a Lutheran attached to the imperial embassy to the Sublime Porte, a copy of Damaskinos Studitis's *Thesaurus,* a work he owned.[94] Gerlach, too, had procured several books and manuscripts during his stay in Istanbul. But these seem to have been exceptions: Gerlach repeatedly mentioned the lack of printed books in Istanbul: "Nothing exists here in print," he wrote, "but the New Testament, the Psalms, sermons of monks," and other works of no importance.[95] The Greeks in the Ottoman Empire, lacking their own printing press, "prefer to read manuscripts over printed books" even though "printed books were imported from Venice," used in church services, and sometimes offered for sale in various shops in Istanbul.[96] Nowhere in Istanbul, Gerlach continued, had he been able to find a map of the city—perhaps Crusius could try a bookseller from Augsburg in Venice (where he knew such a map had been printed).[97] Other books and manuscripts turned out to be not for sale: in one particularly lengthy letter, the chaplain complained that although "some works of Athanasius and Cyrillus were preserved in the patriarchal library," they could not be bought.[98] Having a particular manuscript copied could be expensive as well, sometimes even too expensive: at one point Gerlach bought a set of books from Joannes Zygomalas, but he otherwise deemed the scribal services that the patriarchate's exegetist offered too costly.[99] Istanbul was evidently not a good place to acquire Greek books.

Crusius thus turned to Venice, celebrated then as now as the single most important early modern market for vernacular Greek books, and to a group of Lutherans living there and in nearby Padua. As early as 1564, Engelbert Milander, a Lutheran minister who was accompanying "young noble men on their travels to Italy," sent Crusius from Padua and Venice what appears to have been the latter's first vernacular Greek books.[100] Most of Crusius's contacts there operated at the end of the 1570s, just before the first Greeks arrived on Crusius's doorstep, and were alumni of the University of Tübingen. They had enrolled at the University of Padua to study medicine and joined its German student association, the so-called *Natio Germanica*. Hieronymus Vischer, for example, who matriculated in Padua on September 29, 1579, repeatedly combed the bookstalls of Venice in search of books that Crusius had requested. Through such information agents Crusius also hoped to inform himself about Greeks living in different parts of the Venetian Republic: Jeremias Seng, one of Crusius's former students who matriculated together with Vischer, wrote his former teacher about the community of Greek Orthodox Christians in Venice. Crusius also asked Seng to forward a Greek letter to two Greeks living in Venice and to urge them to write back, while he asked Johann Jakob Haug, another Tübingen graduate, to send him books and to make contact with Greeks studying in Venice and Padua.[101] Just as Crusius depended on Gerlach and later Schweigger in Istanbul, so could he rely on another group of Tübingen graduates living and studying in Italy.

But even Venice, so often celebrated by historians as a major center for the production and trade of (vernacular) Greek books, was a difficult market for Crusius to navigate. In one of his letters, Vischer made it clear to him that "those wishing to buy vernacular Greek books, seldom find them for sale."[102] Italian booksellers could also be untrustworthy: upon his return from Istanbul, Gerlach had given Crusius a model book order, made by Theodosius Zygomalas, that he could (but in the end did not) send to a Greek living in Venice called Nicephorus. Instead, Crusius gave the document to Gruppenbach, who was supposed to bring the form to the Frankfurt book fair and hand it over to Pietro Longo, a prominent Venetian bookseller and courier.[103]

All was said and done, but in letters to Osiander, Crusius complained that no books would be coming from Venice: "Italian booksellers had deceived [them] three times."[104]

Crusius also mobilized his connections in the Holy Roman Empire in search of information about the Ottoman Greek world and for acquiring vernacular Greek books. Bruno Seidel, the physician from Erfurt who had shared with Crusius his suspicions about Gabriel Calonas's identity, also explained to him the difference between two kinds of Greek Orthodox monks: "Those who are made monks after losing their wife are called *hieromonachous*, because if they want to remain priests they cannot marry again. *Kalogeros* comes from 'good old men' and not from 'good' and 'holy.'"[105] David Hoeschel, rector of the St. Anna Gymnasium in Augsburg, sent two vernacular Greek imprints to Crusius, who had them copied by one of his students.[106] Crusius asked Johan Scheurlin, a physician from Augsburg, to see if he could acquire some Greek books from Venice "and to write him about Greek affairs in Italy."[107] Michael Neander, the rector of the *Klosterschule* in Ilfeld with whom Crusius corresponded about all matters Greek, sent him several books in the Greek vernacular.[108] In return, Crusius gave Neander a book that he had earlier received from the Graz-based jurist Wolfgang Finckelthaus. Trading Greek books, probably because they were relatively rare, happened more often: in 1575 Crusius gave Samuel Hailand a copy of a medieval life of Alexander in verse—a duplicate copy that Gerlach had sent him a couple of months earlier—in exchange for the *Tale of Belisarius*.[109] It was through the circulation of such books and information, which moved from one place to the next, that Crusius's knowledge of the contemporary Greek world could expand significantly.

Tracing Crusius's documents, then, renders visible the information agents who aided his inquiries. This small Lutheran Republic of Letters, which extended from Tübingen to Augsburg to Padua to Venice and even to Istanbul, opened numerous windows on the contemporary Greek world. Tübingen facilitated this exchange of information: Vischer, Seng, and Haug were all alumni of the University of Tübingen while the city's reputation as a Lutheran stronghold aided Gerlach's and Schweigger's appointments. Crusius's teaching at the university brought him renown throughout the Holy Roman Empire and fostered connections he could mobilize when in need of information. Yet this network was also constrained by its very nature and possibly more makeshift than Crusius would have wanted: it was by chance that a Lutheran chaplain was assigned to the imperial ambassador and that another one had succeeded him, and who knew how many future Tübingen alumni would comply with Crusius's requests for books and information because they so happened to be continuing their studies in Padua. Yet this imperfect system worked; and it worked because each person offered Crusius a specific set of skills or access to information markets otherwise closed off to him.

Gathering News

Crusius complemented his ethnographic work on the Greeks with inquiries into the history and nature of the Ottoman Turks. The geopolitical changes in the Eastern Mediterranean had made it clear that Greek and Ottoman affairs were deeply intertwined: studying the contemporary Greek world meant reckoning with the rise of the Ottomans at the expense of the Greeks, and thus involved gathering news about Ottoman geopolitics. Here, too, Tübingen's university life and the expertise of others advanced his research in multiple directions.

Humanists like Crusius often began their attempts at understanding the Ottomans with history. The havoc caused by the arrival of the Ottomans propelled humanists across the Italian peninsula to harness their philological skills and investigate the origins and descent of this nomadic people, often by mining medieval chronicles for evidence. In sixteenth-century scholarly circles, their "compulsion to look to the past to make sense of a messy and disturbing present" had lost none of its fire.[110] Crusius, in what was evidently a similar move, turned to Byzantine chronicles for guidance and answers, assuming that reading through the whole of Greek and Byzantine history would reveal more about the perceived unsettling incursions of the Ottoman Turks into Christian territories. Through a comparison of different Byzantine historians, Crusius came to see how the Byzantine and Ottoman Empires came to exist side by side, and how Ottoman sovereignty had come to replace Byzantine authority in the political sphere.[111]

One of his books elegantly illustrates this effort to synchronize Byzantine and Ottoman affairs. In his copy of the 1551 German translation of Martin Luther's *Supputatio annorum mundi*—an eschatological reckoning of the world's expected six-thousand-year history—Crusius filled up the individual columns and margins with references to key passages in late Byzantine and early Ottoman history: the 1204 sack of Constantinople; the restoration of Byzantine rule by Michael VIII Palaeologus; and the bloody military conflicts with the Ottomans that ultimately culminated in the loss of Byzantine political power and the establishment of Ottoman rule. Tellingly, Crusius inserted the names and dates of the reigns and deeds of successive Byzantine emperors and Ottoman sultans, starting in 1261 and continuing to the death of Suleiman the Magnificent in 1566 and the accession of his son Selim II.[112] Crusius thus envisioned the rise of the Ottomans and the fall of the Greeks as key points on the time line of salvation—a powerful reminder that Lutheran attempts at interpreting the Ottomans, and Islam more broadly, were never isolated from broader eschatological discourses that saw the Ottomans as a scourge sent by God to punish his people for their sins.

It is not immediately apparent when Crusius started wading through rumors and reports concerning the Ottomans and their expansion into Christian Europe. His notes in Wolfgang Dreschler's 1550 account of the origins and history of the Ottomans suggest a relatively early date. This otherwise unassuming work revealed to its readers that early in the year 1550 "Suleiman, who for thirty years had tormented the people of God, was rumored to have died."[113] But when Crusius read this entry in 1566, he knew these rumors were "evidently false." Indeed, "if only he had died then!" he exclaimed in the margin, adding with relief that

> the death of this [sultan] was announced in Tübingen, yesterday, October 28, 1566. [It was said] that he died in the month of September of this year in the fortress of Sziget, which he had recently besieged. If it is true, Crusius prays that he may rest in pitch (*quiescat in pice*): just as there today was a lunar eclipse after the third hour in the afternoon.[114]

Many aspects of this note deserve further comment. Crusius evidently experienced that nagging anxiety about the Ottoman advancements that inspired so many publications of the period. His comment also illustrates how he could corroborate historical events described in his historical books with seemingly more accurate evidence brought to Tübingen through the

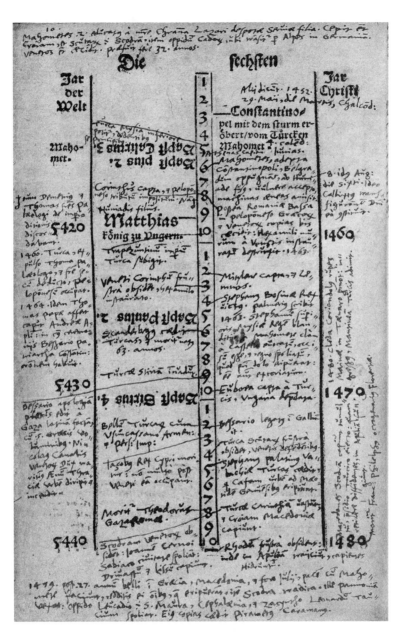

5.5 Crusius's notes in his copy of Luther's *Supputatio annorum mundi* on the fall of Constantinople. *Credit: Universitätsbibliothek Tübingen Ce 1094, fol. 10.*

postal network.[115] His desire to link the sultan's death to a lunar eclipse hints at a more general way in which Crusius sought to interpret the news, on which more follows. And, last, as early as 1566 and thus about a decade before he contacted the patriarch, Crusius was already keeping track of developments in Istanbul by following the news.

Such news arrived in Tübingen through Crusius's overlapping personal and professional networks. Wolfgang Rhoner initially brought this kind of news to Tübingen. Rhoner, the brother of Crusius's first wife, Sybilla Rhoner, lived in Ulm, and culled his information from news originating in different markets, including Rome, Venice, Vienna, and Prague.[116] Later Crusius also began receiving news reports from Heinrich Welling, a classical philologist, who also carried out visitations of the Latin schools in the duchy of Württemberg. Like Rhoner, Welling was on familiar terms with Crusius: Welling's son was one of Crusius's students and at least once Crusius took notes while the boy recited from his father's news reports.[117] Welling himself also came to Crusius's house to discuss the news and once he even recited the news to Crusius when the two met in a bath house.[118] From 1600 onward, Crusius relied solely on Welling's services because—as he noted in his diary—the news reports sent by Rhoner often arrived too late and were short and unreliable. It has been suggested that Welling's reports may have been copies or adaptations of the Fugger newsletter, which would connect Crusius directly to the famous Fugger news service and their expansive commercial network.[119] Through these personal and familial contacts, Crusius was able to keep abreast of the latest developments in and beyond the Eastern Mediterranean.

Communal meals offered particularly attractive occasions to exchange ideas about the latest news. On Easter Monday 1595, for instance, Crusius had lunch with a group of university professors and, although conversation touched upon various topics, they mostly talked "about the Turkish war."[120] At another moment Crusius was explicitly asked to bring the latest news reports that he had received to dinner, which suggests that he might have been the person whom others in Tübingen went to see when they wanted to hear the latest news. The news that Crusius's information agents brought to Tübingen circulated in other households and reached his colleagues through the kind of sociability that this university town offered.

One lurid piece of evidence illustrates just how much Crusius depended on the expertise of others in Tübingen in this process. In 1596 one of Crusius's nephews read him a treatise about a seven-year-old boy from Weigelsdorf, who had reportedly grown a golden tooth in his lower left jaw. The author, Jacob Horst, a professor of medicine at the University of Helmstedt, had examined the golden tooth and asserted its authenticity. His account placed this miraculous affair in an astrological framework: an unusual alignment of the planets at the time of the boy's birth had increased the heat of the sun, causing the bone in the boy's lower jaw to turn to gold. This had to be a portent, in Horst's estimation, that announced the dawn of a new golden age for the Holy Roman Empire and signaled the end of the Ottoman expansion. But because the tooth was located on the boy's left side—usually considered to be the sinister side—the Christian armies of Rudolph II would first face sinister events before achieving a final victory.[121] Crusius concurred with Horst on almost all points, but he believed that it concerned Sigismund Báthory. It had been the Transylvanian prince's name that triggered this conclusion: the etymologist in Crusius realized that Sigismund would be victorious ("*Sieg*") with his mouth ("*mund*"). But the Lutheran in him also entertained the possibility that the golden tooth announced the spread of the evangelical movement in the Mediterranean: "Or shall the Golden Tooth perhaps be a preacher or a book that, winning with its mouth, will plant the pure gospel in the East and nearby places?"[122]

Nearly every aspect of the story was pregnant with significance in Crusius's view and he sought to share his discovery with friends and colleagues, evidently in the hope of obtaining further confirmation and support. This often happened around the university and the *Stiftskirche* and, again, during social events: having just heard mass, and lingering at the spot in the church where the ropes used to ring the church bells hang down, Crusius told Heerbrand and a few others how he interpreted the Silesian boy's golden tooth.[123] He also shared his interpretation with colleagues over lunch, many of whom concurred and expressed their hope that what Crusius predicted would indeed come about. Gerlach, one of the men present, could even add that there were three "teeth, possibly elephant tusks" on Prince Sigismund's shield, suggesting that the Silesian boy's golden tooth indeed referred to Sigismund Báthory.[124] Here we see in detail how Crusius's interpretation of the news could become more authoritative: Gerlach knew from personal experience what Crusius could only piece together from hearsay.

Other forms of confirmation came in writing, and sometimes unexpectedly. On June 15 of that year, one of Rhoner's news reports announced that Sigismund had scored a victory in Temeswar, current-day Bulgaria.[125] Crusius had also discussed "everything [he] knew" on this matter while taking a stroll after mass with Michael Maestlin, the famous mathematician at the University of Tübingen, and Georg Weigenmaier, Tübingen's Hebraist. The latter shared with Crusius some of the news that he in turn had read: in Belgrade, a bolt of lightning had recently destroyed preparations to receive the sultan.[126] Perhaps Crusius and Weigenmaier regarded these to be the sinister events that were supposed to precede the ultimate victory of the Christian forces. In what seemed like a bold move, Crusius even addressed a letter to Báthory, in which he recounted his interpretation, and asked a local preacher by the name of Stephan Ruef to deliver the letter.[127] Though it would never reach its addressee, the move indicates just how much faith Crusius had placed in Báthory.

In an unexpected turn of events, Ruef did show the letter to a recent graduate of the University of Tübingen and of the celebrated *Stift*. This man, who had just accepted his first position as teacher of mathematics and astronomy in Graz, was already corresponding with Crusius and is otherwise known to history as the astronomer Johannes Kepler. In one of his replies, the astronomer intimated that he had seen Crusius's letter to Báthory and sent a poem by the humanist poet Paulus Melissus that supported this interpretation. Such responses were welcome news because it showed that Kepler did not disagree with him. Nevertheless, Crusius also wished that "Ruef would not show the letter to so many others," perhaps fearing that he had not yet gathered enough evidence to back up his claims.[128] In another message, Kepler was more forthcoming: he acknowledged that the heavens agreed with Crusius and attached one of his own prognostications as evidence.[129] The prognostication announced a universal mutation of the whole world and as such corresponded neatly with Crusius's belief that the Ottoman Turks would be defeated.[130]

Prognostications such as these provided a kind of proof that Crusius eagerly sought, but that he could not easily produce himself. Claudia Brosseder has shown that "throughout the sixteenth century . . . German scholars were under the spell of astrology" and "collected observations on comets and eclipses and painstakingly related them to singular historical events."[131] Crusius was no exception: his own interpretation of the boy's golden tooth was founded on certain astrological assumptions. Like early modern astrologers, he searched the skies for celestial signs, connected them to contemporary political events, and occasionally even drew images of unusual heavenly phenomena in his notebooks.[132] But Crusius does not seem to have read the *arcana* of early modern astrological writings: of the more than seven hundred books that have survived from his private library, there are no works of astrology, apart from Regiomontanus's *Tabulae astronomicae,* in which he left no annotations. Nowhere in his diary or in his other manuscript writings did he, to my knowledge, dabble in astrological predictions. The skies intrigued him, but he did not possess the skills to unlock their mysteries.

Crusius instead deferred to the expertise of those who could read the skies: with Philipp Apian, a professor of mathematics in Tübingen, whose father Peter Apian was the author of the celebrated 1540 *Astronomicum Caesareum,* he discussed the famous 1577 comet that appeared above Istanbul and that so many in Europe observed.[133] Philipp Apian's student Michael Maestlin was one of the first people Crusius contacted about his interpretation of the golden tooth. This mathematician had earlier calculated on Crusius's instigation the year in which Duke Friedrich of Württemberg was born, which was crucial evidence for this sort of astrological prediction.[134] And it was Maestlin who had introduced Kepler, who was *his* student, to the works of Copernicus.[135] Crusius thus talked to three generations of astrologers and was part of a community that thought and talked about the meaning of celestial portents. No wonder that he contacted all three of them when he sought further support for his interpretation of the golden tooth.

Portents were not the only kind of evidence that captivated Crusius. On June 15, 1596, just two days after having given Crusius his prognostication, Kepler sent a *thaler* to Tübingen that bore the image and the weapon of Báthory. The coat of arms did indeed, as Stephan Gerlach had earlier suspected, consist of three tusks. In addition to the numerous rumors and report that Crusius had read and heard, in addition to the support that several of his colleagues and correspondents had given him in writing or in person, and in addition to Kepler's prognostication, Crusius now had material evidence as well: an object that came from the very lands that the portent was supposed to talk about and one that provided near irrefutable evidence that Báthory was indeed the "Golden Tooth" that would crush the Ottoman Turks. How else could the teeth in the prince's crest be interpreted?[136]

Crusius, then, sought confirmation for rumors and news reports, like many of his contemporaries did, by deferring to the expertise of others. Gerlach, having himself lived in the Ottoman Empire, knew about the imagery of Báthory's crest. As astronomers and mathematicians, Apian, Maestlin, and Kepler were qualified to read the heavens. In the case of the news reports, Crusius ultimately subscribed to the service that he deemed the most reliable one. Keeping track of the news supplemented inquiries of a different kind, such as reading historical chronicles and interviewing wandering Greeks. Not all the details of the story are known, and some of the evidence is circumstantial. The contents of Kepler's prognostication, for instance, are lost. Neither do we know exactly whether Apian and Crusius discussed the "Golden Tooth" in any comparable depth. I also have not been able to locate his reaction to the fact that, in actuality, Báthory did not deliver a decisive defeat to the Ottomans. Maestlin's exact involvement in the matter remains somewhat unclear as well. In the end, this was also a relatively open-ended and serendipitous investigation: Crusius's inquiry operated as much on chance and contingency as it did on regular lines of communication. Yet even the outline of the story reveals how his position within the university town of Tübingen, and the sociability and the epistolary networks it fostered, made such intellectual exchanges possible.

Conclusion

On June 7, 1597, one of Crusius's remarkable dreams reproduced the rich social and intellectual life that could develop over a meal in Tübingen at the court of the Ottoman sultan:

> A dream: 3rd hour before sunrise. We were seated at a table in Constantinople, my mother, Crusius, and the Turkish emperor. The Turk drank to my health (kindly and with seemly merriment), and I, rising to my feet, said: "Most gracious emperor," after which he, still seated with us, spoke in German to some people at another table (I do not know what he said). I therefore said humbly: "Most gracious em-

peror, where did your Imperial Majesty learn German?" He replied: "From people around me." Then I awoke. I later got up at the 4th hour. This too I asked: "Most gracious emperor, is there not something, perhaps an old Greek book, that I could take home with me (to Germany)?" He replied: "Oh yes, let us have a look among our books." So much for this.[137]

Only in his dreams could Crusius, unbothered by geographical distance, obtain materials directly from the Ottoman sultan. Only in his dreams was the sultan part of the sociability and intellectual exchange that Tübingen, as a university town, fostered. And only in his dreams, as Crusius discovered later in yet another dream, could books be taken from him with the ease with which he dreamed of acquiring them: "a woman carried from my attic, on her head, two large books written by hand, among other things."[138] Only in his dreams, then, could books and the knowledge they contained move effortlessly to and from his Tübingen home.

Once Crusius had woken up—perhaps to copy a manuscript with a single quill while standing up; perhaps to mark his student papers; but most certainly early in the morning—obtaining and understanding information about the Ottoman Greek world required a more sustained effort. Books and manuscripts did indeed come from the Ottoman capital, and so did news about the Ottoman advancement and the military exploits of the sultan, but their circulation was contingent upon the continuous efforts of Crusius's friends and acquaintances. Some of them were living in Istanbul, others in and around Venice, but a surprising number of them were Lutherans connected to Tübingen and its university. And the documents acquired by Crusius only began to reveal their mysteries through conversation and collaboration with yet another group of Lutherans who could each claim expertise in a particular field. Crusius was no isolated mind: his was a communal project, the growth of which was made possible through the help and support of other experts.

Early modern university towns like Tübingen can thus best be approached as knowledge communities that made scholarly inquiry possible through different forms of sociability. As a complex social-religious conglomeration, the town of Tübingen offered exactly the right environment for the research that Crusius was engaged in and allowed for a kind of scholarly intimacy that guaranteed that everyone was aware whom to ask what: through everyday face-to-face interaction in Tübingen's *Altstadt,* Crusius knew exactly whose expertise complemented his own and who could assist him in his studies. That is not to say, of course, that the university town alone determined what Crusius was able to discover. Some informants, including the Greek ones, had no direct connection to Tübingen. But to some extent, even that small network of Greeks living in Venice and Istanbul was an extension of Crusius's Tübingen exchanges and contributed, from afar, to the symbiosis of sociability and scholarship that the university town fostered.

Crusius knew full well that much of his inquiry depended on the expertise of others. Throughout his books, notebooks, and manuscripts, he recorded the contributions of his friends and acquaintances, labeled specific transcriptions as his students', and drew the seating arrangements of dinner parties at which the news was discussed. In his published works, as we will see in Chapter 6, Crusius would continue to acknowledge the works of others, even when it impeded the printing of his findings. He did so because he realized that being part of a community of scholarly experts was more than the sum of its parts—and that to benefit from the community one needs to acknowledge the contribution of others. "Friendship," Crusius intimated as early as 1554 when he was still teaching young boys in Memmingen, and perhaps encouraging them to undertake the kind of collaborative work he would later engage in, "often pushes us to do things that we would otherwise have been slow to undertake."[139]

6

TRAVEL IN THE MIND'S EYE

Over the years, Crusius amassed a massive amount of material through writing letters, reading books, and interviewing Greeks, and through learned exchange in and around his Tübingen home. His seminal publication on the Ottoman Greek world, the *Turcograecia,* published in Basel in 1584, reproduced some of that material and became, in Crusius's lifetime, a major source for early modern Greek history and the Greek vernacular. Its eight books brought together a unique collection of visual, textual, and material evidence that documented the changes the Greek world had witnessed since the late fourteenth century. It reproduced and explicated a set of Greek chronicles, unknown until then in the Latin world, which narrated how the Ottomans had deprived the Greeks of their political independence and contested their ecclesiastical authority. It offered hundreds of letters, in various Greek registers, that Greek Orthodox Christians living in different parts of the Mediterranean had written. It contained unique documents related to sixteenth-century vernacular Greek education. It did not reproduce everything that Crusius had assembled, but it was a copious documentary record that allowed for an extensive survey of Ottoman Greek culture and society, from religion to topography, from linguistics to education, and from dress to politics.

One of its greatest accomplishments was that it connected the fate of the Greeks thematically and systematically with the Ottoman expansion into the Mediterranean and that the numerous primary sources Crusius reproduced, as well as his layers of commentary on these materials, brought the Ottoman Greek world to life like few other books of the period did. Yet because of its complexity and idiosyncrasy, the *Turcograecia* was also a work that proved difficult to print and one that sold poorly while Crusius was alive. Today it is more often referenced than read, and it has not received the critical attention that its scope demands. A seemingly miscellaneous work not easily categorized, the *Turcograecia* functioned as an important entry point into studying Ottoman Greece, but also one that readers then and now have found difficult to situate.

This chapter demonstrates that Crusius designed his masterpiece not as some miscellaneous work but as a very particular kind of travel guide. Up until the late sixteenth century, most conventional histories, a genre that included the description of other civilizations, came in narrative form and offered chronological analyses. In the late sixteenth-century learned world, however, many scholars began experimenting with new ways to present their research and were choosing in ever greater numbers to insert primary source material into their texts. Crusius followed these developments and in the *Turcograecia* replaced narration almost entirely with reproductions of primary sources, relegating to the commentary explications based on the information he had amassed through reading and interviewing. In the footnotes to his publications, he referred repeatedly to the informants who lodged with him. In this way, the notes themselves became an organic and visible part of the whole. The result was a work that was unprecedented in its choice of sources (many of which were not yet known at the time), its presentation (few early modern books contained such little narration), and in the kind of intellectual work it did: the *Turcograecia* offered an intricate mosaic of Ottoman Greece that Crusius hoped would serve as a replacement for an actual journey to these parts. Without having to travel, readers could encounter directly and in a variety of original documents what Greek life under Ottoman rule was like.

To understand Crusius's vision for how the *Turcograecia* would facilitate such intellectual travel, it is necessary to dissect the book's composition, content, methods, and models, as he himself never explicitly discussed the logic behind the book. Tracing such details—including the nature of the firsthand evidence that Crusius chose to include, the scholarly traditions from which he drew to organize this material into a coherent whole, and his efforts to find a printer—allows us to see how and where Crusius translated his reading, collecting, and conversing into a public, published form of writing. An examination of the *Turcograecia*'s constituent components also reveals the collaborative and interdisciplinary nature of early modern ethnography. Crusius drew heavily from the work of travel writers, ecclesiastical historians, antiquaries, and philologists, creating a template for understanding other cultures that solidified his reputation as a Hellenist. Only when we situate the book within the learned traditions from which it emerged can we see the *Turcograecia* not as a simple accumulation of data but as an ethnographic treatise that presented a particular way of "traveling" to Ottoman Greece. Finally, the process of compiling and especially publishing the *Turcograecia* reflects the ways in which his religious sympathies continued to shape his "discovery" of Ottoman Greece. Though religion is only one of the many topics discussed in the *Turcograecia*, Crusius very much envisioned printing his findings to be fulfilling God's work in the world. Getting the book published in the deeply divided confessional landscape of the sixteenth century, where books were used as ammunition in religious warfare, was therefore a difficult affair, not made easier by the fact that Crusius, as a staunch Lutheran, was always explicit about his religious sympathies.

Composition and Content

The direct origins of the *Turcograecia* remain obscure. Nowhere in his diary or elsewhere does Crusius explicitly state when he first conceived of the work. It probably began its life in 1579, though, after Gerlach had given Crusius two otherwise unknown Greek chronicles that he had brought from Istanbul and that would make up the *Turcograecia*'s first two books. Over the years, as Crusius amassed more and more material, the book grew into a vast and learned tome. The final version, published by Sebastian Henricpetri and printed by Leonard Ostein in 1584, was 554 folio-sized pages thick and divided into eight books. Each book was composed of precise reproductions of one or several original Greek documents, Crusius's Latin translations, and copious sets of notes, in which he added choice passages and full texts from the relevant books in his study and incorporated the firsthand evidence he had gathered by interviewing his informants. The work was prefaced by a long dedicatory epistle to three sons of Philip I, Landgrave of Hesse. It also contained introductory poems in praise of Crusius and his scholarly accomplishments, an eighteen-page index, a list of authors referenced in the work, and a substantial errata list.[1] Together this material offered, according to

TVRCOGRAECIAE
LIBRI OCTO
A̓
Martino Crvsio, in Academia
Tybingenſi Græco & Latino Profeſſore,
vtraque lingua edita.

QVIBVS GRAECORVM STATVS SVB IMPERIO
Turcico, in Politia & Eccleſia, Oeconomia & Scholis, iam inde ab
amiſſa Conſtantinopoli, ad hæc uſq̧ tempora, luculen‐
ter deſcribitur.

CVM INDICE COPIOSISSIMO.

Cum Gratia & Priuilegio Cæſ. Maieſt.

BASILEAE,
PER LEONARDVM OSTENIVM,
SEBASTIANI HENRICPETRI
IMPENSA.

6.1 Frontispiece of the *Turcograecia*. Credit: Universitätsbibliothek Tübingen
Fo XVI 18.2, title page.

the title page, insights into "the status of the Greeks under Turkish rule with regards to politics and the church, the household and schooling."[2]

How did Crusius communicate these insights to his readers? He divided the main body into four equal parts: books one and two, three and four, five and six, and seven and eight. In the first part, readers could contemplate the political and ecclesiastical history of the Greek world.[3] Book one concentrates on the political history of Constantinople from the end of the fourteenth century. It consists of a Greek chronicle and a long letter that Zygomalas had written in 1581 about the events following the capture of Constantinople. Book two traces the development of the patriarchate of Constantinople, using a chronicle that Crusius believed had been translated into vernacular Greek by Manuel Malaxos, a Greek scholar with close ties to the patriarchate.[4] Several woodcut images adorn these books, including ones of a Byzantine emperor, the patriarch of Constantinople, the Greek Orthodox patriarchate and the *Seraglio*, the Ottoman harem.[5]

The second and third parts of the *Turcograecia* reveal, according to the preface, how "Greeks live amongst each other and go about their business."[6] Book three offers a collection of letters that different Greek scholars had exchanged among themselves between 1556 and 1580. It is subdivided into three parts: the first part contains letters in the Greek vernacular that Zygomalas had translated into "purer" Greek (that is, ancient Greek). The second part consists of twenty letters in ancient Greek, the first ten of which also appear in a vernacular Greek version made by Zygomalas. In the third part, Crusius gathered seven letters in ecclesiastical Greek—that is, a mixed form, between classical and vernacular Greek. Book four presented another sixty letters in different Greek registers. Together these two books showed Crusius's readers how Greeks "discussed ecclesiastical, political, and social matters."[7]

Books five and six concern the realm of education. Here Crusius hoped that his audience would see how young Greeks grow up and are educated. Book five consists of sixty-one school exercises in vernacular Greek (*themato-epistolae*) that Zygomalas had sent Crusius in 1578. These assignments required students to translate a short text in the vernacular back into classical Greek. Book six is concerned with vernacular Greek poetry. It is subdivided into two parts. The first is an edition of the Cretan Demetrio Zeno's vernacular Greek translation of the *Batrachomyomachia* (*Battle of Frogs and Mice*), a Late Antique parody of the *Iliad*, long attributed to Homer, that Crusius had also taught in Tübingen. He received the 1529 Venetian edition of this text from one of his Lutheran contacts in Venice. The second part consists of seven poems that Crusius wrote for various occasions, which the hierodeacon Symeon Cabasylas had translated into vernacular Greek. According to Crusius's preface, the materials in book six could teach readers about warfare, while in book five they could find information about all sorts of nonviolent matters.[8]

Crusius hoped that the fourth and final part of the *Turcograecia* would introduce his readers, "through friendly conversation," to the Greeks with whom he had been exchanging letters.[9] Book seven collects a total of twenty-eight letters that Crusius, Andreae, and Gerlach exchanged with different members of the patriarchate. Book eight consists of eighteen letters, written between 1570 and 1583, that Crusius had exchanged with Greek Orthodox Christians living in Egypt and places outside the Ottoman Empire, including Gabriel Severus in Venice and Franciscus Portus in Geneva.

The last three parts of the *Turcograecia*, thus, provide a snapshot of Greece's social, political, educational, and religious landscape, while the first offers a journey into its past to see where that world originated. Initially, though, Crusius had envisioned an even longer work, one that would not just encompass his findings on the Ottoman Greek world but would include documents that testified to the ways in which Greek studies had migrated to the Holy Roman Empire. For what seem to have been reasons of length, this material ultimately appeared as a separate volume, the *Germanograecia*. This book, published in 1585, shared with its companion piece a focus on original documents: the *Germanograecia* included several of Crusius's orations on topics as diverse as Homer's *Odyssey*, the development of the Greek language since antiquity, and the value of studying *sententiae*. It presented editions of the Greek problem sets that his students had to solve in class. And three of its six books reproduced Greek poems that Crusius had written for different occasions. The documents included in the *Germanograecia* thus painted a vivid picture of the kind of Greek learning with which Crusius's audience would have been all too familiar.

Crusius's elegant division of the *Turcograecia*, as set out in the preface, does not completely capture the actual arrangement of the material. Every document, whether it was a chronicle, a poem, or a letter, was explicated in lengthy sets of notes. In these commentaries, even more than in the original Greek documents, readers could find a wide range of information: from comments on Greek marriages and the ways in which Greeks dated the years to observations about the various types of coins in circulation in the Ottoman Empire and the ancient monuments that were still extant in Istanbul and other cities. Readers could learn that Christian boys, who had been taken by the Ottomans to receive an elite education at court through a practice known as *devşirme*, filled the ranks of the Janissaries. They could find information about the origin of their name—"new soldier" (*yeni-çeri*)—and that they differed from the *Sipahi*, the Ottoman cavalry corps. One set of notes included the names and locations of the various Orthodox monasteries on Mount Athos, as well as the number of monks inhabiting the peninsula. Another note described what customs dictated contact with the patriarch— one approached him with one's hand on one's chest. Crusius's comments also described the funerary rites of the Greeks, the feasts held in honor of the deceased, and the laments sung at such ceremonies. His notes made mention of Greek Orthodox chanting, the garments that Greek ecclesiastics wore, and the images of the saints, apostles, and Church Fathers that decorated churches in Istanbul. Elsewhere readers could learn how Greeks performed their liturgy and celebrated mass—a question of central interest, given the belief that the Orthodox churches followed particularly ancient rituals, and given the fascination of Protestant scholars, from Luther on, with the early history of Christian liturgy.[10] The *Turcograecia*, in short, covered not all but numerous aspects of Ottoman Greek life.

Crusius's commentaries also require our attention exactly because they offered the kind of guidance, in the literal and metaphorical sense, that antiquaries and travelers usually provided in their works. Topography was an important theme, for instance. Crusius's note on the many gates of the Ottoman capital might have attracted his readers' attention, as would perhaps his explanation of the names and locations of Greek islands in the Aegean as well as the languages spoken there. Readers may have found his short description of Adrianople useful.[11] But they would not have seen such topographical material in visual form: the *Turcograecia* does not contain any maps. It is not that Crusius did not possess any. He once pasted a map of Istanbul that he had taken from Pierre Gilles's account of his travels to the Ottoman capital—and that he had enriched with layers of interpretative annotation—into the back of one of his Byzantine books.[12] Instead, the

Turcograecia offered information that Crusius believed could function as a stand-in for an actual journey. In his notes to book eight, for instance, Crusius had inserted a lengthy German quotation from Schweigger's description of his journey from Istanbul to the Holy Land. Readers could follow Schweigger to every stop on the way: from Troy, the Cyclades, Samos, Rhodes, Alexandria, Rosetta, Jaffa, all the way to Jerusalem.[13] Elsewhere, Crusius included the distances—which Apian had calculated for him—between Tübingen and Istanbul.[14] His notes to a letter of recommendation that the patriarch of Alexandria had written for one Albert of Lowenstein offered a similarly precise reconstruction of the route that pilgrims like this count took to get from Venice to the Holy Land: a hundred German miles from Venice to Ragusa, sixty from Ragusa to Corfu, from there another sixty to Methoni and then another sixty to Crete, another sixty from Crete to Rhodes, then fifty miles from Rhodes to Cyprus, sixty from Cyprus to Jaffa, and from there the last eight miles over land to Jerusalem. The list Crusius had included of other Protestant travelers, culled from the books in his study, offered further evidence of the vibrant Protestant culture of devout Holy Land pilgrimage and of the great popularity of such accounts in the first century after the advent of print.[15] The descriptions that these pilgrims offered of Christian churches in Alexandria or the Christian cemetery in Damascus may also have whetted the reader's appetite for information about the Christian landscape of the Eastern Mediterranean.[16]

Crusius's commentaries, like other travel books, sometimes adopted a distinctly ethnographic flavor. The notes to book seven, for instance, listed the cities that Gerlach had encountered on his journey to the Ottoman Empire and included Gerlach's extraordinarily graphic description of the way in which Greek women dressed, discussed in Chapter 5.[17] Elsewhere Crusius's comments on the island of Chios, meant to elucidate a letter sent to a Greek physician from that island, revealed not only that its port was small and that mastic—the tasty resin obtained from the mastic tree—came from there but also that "men are nowhere more courteous than on Chios where the women were extremely courteous and beautiful." And "although this was a Greek island," the note continued, "the customs" of the people living there "were Western." The population spoke not only Greek but also a "corrupt" Italian, "just as the Genoese," whom they resembled in their way of life and in how they dressed.[18] In just a few descriptive sentences, Crusius brought to life an island culture and offered his readers powerful clues about its Italian past.

Crusius frequently peppered his notes with explanations of vernacular Greek words and comments on the linguistic diversity of the Ottoman Greek world. Readers with an interest in language may have appreciated his translations of the different titles of members of the patriarchate, the vernacular Greek names of certain musical instruments, his discussion of the correct vernacular Greek words for bread and wine—two words that any Lutheran with an interest in Greek would have wanted to know—and the letter of Zygomalas that described the nature of contemporary Greek.[19] Crusius's observations on the many letters edited in the *Turcograecia* are a particularly rich repository for information on the different ways in which Italian and Ottoman rule had affected the language Greeks spoke: at one point, for instance, Crusius explained how the expression καλὰ καὶ—which introduced a subordinate clause in one of the letters, but which readers steeped in classical Greek might not have immediately recognized—was a nonclassical way of saying "although" that was a direct translation of the Italian *ben che*.[20] Readers may also have noticed how some of Crusius's observations belonged to a larger cluster of texts. His lengthy comment on the different Greek names for the octopus, for example, did not only reference the relevant passages in Aristotle and Gesner—the ancient and modern authorities on this subject. It also cited the less canonical, but for Crusius equally pertinent, didactic poem that the second-century Greco-Roman poet Oppian had written on fishing.[21] Yet his contemporaries may not have known that Crusius was not always exactly right: at one point, he wrote that Greeks use the term "Franks" (φρανκοῦς) for "all the peoples of the West perhaps because of the nobility and virtue of the Franks."[22] In light of the many malicious rumors about Lutheranism that, according to Gerlach, circulated in Istanbul, this seems to have been wishful thinking rather than the product of actual research.

Crusius, then, annotated the sources he had edited with copious and varied information. Ultimately, though, he wanted readers to experience his findings directly through the original source material. He envisioned his ideal reader to be a pilgrim (*peregrinus*), who, "standing at a distance," would encounter in each of the *Turcograecia*'s eight books different aspects of the Ottoman Greek world.[23] Only through engagement with original documents,

Crusius seemed to have believed, would his readers experience Ottoman Greek culture in its full complexity. Only reading original documents could serve as a replacement for a physical journey through space.[24] Only original documents would turn his readers into the pilgrims he wanted them to be. And only original documents would "provide the occasion for others to search for more [evidence] and to see Athens itself and other places in Greece."[25] No wonder that Crusius drew so heavily from the criteria for source criticism developed in different scholarly fields: for such a hermeneutics, precise reproductions of authoritative testimonies by far surpassed the potential of narrative and analytical history.

A single example may illuminate precisely how various bits of evidence, both oral and textual, formed an intricate mosaic that must have conveyed a strong sense of immediacy to Crusius's readership. One of his principal aims had been to find out as much as he could about the Orthodox Church. It was Gerlach, more than anybody else, who had helped Crusius acquire such knowledge. From his precise and empirical observations, packed with spellbinding detail, Crusius assembled what was arguably the most accurate representation of patriarchal complex in Western Europe.[26] Word for word and line for line, Crusius reproduced what he had read and seen in Gerlach's letter, first in his diary, and then in his notes to the second book of the *Turcograecia*. The resulting image, in combination with an elaborate legend, identified the entire layout of the patriarchal complex, including the house of the patriarch, the visitors' rooms, and the ancient cisterns.[27]

But Gerlach's testimonies alone did not suffice to explain the full richness of Greek Orthodox life, however dense in empirical detail they were. When Crusius sought to understand the set of images from Gerlach, including one of the Orthodox patriarch, he relied heavily on the linguistic expertise of Donatus, his first Greek visitor. Donatus not only labeled all the individual elements and colors of the patriarch's garment but also placed the image, and especially the clothing it depicted, in its proper religious context. He told Crusius that "twelve ecclesiastics . . . chose, crown, and consecrate the patriarch" by vesting him with his patriarchal attire.[28] It was rituals like this one that interested Crusius, who had highlighted exactly that passage in the patriarchal chronicle that discussed the custom to create a patriarch.[29] Knowing full well the importance of dress to understand a culture, Crusius included the very image that Gerlach had sent him, as well as Donatus's

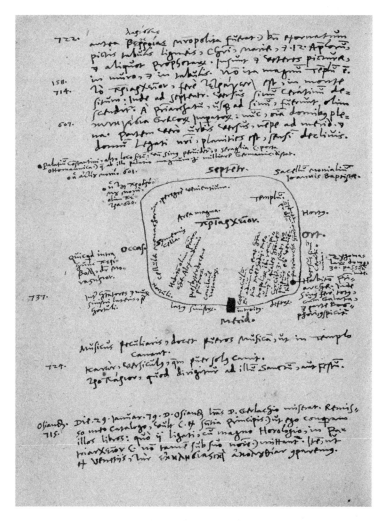

6.2 Manuscript reconstruction of the patriarchate of Constantinople based on the information that Crusius received from Gerlach. *Credit: Universitätsbibliothek Tübingen Mh466 vol. 1, fol. 722.*

explications and notes, in the *Turcograecia*, creating an evocative set piece about the patriarchate of Constantinople.

In collecting and reproducing such a variety of documents, Crusius created a work that is not easily categorized. The *Turcograecia*'s eight books took readers on a lengthy journey through the Ottoman Greek world—from its social fabric, as found in the letters, to its ecclesiastical and political institutions, as described in the chronicles—and guided them through a wealth

190　In Historiam Ecclesiasticam

ornatum, pictis tabulis ligneis, Christi, Mariæ, 12. Apostolorum, & aliquot Prophetarum. Insunt & ueteres picturæ, in muro, & in tabulis. Metuendum est, ne quando Saltanus pro Patriarcheio aliquid aliud ibi ædificet. Non longè inde, Ortu uersus, est D. Ioãnis Zygomalæ domus: habēs tres cõtignationes (drei stock ob einander) in supremo plana, & amœna: unde in Mare despectus est. Ad Occasum, Boreum uersus, Prodromi μονή est, olim μετρα: longius inde, Aetij μονή: postea, Palatium Constantini: unde sinus peruidetur, & Saraglia (porta Ottomanica) ab illo palatio magnum dimidiatum milliare Germanicum distans. Quando Monachus, aut matrona Græca, portam Patriarchatus præteriit: tunc manu dextera pectori applicata, id flectit, non genua: & crebris crucibus frontem ac pectus signat. Postquam primam portam Patriarchatus (ea autem meridiem spectat) intraueris: occurrit altera, sub fornice: ad cuius fornicis dexterum latus, uetus imago Imperatoris & Augustæ picta est, sine nomine: ad sinistrum uerò, duo Apostoli. Gerlachius, Patriarchã accedens, manu pectori apposita, id inflexit: postea dextram Patriarchæ osculatus est. Sic etiam in Turcis honorandis, manus pectori applicatur, & id inflectitur. Pileis non solent capita nudari.

Patriarcheij delineatio, quantum intelligere potui, ferè hæc est.

Reuerentia Græcorum.

Quicquid intra hunc ambitum est, dicitur μοναστέριον.

A habitatio domini Patriarchæ, usq; ad templum extensa. Ex ea sinus ferè totus, cum oppido Galata & parte Bosphori conspicitur. B. C. D. Sepulchra quorundam Monachorum ueterum, quæ inscriptionibus carent, excepto C, quæ obliterata est. Reliqua structura ab E usq; * continet conclauia Monachorum Metropolitarū & Episcoporum, quando ab externis locis ueniunt, in his cubiculis hospitia habent. E Conclauia clericorum, scribarum & officialium D. Patriarchæ. F Tablinum D. Theodosij & suorum collegarum, ut Σαγχεδοι τ̃ μεγαλα, &c. G Puteus, quorum tres in atrio, quartus in tempo est, nam totum hoc ædificium Cisternæ superstructū est ab antiquis. H Chorus ubi Patriarcha licet liturgias habent: urbi inscriptio quædam munia. Μογκλη πρωτοψαλτῳ και ψαλτολογυμ. Itectum templi plumberū ab antiquo. K καλαι in hoc tractu ẽ παλαιηαι. L Cupressus. M Ficus. N equile Patriarchæ. O Hic murus superiore muro humilior est: habens tantum terrestria cubicula, non ανώγαια. P Δάρνη arbor.

Addam & hæc: cū eorū mentio supra facta sit. Πρωτέκθικως, ὁ μακρονείλω. Choniat in Balduini Flandri imperio. Manuscriptū Augustanus Barbaro Græcus codex habet. μακροπείλω. In illustri arcis Tybingens.

Tybing. Bibliotheca.

Bibliotheca (cuius Bibliothecarius, præstans uir, D. Andreas Rittelius est) pars operum D. Basilij manuscripta extat: in cuis margine quodã, scriptũ fœminea (ut uideatur) manu est, μερίμ πολεί. Ibi, defecta est mēbrana. Credo fuisse, κομμα ιωακυλλαγίνι cuius ille codex fuerit. In eadem Bibliotheca, liber pulcherrimè in mēbranis descriptus extat: continens aliquot Sanctorũ uitas: per mēsem Martiũ, Aprilē, Maiũ: unde & τέτρον τρίμύνον appellatur. Ibi in quodã margine infrà scripti est, τ βλαχερνίν, initio uerò libri, & in fine: ἡ βίβλος αὐτὴ, & μο νῆς ἕ προσβρίας: & καιρᾶσα έγχειρι ἀ δετὶς χεχώλθου τὸ μοναχιλι, μέτρω. Huius loci explicationem, Gerla-

Cœnobium Præcursoris.

chius 7. Martij 78. Byzantio mihi perscripsit: τῶν μονῶν ὲ προδρόμου, Constantinopoli satis amplū Monasteriū fuisse: cuius Tēplū adhuc reliquā, pulcherrimis picturis imperatorũ Græcorū, & Sanctorū, exornatũ sit. Hodie uerò negari usũ Græcorū, propter templũ Turcicũ uicinũ. Manere etiã cellulas, à Sanctimonialibus Græcis habitatas: quæ elemosynis Patriarchæ, & reliquorũ Græcorũ, alantur. In προσκυναίῳ esse elegantes picturas τ προδρόμου, Eremitarũ, Patrũ Græcorũ, & Christi, aureæ sellæ insidentis, cũ inscriptione, μέτρα. Vicinũ esse,

Et Aetij.

templum ἁ άετιξ: exornatũ uario marmore, et picturis (quib. singulis facies erasæ esse: sicut & in reliquis Monasterijs ac Tēplis, quæ Turcica manus polluerit) hodieq; Mahometano cultui addictũ. Hisce uicinū esse locū ἐ βλαχερνῶν, in angulo sinus ceratini: Templis, porticibus Regijs, alijsq; ædificijs, olim illustrem: nunc casis

Græco-

6.3 Crusius's printed reconstruction of the patriarchate of Constantinople from the *Turcograecia*. It identified the entire layout of the patriarchal complex, including the garden, the house of the patriarch on the right (A), the visitors' rooms on the left (*), and the ancient cisterns next to the tower (G). Credit: Universitätsbibliothek Tübingen Fo XVI 18.2, p. 190.

of miscellaneous historical, topographical, linguistic, and political information about the Ottoman Greek world. That is not to say that Crusius knew all there was to know: he openly acknowledged his inability to verify specific bits of information. He also missed parts of the story and misinterpreted others. It is therefore important to bear the limits of Crusius's scholarly enterprise in mind. His interactions with his Greek Orthodox informants were irregular; the arrival of letters from the Ottoman Empire was subject to the vagaries of the postal network; and unlike some of his German informants and contemporary orientalists, Crusius never sought to enrich his vision by studying Arabic and Ottoman Turkish or materials in these languages. For all its copiousness and originality, the *Turcograecia* was more piecemeal and idiosyncratic than Crusius may have cared to admit.

Methods and Models

As a repository of predominantly primary sources, the *Turcograecia* tells us very little about the methods and models that Crusius used to compile and organize his material. His own documents, however copious, are equally silent on this issue. No drafts or working papers have survived. Neither do we have his commonplace books, if he ever used them. Yet it is clear from the books in his library that Crusius drew heavily from the work of travel writers, ecclesiastical historians, antiquaries, and philologists, as he brought this material to print. His numerous surviving annotated books cannot always tell us with a satisfying degree of certitude which specific criteria for source criticism and which authors inspired him while he compiled his own material. But placing his books side by side, and reading between the lines of the *Turcograecia,* enables us to situate the book in the intellectual traditions from which it emerged.

One notebook in particular lies at the origins of the *Turcograecia.* In Mb 37, currently in the Tübingen University Library, Crusius collected evidence on "the affairs of the Greeks of Byzantium" and recorded the Greek letters he received as well as the conversations he had with his Greek guests. Some of this material made it into print, including the abovementioned information on the patriarchate and Donatus's explications. Other information was not reproduced. But not even this notebook contained everything that would end up in the *Turcograecia*: much actually came from other books and manuscripts in Crusius's possession. It is not easy to infer how this material was selected: letters that appear next to each other in one of Crusius's letter books are printed in different parts of the *Turcograecia*. The paratextual notes printed in the margins of the political history in book one are lifted almost to the letter from Crusius's richly annotated copy of this manuscript, which has survived in Paris. Yet his commentary in the notes is based on material from his other manuscripts.[30] It is possible, then, that he relied on an organizational principle that is unfortunately not visible in the surviving materials—his manuscripts contain internal cross-references, but hardly ever does one set of papers refer to another. It is also possible that Crusius, as he compiled more and more material for the *Turcograecia*, worked at least partially from memory, as other scholars of the period did.

No direct models for the *Turcograecia* survive. No ethnographies of Ottoman Greece existed and no other early modern ethnography on any culture amassed primary sources, paratextual notes, and commentary in the way Crusius would. Yet in reproducing so much firsthand evidence, the book was a product of its time. Early modernity was a period of great experimentation and change for those who sought to document the intricacies of other people's cultures, religions, and histories. Questions of evidence would prove to be especially transformative for the genre. Humanists reinvented history by advocating for a deeper engagement with primary sources while simultaneously remaining wedded to the classical models of Livy, Polybius, and others. Ecclesiastical historians shaped history writing through the critical study of primary sources—an operation that was vital in the religious wars over theology, church doctrine, and tradition fought out in Catholic and Protestant camps alike. Travel writers, who maintained a vexed relationship with established standards of truth, regularly found themselves confronted with the similarly pressing problem of credibility: How to entertain, convey to an audience the known and unknown, and portray incredible facts and marvelous fictions, without compromising their authenticity and reliability? And how was one to escape the long shadow cast by a tradition of travel writing known for its fabulous tales and wondrous creatures?[31] The result of these revolutions, which were hotly debated in the *ars historica* tradition, was that narrative formats were increasingly often enriched by quotations from original sources and lengthy discussions of what counted as reliable evidence.[32] Crusius followed these trends, reproducing a wealth of primary sources to offer his readers a journey of discovery.

Different parts of the book belonged to different intellectual traditions. The histories in books one and two, for instance, were part of two strands of history writing that blossomed in the second half of the sixteenth century. On the one hand, the history of the patriarchate of Constantinople that Crusius reproduced was a form of Church History. Early modern Church historians searched meticulously and restlessly for an accurate image of the Early Church, producing vast repositories of direct evidence that, as the Reformations unfolded, became powerful tools in the hands of scholars across the confessional divide.[33] On the other hand, by including political history in the *Turcograecia*, Crusius entered the scholarly arena occupied by those writers whose (literary) narrations of past and present civilizations were hotly debated in the *ars historica* tradition.[34] For the letters inserted in the final parts of the *Turcograecia*, Crusius drew inspiration from letter collections. Editing letters was not a prevalent method for describing a country and its peoples, but important precedents existed. Cicero's *epistolae familiares*, a collection that illuminated connections between different Roman elites, was considered an incredibly insightful form of history writing by the Roman biographer Cornelius Nepos. Ogier Ghiselin de Busbecq's account of his travels through the Ottoman Empire, which Crusius finished in three days, had also started as a correspondence. Many accounts from travelers to the New World arrived in epistolary form as well—Columbus's letter of his first voyage, Cortés's *Carta de relación*, and Pietro Martire d'Anghiera's *Decadas del nuevo mundo* being particularly prominent examples. In terms of content, then, the *Turcograecia* drew on various contemporary modes of presenting to readers other cultures and civilizations.

For the *mise-en-page*, Crusius may have looked to the bilingual editions of Greek authors in his library. Like these tomes, which were frequently printed in Basel and began to flood the learned book market in this period, the *Turcograecia* offered a Latin translation facing the Greek original. Crusius's rich sets of notes, often printed after the text, offered linguistic and historical guidance, not unlike commentaries that helped readers navigate works of Greek and Latin prose and poetry. The *Turcograecia* also reflected Crusius's long-standing interests in humanist pedagogy: his set of Latin and Greek grammars for pupils had included school exercises comparable to the vernacular *themato-epistolae* included in book five. In 1566 Oporinus had printed a collection of Crusius's Greek poems and orations in Latin and Greek that taught students, according to its author, about piety and decency, and sought to improve their knowledge of the Greek language.[35]

Three fields of inquiry proved particularly influential in how Crusius designed the *Turcograecia*: antiquarianism, ecclesiastical scholarship, and travel literature. Crusius's commitment, for instance, to offer full reproductions of the evidence rivaled the zeal with which antiquaries scrutinized and recorded aspects of ancient artifacts and objects both local and exotic. Since antiquity, a whole tradition of scholars chose to reproduce evidence and establish facts rather than narrating a story.[36] They organized their material systematically rather than chronologically, and while they pieced together various kinds of evidence, they generally expressed a preference for nonliterary materials: coins, inscriptions, and statues. But antiquaries also expressed an abiding interest in the materiality of sources and often presented their findings in visual form.[37] It was crucial, in any given case, to record evidence at first hand and to disclose under what conditions an observation was made. If you had been unable to examine the object yourself, you made sure to rely on a trustworthy informant who had, even if in practice antiquaries did not always adhere to these standards. Antiquarian writings, moreover, evince a propensity for systematic collecting and encyclopedic comprehensiveness: antiquaries believed—just as Crusius did—that the gradual accumulation of evidence would allow for an extensive survey of not just individual items but of all the individual threads of a civilization's social fabric.

The *Turcograecia* also demonstrates how Crusius drew heavily from the criteria for source criticism that ecclesiastical historians and travelers applied in their publications. Their works helped Crusius think about how he could communicate, in print, not just the sheer enormity and diversity of Greek life but also the prominence of his testimonies, as well as the results of his laborious practice of establishing credibility in his testimonies. Travel writers showed Crusius the full complexity of reporting a world that lay beyond what was directly discernible. Most writers deployed elaborate rhetorical strategies or adduced firsthand experiences to bolster their credibility. In their writings—and Crusius's library shows he read many—he found a format for citing reliable informants and their testimonies. From ecclesiastical historians he learned that the inclusion of full text, rather than scant quotation, offered readers the possibility of verification. Following the fourth-century *Church History* of Eusebius—the archetype of such a documentary history—Church historians cited documents in many ways. Eusebius tended to quote whole documents with headnotes, which would justify accepting them as genuine or would otherwise localize them in time and space. Johannes Nauclerus—whose early sixteenth-century *World Chronicle* Crusius knew well—usually jammed documents into the text with very little explication and no typographical separation. In the *Magdeburg Centuries*—another collaborative and compilatory project that Crusius referenced often—Matthias Flacius and his team of collaborators steered a middle course. In some cases, they inserted whole documents into their work, explicated by sets of headnotes. In others, they simply summarized or excerpted them. Crusius adopted their eclectic methods eclectically.

Publishing the *Turcograecia*

Not everyone understood Crusius's goals for the *Turcograecia*. Publishing the book became a protracted process in which Crusius had to enlist the help of his acquaintances and literary agents who, often unpaid, acted as his go-betweens with publishers and printers. About a dozen presses all over the Holy Roman Empire considered and rejected the book before it was finally printed in Basel. In addition to the financial and technical issues with printing such an elaborate text, Crusius faced the additional challenge of seeking a publisher in a deeply confessional landscape: getting the work published in a reformed city was no mean feat for a Lutheran who envisioned his scholarship to be God's work. Tracing the *Turcograecia*'s long and winding path to publication thus highlights the collaborative nature of Crusius's big book as well as the ways in which religion impeded his inquiry into the Ottoman Greek world.

One of the biggest challenges that aspiring authors like Crusius faced was finding someone willing to bear the financial burden of printing.[38] The *Turcograecia* was a big and complex book, and getting published was a costly business. University professors like Crusius did not usually earn enough to pay for their own publications. When the publisher would not finance the publication, which was all too common, those without financial means had to find a patron or secure funding through another party. Crusius tried both approaches: in some cases he asked the publisher to bear the costs for the *Turcograecia*; in other cases he urged his contacts to find him patronage.[39] More often than not this led to nothing: one of his contacts urged Crusius to send the *Turcograecia* to Wittenberg, but when it became clear that more than two thousand florins were needed to fund the printing, he decided to look for alternatives. The remuneration that Crusius wished to receive beyond free copies of the books further complicated the search for the right publisher. In March 1581, when he first started contacting his acquaintances about printing the *Turcograecia*, he wrote to Matthaeus Ritter in Frankfurt to see if the famous Wechel press would perhaps be interested in the work. He made it clear that, should Wechel be unable or unwilling to give him an honorarium, the *Turcograecia* had to be immediately sent back to Tübingen.[40]

Images also increased expenses. One of the reasons that Wechel would eventually decline to print the *Turcograecia* was that Crusius wanted him to pay for the images, while the printer believed Crusius should bear the costs.[41] When Henricpetri, who would end up publishing the book, had shown interest in printing the *Turcograecia*, Crusius bluntly told him that the publisher would have to pay for the roughly ten images he hoped to include.[42] The publisher's solution was as simple as it was effective: he ignored Crusius's request, printed fewer images, and sent the originals back to Tübingen.

Many printers did not have the right technical apparatus to produce a learned works of the scope and complexity of the *Turcograecia*. Crusius immediately realized that Gruppenbach's press in Tübingen was not an option because it could not print Greek.[43] One of his contacts told him that he ought not to expect much from Nuremberg because there was no capable printer there either.[44] In a scholarly world where books in Greek were not often a commercial success—even classical commentaries and editions of leading scholars of Greek often sold poorly—one wonders how Crusius eventually convinced his publisher not only to print Greek and Latin face-to-face but also to incorporate the signatures of prominent Greeks, which would have required the cutting of a specific and expensive set of woodcuts.[45] In a later publication, published by a different printer, Crusius confided that he had been unable to reproduce similar Greek signatures with their elegant ductus because the printer lacked the right equipment for the job.[46]

The book's size deterred printers as well. The problem here was not just that bigger books carried bigger risks for the publisher but also that the samples of the *Turcograecia* that Crusius had sent to prospective publishers did not completely represent the nature of the work: Crusius had shared for evaluation only what ultimately became the first two books of the *Turcograecia*. But while he was talking to different publishers the work expanded significantly: by September 1581, when Wechel knew only of the translation of the political history in the first book, Crusius had already completed no fewer than eight other books.[47] Over time the work grew so significantly that Crusius began to envision two separate works: "I expanded the *Turcograecia* and the *Germanograecia* on both sides," he noted in his diary, "so that it [contains] the lives of Trucello and Calonas, many letters, and the orations that I held in Latin and Greek in the auditorium."[48] But at the same time, he kept sending only the first part of the *Turcograecia* to potential publishers. Even Henricpetri was initially given just the first two books.[49] Only in November 1583 did Crusius plan to send the remaining books to Basel.[50] This may have been an astute business technique—Crusius's diary tells us that he knew the size of the book would be an issue—but it was also risky: as the work grew, its nature and scope changed markedly. While the first book of the *Turcograecia* could easily have fitted into the established genre of history writing, the inclusion of the letters and other materials turned Crusius's work into a miscellany that was harder to market, and consequently a bigger commercial risk. No wonder that printers like Wechel and Henricpetri told Crusius they were hesitant to decide without having seen the whole work.[51]

Religion was an important reason why the *Turcograecia* proved so difficult to print. Crusius recorded how confessional motivations impeded Wechel, whom he believed to be "untrustworthy" because of his adherence to Zwinglianism, from printing the *Turcograecia*.[52] Shortly thereafter, Crusius sent no fewer than eight letters to contacts in places across the Holy Roman Empire, seeking a printer in perhaps Wittenberg or Leipzig because it appeared he would not find a printer "amongst the Calvinists."[53] On February 15, 1583, when Crusius suspected that the *Turcograecia* and the *Germanograecia* would be rejected by publishers in Wittenberg, he voiced his frustrations about the lack of progress and the confessionalization of the learned book market: "The Zwinglians have the best presses, but they hate the free arts and sciences. And why do we refuse to expand our true religion to others while the Jesuits scatter their mistakes all the way to new islands and India and the pope feeds Greek young men, whom are brought from Greece at his expense, and pays to have them educated in private schools in Rome?"[54] Just as Crusius had feared the influence of the Roman Curia on Eastern Christians while corresponding with the patriarch, so he could not hide his frustration over the efficiency of the Jesuits when he sought to bring his vision of the Ottoman Greek world to print.

Wittenberg's indifference was particularly painful. Crusius had received other rejections before—"this is [already] the ninth setback," he sighed in the margins of his diary—but Wittenberg, the town of Luther, was different.[55] In his diary, Crusius recorded a dream he had right after hearing about the sum of money needed to print the work:

> There was a high mountain, on both sides adorned with tall and beautiful pine trees. The ground was white, without a single plant, completely smooth. A friend of mine (I do not know whom) preceded me and I followed him wanting to ascend, conquer the mountain. But the mountain was steep almost as if the slope was vertical. He went on while I got stuck, unable to go on because my knees would not bend. I tried so hard to move them, but in vain. I also told my friend to wait. But he moved on without caring about me. From the back and from left and right I feared men, as if perhaps there were bandits. After these attempts to go up failed because of my struggles, I woke up. That white and high mountain that I could not ascend was of course Wittenberg (λευκορέη). My *Turcograecia* could not ascend it. But the other who went first, went on. What if the *Acta Constantinopolitana* could be printed there? Yes, Christ, may it happen![56]

The dream confirmed what he already feared: Lutheran Wittenberg would not print the *Turcograecia*—though it would indeed, as Crusius hoped, print the *Acta*, in which the correspondence with the patriarch was documented.[57] Crusius's expectations for his scholarship, though perhaps at times unrealistic, were always fed by his confessional sympathies.

One can gauge from his diary and the other dreams that he recorded, whenever there was either a breakthrough or a setback, just how closely intertwined his piety and scholarship were. On August 9, 1583, when Grynaeus and Bauhin confirmed in writing that the printing of the *Turcograecia* would begin that fall after the Frankfurt book fair, Crusius had a similar dream. Even though he had forgotten the details once he had woken up, he thanked God in his diary for confirming that the printing of the *Turcograecia* would now succeed.[58] Conversely, in moments when he received rejections, he prayed to God to find him a printer and help his work along the way.[59] For Crusius, as for many of his contemporaries, printing was fulfilling God's work in the world, and not finding a printer thus prevented him from performing their godly tasks. No wonder that the search for a printer haunted his dreams.

Nevertheless, when his Lutheran sympathies hindered the printing process, Crusius would not yield. This is particularly clear from his decision to acknowledge Gerlach with his full name in the *Turcograecia*. By the time Crusius was looking for a printer in Basel, Gerlach had become embroiled in a dispute with the Calvinist theologian Lambert Daneau. Crusius's contacts in Basel were therefore not too sure about acknowledging the former chaplain: a letter from Johann Jacob Grynaeus, one of Crusius's contacts in Basel, suggested that it would be easier to persuade printers in Basel if Gerlach's name were removed from the work. Even the esteemed press of the French printer Henri Estienne would then be an option. But for Crusius this was absolutely nonnegotiable: "You Zwinglians will sooner die," Crusius confided to his diary in no uncertain terms, "than I remove the name of my good friend Gerlach."[60] In his next letters to Basel—this time to the humanist scholar Theodor Zwinger and the botanist Caspar Bauhin—he implored them to reason: surely this "work of history and philology" ought not to be rejected because of the inclusion of Gerlach?[61] Even after Grynaeus and Zwinger had agreed that Gerlach's name ought not to be removed, Crusius still made a point of emphasizing that the inclusion of the chaplain's testimonies would not be a problem because they contained "nothing about today's controversies."[62]

Crusius, like other aspirant authors of the period, heavily relied on the (unpaid) labor of his contacts to ensure that his book would make its way into print.[63] Gruppenbach was Crusius's first and last point of contact; many correspondences with potential publishers went via him.[64] Other acquaintances acted as his agents in other places: once Frankfurt seemed not to have been an option anymore, Crusius wrote to Chytraeus in Rostock, to Grynaeus in Basel, to Polycarp Leyser in Wittenberg, and to others elsewhere, hoping one of them could find him a printer.[65] It is not always possible to reconstruct their brokering, but they probably acted precisely like those literary agents who, as Ann Goldgar has shown, "placed manuscripts, negotiated terms, and provided a link" between the author and the print shop."[66] His connections also helped him acquire further materials: from the moment he decided to bring some of his findings to print he started requesting materials and all sorts of aid from his acquaintances, including Georg Tanner, a philologist from Vienna, and Johannes Sambucus, the famous Hungarian humanist.[67] In that sense, the process of collecting the materials that appeared in the *Germanograecia* was as deeply collaborative as the process of gathering information about the Ottoman Greek world for the *Turcograecia*. Yet, ironically, it was precisely the wealth of information, and its diversity, which made it so hard to bring the book to the world of print.

Printing the *Turcograecia* was thus no mean feat. It required the help of others and was in some ways hindered by Crusius's Lutheran beliefs—to say nothing of the regular setbacks that aspirant authors faced. For even after Henricpetri had expressed an interest in printing the work, the project continued to be plagued with difficulties. In April 1583, for instance, Gruppenbach had to tell Crusius that Henricpetri had indeed received the first two books, but could not yet examine them due to other commitments.[68] Later, when Crusius finally heard his book would be sold at the Frankfurt book fair, he was also told by Henricpetri that Leonard Ostein had done a poor job and that many errors had crept into the work.[69] Ostein's alleged incompetence even discouraged Henricpetri from publishing the *Germanograecia*.[70] This prompted Crusius to write various contacts that he was still hoping to find a printer for the *Germanograecia*.[71] He begged Matthaeus Ritter, for instance, not only to encourage Henricpetri to print the *Turcograecia*'s companion piece but also to contact Wechel again and see if he might be interested in printing it.[72] Though exceptional in the kind of intellectual travel that it offered to Ottoman Greece, the *Turcograecia* was thus representative of the many difficulties that scholars faced when it came to securing publication in a world rife with religious turmoil.

Conclusion

On April 22, 1584, the catalog for that year's Frankfurt book fair arrived in Tübingen. Much to Crusius's satisfaction, it listed his *Turcograecia*. The book had been published shortly before by Sebastian Henricpetri and printed by Leonard Ostein, whose printer's device—three lions, one of which holds an hourglass in his paw—was included both on the frontispiece and the final page of the work.[73] Two days later Crusius received twelve copies of the book. Three of these he had bound in luscious red leather and, enriched with a personal inscription, sent to the three sons of Philip I, to whom the work was dedicated.[74] In the next few months, Crusius told everybody who would listen about its publication and encouraged his correspondents to buy a copy. Not many seem to have done so: the book was a commercial disaster. When, in 1593, he completed his other monumental work—his *Annales Suevici*, a massive history of Swabia, in three parts, that continues to be one of the main sources for the sixteenth-century history of this region—one of his agents contacted Henricpetri to see whether Basel would be interested in publishing it. Politely, but in no uncertain terms, the publisher declined: much to his own detriment, both the *Turcograecia* and the *Germanograecia* had proven impossible to sell.[75]

Filled with original sources that touched on a wide range of topics, the *Turcograecia* offered its readers a journey that was unprecedented. Never before had such a massive amount of information about Greek life under Ottoman rule been accumulated. Never before had European scholars had access to such a great number of firsthand testimonies about this world. Never before had there been any comparable book that would—at least as Crusius hoped—facilitate a kind of virtual journey to Ottoman Greece. To be sure, other, often elaborate, ethnographies of the world's many peoples have survived from this period. Pierre Belon's travelogue, which was an important source for the *Turcograecia,* is a case in point for the Ottoman Empire. Yet few such books offered as diverse a collection of firsthand testimony as Crusius's work, and none focused exclusively on the Greeks. Though a work that defied easy categorization, the *Turcograecia* was thus novel in its subject matter and the way in which it told its story—two aspects of the book that were inextricable for achieving the goals Crusius had set for himself in writing this work of ethnographic scholarship.

Why was the book such a commercial failure? Perhaps it was the book's eclecticism combined with its content—as distinct as it was diverging—that made it such a difficult sell. Crusius's refusal to remove Gerlach's name did not make it any easier in a confessionalized world where the stakes were high. Yet such was not always the fate of comparable works. Early modernity was an era of big books with big theses, and writers like Bodin, Bruno, Scaliger, and Lipsius knew how to sell arguments few had heard before as well as modes of exposition that were strikingly novel—as famously in the case of Montaigne's *Essais*. Perhaps, then, the *Turcograecia*'s failure to sell might be explained by the fact that Crusius was in some ways cut off from the intellectual centers and printing hubs where books were made. Although his relationship with Oporinus was affectionate and familiar, Crusius often had to approach printers for the *Turcograecia* in an indirect way, and it appears he had little influence over how such an eclectic piece of scholarship was advertised.

Yet however few copies Henricpetri managed to sell, the *Turcograecia* solidified Crusius's reputation as one of Europe's foremost Hellenists. Few scholars have used the book in exactly the way that Crusius intended—that is, for a virtual journey through Ottoman Greece. But it was mined throughout the sixteenth and seventeenth centuries as a rich repository of evidence on the language and religion of the Greeks, and its unique content continues to be of interest to scholars today: one of the unintended consequences of Crusius's unquenchable thirst for information on Ottoman Greece was, ironically, that his big book is today often the only surviving source for the documents that Crusius included in its pages. It is thus the book's eclectic content and its methodological innovation that continue to make the *Turcograecia* such a rewarding text. Open-ended and full of indiscriminate facts, Crusius's seminal work offered information unavailable in any other early modern document.

7

VISIONS OF OTTOMAN GREECE

By encouraging the reader to embark on a journey of their own through original sources and thick layers of commentary, the *Turcograecia* introduced politics, religion, education, and many other aspects of Ottoman Greek life. It offered a portrait of Ottoman Greece that was full of glistening details. Yet Crusius allowed his readers to arrive at just one inescapable conclusion: that once mighty Greece had fallen under Ottoman domination. "Greece had been Turkified," Crusius concluded pointedly in the preface of the *Turcograecia*. Greeks had erred and fallen into superstitious ways, and Greece's "misfortune should therefore be lamented" by all who cared about that world.[1] Crusius also noted that the "Greek language used these days in Constantinople, in Greece, on the islands, and in large parts of Asia" did not come close to "that old purity" of ancient Greek.[2] Using religion and language as his yardsticks, Crusius observed Greece's decline and fall in dramatic fashion. He set all the *Turcograecia*'s colorful vignettes, and all its vibrant evidence about the survival of Greek life under Ottoman rule, into a frame that left nothing to the imagination. Greece had become a ruin, both literally and metaphorically.

Crusius was neither the first nor the last to project onto Greece a narrative of decline, but his big book is the fullest and clearest window into broader European attitudes about Greece during this period. Throughout early modernity, comparison determined how European scholars and travelers evaluated Ottoman Greece, turning a variegated world into a vehicle of a deep yearning for a timeless Greek antiquity that only ever existed in the minds of the people who created it. Ancient Hellas had cast such a powerful spell over the imagination of Crusius and a legion of other scholars and travelers that later periods in Greece's history were inevitably measured against its most compelling ancestor. Such thinking continued for centuries. Few of the Romantic philhellenes may have known Crusius's work intimately—if at all—but they shared with him a distinct way of envisioning Greece: not simply as a place worthy of studying or visiting in its own right but as a canvas unto which they could also project their own sentiments and beliefs. For them, and for so many others, Greece's venerable past, to reference Terence Spencer's magnificent study, "seemed to bear little relation to the contemptible present."[3] Crusius thus embodies what Eliza Marian Butler famously called "the tyranny of Greece over Germany"—an admiration for an otherworldly Greek past that ran deep and enthralled generations of German writers and scholars.[4]

This tradition of European philhellenism has most often been studied in its eighteenth- and nineteenth-century manifestations. Yet extending our view to the sixteenth century allows us to see it in its full complexity and length. The *Turcograecia* occupies a central position in this history. It functioned in some cases as a key methodological node that shaped later accounts of Ottoman Greece. Its arguments, rich and diverse contents, and meticulous attention to detail conjured up an Ottoman Greek world whose contours directly determined how some later accounts of Ottoman Greece were framed. In other cases, Europeans came to their pessimistic assessments of Greece's current state seemingly independently. Crusius is thus representative of larger patterns and, at times, serves an important origin point for the ways in which Europeans envisioned Ottoman Greece. Situating him in this tradition and comparing the *Turcograecia* with texts that were and were not based on it, allows us to grasp how his representation of Ottoman Greece echoed throughout early modernity.

What makes the *Turcograecia* stand out from this tradition, moreover, is that we can trace in greater detail than for any other text how Greeks themselves contributed to European visions of Ottoman Greece. Crusius narrated a story of decline that, at first sight, appears to stem entirely from cultural biases and religious prejudices. Yet to dismiss his pessimistic diagnosis of Ottoman Greece as an unfounded opinion would be to miss the mark. He may have been biased; his confessional beliefs, combined with his love for ancient Greece and its language, may have clouded his vision; his conclusion that Ottoman Greece was but a shadow of its ancient self may have been extremely narrow; but Crusius was—crucially—not uninformed. From the chronicles he reproduced in the *Turcograecia*'s first two books to the letters he inserted in its final parts, a variety of documents appeared to confirm Greece's decline. Much of that evidence came, paradoxically, from Greeks themselves, who had narrated a story of decline that Crusius adopted all too willingly. Members of the Greek patriarchate communicated the dire predicament of their Church, while also lamenting the lack of proper schooling for Greeks living under Ottoman rule. Crusius's various visitors told a similar story about Ottoman tyranny, as did the Greek texts that he read. Crusius's views on Greek life under Ottoman rule were thus grounded in Greeks' day-to-day experiences, and so were, by extension, the visions of Ottoman Greece that circulated in Western Europe from the sixteenth century onward. But this does not mean that Crusius took all experiences into consideration: the Greeks who contributed to European notions of Greek decline and degeneration were a specific group—a handful of mobile Greeks and some elite Greek Orthodox ecclesiastics—whose pessimistic views of Ottoman Greece were corroborated by evidence that Crusius took from the Greek chronicles he reproduced.

Here Crusius's story exemplifies larger patterns in the early history of orientalism and Europeans' engagement with the cultural and religious landscape of the early modern Mediterranean. Historians have in recent years shown how early modern European ideas about the "Orient" were the product of prolonged exchange and encounter between Europeans and Ottomans. European scholars developed a sophisticated understanding of the Islamic world by studying the literature and scholarship of their Ottoman colleagues, including Turkish, Persian, and Arabic dictionaries, commentaries, books, and manuscripts. In Istanbul and other diplomatic hubs in the Islamic world, dragomans communicated perspectives on the Ottoman world, and a powerful discourse of alterity, that shaped how European knowledge about the Ottomans developed. The news that circulated in Europe about the Ottoman Empire and other great early modern Islamic powers was similarly brokered by a range of Ottoman subjects. How Europeans came to understand the "Orient" was thus not simply a classic expression of orientalism—a discursive formation produced outside the world it was supposed to represent—but a field of knowledge made possible through various forms of intellectual and material exchange between two deeply entangled worlds.[5]

Visions of Ottoman Greece developed in similar ways and operated on the same logic: they were not solely the by-product of Europeans' imagination but an amalgam of Europeans' cultural biases and testimonies from a wide range of Greek and non-Greek observers.

GREECE'S DECLINE AND FALL

As Crusius evaluated his findings, one method determined more than any other how he came to his conclusions about Greece's decline: comparison across time and space. Early modern scholars who studied other cultures and places knew that comparison made it possible to trace how the present emerged from the past, to understand how once great nations had fallen into decline, and, conversely, to recover how past greatness had continued into the present. Comparison allowed scholars to probe the nature of change itself and to grasp the fickleness of fortune. Especially from the late fifteenth century onward, humanists and antiquaries—first in Italy, later north of the Alps as well—embraced comparison as a method for understanding a given country. One influential and innovative early modern practitioner of this approach was Flavio Biondo, whose *Italia Illustrata, Roma Instaurata,* and *Roma Triumphans* broke much new ground. His work offered sophisticated tools for reconstructing a country's national past and linking it to the present. This kind of inquiry, which was variously called chorography, historical topography, or descriptive geography, had deep roots: ancient authors such as Strabo, Ptolemy, and Pomponius Mela produced extensive surveys of the ancient world, which, however different in execution, offered early modern readers a template for reviewing the particulars of a given place or country. Comparison, they taught, was key in any such endeavor.[6]

Crusius shared with these authors a desire to understand a country through a parallel description of its ancient and modern incarnations. Though he never said so explicitly, comparison is the underlying principle of his *Turcograecia,* which offered the kind of comparative analysis and the types of insights that historical geographies presented: "First in the times of Alexander," he reminisced in the preface, "and then again in those of Constantine the Great the glory and dignity of the Greeks and the Eastern empire reached for centuries to the heavens. Today, now that the Turks rule, they have been pressed almost to the lowest regions of the earth."[7] Crusius did insist that "by my inquiry, as if by mattocks" ancient Athens, which was thought to have been destroyed, and other places in Greece could "be excavated again, brought to light, and as it were restored (*instaurata*) in the minds of the people."[8] Just as Biondo and his compatriots had compared Roman antiquity with Renaissance Italy, as a way to understand change over time, so Crusius compared ancient to Ottoman Greece.

Yet Crusius placed different accents. In the *Italia Illustrata, Roma Instaurata,* and *Roma Triumphans,* Biondo had told a double story. On the one hand, he had traced the remains of Republican and imperial Rome, sifting the ruins for evidence of how great the city and the state had been and how low time had brought them. On the other hand, Biondo, and many of his contemporaries, believed that the destruction of ancient Rome had enabled the rise of Christianity, as temples were literally transformed into churches, and made possible the creation of Italian cities and states—the little trees that could not grow until they were no longer under the vast shadow of Rome. Crusius's pessimistic vision contrasted sharply with the optimism of Biondo and other early modern practitioners of descriptive geography. For Crusius's story went in only one direction: he observed how fortune changed to misfortune and how "in the history of the Greek empire one could see how on Earth nothing is stable and permanent."[9] The *Turcograecia* thus traced how the original church of the Greeks and the particularly ancient principles to which they adhered had degenerated over time, as had their language. In Crusius's hands, then, a parallel description of Greece's past and present confirmed much of what he set out to prove: Greece was no longer the world that he and his audience had known through the study of Plato and Homer, nor was it a world upheld by the orthodoxy of the Church. Ironically, it is not immediately apparent what exactly Crusius considered the high period of Greek life from which decline ensued. He did not divide Greek history into clear-cut periods— not in the *Turcograecia* or in any of the manuscripts I have examined.

Crusius's execution also differed from that of some of his colleagues who practiced descriptive geography more broadly. In his *Turcograecia,* he did not survey the Greek archipelago in granular detail or describe its mountain ranges and coasts with microscopic precision. Nor did he offer systematic lists of the ancient and modern names of cities or present other noteworthy topographical features—as historical geographers often did. Crusius had collected such data through reading and interviewing his Greek informants and, indeed, some of it can be found inserted in different parts of his commentary. But in the end, Crusius sought to measure change over time and to recover what was left of ancient Greece in two primary ways: through analysis of changes in the Greek language and religion. Long before he published the *Turcograecia,* his understanding of both language and religion shaped how he approached the Ottoman Greek world, Greek Orthodox and Byzantine books, and the people who visited him in his Tübingen home.

Language, and its manifestation in written form, became an especially important yardstick for measuring decline. In a period when language and culture were thought to be deeply intertwined, such an assessment could easily be applied to the history of Greece as a whole. In an oration on why the Greek language needed to be preserved, Crusius exclaimed "how many corruptions in all the arts have poured out of the ignorance of this [Greek] language, how much darkness in philosophy, and how big a perversion of the Christian religion." Only the recent and fortunate "rebirth of Greek letters" in Germany and Italy had "dispelled this darkness."[10] Crusius's deep consciousness of decline was thus not calibrated as Western visions of development and decline normally were. His pessimism implied a timeless period of purity and florescence somewhere in the ancient Greek past—a vision that projected Homer and Hesiod, Herodotus and Thucydides, Pindar and Plato, and Aeschylus and Aeschines onto the same canvas.

Many of Crusius's contemporaries approached not just Greek but languages in general in similar ways. Throughout the early modern period, in their attempts to establish historical epochs, scholars had to grapple with the diversity of the past and come to terms with the period in between antiquity and the present. The threefold scheme of ancient/medieval/modern that they devised, which eventually crystalized during the late seventeenth and early eighteenth centuries, was strongly influenced by ideas about the postclassical development of an ancient Latinity. Ideas about the proper way to temporally classify and organize Latin texts and their authors varied. Some scholars knew that Christian texts were written in a Greek and Latin that was unclassical, but they still showed great enthusiasm for such documents. Yet the ambivalences that other scholars expressed toward later Latin, which they studied with great zeal even as they decried its decadence, closely resembled Crusius's attitude toward Greek.[11] In such cases, the language in which a given text was written offered valuable clues about its position in history and its relationship to developments in the world at large—be they corruptions or rebirths. Yet few of his contemporaries adopted language rather than historical geography as the central framework for organizing their description of a given place or country.

Religion was another pervasive criterion for evaluating Greek life under Ottoman rule. The correspondence with the patriarch had already made Crusius aware of the divergences in doctrine between Lutherans and Greek Orthodox Christians. Reading Greek Orthodox books and manuscripts had only confirmed that assessment. Now, when he sought to inform his colleagues about what really went on in the Ottoman Greek world, he did not hide his Lutheran sympathies. In his preface, he noted that readers would see how the religion of the Greek, which he had "initially hoped to be purer," turned out to contain many "mistakes."[12] Ironically, however, very few of the many sources that Crusius included in the *Turcograecia* are explicitly religious or theological in nature. Indeed, the deviations from the Lutheran norm that Crusius had detected in Greek Orthodox treatises are hardly mentioned in the *Turcograecia*. Nor is there the kind of detail about Greek Orthodox beliefs that dominated his exchanges with the patriarch, which would later come to be published in the *Acta*. Even his depiction of the patriarchate—an age-old institute that dated back to at least the fourth century—showed continuity rather than decline: though the patriarchal history narrated how the Greek Orthodox patriarchate had lost some of its political independency, it had survived into Ottoman times, sometimes even with support from the sultan.[13] It may not have appeared to be thriving, but it existed. In his preface, then, Crusius projected ideas about religious purity instead of examining closely how Greek Orthodoxy had changed with the arrival of the Ottomans.

Such evaluations of the Greeks' language and religion led Crusius to narrate a triumphant story about the cultivation of Greek studies in Lutheran Germany. Nowhere is this more visible than when we compare the *Turcograecia* to its companion piece, the *Germanograecia*. The central thesis of the latter book held that after the fall of Constantinople, Greek studies had blossomed in the West and had come to full fruition in Germany. Thus, while the *Turcograecia* implied that Lutheran Germany had replaced the Greek Orthodox world as the true custodian of Christian orthodoxy, the *Germanograecia* advanced the same argument about scholarship, perpetuating that intrinsically humanist concept of the transfer of learning (*translatio studii*). For Crusius it was a truism that Greek studies in Germany inspired piety, while as pious Christians—and the true guardians of the original Church—Lutherans cultivated the study of the Greek language.

At the same time, Crusius's understanding of the place of Ottoman Greece in the longer expanse of Greek history was more complex than the distinction between "ancient" and "modern" suggests. Crusius was one of early modernity's most voracious readers of Byzantine histories. Not only had he worked his way through the monumental volumes of Zonaras, Choniates, Gregoras, and Chalkokondyles—the four Byzantine historians that the printer Oporinus had famously arranged into a single narrative—he had also covered many other Byzantine texts in dense of layers of annotation. His library was stocked with the works of Anna Komnene, John Skylitzes, George Pachymeres, George Kedrenos, Pseudo-Kodinos, Michael Glykas, Constantine Manasses, and Late Antique historical works such as Eusebius's *Church History*. Reading these different Byzantine authors gave Crusius an unusually capacious understanding of how the history of the Greeks had developed from creation all the way to 1453. In the *Turcograecia*, Crusius continued the story of the Greeks where those Byzantine historians had left it. In books one and two, readers could find not only detailed accounts of how the Ottomans had gradually diminished Byzantine political authority and established their own rule but also firsthand evidence of how Greek religious life had continued in some form deep into the sixteenth century. In the first chronicle, they would have read about the deeds of different sultans, such as the Ottoman conquest of the Arab world in 1516–1517, the wars they waged against the Persians, and the coups plotted at the Ottoman court. In the second, they would have learned how successive patriarchs tried to carve out a space for the Greek Orthodox Church in this new political reality. In placing these narratives alongside one another, Crusius underscored that present-day Ottoman and Byzantine affairs were deeply intertwined: for him, every Greek period, including Ottoman times, formed part of a single, coherent, though not exactly uniform tradition.[14] Yet none of these insights returned in the conclusions that Crusius drew, which compared ancient to Ottoman Greece with little consideration of what happened in between.

Crusius's vision of Greek life under Ottoman rule thus depended on a series of comparisons between Greece and Germany, between ancient and Ottoman Greece, and between different periods in Greek history, as told by different Greek historians. Crusius's approach mirrored those of other early modern practitioners of descriptive geography who embraced comparison to understand a given country. Yet comparison, however powerful, was no neutral tool: as Crusius's comparisons were strongly calibrated by ideas about the purity of language and religion, they quickly revealed a dual story of decline in Ottoman Greece and the triumphant ascent of Lutheran Germany, where Greek studies blossomed once more. Reading Byzantine authors had made Crusius see all periods in Greek history as existing on a continuum. But his focus on language and religion ultimately yielded a binary that effaced all that lay in between, including the vibrant political and religious history of Byzantium.

Ottoman Greece in the Early Modern Imagination

How did Crusius's vision of Ottoman Greece compare to those of other Europeans? Throughout the early modern period, texts appeared that lamented Greece's decline and fall just like the *Turcograecia* did. Theologians from all over Europe penned treatises on the sorry state of the Greek Church, while travelers merged observation with textual references in their attempts to capture the deplorable nature of Greek life under Ottoman rule. Even in Latin and vernacular poetry the trope of Greece's decline gradually became commonplace. Much like the ruins that populated the landscape of the Ottoman Greek world, the Greeks themselves were believed by Europeans to have degenerated. Some of these authors knew Crusius's work intimately and peppered their accounts with references to the *Turcograecia*. But not all writers on early modern Greece seem to have been familiar with his work. Yet, whatever their relationship to Crusius was, most—if not all—early modern visions of Ottoman Greece operated on the same logic as the *Turcograecia* did: comparison of the "old" and "new" Greece revealed how deeply the Greeks had sunk. Comparing Crusius to his contemporaries and later writers thus confirms that his rather bleak assessment was no aberration. On the contrary: even after the Greek war of Independence (1821) restored Greek autonomy, diagnoses of the Ottoman Greek world were punctuated by ideas about decline and purity.

Comparisons of Greece's current state with its ancient splendor led many early modern observers to conclude, just as Crusius had, that the Greeks were marred by ignorance and moral degradation. From the sixteenth-century Dutch scholar George Dousa to the English traveler George Sandys, from the French botanist Pierre Belon to the eighteenth-century German theologian Johann Michael Heineccius, European writers of diverse backgrounds bemoaned the lack of educational opportunities for Greeks under Ottoman rule and the corruptions that had crept into their beliefs. Many deplored Athens's transformation from the archetypical model of a learned city—whose cultural legacy had given birth to the civilized world—to a place where there were no schools and universities. Others commented negatively on the type of Greek that Greeks spoke and considered their religion to be marred by superstitions, not at all comparable to the purity of the original church. Some noted that there were hardly any books in Greece, while others described how Greek priests, and the Greek clergy more generally, were poorly educated. Still others found confirmation of Greece's decline and decay in the numerous ruins that they saw with their own eyes or read about in the books in their study.[15] In the words of perhaps the most popular English traveler to mention Greek life under Ottoman rule, George Sandys, the knowledge of the Greeks "is conuerted . . . into affected ignorance (for they haue no schooles of learning amongst them)." Sandys also lamented that "their liberty" had turned "into contented slauery, hauing lost their minds with their Empire."[16] For Sandys, as for Crusius and others, little was left of Greece's ancient splendor.

Reasons for Greece's decline varied from writer to writer. It was commonplace for early modern observers to state that the Ottoman sultan had deprived the Greeks of their independence and forced them into servitude. It was believed that this had had disastrous consequence in many areas of Greek life. It had led, for instance, to the corruption of the Greek language, to say nothing of the indignities that Greeks had to endure as an enslaved nation. The Greek Church saw some of its buildings confiscated, which was considered further evidence of Turkish tyranny. Greece's status as an enslaved nation was sometimes also seen as divine punishment for having strayed from the true path or as the result of the very nature of empire: history had shown that great civilizations would inevitably collapse and be succeeded by others. Yet some Europeans thought that Greece's decline had begun long before the Ottoman conquest. Some even argued that the Greeks themselves were to blame: their "weakness" had enabled the Ottomans' swift conquest of what was left of the Byzantine Empire and, content with their servitude, they were now too "lazy" to take up arms.[17] Ultimately, though, the notion of Greece as an enslaved nation was so enduring that this period in Greek history came to be known as the "tourkokratia."

Comparison could be deployed not simply to prove Greece's decline but also to understand what remnants of ancient culture had survived. We see this repeatedly in the many early modern travelogues that comment on the ancient ruins in cities such as Athens as well as in some travel writers' attempts to frame Greek people as somehow the heirs of ancient culture. Observing how peasants in Crete danced from the hottest time in the day to nightfall during a summer festival—every man laden with weapons and dancing with his wife or sweetheart—Pierre Belon realized that their dance was related to the Pyrrhichios, the famous dance performed in ancient Greece before going to war. Belon and others also noticed that, while some Greeks dressed as Venetians and some *alla Turca,* common people wore their hair the way the ancients had done—an ethnographic observation that in its richness rivaled those that Gerlach communicated to Crusius.[18] Not all such assessments were positive, though. Various travelers, following stereotypes already current in antiquity, saw the Greeks as a cunning people prone to lying and deceit. Numerous travelers and pilgrims commented in similar ways—and with comparable disapproval—on the drinking habits of the Greeks: Greeks living under Ottoman rule were thought to be heavy drinkers just like their ancient ancestors.[19] So pervasive were such ideas that the English cleric Fynes Moryson, who traveled through the Ottoman Empire in the 1590s, noted in his diary that Greeks were heavy drinkers but also that he had not personally experienced this on his journeys.[20] Comments such as these illustrate not only the power of comparison in the early modern imagination but also how extremely difficult it was for Greeks to shed their cultural traits in the eyes of European observers. Steeped in a classical tradition that showed what Greece once was—and thus what it ought to be—Europeans could not help but feel "betrayed by the failure of contemporary Greeks to live up to the high ideals attributed to the ancient Greeks."[21]

Framing accounts of the Greek world in terms of decline and decay did not preclude impartial description. It is one of the great ironies of early modern accounts of the Ottoman Greek world—and of early modern travel writing and scholarship more generally—that these works, just like the *Turcograecia,* combined accurate observations on various aspects of the Ottoman Greek world with pessimistic assessments of these findings and at times deeply jaundiced remarks. In the eloquent treatises on the Greek Church that the seventeenth-century scholars Thomas Smith and Paul Rycaut produced—perhaps the period's best-known treatments of this topic—readers could learn about nearly all aspects of Greek Orthodoxy, from fasting to feast days and from sacraments to saints. However, the overall sentiment was that the Greek religion was contaminated by superstition: for all their detailed descriptions of the Greek rites and nuanced appraisals of Greek piety, both Smith and Rycaut, like Crusius, also mentioned the ignorance of the Greeks, their "errours and defects," their "factious temper," as well as the "mixture of odd opinions and fancies" that had in their eyes infected Greek Orthodoxy.[22] However irenic these authors claimed to be, their investigations ultimately sought to ascertain the superiority of their Anglicanism over the religion of the Greeks—and they were guided by the same notion of decline and decay as Crusius had been. Compilations created to confute could thus easily, though inadvertently, preserve practices of those whose religious beliefs were scrutinized.

Many of these elements merged in the most extensive treatise to emerge from this tradition, and one for which Crusius's *Turcograecia* was an important model: the twelve-hundred-page exploration of Greek Orthodoxy by the German theologian Johann Michael Heineccius. Not as influential as Rycaut's seminal work, and now all but forgotten, the *Eigentliche und wahrhafftige Abbildung der alten und neuen Griechischen Kirche* (1711) treated in three books nearly every aspect of the Greek religion, from the offices and the liturgy to theology and dress. Heineccius culled his evidence from a variety of sources, including Rycaut and other seventeenth-century authors, but also Crusius, Gerlach, Schweigger, and a host of other Greek writers from Late Antiquity all the way to the early modern period. The result was a synthesis of other people's work more than an original treatise, but one that operated on the same logic as the *Turcograecia*: through a comparison of the "old" and "new" Greek Church, the treatise sought to demonstrate that the Greek Church was in decline, as its second chapter made unequivocally clear. Their faith was no longer uncorrupted, and their ceremonies were incorrect. Different factions vied for the patriarchal throne. Bishops did not execute their offices and only few had any substantial knowledge of their religion, which meant that ignorance ran rife among Greek Orthodox congregations, who were also affected by grinding poverty. None of this, however, was acknowledged by Greek Orthodox Christians themselves: "There is no people," Heineccius stressed, "with more love and reverence for its Church than the Greeks."[23] Although Heineccius believed that decline had set in as early as the fourth century, when Christianity became the official religion of the Roman Empire, he also believed that one of the reasons for the Greek Church's further deterioration was its subjugation to Ottoman rule after the conquest of Constantinople: Greeks lost their piety and converted to Islam, while their Churches were destroyed or turned into mosques.

Heineccius's vivid account of the Greek Church also affords insight into how exactly the *Turcograecia* shaped early modern accounts of Greek life under Ottoman rule. Many early modern writers mentioned Crusius only in passing, citing his work in their footnotes, often solely to reference one of the sources he had edited. In other words, they treated the *Turcograecia* as a repository of evidence on a variety of topics related to the Ottoman Greek world. Heineccius was no exception. He, too, peppered his notes with references to Crusius and the *Turcograecia,* often only to direct readers to information provided by Gerlach, Zygomalas, or other Greeks. It is thus no coincidence that Heineccius diagnosed the sorry state of the Greeks by the same metrics that Crusius had used: poverty, ignorance, lack of learning among the clergy, and a general decline due to the arrival of the Ottomans. Yet his engagement with Crusius's work ran deeper: the passage where Heineccius discussed the Greek Orthodox patriarchate of Constantinople includes a stunning image of the patriarchate. Although it is made from a different plate and completely updated so that the contours of the buildings and the walls enclosing the property are more symmetrical, the image was lifted, without acknowledgment, from the *Turcograecia*. Some of the exploratory notes were taken verbatim from Crusius.[24] So even when Crusius was not explicitly referenced as a standalone source, his shadow haunted scholarship on early modern Greece.

The kind of story that Crusius and his colleagues told continued to have currency for centuries to come. The writings of numerous other authors, famous and infamous ones as well as those now forgotten, could corroborate just how pervasive this way of looking at Greece was. Not long before Johann Joachim Winckelmann would famously project his ideas about ideal beauty, harmony, and proportion on ancient Greek art, and not long before other Germans—who never set foot in Greece—idealized Greece and fully embraced a classicizing aesthetic, texts like that of Heineccius operated on the same logic as the works of Belon, Crusius, and other early modern writers about Greece. For the philhellenes of the eighteenth and nineteenth centuries, Greece existed similarly not on its own terms but as a "composite dreamworld," in which the historical reality of ancient Greece was replaced by whatever ideal Europeans projected onto this world.[25] Nineteenth- and twentieth-century travelers from Germany approached Greece, like so many of their ancestors who had gone there on their grand tour, similarly as a "projection room" where they hoped to find not a Greek reality but a way to construct the self.[26] Eminently adaptable, Greece functioned for poets and scholars from the early modern to the modern period, as Constanze Güthenke has eloquently shown, as "a placeholder, standing in for its past or someone else's present, and not quite 'itself.'"[27]

Obviously, these writers differed from one another as much as their cultural-intellectual worlds did. The secular and aesthetic and far more political philhellenism of figures like Winckelmann marks a strong departure from the more religiously motivated scholarship of Crusius, Smith, Rycaut, and Heineccius. Crusius also seems far more meticulous about cataloging the here and now of Ottoman Greece and the postclassical transformation of the Greek world than the eighteenth- and nineteenth-century philhellenes, who cared deeply about the Greek War of Independence and the plight of the Greek people but whose work transmits a weaker impulse for collecting everything there was to know about the culture and languages of the Greeks. But what all these Europeans shared, even if the lines connecting them are tenuous, is a tendency to suspend Greece somewhere between an ancient purity and a modern corruption.

Crusius's *Turcograecia*, then, was part of a long and influential tradition that measured any period in Greek history against its classical counterpart. Early modern travel writers and scholars from England, France, and Germany saw in contemporary Greece, just as he did, a world that was in decline. For some, like Heineccius, Crusius's *Turcograecia* served as something of a blueprint. Others, too, recognized Crusius's importance for the study of Ottoman Greece: no less a historian than Leopold von Ranke praised Crusius as Europe's first philhellene. So did the now lesser-known nineteenth-century classicist Friedrich Wilhelm Thiersch, whose various plans for a liberated Greece were never realized.[28] For other Europeans who looked in the mirror of Greece and saw their own hopes and ambitions reflected, Crusius was not a household name. But comparison proved to them, too, that Greece was but a shadow of its former self.

Proof and Prejudice

Such visions of Ottoman Greece may at first appear to be largely figments of the European imagination. Crusius's deeply pessimistic assessment did indeed reflect at least partially his bias as a Lutheran with a command of the Greek language perhaps unmatched in the sixteenth-century Latin world. The exchange of letters with Jeremias II had convinced him that the Greek Church was no longer the true guardian of Christian orthodoxy, and Crusius's reading of Greek Orthodox materials confirmed him in this view. Later accounts of Ottoman Greece were similarly marred by preconceived ideas about ancient purity and modern degradation.

Yet this one-sided genealogy obscures the different information flows that converged in the creation of European depictions of Greek life under Ottoman rule. More than any other published text, the *Turcograecia* reveals to us the many firsthand testimonies that shaped Crusius's journey of discovery, all of which demonstrate that elite Greeks themselves—as well as Westerners whom Crusius trusted—contributed greatly to his conclusions, and by proxy, the jaundiced views of Ottoman Greece that came to circulate in early modern Europe. Like his letters, his diaries, and his interviews, the *Turcograecia*—through its annotations and paratextual notes—reveals how Crusius's seemingly stereotypical views of the Greeks were grounded at least partially in historical exchanges of information with particular groups of Greek interlocutors. In this way, the *Turcograecia* reminds us that this longer tradition of envisioning Greece originated not simply in the classrooms and studies of European observers but through moments of mediation between Europeans and Greeks themselves.

One powerful piece of evidence for Crusius's decline theory was the testimonies of Greeks themselves regarding their lost independence. Based on his interviews and correspondence, as well as a variety of printed works by Greek Orthodox Christians living under Ottoman rule, Crusius concluded that the arrival of the Ottomans had affected Greek life in myriad ways, few of which were positive. Much of this information made it into the *Turcograecia*. In the chronicles, for instance, readers could discover how different Christian churches had been turned into mosques or were barely saved from that fate through the intercession of successive patriarchs. The tragic lives of Crusius's Greek informants, which he referenced in his notes, revealed the conditions of Christians living in Ottoman captivity.[29] Crusius had also included information about the numerous Greek Orthodox Christians who had to collect alms because the Church was being "suppressed into slavery by the Barbarians."[30] One of the letters in the *Turcograecia* called upon everyone to support a Greek from Cappadocia "who had been cruelly afflicted by the Turks."[31] Crusius had even reproduced evidence from the printed works that former captives published: in his notes on the ecclesiastical history, he included a lengthy passage on the circumcisions of the Ottomans that was based almost verbatim on the *De Turcarum moribus epitome* of Bartholomeus Georgievicz, a Dalmatian who had been taken captive in the 1526 Battle of Mohács.[32] Much like the captivity narratives that his guests told him in Tübingen, these testimonies painted a world in black and white, with only an occasional shadow.

The *Turcograecia* contained evidence that visually represented this transformation in Greek life. Two elaborate genealogies, laid out in branching diagrams of different sizes, showed how the Byzantine and Ottoman Empires had come to exist side by side, and how Ottoman sovereignty had come to replace Byzantine authority in the political sphere. The first showed the Palaeologan dynasty that ruled Constantinople "from the moment when the city was taken from the Latins until the Turkish Siege." The second reconstructed the Ottoman imperial house from its founding father all the way to the moment when Murad III inherited the throne in 1574.[33] Crusius's inclusion of these genealogies reflected a period preoccupation: in an early modern political climate of predominantly noble families and hereditary monarchies, genealogy constituted a vital branch of scholarly research that was used to substantiate dynastic claims or confirm royal status.[34] But genealogy, historical chronology's twin sister in the pursuit of knowledge, was also a crucial method for understanding historical writing. Reiner Reineccius, a German professor of history and an acquaintance of Crusius, would go as far as to claim that genealogy illuminated "all the other parts of history, and without it they bear basically no fruit at all."[35] Genealogical tables

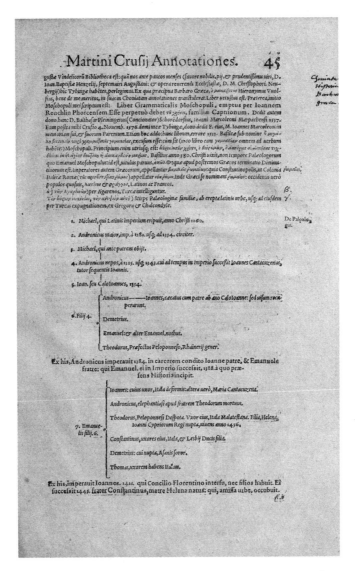

7.1 Crusius's genealogy of the Palaeologan dynasty that ruled Constantinople. It starts with Michael VIII Palaeologus, "who took the empire from the Latins," and ends with Constantine XI Palaeologus, who died after the Ottomans had captured Constantinople in 1453.
Credit: Universitätsbibliothek Tübingen Fo XVI 18.2, p. 45.

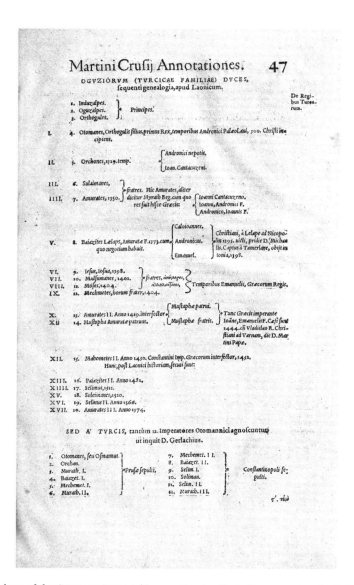

7.2 Genealogy of the Ottoman imperial house. Crusius first offers an extensive list of twenty Ottoman Sultans, which he had taken from the Greek historian Chalkokondyles, before copying information he received from Gerlach: that the Ottomans themselves only recognize twelve of these. Credit: Universitätsbibliothek Tübingen Fo XVI 18.2, p. 47.

and diagrams helped readers resolve chronological inconsistencies and find links between past and present: history offered precedent while genealogy uncovered pedigree. In Crusius's case, this interest in genealogical data helped him synchronize the new Byzantine history with the even newer Ottoman history: individually the genealogies in the *Turcograecia* can be read as condensed, but tidy and easily navigable, records of the last Byzantine and first Ottoman rulers of Constantinople since 1056. But together, they demonstrate how the Ottomans had deprived the Greeks of their political independence: as Ottoman sultans replaced Byzantine emperors, Greeks were no longer a free people but one governed by a foreign ruler. And, crucially, Crusius had found these genealogies in his Byzantine sources.

The *Germanograecia* presented a similar narrative of Greek subjugation under the Ottomans. On one page, readers would have encountered Gerlach's lengthy assessment of the Ottomans: "The Turks," according to the chaplain, "show no humanity to Christians unless they are merchants or when there is a profit to be made. Otherwise, they shout in their language: 'You dog, you unbeliever.'" In that same set of notes, readers would also have found the story of a German slave who had lived in captivity for thirty years and the miraculous story of how seventy-two Christians had escaped from the Ottomans—this latter being a direct quotation from a book published in Barcelona in 1568.[36] Elsewhere in the *Germanograecia*, Crusius included the wedding hymn that he had composed for Gerlach, which described—very much in line with the genre—how the chaplain "had fought the ferocious Turk with sword and fire."[37] But perhaps knowing that this might be taken for a rhetorical flourish, he added a note citing Gerlach's own words as evidence that such was indeed how Ottoman Turks behaved.[38] In yet another part of this work, Crusius expressed his fears that the Greek language might die, just as politics had died after the arrival of the Turks.[39] Here, too, Crusius relied on firsthand evidence and testimonies by Greeks themselves. Even the book's central thesis echoed the sentiments of a native Greek: the celebrated Greek teacher Joannes Argyropoulos once exclaimed upon hearing Johannes Reuchlin, one of his students, pronounce Greek "that with our exile Greece has crossed the Alps."[40] Both in the *Turcograecia* and the *Germanograecia*, then, Crusius cast the Ottomans as a people bent on the subjugation of everything Greek, with devastating consequences.

220   THE DISCOVERY OF OTTOMAN GREECE

Crusius went to great pains to document the fate of the Greeks at the hands of the Ottomans. One of Crusius's concerns was finding out what had happened to the last Byzantine emperor, Constantine XI, and his wife—lest his readers get the impression that the Ottomans had completely replaced the Greeks. But he was unable, as the *Turcograecia* testifies, to locate Constantine's grave or to identify his wife's name correctly. Zygomalas, to whom Crusius had turned with great expectations, had to admit not knowing her name. This Greek had only heard rumors that the emperor had had his wife and children killed so that the sultan would not capture them alive.[41] The Greek books in Crusius's study had been only marginally more informative. The late Byzantine historian Chalcocondyles revealed that Constantine had married not once but twice. But no name was given. Crusius conjectured that it was the emperor's second wife whose tragic fate other historians had also chronicled: the Ottoman sultan had supposedly "invited her to a dinner together with her daughters and other noble women" where "they were mistreated" and cruelly "cut into pieces." When he incorporated these findings into the *Turcograecia,* he not only expressed his astonishment over the fact "that a person of such repute remains unknown in history" but also inserted a short epitaph that lamented the unknown location of their graves and anticipated the pity that the merciful God would take on them.[42] Even when the exact details kept eluding Crusius—which of the two wives was murdered by the Ottomans; which one by the emperor himself, if there was any truth to these rumors?—his Greek testimonies ultimately shaped his pessimistic assessment of Greek life under Ottoman rule.

Greek learning was another area in which Crusius saw decline. Different parts of the *Turcograecia* made it unequivocally clear that Greek books were difficult to come by, that levels of literacy among Greeks were distressingly low, and—something that must have disheartened Crusius's Lutheran audience in particular—that few Greeks had access to scripture, and even fewer were able to understand it, since the Bible was not readily available in vernacular Greek. In addition to Gerlach's assessment of the lack of schooling in the Ottoman Empire, Crusius also incorporated a letter from Theodosius Zygomalas that implied as much: when the *protonotarius* wrote that Crusius's students have knowledge because they have a king—that is, a just ruler—Crusius concluded that only under a just ruler is there freedom and only when there is freedom is there knowledge.[43] From reading another of

Zygomalas's letters, which listed the small number of learned men left in Greece, Crusius realized just how much damage the "evil of slavery" had done.[44] His conclusion, then, was inescapable: producing knowledge in the humanist sense was impossible in Greece now that the Ottomans ruled there. No wonder, Crusius noted, that many Greeks with an insufficient knowledge of classical Greek moved to academies across Italy to learn their own language.[45] And no wonder that he considered himself and other Lutherans "lucky . . . because of our liberty, our true doctrine in God, and the schools that we have set up."[46]

The postclassical development of ancient Athens confirmed Crusius's diagnosis. For many, including Crusius, ancient Athens served as both metaphor and model of a cultured city. The Swiss humanist Theodor Zwinger, who would help bring the *Turcograecia* to print, had even chosen ancient Athens, along with Paris, Basel, and Padua—which he called the Athens of, respectively, France, Switzerland, and Italy—as one of his case studies in his praised treatise on travel.[47] Many of Crusius's informants showed him how this iconic city, once the center of culture, had become an insignificant point on the map of letters and learning. Symeon Cabasylas, for instance, had revealed in a letter to Crusius that the inner city of Athens was completely populated by the Ottomans while the Greeks had to make do with the outer circles.[48] Though the Greeks whom Crusius invited into his home told him about the churches that were still standing, few of them could assuage his fears that little had remained of the city of Plato, Aristotle, and those other ancient luminaries that early modern scholars revered. On the contrary: perhaps the most captivating image of Athens in the *Turcograecia* was found in a reproduction of a lengthy letter by Zygomalas, which communicated in detail what he had seen during his visits to Athens. Initially, it seemed all was well: Zygomalas described how he had examined the Areopagus; the old Academy, Aristotle's Lyceum; the Parthenon, which depicted the "histories of the Greeks as well as those of the Gods"; and even two statues of horses that were said to have been made by Praxiteles "so that virtue and human ingenuity appear to pass through stones." But although he gave Crusius—and any reader of the *Turcograecia*—a glimpse of what had remained of ancient Athens, Zygomalas ultimately painted a rather bleak picture: though the variety of songs that Athenians sang sometimes moved their audiences, Athenians had, according to Zygomalas, "degenerated into barbarity." Indeed, he sighed that only "the skin has remained of something that was once alive." He did not neglect to mention in an overt attempt to appease Crusius that while the Greeks themselves "as slaves were deprived of wisdom and learning," Greek learning now migrated to Germany. "Nothing remains but to keep quiet," Zygomalas concluded poignantly.[49]

Crusius's narrative of decline was not always consistent. In preparing texts for inclusion in the *Turcograecia,* and in reading Greek manuscripts and books, he had discovered what he considered a great many "errors" in the way specific words were spelled—that is, deviations from ancient Greek. But instead of replacing them with their classical equivalents, which was not uncommon in this period, Crusius believed that maintaining "these orthographic mistakes" would allow readers to see "that today in Greece there is no difference between the ι, η, υ, ει, and οι, neither in writing nor in pronunciation." These changes could teach his readers about the "ignorance and the negligence of those that transcribed" these manuscripts.[50] Ironically, though, Crusius's explications of when these "errors" first started to appear undermined the very idea that the Ottomans were to blame for the Greeks' demise. He noted that such deviations from the classical norm had begun to appear before the Ottomans had taken Constantinople: "Even in older manuscripts from the period when the [Byzantine] Empire was still standing" these changes "can be observed."[51]

Crusius's claims about Greek decline in the *Turcograecia* and *Germanograecia,* then, relied not only on his own assumptions but also on accounts by eyewitnesses of the indignities that Greeks suffered at the hands of the Ottomans. Many such testimonies came from Greeks themselves. Zygomalas spoke about servitude and the decline of learning, as did the Greeks who visited Tübingen, while in Greek chronicles Crusius found further confirmation that Greece was in decline. Crusius's conclusions, while informed by dialogue with Greeks, did reflect a particular set of Greek sentiments. Crusius relied on a circumscribed number of itinerant Greeks, who, despite being a varied group of people from different social strata, had a vested interest in painting a picture of servitude and suppression, as did the small number of elite Greek Orthodox clerics with whom Crusius corresponded. Other voices from the Ottoman Greek world, such as those of merchants or converts to Islam, do not appear in the *Turcograecia* or Crusius's other documents; he only seems to have cared for positions that confirmed his pessimistic assessment of Ottoman Greece. Focusing on this narrative of decline, the *Turcograecia* did not capture the full range of Greek visions of Ottoman Greece.

Crusius's vision rested not solely on Greek testimonies either. His dismissive comments on Greek orthography were all his own. Evidence that his trusted Protestant colleagues provided also frequently corroborated his conclusions. Gerlach, for instance, had once intimated—in a letter that Crusius must have read with great interest and reproduced in part in the *Turcograecia*—that Greeks claimed that the Greek vernacular was "very old," although "they did not know when it truly began." The purest form of the Greek language was, according to Gerlach, spoken in Istanbul, while Athenians spoke "the most corrupt form." There were also a great many differences in pronunciation across the Greek-speaking world, but Gerlach wrote that all Greeks, "wherever they are from," still "understand each other, with the exception of the Ionians who, living in fourteen villages in the Peloponnese between Nafplio and Monemvasia, speak the ancient language" albeit with many grammatical errors. These Ionians did understand "those who speak grammatically, but speakers of the vernacular" they understood "not very well."[52] Such insights, which Gerlach had acquired either through hearsay or through conversation with Greeks living in different parts of the Ottoman Empire, spoke to Crusius's interests in the whole history of the Greek language—and they shaped his pessimistic conclusion.

Crusius's vision of Ottoman Greece thus resulted from a merging of perspectives and positions: Greek testimonies, eyewitness observations by trusted colleagues such as Gerlach, and his own ideas about purity. Obviously, not all early modern accounts of Ottoman Greece operated on the same logic. Firsthand exchange with a range of Greek informants, for example, was possible to a greater extent in the eighteenth and nineteenth centuries—when travel to Greece was not easier but more common—than in earlier centuries. By then, the gradual accumulation and proliferation of textual as well as material documentation by Greeks about Greece ensured that "evidence" was also more readily available than in Crusius's days. Yet, despite these developments, the *Turcograecia* continued to be a seminal text in this long tradition of envisioning Greece. It produced conclusions that resonated strongly among people who believed in the Ottomans' destructive power. And Europeans eagerly reproduced its firsthand evidence: Heineccius, tellingly, cited a letter by Zygomalas from the *Turcograecia* as evidence of the plight of the Greeks, demonstrating just how enduring elite Greeks' assessments of their Church's dire predicament were.[53]

READERS OF THE *TURCOGRAECIA*

One of the great ironies of this story is that despite Crusius's strong emphasis on Greece's decline, early modern readers appreciated the *Turcograecia* for what it had become: a repository of miscellaneous material, ready to be brought to bear on a variety of scholarly discussions. Some scholars adopted Crusius's decline theory all too willingly: in his 1586 *Chronicon sive Synopsis Historiarum,* the Lutheran schoolmaster Michael Neander repeated a point that he had found in one of the letters edited in the *Turcograecia*—namely, that "nowhere in Greece nowadays do people use a more barbarous idiom than in Athens."[54] Other readers, however, found other evidence. The actual copies of the *Turcograecia* that have survived, about a hundred, tell us very little about this reception. Most contain no annotations beyond some scant provenance notes. But casting a wider net, we can see how early modern Europeans brought the firsthand evidence collected in the book to bear on a variety of scholarly discussions.

Perhaps the most important arena in which the *Turcograecia* was valued was lexicography. Dictionaries published throughout the sixteenth and seventeenth centuries copied linguistic material from the *Turcograecia*. One of the earliest and most influential glossaries of vernacular Greek was published by the Dutch classical scholar Johannes Meursius. His 1614 *Glossarium graecobarbarum* would lay the groundwork for DuCange's celebrated dictionary of medieval Greek. Yet Meursius, although innovative, did not work in isolation: some of the entries in his glossary were lifted verbatim from the *Turcograecia,* reproducing the exact words that Donatus had spoken to Crusius when he was in Tübingen in 1579.[55] The conversations that Crusius had with his Greek guests, and the moments in which they pored over his books, contributed decades later to the rise of vernacular Greek lexicography.

In the early eighteenth century, lexicographers continued to use Crusius as a point of departure for their inquiries. Johannes Tribbechovius, who would make a name for himself as professor of theology in Halle, referenced the *Turcograecia* in his 1705 introduction to the Greek vernacular.[56] The Lutheran theologian Johannes Langius reprinted Crusius's bilingual edition of the

Batrachomyomachia and lifted the latter's annotations on this poem for inclusion in his two-volume *Philologia barbaro-Graeca* of 1708.[57] This now forgotten work was an extensive survey of the development of the Greek vernacular. It offered readers an account of the origin of the vernacular, an analysis of the first vernacular Greek translation of the New Testament, a synopsis of the vernacular Greek grammar, an introduction to vernacular Greek poetry, and a compendium of vernacular Greek vocabulary. It was the first of its kind, but it explicitly identified Crusius "as the first to introduce vernacular Greek into our Germany."[58] Though Langius was only repeating Crusius's own boastful comment that he was the first to introduce this language in Germany, its inclusion here clearly indicates the reputation Crusius enjoyed in eighteenth-century scholarly circles as a lexicographer and linguist.[59]

Even one of Crusius's most notable readers—Joseph Scaliger—situated the *Turcograecia* in the larger world of lexicography. His strikingly annotated copy has survived in Leiden, in part through Gerard Vossius and his son Dionysius, who possessed the copy after Scaliger's death. It contains marginal notes throughout, which, though often short, reveal that the great scholar devoured the chronicles in books one and two. He approached them, characteristically, as a chronologer, inserting in the margin the results of his own chronological inquiries and correcting Crusius when his dating was off.[60] Scaliger's notes also demonstrate a profound engagement with the linguistic material included in the *Turcograecia*: he recorded which vernacular Greek words had Arabic, Turkish, French, and Italian origins or cognates.[61] Occasionally, he also expressed disagreement with Crusius, corrected his spelling of certain words, and provided alternative readings.[62] The copious index, advertised on the title page, was not copious enough for Scaliger, who knew exactly how useful a good index, printed or manuscript, could be for a reader hoping to exploit a mass of documents and materials. Scaliger, who compiled a great index to Janus Gruter's corpus of inscriptions, inserted many new headings and pointers in the margins and between the lines of Crusius's index, evidently to make bits of information in different parts of the *Turcograecia* more easily retrievable. His many cross-references served a similar goal.[63] Not all pages referenced contain traces of reading, indicating that—as is so often the case for early modern books—seemingly untouched pages may still have been read.

Perhaps the most revealing set of notes in Scaliger's copy pertains to the image of the Greek Orthodox patriarch. Its inclusion next to the title page of the ecclesiastical chronicle in book two seems to have been largely ornamental: there is no legend, only a short note identifying it as the patriarch of Constantinople.[64] Instead, readers interested in understanding the intricacies of the patriarch's garment had to look elsewhere in the *Turcograecia* for guidance. This is exactly what Scaliger did: he copied from page 188 the information that Donatus had given Crusius about the patriarch's dress and tried to identify which item of clothing was which. In short, even though he did not mark up every single page, Scaliger seems to have understood the scope of Crusius's project and knew how to connect the different pieces of the mosaic that was the *Turcograecia*. It is no surprise therefore that in the second edition of his *De emendatione temporum*, Scaliger referenced the *Turcograecia* and praised Crusius as an important philhellene.[65]

Already in Crusius's lifetime, his work was known in Catholic circles. In this case, though, it was not just the lexicographical material or the chronicles that drew attention but also the fact that the book betrayed its author's deeply Lutheran sentiments. One consultor of the Congregation of the Index of Prohibited Books was given the task of determining whether the *Turcograecia* needed to be censured, expurgated, or even included on the *Index*. His two-page report, which has survived in Rome in the Archive of the Congregation for the Doctrine of the Faith, concentrated exclusively on those passages that opposed proper Catholic doctrine: the "heretical author" of the *Turcograecia*, the assessment began, "praised many heretics, exalted the Augsburg Confession" and "did not follow the text of the Holy Scripture according to the vulgate edition, but the versions of the heretics." The rest of the report listed about two dozen pages from the *Turcograecia* that were potentially suspect and thus required attention from the congregation.[66] No wonder that when the theologian and future prefect of the Biblioteca Ambrosiana Francesco Bernardino Ferrari wanted to read his copy of the *Turcograecia*, he had to request a reading license.[67] The *Turcograecia* was evidently read at the Curia with the correspondence between Tübingen and Jeremias in mind—the *Acta* of which, once published, had drawn Crusius into that acrimonious dispute with different Catholic scholars.

Not much is known about the *Turcograecia*'s circulation in the contemporary Greek world. Hieremias, the archbishop who visited Tübingen in May

1599, told Crusius that he had seen the *Turcograecia* in Prague and that he believed that "everything" mentioned in it "was true." He even bought a copy from Crusius that was bound with the 1585 *Acta*, "which he had not seen before."[68] More than a century later, and a decade after the conclusion of the Synod of Jerusalem, Patriarch Dositheos II hoped that John Covel, Master of Christ's College and former chaplain to the Levant Company, could acquire a set of books for him, one of which was the *Turcograecia*.[69] One tiny bit of evidence, though, suggests that the *Turcograecia* was not as well received in the higher echelons of the Greek Orthodox Church as Hieremias's estimation and Dositheos's interests imply. In June 1599 Crusius received a letter from the Metropolitan of Philadelphia, requesting a copy of the *Turcograecia*. It was a polite and friendly note but one with quite a critical conclusion: "Know that those amongst the Greeks who hold you in high regard are annoyed by the composition of the title because it is not our custom to call much-loved and much-praised Greece Turkish-Greece in such a barbaric way."[70] Crusius, of course, had not meant to insult the Greeks—he had chosen the title merely "to show the status of Greece under the Turks"—but he nevertheless felt he needed to write "a defense against the awful suspicion of the Greeks about [him] on account of the title of [his] work."[71] In these letters, addressed to Gabriel Severus and Maximus Margunius, Crusius repeated what he had intimated to his diary:

> I have written and edited two works: of which the first is called, *Turcograecia*, because it shows what the state is of present-day Greece after the Barbarians suppressed it in such a deplorable manner. . . . But there is otherwise nothing that could damage the reputation of that famous people that I so dearly love. On the contrary: everywhere in that work my love and affection for them is visible. I called the other work the *Germanograecia* to show how, by the grace of god, Greek studies are now in Germany, to which they . . . migrated after the fall of Constantinople.[72]

The responses that these letters provoked appear not to have survived. This exchange nevertheless illustrates three important points. First, it is no surprise that the only evidence of the *Turcograecia*'s reception in Greek Orthodox circles comes not from Istanbul but from Venice, a place with a strong émigré

Greek community and a city whose book markets and news networks reached all the way to the Holy Roman Empire. Second, Severus's complaint suggests that the language of fluidity and hybridity, which historians of the early modern Mediterranean have recently adopted to understand cross-cultural interactions, did not resonate with some of our historical actors: the suggestion that there was something like an Ottoman Greek world was as insulting as it was repulsive in the eyes of the sultan's Greek subjects. Third, the letter illustrates how Crusius relied on only a particular group of Greeks who narrated a story of decline.

Its miscellaneous nature ensured that the *Turcograecia* enjoyed widespread currency in a variety of scholarly fields across several centuries. Readers appreciated the historical and linguistic data that it provided—and especially the insights it offered into the Greek vernacular—as much as the narrative of decline that it presented. It was thus the content of what Crusius had discovered, the historical and linguistic data he printed as well as Crusius's choice to present that in a direct way, that appears to have found greatest appreciation among his readers. Early modern readers mined the *Turcograecia* not solely as an account of present-day Greece but as the miscellaneous treasure trove that it had grown to become. This is exactly how the book is still read today: known primarily among Byzantinists and scholars of the Greek vernacular, the *Turcograecia* has drawn scant attention from historians working in other fields.

CONCLUSION

In chapter 68 of the sixth and last volume of *The History of the Decline and Fall of the Roman Empire*, Edward Gibbon explained that shortly after 1453 "the churches of Constantinople were shared between the two religions: their limits were marked; and, till it was infringed by Selim, the grandson of Mahomet, the Greeks enjoyed above sixty years the benefit of this equal partition."[73] Here, as earlier in his narration, the English historian had culled his information from Crusius's *Turcograecia*. Together with other early modern treatises about the Ottoman Greek world, it gave Gibbon, who truly despised the Greek church, exactly the kind of information he was looking for: evidence for the decline and fall of the Roman Empire in the East. One particularly powerful indication of this story was the fact that "the patriarch who succeeded Gennadius threw himself in despair into a well."[74] Yet at the same time Gibbon could not hide his admiration for the Ottomans: even though he dismissed Voltaire for his preference of "the Turks to the Christians," Gibbon realized all too well that Mehmed II would not let Constantinople "be despoiled of the incomparable situation which marks her for the metropolis of a great empire." On the contrary: since the sultan "established his own residence, and that of his successors, on the same commanding spot which had been chosen by Constantine," it was guaranteed that "the genius of the place will ever triumph over the accidents of time and fortune."[75]

Gibbon's reading of Crusius mirrors Crusius's own reading of his sources and gestures at something broader: that numerous scholars and travelers to the Greek world—from Renaissance humanists to Enlightened intellectuals and Romantic poets—created their own Greece and made the evidence that they found there serve their scholarly and confessional agendas and confirm their cultural biases. For, ultimately, Crusius's conclusion was meant to support just one interpretation: that Greece was in decline and that Lutheran Germany supplanted the Greek Church as the guardian of Christian orthodoxy. Yet, crucially, Crusius was not uninformed. Neither was Gibbon, for that matter, and we could posit the same for some of those who traveled through the Ottoman Greek world in search for antiquities and other ancient remains. In the *Turcograecia* and the *Germanograecia*, Crusius reproduced a bewildering amount of firsthand evidence, some of it by Greeks themselves, that recorded the intricacies of the Ottoman Greek world in all its vividness and diversity.

One seminal lesson to be learned from tracing early modern visions of Ottoman Greece is thus that the tropes and stereotypes that circulated about this world in early modern Europe were not just based on European assumptions. Evidence as much as conviction were central to how such ideas emerged and crystalized. Greeks corroborated, perhaps unwittingly, what Crusius believed was true—what he wanted to be true. They offered him exactly the kind of information that confirmed his own opinion and fed into his misguided sense of cultural and religious superiority. In so doing, their categories became his—at least as long as they were compatible with what Crusius deemed was right. The outcome of this complex process of cultural brokering was an East–West binary that flattened the complexity of Greek life under Ottoman rule. We should therefore do well to remember that such visions of the Ottoman Greek world, however partial, were not always some orientalist figment of the imagination but the result of information brokering between two entangled worlds. The irony here is that Crusius nevertheless fell victim to the same fallacy that would mislead countless other early modern scholars who wished to inform themselves about cultures that were not their own: their penetrating visions were not uninformed, but they were nevertheless seamed with contradictions. They were the products of their own prejudices and religious sympathies, combined with the results of systematic inquiry and the knowledge and testimonies of local informants.

The global exchange of knowledge, then, so characteristic of early modernity as well as of Crusius's learned life, did not always yield deeper insight into other cultures and civilizations. On the contrary: sometimes it confirmed preexisting biases as much as it broadened cultural horizons. This too was typical for the period: more than one great early modern ethnographic enterprise stimulated brilliant, sophisticated inquiries into local traditions and customs, revealing culture in all its diversity but yielding very little beyond the accumulation of data. For once the evidence had been collected, scholars could be quite unsure what to make of it. Sometimes sources were simply laid out as *acta* with little to no contextualization, as happened in the famous Florentine Codex and the questionnaires that Spanish scholars compiled to inform themselves of the Americas. Sometimes, as in the case of Buxtorf's work on Jewish customs, the material was published, but in a form so warped by presuppositions, often confessional, that the research on which everything rested could quickly disappear from view. Crusius's *Turcograecia* sits between these two extremes, allowing readers at once to experience Greek life under Ottoman rule through numerous documents and to draw from this journey a specific lesson about Greece's decline.

CONCLUSION

On September 3, 1594, Tübingen's Faculty of Arts received a rather curious gift for its newly founded library: Crusius's four-hundred-page family history. Copied from his autograph exemplar by six of his students, and beautifully bound, the manuscript chronicled his life and those of his parents. Two elaborate genealogies, one detailing his father's side of the family, one describing his mother's lineage, branched out over its opening pages. Organized year by year, Crusius's family history began in 1490, with the birth of his homonymous father, Martin Kraus, and continued until the 1590s. Crusius knew, however, that these "Crusiades"—named in true humanist fashion after the ancient epics that he had been teaching for nearly four decades—made for an odd textual record. In his preface, Crusius staged a debate with a hypothetical critic who questioned his decision to narrate his own family history: Why had he written about himself and not about the great kings and queens of the past? Was that not an act of arrogance? And who would care about people of low birth anyway?

Crusius's defense was as ingenious then as it is revealing today. Nowhere in his writings is he more explicit than here about how he conceptualized his own position in the world around him: "May other people write genealogies of noble and illustrious people. I want to write a chronology, or a history, of my family and myself. We cannot all be of noble or illustrious birth." Yet according to Crusius, "by the gift of God" people could "live their lives piously and honorably, each fulfilling what is accorded to them honestly and laudably." It was not people's background but their accomplishments in life that determined whether they merited inclusion in the historical record. Twice, Crusius resorted to horticulture to stress this point: "It is not be-

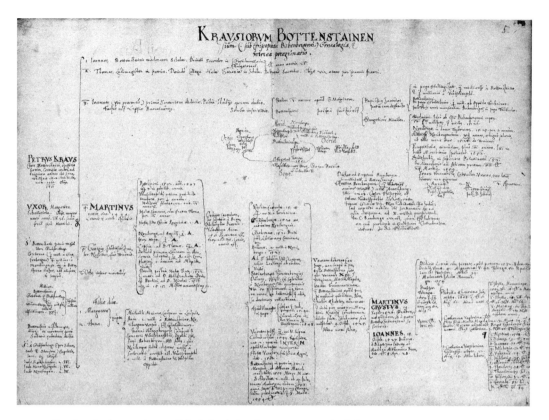

C.1 Crusius's genealogy of his father's family. It starts on the left with Crusius's grandfather Peter and father Martin (nr. 4). Crusius himself and his family are located on the bottom right. The drawing in the middle is of the region around Pottenstein, where his grandfather was from. Credit: *Universitätsbibliothek Tübingen Mh 443, vol. 1, fol. 5.*

cause some plants are beautiful and famous, that others are worthless and despised," and "in a decorated and delightful garden there are not only remarkable plants and flowers," he intimated using a period metaphor. Moreover, Crusius's apology continued, the ancestors of many farmers and artisans once belonged to the upper classes: "Since Noah's Ark" many "noble and illustrious families, whose names time itself has consigned to oblivion, have sunken into poverty and obscurity through the fickleness of fortune." It was therefore justifiable "to write about people of little renown." There was also historical precedent, as "others had written about their own affairs as well: such as Emperor Julius Caesar, the Jew Josephus, and the theologian Gregory of Nazianzus." So why, Crusius asked, "should I cheat myself and

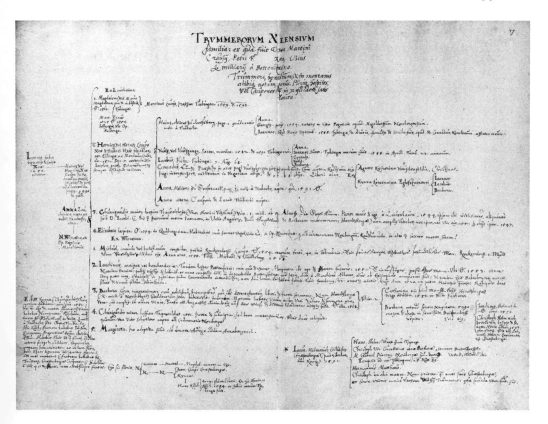

C.2 Crusius's genealogy of his mother's family. It includes on the top his parents, Maria Magdalena Trummer (nr. 1) and Martin Kraus, as well as Crusius himself, identified by his profession: professor at the University of Tübingen. *Credit: Universitätsbibliothek Tübingen Mh 443, vol. 1, fol. 7.*

my family by not writing about them?" Had he not already "written about many other people" in the *Turcograecia* and his other published works? In any event, this particular historical document, like Crusius's other writings, was a "work of piety toward God," not born out of vanity, and it was one for the ages: "In about a hundred years someone will find here something about their ancestors that will entertain."[1]

Not one hundred but over four hundred years have passed since Crusius penned these words. I have not discovered anything about my own ancestors in any of his documents, but I have found much that is, by turns, productive, entertaining, compelling, surprising, and even moving. Readers of this book have hopefully found Crusius's story equally rewarding. His hunger for knowledge and desire to record not only the results of his inquiry but also the mechanisms in all their gritty, granular detail have afforded us more than the occasional glimpse behind the curtain: Crusius portrayed moments of knowledge making in just as much, if not more, detail as the published works they yielded. His journey of discovery was not predicated on travel but on the fruitful exchange of different forms of expertise in the university town where he resided. It was made possible by gendered labor within Crusius's household, as well as by forms of mobility spurred by the arrival of the Ottomans in the Eastern Mediterranean. His scholarship developed through exchanging letters, reading books, interviewing Greeks, and collecting all sorts of information about their culture and religion. Every detail mattered, from "readings" of Greeks' appearances to the formal features of old manuscripts to the suffixes used by some of his Greek informants. His Lutheran sympathies inspired him to collect material unknown to most of Crusius's scholarly peers, but they also clouded his vision: Greeks could not live up to the purity of their ancient ancestors, not in their religion, not in their language—and once Crusius realized this, he began to harbor high hopes for spreading his Lutheran truth among them. In the end, then, this was a double story in which new knowledge also confirmed preexisting beliefs, even as Crusius's intellectual horizon expanded dramatically.

In the process, although without ever explicitly aiming to do so, Crusius rendered visible people and phenomena previously thought to have been sufficiently understood. Therein lies Crusius's value as a subject of scholarly inquiry: the documentary record that he left of his life may at first appear singular, but on closer inspection it illuminates experiences that transcend the contours of his Tübingen life. Following Crusius on his journey of discovery demonstrates how the Lutheran Reformation, Mediterranean history, and the history of ethnography and encounter were inextricably connected in early modernity. Once we recognize these deep cross-cultural entanglements, we begin to see the full range of how Western Europeans examined the early modern world: some traveled far and wide, while others, like Crusius, stayed at home, traveled in the mind's eye with the help of informants, and encouraged their colleagues and readers to embark on similar mental journeys. The massive archive of surviving documentation that Crusius left has made it possible to uncover the historical realities lived by him, his

CONCLUSION 235

family, his colleagues, and the other individuals—Greeks and non-Greeks—who populate this book. Not all of these correspond to familiar types. What Crusius's story reveals to us is thus most of all the horizon of possibilities in the sixteenth-century world: global lives could be lived in various ways and on various scales, not all of which required travel or mobility.

Entering Crusius's world also illuminates the sometimes unexpected genealogies of the ways in which European constructions of both the Middle East and postclassical Greece developed in the centuries after Crusius's death as well as Protestant missionary enterprises in the Mediterranean. The knotty circumstances that enabled his inquiry adumbrate the ways in which knowledge about the cultural and religious other was produced in colonial contexts more familiar to us today. Centuries separated him from high colonialism, and geopolitics changed dramatically in that period of expansionism. Yet Crusius's investigation, which turned Ottoman Greece into a site of his own anxieties and expectations, belonged to a broader orientalist discourse from which so much early modern scholarship on the "Orient" gained its pernicious strength. Crusius's "orientalism" was obviously not directly wedded to a state-colonial project, nor did it do the cultural work of empire. Nor was it focused on Islam and the Muslim Other. Yet Crusius, too, reduced a vibrant and diverse world to a set of stereotypes, producing an essentializing construct as pervasive as later articulations of cultural and religious difference in the "Orient." And it all took place in the intimacy of his scholarly household in Tübingen—a town that after his death would become, like Leiden and Paris, an important center for oriental studies. Crusius's Tübingen life was thus one area through which the roots of orientalism moved. Recognizing that is valuable for understanding early modern orientalism, as recent scholarship has emphasized, not as "a myopic yet all pervasive representation by and for Europeans" but as a confluence of "specific communicative circuits and institutionalized genres of knowledge production" that connected European and Ottoman actors, and which concerned not only Islam but also the Christian Other.[2]

Crusius's scholarship also lays bare the deep roots of nineteenth-century Protestant missionary work. In most traditional accounts, the Protestant mission only really took off with the Pietists and their institutionalized, church-supported evangelizing across the world. Especially in the nineteenth century, the Middle East emerged as a prime site of proselytization in the eyes of Protestant groups across Europe and America. Muslims and Eastern Christians were believed to be susceptible to God's true message, if only they knew about it. Such beliefs gave rise to a kind of missionary work that, as in Crusius's case, fused an absolute confidence in the written word with an almost condescending desire for the edification of Middle Eastern peoples. Many important differences existed, of course: whereas later institutionalized religious expansionism was placed in the service of colonialism, Crusius's hopes of spreading the faith never acquired such imperialist contours. Nineteenth-century missionaries could rely on instruction manuals, while no such documentation was available when Tübingen set out to convince the Greek Orthodox Church of its Lutheran truth. Colonialism facilitated the construction of schools and the education of local boys and girls by both men and women—a missionary infrastructure of which sixteenth-century Tübingen, again, could only have dreamed. Given the immense power of the Ottoman realm in Crusius's day, he was more prone to fears of Turkish expansion than to hopes for European conquests. Yet, despite these and other differences, Crusius and his Lutheran colleagues were inspired by the same evangelizing zeal that motivated their nineteenth-century descendants. Throughout the early modern period, Lutheranism—and Protestantism writ large—was looking outward as much as it was looking inward.

One final implication of Crusius's story concerns the longer history of European representations of Greece. In the centuries after Crusius's story ended—and indeed up to this very day—Europeans have almost invariably infused their love of Greece with a deep sense of disappointment: in hardly any context could Greeks live up to the expectations others had of them. European philhellenism, for instance, really took off in the nineteenth century when Europeans encountered antiquity's splendid monuments in ruins, and new forms of art and scholarship taught them to believe that to be Greek was to admire the beautiful—a way of life that did not require any change in the way Europeans regarded contemporary Greeks. Discussions of the return of the Elgin Marbles to Athens have been framed to this day by spurious assumptions that the Greeks are somehow unable to look after and preserve these infamous artifacts properly. And even international media's coverage of the economic crisis that hit Greece after the US housing market crashed in 2007 was marred by idealized notions of ancient Greece and assumptions that the Greeks—in a plot twist reminiscent of an ancient tragedy—were themselves to blame for their misfortune.[3] European and American economists and politicians freely used such language as well. Framed as unworthy successors and uncultured custodians of Greece's ancient splendor, the Greek people have been consistently compared in unfavorable terms to their famous ancestors. This book has offered one deeply contextualized analysis of how such comparisons developed across cultural and confessional contexts. It serves as a reminder that, though the roots of such ways of seeing run deep, their development was the result of deliberate effort.

Understanding how Crusius envisioned Ottoman Greece does not explain how we got from one place to another. Neither does it allow us to draw precise genealogies of orientalism, philhellenism, and the Protestant mission with easily identifiable branches. But it offers historical perspective and analytical leverage on phenomena that stretch over centuries, laying bare the distinct forms they took in a sixteenth-century world of exchange and encounter—a world that resisted simple binary distinction between "East" and "West." Recovering these forgotten realities shows a Lutheran community bent on spreading its religious principles through exchange with Greek Orthodox Christians. It reveals the Middle Sea and its reverberations in Crusius's Tübingen home as key sites in the formation of a distinct way of envisioning Greece and as crucial templates for studying cultural and religious difference. And it uncovers how mobility and encounters both in and beyond the Mediterranean made possible such visions of Ottoman Greece as well as the creation of early modern Europe's richest archive on Greek life under Ottoman rule.

When Crusius made his modest contribution to the library of Faculty of Arts, and shared with the world the history of his family, he inadvertently created evidence that can tell us how he attempted to preserve his memory. It is also a testament to the painful reality that Crusius would be more often forgotten than remembered.

His gift of what was essentially a *Gedenkbuch*, a memory book, was part of a larger effort to rebuild Tübingen's university library. Most of the books the university collected before the Reformation were destroyed in a fire in 1534. Although the university and its faculties continued to acquire books in the next few decades, a librarian was not appointed until 1591. Still later the Faculty of Arts had two wooden cabinets made to store its book collection.[4] The materials that Crusius entrusted to the university, which included not only his *Gedenkbuch* but other books as well, were meant "to be kept" there "in perpetuity."[5] He also promised to bequeath his other books to the university library, the library of the Collegium Illustre, and the library of the Faculty of Arts, technically a different collection from the university library. He hoped, though, that he would be allowed to keep them until the end of his life and that some of the books would be given to any of his grandchildren who would obtain a degree.[6]

No shortage of means would prevent his descendants from seeking a higher education—that much Crusius knew. Only two of his daughters were still alive by the time he drew up his will in February 1605 and made provisions for establishing a scholarship (*stipendium*) in his own name to provide for the education of his heirs. The primary beneficiaries of the funds, worth no less than fourteen hundred florins, were the children of his daughter Maria Magdalena and her husband, Jakob Maier—whom we have met as one of the amanuenses who helped Crusius transcribe letters and collate manuscripts—and any (male) descendants down that line. Should there be none, or should they be found unqualified for pursuing a university degree, any relatives on his mother's side of the family, the Trummers, would become the beneficiaries. In case there were none in that part of the family either, Crusius's friend and colleague Veit Müller would have to allocate the funds, which were meant to cover room and board for up to two students in the Bursa. Crusius also stipulated that stipend holders "zealously pursue philosophical study and the Greek language in particular" and make every effort to get a position in the Faculty of Arts or as a teacher of Greek. Every year, on September 19, Crusius's birthday, two inspectors would have to determine whether the stipend holders had made satisfactory academic progress and, at small dinner parties paid for by the fund, were supposed to "amuse themselves and commemorate [Crusius] with great gaiety."[7]

Tragically, none of his heirs seem to have become the studious scholar of Greek Crusius wanted them to be. His grandson, Johann Wolfgang Maier, owned one of his grandfather's manuscripts, which he gifted to Veit Müller before the latter's death in 1626, and obtained an MA degree.[8] But none of Maier's cousins followed suit. One of Crusius's great-great-grandsons, Ernst Gottlieb Maier-Crusianus, recipient of the *stipendium* in 1667, perhaps came closest to what the fund was meant to achieve: born in neighboring Lustnau, Ernst Gottlieb graduated from the University of Tübingen in 1667 with a degree in philosophy before defending a dissertation in Tübingen's Faculty of Law on property and inheritance law.[9] He spent much of the rest of his life as a professor there, and his portrait was eventually included in Tübingen's famous *Professorengalerie*—that same portrait collection of the university's professors, rectors, and chancellors that began its life in the late sixteenth century when Crusius, whose portrait was also included, still delivered his celebrated Homer lectures.[10] Ernst Gottlieb's only son, Johann Adam Maier-Crusianus, was the end of the line, the last to carry the patronymic "Crusianus." Johann Adam died without issue in 1751. Only one tiny bit of evidence about Johann Adam's intellectual life survives: in Stuttgart's Hauptstaatsarchiv there is a short treatise that he wrote on the imperial banner. It offers nothing original in terms of content, but its focus was not very different from the heraldic documents Crusius had perused for his *Annales Suevici*—documents that, ironically, are kept in the same archive.[11]

Here Crusius's story, and his extraordinary journey of discovery, comes to a close. True, the *Turcograecia*, however much of a commercial disaster, cemented his reputation as one of Europe's first philhellenes and his legacy as a scholar of the contemporary Greek world and its language. The *Annales Suevici*, the chronicle Crusius proudly mentioned in the preface to his family history, ensured that his name was not forgotten by historians of Swabia, certainly after this work was translated into German and continued by Johann Jacob Moser, a German jurist whose work earned him the title "the father of German constitutional law" in the early eighteenth century.[12] Until well into the seventeenth century, the correspondence with the patriarch, and Crusius's role therein, served as ammunition for Catholics against Lutheran pretentions.[13] But Crusius's annotated books and manuscripts, the bulk and in many ways the real meat of his findings, were forgotten, dispersed as they were over Tübingen's libraries. Occasionally, items from his library have reappeared on the rare books market, confirming that at least a part of his book collection traveled beyond the confines of Crusius's Tübingen: in 1982, Tübingen's University Library bought Crusius's personal, and richly annotated, copy of the *Annales Suevici*; in 2000, Crusius's working copy of Homer, equally densely annotated, was bought by the Princeton University Library; in May 2016, I stumbled upon the copy of the *Annales Suevici* that

Crusius had gifted to Tübingen's Faculty of Arts and which Princeton also managed to acquire.[14] Yet in a general sense Crusius's real *Nachlass,* his private archive, forgotten though not exactly lost, remained in Tübingen, unexplored for centuries.

Only in the early nineteenth century did knowledge of Crusius's personal papers begin to reemerge. This was initially a local affair. For his entry on Crusius, in the second volume of his *Wirtembergischer Plutarch,* a biographical dictionary of famous Württembergers, the nineteenth-century historian Karl Pfaff referenced Crusius's diary and praised the scope and quality of the books and manuscripts he had left behind.[15] Educated at Tübingen's *Evangelisches Stift,* and later *conrector* at Esslingen's Latin school, Pfaff shared with his father, a clerk and archivist in Stuttgart, a predilection for archivalia. For the numerous publications that he dedicated to the history of Württemberg, among which the *Wirtembergischer Plutarch* was one of the shortest, Pfaff collected materials from archives all over the duchy and the State Archive in Stuttgart in particular. I suspect that Pfaff—if he indeed went to Tübingen to study Crusius's diary as he claimed—would have informed himself about Tübingen's holdings by drawing on two descriptions of them by its former librarian Jeremias David Reuss. Pfaff may even have browsed through Reuss's manuscript catalogs, preserved to this day in Tübingen, which mentioned Crusius's Greek manuscripts as well as his diary and family history.[16] Yet it is also possible that Pfaff became aware of the diary from reading Veit Müller's funeral oration, which he knew had drawn from the diary. Whatever may have directed him to Tübingen, it was Pfaff's attempt at illuminating the glorious history and the *viri illustres* of Württemberg— in many ways a project similar in ambition and scope to Crusius's *Annales Suevici*—that brought the diary to his attention and, consequently, that of his German readership.

But history had one last trick up her sleeve. It is no small irony, and surely one that Crusius would have greatly appreciated, that it took a Greek from Istanbul, after a three-year sojourn in Tübingen in the late nineteenth century, to draw attention to Crusius's *Nachlass* as an important but untapped source for Greek history. Basileos Athanasiou Mystakides called the *Crusiana* in Tübingen "truly a treasure, or better still a mine of treasures" in what was the first of several articles dedicated to Crusius.[17] Born in Istanbul in 1859, educated in Athens and Germany, employed first as a journalist, later as a representative of Istanbul's Archaeological Museum, and still later as a teacher at the Phanar Greek Orthodox College in the Ottoman capital, Mystakides was enthralled by Crusius and the extraordinary record he had left of a bygone age of German-Greek interactions. I have been unable to discover anything about his time in Tübingen other than that he was there, but I imagine him sitting in the old library in the *Altstadt*—its current location, the Bonatzbau, was only completed in 1912—sifting through manuscripts, one after another, and gradually building himself an image of Crusius and his Greek guests. The publications that resulted from Mystakides's studies, which were often little more than lengthy excerpts from Crusius's diary and manuscripts, made that lost story visible for the first time in centuries. From the *Turcograecia* some early readers may have gleaned its contours, but Mystakides, who continued to publish about Crusius until he died in 1933, was truly the first to reveal in living color Crusius's discovery of the Ottoman Greek world and the richly textured encounters that made it possible.

Although he had no such goal in view, Mystakides highlighted one hugely important point about Crusius's story—and those told in recent years about countless other early modern luminaries. It is in the layers of marginal annotation and in manuscript notebooks; in working papers, discarded drafts, and letters; in the dustbin of ideas and other material remains of learned sociability; in the scores of unbundled papers that outlived their creators—in short, in scholars' private archives—that we can appreciate early modern scholarship for what it really was: a deeply human pursuit, involving a diverse array of individuals, whose lives and deeds, hopes and anxieties, thoughts and emotions have for centuries lain dormant, known to but a handful of archivists, librarians, and local experts, just waiting for curious scholars of Mystakides's ilk to make them speak to the world again. Only by setting published work against scholars' private archives, their letters and their notebooks, their diaries and their papers, do we learn to read publications like the *Turcograecia* properly. Only from juxtaposing printed to unpublished material do early modern scholars like Crusius and his colleagues begin to emerge as real people. Crusius's consequence, in other words, his real contribution to the world as we know it, can only be measured by pondering his private archive; by painstakingly piecing together the countless clues that he left in his books and manuscripts; and by reducing the scale of observation to a level where all the details and the human dimensions come into full focus. It is up to us to descend into archives and libraries, to bring the many stories they preserve back to life, to read the world of print against the manuscripts and bundles of paper that have survived the accidents of time. Only then will we be able to see the world they inhabited, and which inhabited them, with new eyes. Only then will we be able to meet the great scholars of the later sixteenth century, including those whose importance we at this point can only suspect, on terms of intimacy.

ABBREVIATIONS

NOTES

ACKNOWLEDGMENTS

INDEX

Abbreviations

Acta

Acta et scripta theologorum Wirtembergensium, et patriarchae Constantinopolitani D. Hieremiae: quae utrique ab anno 1576 usque ad annum 1581 de Augustana Confessione inter se miserunt: Graece & Latine ab ijsdem theologis edita (Wittenberg: heirs of Johannes Krafft, 1584)

Crusius, Germanograecia

Martin Crusius, *Germanograeciae libri sex* (Basel: Leonard Ostein, 1585)

Crusius, Turcograecia

Martin Crusius, *Turcograeciae libri octo* (Basel: Leonard Ostein, 1584)

UBT

Universitätsbibliothek Tübingen

Notes

Introduction

1. For the fullest account of Crusius's life, see UBT Mh 443 (his history of his family), UBT Mh 466 (his nine-volume diary); Veit Müller, *Oratio de vita et obitu . . . Martini Crusii* (Tübingen: Philipp Gruppenbach, 1608), which is largely based on the diary and the family history; and Melchior Adam, *Vitae Germanorum superiori, et quod excurrit, seculo philosophicis et humanioribus literis clarorum* (Frankfurt: Nicolaus Hoffmann, 1615), 481–495, which is largely based on Müller's funeral oration. No modern biography exists. For Crusius's place of birth and his death, see Johannes Michael Wischnath, "Fakten, Fehler und Fiktionen: Eine forschungsgeschichtliche Fußnote zu Herkunft und Todestag des Tübinger Gräzisten Martin Crusius (1526–1607)," in *Tubingensia: Impulse zur Stadt- und Universitätsgeschichte. Festschrift für Wilfried Setzler zum 65. Geburtstag*, ed. Sönke Lorenz and Volker Schäfer (Ostfildern: Jan Thorbecke Verlag, 2008), 225–246.

2. For an account of Crusius's life and that of his father, in addition to Crusius's own family history, UBT Mh 466, see Albert Gaier, "Pfarrer Martin Krauß," *Blätter für Wüttembergische Kirchengeschichte* 68/69 (1968/1969): 497–521.

3. For the little that is known about Crusius's time there, see Herbert Schallhammer, "Das Schulwesen der Reichsstadt Memmingen von den Anfängen bis 1806," *Memmingen Geschichtsblätter* (1963): 5–103.

4. For Crusius's own account of his appointment, see UBT Mh 443, vol. 1, fol. 45^v.

5. UBT Mh 466, vol. 1, fol. 642.

6. For Crusius lamenting the fall of Constantinople, see UBT Mh 466, vol. 5, fol. 733; vol. 6, fol. 742; vol. 8, fol. 171, 519. For his doubts about the year of this event, see UBT Mh 519, fol. 14^r.

7. John W. Bohnstedt, "The Infidel Scourge of God: The Turkish Menace as Seen by German Pamphleteers of the Reformation Era," *Transactions of the American Philosophical Society* 56, no. 9 (1968): 1–58; Winfried Schulze, *Reich und Türkengefahr im späten 16. Jahrhundert: Studien zu den politischen und gesellschaftlichen Auswirkungen einer äußeren Bedrohung* (Munich: Beck, 1978); Almut Höfert, *Den Feind beschreiben: "Türkengefahr" und europäisches Wissen über das Osmanischen Reich, 1450–1600* (Frankfurt: Campus-Verlag, 2003); Thomas Kaufmann, "Aspekte der Wahrnehmung der "türkischen Religion" bei christlichen Autoren des 15. und 16. Jahrhunderts," in

Wahrnehmung des Islam zwischen Reformation und Aufklärung, ed. Dietrich Klein and Birte Platow (Paderborn: Wilhelm Fink Verlag, 2008), 9–26; Felix Konrad, "From the 'Turkish Menace' to Exoticism and Orientalism: Islam as Antithesis of Europe (1453–1914)?," European History Online (2011), online: http://ieg-ego.eu/en/threads/models-and-stereotypes/from-the-turkish-menace-to-orientalism (last accessed: November 25, 2023).

8. UBT Mh 466, vol. 5, fol. 639. For these kinds of prayers, see those that Crusius collected in UBT Mh 545, fol. 44^r–46^r.

9. Müller, *Oratio*, 68.

10. For Crusius as a teacher of Greek, see Franz Brendle, "Martin Crusius: Humanistische Bildung, schwäbisches Lutherthum und Griechenlandbegeisterung," in *Deutsche Landesgeschichtsschreibung im Zeichen des Humanismus*, ed. Franz Brendle, Dieter Mertens, Anton Schindling, and Walter Ziegler (Stuttgart: Steiner, 2001), 145–163; Walther Ludwig, *Hellas in Deutschland. Darstellungen der Gräzistik im deutschsprachigen Raum aus dem 16. und 17. Jahrhundert: Vorgelegt in der Sitzung vom 30. Januar 1998* (Hamburg: Joachim Jungius-Gesellschaft der Wissenschaften, 1998), 28–82. For Crusius's philhellenism, see George Elias Zachariades, *Tübingen und Konstantinopel: Martin Crusius und seine Verhandlungen mit der Griechisch-Orthodoxen Kirche* (Göttingen: Gerstung and Lehmann, 1941); Panagiotis Toufexis, *Das Alphabetum vulgaris linguae graecae des deutschen Humanisten Martin Crusius (1526–1607): Ein Beitrag zur Erforschung der gesprochenen griechischen Sprache im 16. Jh* (Cologne: Romiosini, 2005). For the correspondence with the patriarch, see Walter Engels, "Tübingen und Byzanz: Die erste offizielle Auseinandersetzung zwischen Protestantismus und Ostkirche in 16 Jh.," *Kyrios* 5 (1940–1941): 240–287; Ernst Benz, *Wittenberg und Byzanz; zur Begegnung und Auseinandersetzung der Reformation und der Östlich-orthodoxen Kirche* (Marburg: Elwert-Gräfe und Unzer, 1949); Ernst Benz, *Die Ostkirche im Lichte der protestantischen Geschichtsschreibung von der Reformation bis zur Gegenwart* (Freiburg: K. Alber, 1952); Steven Runciman, *The Great Church in Captivity: A Study of the Patriarchate of Constantinople from the Eve of the Turkish Conquest to the Greek War of Independence* (London: Cambridge University Press, 1968), 247–256; Wayne James Jorgenson, *The Augustana Graeca and the Correspondence between the Tübingen Lutherans and Patriarch Jeremias: Scripture and Tradition in Theological Methodology* (PhD diss., Boston University, 1979); Dorothea Wendebourg, *Reformation und Orthodoxie: Der ökumenische Briefwechsel zwischen der Leitung der Württembergischen Kirche und Patriarch Jeremias II. von Konstantinopel in den Jahren 1573–1581* (Göttingen: Vandenhoeck and Ruprecht, 1986); Zacharias Tsirpanlis, *The Historical and Ecumenical Significance of Jeremias II's Correspondence with Lutherans (1573–1581)* (Göttingen: Vandenhoeck and Ruprecht, 1986); Gerhard Podskalsky, *Griechische Theologie in der Zeit der Türkenherrschaft (1453–1821): Die Orthodoxie im Spannungsfeld der nachreformatorischen Konfessionen des Westens* (München: C. H. Beck, 1988). For an excellent catalog of Crusius's documents, see Thomas Wilhelmi, *Die griechischen Handschriften der Universitätsbibliothek Tübingen: Sonderband Martin Crusius: Handschriftenverzeichnis und Bibliographie* (Wiesbaden: Harassowitz, 2002).

11. For the edition of the diary, see Wilhelm Göz and Ernst Conrad, *Diarium Martini Crusii 1596–1597* (Tübingen: Verlag der H. Laupp'schen Buchhandlung, 1927); Wilhelm Göz and Ernst Conrad, *Diarium Martini Crusii 1598–1599* (Tübingen: Verlag der H. Laupp'schen Buchhandlung, 1931); Reinhold Stahlecker and Eugen Staiger, *Diarium Martini Crusii 1600–1605* (Tübingen: Verlag der H. Laupp'schen Buchhandlung, 1958); Eugen Staiger, *Diarium Martini Crusii. Gesamtregister* (Tübingen: Verlag der H. Laupp'schen Buchhandlung, 1961). For studies of the diary, see Wilhelm Göz, "Martin Crusius und sein Tagebuch," *Literarische Beilage des Staats-Anzeigers für*

Württemberg (1921): 362–370; Reinhold Stahlecker, "Das Tagebuch des Martin Crusius," *Tübinger Blätter* 33 (1942): 25–31; Josef Forderer, "Tübingen am Ende des 16. Jahrhunderts. Interessantes und Amüsantes aus dem Tagebuch des Professors Crusius," *Heimatkundliche Blätter für den Kreis Tübingen* 10, nos. 1–3 (1959): 54–64; Wolfgang Zeller, "Tübinger Universitätsrecht in der Dekade 1596–1605 überliefert von einem Altphilologen," *Attempto* 57–58 (1976): 90–102; and, most recently, Wolfgang Mährle, "Der Tag des Gelehrten. Das „Diarium" des Martin Crusius als frühneuzeitliches Selbstzeugnis," in *Spätrenaissance in Schwaben: Wissen—Literatur—Kunst*, ed. Wolfgang Mährle (Stuttgart: W Kohlhammer GmbH, 2019), 229–247.

12. E.g., Peregrine Horden and Nicholas Purcell, *The Corrupting Sea: A Study of Mediterranean History* (Oxford: Blackwell, 2000); William V. Harris, ed., *Rethinking the Mediterranean* (New York: Oxford University Press, 2006); Eric R. Dursteler, "On Bazaars and Battlefields: Recent Scholarship on Mediterranean Cultural Contacts," *Journal of Early Modern History* 15 (2011): 413–434; Natalie Rothman, *Brokering Empire: Trans-Imperial Subjects between Venice and Istanbul* (Ithaca, NY: Cornell University Press, 2012); Daniel Hershenzon, *The Captive Sea: Slavery, Communication, and Commerce in Early Modern Spain and the Mediterranean* (Philadelphia: University of Pennsylvania Press, 2018).

13. Important exceptions exist of course. See, for instance, Molly Greene, *A Shared World: Christians and Muslims in the Early Modern Mediterranean* (Princeton, NJ: Princeton University Press, 2000), and Molly Greene, "Beyond the Northern Invasion: The Mediterranean in the Seventeenth Century," *Past & Present* 174, no. 1 (2002): 42–71.

14. Carina L. Johnson, *Cultural Hierarchy in Sixteenth-Century Europe: The Ottomans and Mexicans* (Cambridge: Cambridge University Press, 2011). Anthony Grafton has similarly argued that the period's "most vivid accounts of Jewish life and customs" written by Catholic and Protestant authors and even by converts "showed little sympathy for the world they described." Even an emotion as elusive as sympathy, as Alexander Bevilacqua has shown for the Enlightenment study of Islam, "did not always lead to deeper understanding." See Anthony Grafton, "Christian Hebraism and the Rediscovery of Hellenistic Judaism," in *Jewish Culture in Early Modern Europe: Essays in Honor of David B. Ruderman*, ed. Richard I. Cohen, Natalie B. Dohrmann, Adam Shear, and Elchanan Reiner (Pittsburgh, PA: University of Pittsburgh Press, 2014), 169; and Alexander Bevilacqua, *The Republic of Arabic Letters: Islam and the European Enlightenment* (Cambridge, MA: Belknap Press of Harvard University Press, 2018), 2.

15. In arguing for the central role of religion in the study of other cultures, this book contributes to a robust body of Anglophone scholarship. For an erudite overview, see Dmitri Levitin, "Introduction: Confessionalisation and Erudition in Early Modern Europe: A Comparative Overview of a Neglected Episode in the History of the Humanities," in *Confessionalisation and Erudition in Early Modern Europe: An Episode in the History of the Humanities*, ed. Nicholas Hardy and Dmitri Levitin (Oxford: Oxford University Press, 2020), 1–94.

16. Rothman, *Brokering Empire*, 6 (with further references).

17. Fernand Braudel, *The Mediterranean and the Mediterranean World in the Age of Philip II. Volume I. Translated from the French by Siân Reynolds* (New York: Harper and Row, 1972), 17; Peregrine Horden and Nicholas Purcell, *The Corrupting Sea: A Study of Mediterranean History* (Oxford: Blackwell, 2000), 121, 172.

18. The literature is vast. See, for instance, Surekha Davies, *Renaissance Ethnography and the Invention of the Human: New Worlds, Maps and Monsters* (Cambridge: Cambridge University Press, 2016); Yaacov Deutsch, *Judaism in Christian Eyes: Ethnographic Descriptions of Jews and Judaism in*

Early Modern Europe (Oxford: Oxford University Press, 2012); Christine R. Johnson, *The German Discovery of the World: Renaissance Encounters with the Strange and Marvelous* (Charlottesville: University of Virginia Press, 2008); Joan-Pau Rubiés, *Travel and Ethnology in the Renaissance: South India through European Eyes, 1250–1625* (Cambridge: Cambridge University Press, 2000); Anthony Pagden, *European Encounters with the New World: From Renaissance to Romanticism* (New Haven, CT: Yale University Press, 1993); Stephen Greenblatt, *Marvelous Possessions: The Wonder of the New World* (Chicago: University of Chicago Press, 1991).

19. Elizabeth Horodowich, *The Venetian Discovery of America: Geographic Imagination and Print Culture in the Age of Encounters* (Cambridge: Cambridge University Press, 2018), 12.

20. Lorraine Daston and Glenn W. Most, "History of Science and History of Philologies," *Isis* 106, no. 2 (2015): 378–390, at 378.

21. Lorraine Daston, "The Sciences of the Archive," *Osiris* 27, no. 1 (2012): 156–187, at 156.

22. For the study of the patristic corpus in the early modern period, see the articles collected in *Auctoritas patrum: Zur Rezeption der Kirchenväter im 15. und 16. Contributions on the Reception of the Church Fathers in the 15th and 16th Century*, ed. Leif Grane, Alfred Schindler, and Markus Wreidt (Mainz: Phillipp von Zabern, 1993); Irena Backus, ed., *The Reception of the Church Fathers in the West: From the Carolingians to the Maurists*, 2 vols. (Leiden: Brill, 1997); Günther Frank, Thomas Leinkauf, and Markus Wreidt, eds., *Die Patristik in der frühen Neuzeit: Die Relektüre der Kirchenväter in den Wissenschaften des 15. bis 18. Jahrhunderts* (Stuttgart: Frommann-Holzboog, 2006); Jean Louis Quantin, *The Church of England and Christian Antiquity: The Construction of a Confessional Identity in the 17th Century* (Oxford: Oxford University Press, 2009); Katherine Van Liere, Simon Ditchfield, and Howard Louthan, eds., *Sacred History: Uses of the Christian Past in the Renaissance World* (Oxford: Oxford University Press, 2012).

23. Mack Walker, *German Home Towns: Community, State, and General Estate, 1648–1871* (Ithaca, NY: Cornell University Press, 1971).

24. For this revisionist historiography, see Renate Dürr, Ronnie Po-Chia Hsia, Carina L. Johnson, Ulrike Strasser, and Merry Wiesner-Hanks, "Forum: Globalizing Early Modern German History," *German History* 31, no. 3 (2013): 366–382; Renate Dürr, "The World in the German Hinterlands: Early Modern German History Entangled," *Sixteenth Century Journal* 50, no. 1 (2019): 148–155.

25. For a comparable argument in a later (imperial) context, see Emma Rothschild, *The Inner Life of Empires: An Eighteenth-Century History* (Princeton, NJ: Princeton University Press, 2011).

26. For a recent reflection on microhistory (and its connection to the global), see the articles collected in John-Paul Ghobrial, ed., *Global History and Microhistory, Past & Present Supplement 14* (Oxford: Oxford University Press, 2019).

27. Giovanni Levi, "Intervista a Giovanni Levi" in *Microstoria: a vent'anni da L'eredità immateriale; saggi in onore di Giovanni Levi*, ed. Paola Lanaro (Milan: FrancoAngeli, 2011), 169–177, at 175.

28. UBT Mh 466, vol. 7, fol. 91. His contemporaries readily accepted his self-assessment. See UBT Mh 466, vol. 6, fol. 275.

29. E.g., Carla Roth, *The Talk of the Town: Information and Community in Sixteenth-Century Switzerland* (Oxford: Oxford University Press, 2022); Peter Miller, *Peiresc's Mediterranean World* (Cambridge, MA: Harvard University Press, 2015); Matthew Lundin, *Paper Memory: A Sixteenth-Century Townsman Writes His World* (Cambridge, MA: Harvard University Press, 2012).

30. Crusius, *Turcograeciae*, 516.

31. Mary Laven, *Mission to China: Matteo Ricci and the Jesuit Encounter with the East* (London: Faber and Faber, 2011), 30; Erin Maglaque, *Venice's Intimate Empire: Family Life and Scholarship in*

the Renaissance Mediterranean (Ithaca, NY: Cornell University Press, 2018), 19–21; Suzanne Marchand, "Weighing Context and Practices: Theodor Mommsen and the Many Dimensions of Nineteenth-Century Humanistic Knowledge," History & Theory 59, no. 4 (2020): 144–167.

32. Sabine MacCormack, Religion in the Andes: Vision and Imagination in Early Colonial Peru (Princeton, NJ: Princeton University Press, 1991), 6.

33. Sabine MacCormack, On the Wings of Time: Rome, the Incas, Spain, and Peru (Princeton, NJ: Princeton University Press, 2007), xvii. See also Margaret T. Hodgen, Early Anthropology in the Sixteenth and Seventeenth Centuries (Philadelphia: University of Pennsylvania Press, 1964); John Howland Rowe, "The Renaissance Foundations of Anthropology," American Anthropologist 67, no. 1 (1965): 1–20; Anthony Pagden, The Fall of Natural Man: The American Indian and the Origins of Comparative Ethnology (Cambridge and New York: Cambridge University Press, 1982); David A. Lupher, Romans in a New World: Classical Models in Sixteenth-Century Spanish America (Ann Arbor: University of Michigan Press, 2003). Joan-Pau Rubíes, "Travel Writing and Humanistic Culture: A Blunted Impact?," Journal of Early Modern History (2006): 131–168.

1. Christian Purity

1. On Jeremias, see, most recently, Christian Hannick and Klaus-Peter Todt, "Jérémie II Tranos," in La théologie byzantine et sa tradition, ed. Carmelo Giuseppe Conticello and Vassa Kontouma (Turnhout: Brepols, 2002), 2:551–615, with further bibliography.

2. Acta, 143. Two modern translations exist: Wort und Mysterium: der Briefwechsel über Glauben und Kirche 1573 bis 1581 zwischen den Tübinger Theologen und dem Patriarchen von Konstantinopel (Wittenberg: Luther-Verlag, 1958) and George Mastrantonis, Augsburg and Constantinople: The Correspondence between the Tübingen Theologians and Patriarch Jeremiah II of Constantinople on the Augsburg Confession (Brookline, MA: Holy Cross Press, 1982).

3. Georges Florovsky, "An Early Ecumenical Correspondence," in World Lutheranism of Today (1950), 98–111; reprinted as "Patriarch Jeremiah II and the Lutheran Divines," in Collected Works of Georges Florovsky, volume 2, Christianity and Culture (Belmont, MA: Norland Publishing, 1974), 143–155, at 149–150.

4. Walter Engels, "Tübingen und Byzanz: Die erste offizielle Auseinandersetzung zwischen Protestantismus und Ostkirche in 16 Jh," Kyrios 5 (1940–1941): 240–287; Florovsky, "Patriarch Jeremiah II and the Lutheran Divines"; Steven Runciman, The Great Church in Captivity: A Study of the Patriarchate of Constantinople from the Eve of the Turkish Conquest to the Greek War of Independence (London: Cambridge University Press, 1968), 247–256; Wayne James Jorgenson, The Augustana Graeca and the Correspondence between the Tübingen Lutherans and Patriarch Jeremias: Scripture and Tradition in Theological Methodology (PhD diss., Boston University, 1979); Dorothea Wendebourg, Reformation und Orthodoxie: Der ökumenische Briefweschsel zwischen der Leitung der Württembergischen Kirche und Patriarch Jeremias II von Konstantinopel in den Jahren 1573–1581 (Göttingen: Vandenhoeck & Ruprecht, 1986); Zacharias Tsirpanlis, The Historical and Ecumenical Significance of Jeremias II's Correspondence with Lutherans (1573–1581) (Göttingen: Vandenhoeck & Ruprecht, 1986); Gerhard Podskalsky, Griechische Theologie in der Zeit der Türkenherrschaft (1453–1821): Die Orthodoxie im Spannungsfeld der nachreformatorischen Konfessionen des Westens (München: C. H. Beck, 1988).

5. UBT Mh 466, vol. 1, fol. 1–4.

6. Hauptstaatsarchiv Stuttgart A63 Bü44.

7. Hauptstaatsarchiv Stuttgart A63 Bü44.

8. On Gerlach, see Martin Kriebel, "Stephan Gerlach. Deutscher evangelischer Botschaftsprediger in Konstantinopel 1573–1578. Diasporafürsorge in der Türkei und die ersten Beziehungen zur Griechisch-orthodoxen Kirche im 16. Jahrhundert," *Die evangelische Diaspora* 29 (1958): 71–96; Ralf C. Müller, *Prosopographie der Reisenden und Migranten ins Osmanische Reich (1396–1611): Berichterstatter aus dem Heiligen Römischen Reich, ausser burgundische Gebiete und Reichsromania*, 3 vols. (Leipzig: Eudora-Verlag, 2006), 3:46–123; and Richard Calis, "The Lutheran Experience in the Ottoman Middle East: Stephan Gerlach (1546–1612) and the History of Lutheran Accommodation," *English Historical Review* 139, no. 596 (2024): 94–125.

9. UBT Mh 466, volume 1, fol. 5.

10. Robert Kolb, *Andreae and the Formula of Concord: Six Sermons on the Way to Lutheran Unity* (Saint Louis, MO: Concordia, 1977), and Kolb, *Die Konkordienformel. Eine Einführung in ihre Geschichte und Theologie* (Göttingen: Mohr Siebeck, 2011); Jobst Ebel, "Jacob Andreae (1528–1590) als Verfasser der Konkordienformel," *Zeitschrift für Kirchengeschichte* 89 (1978): 78–199; and Rosemarie Müller-Streisand, "Theologie und Kirchenpolitik bei Jakob Andreä bis zum Jahr 1568," *Blätter für württembergische Kirchengeschichte* 60/61 (1960–1961): 224–395.

11. UBT Mh 446, vol. 1, fol. 13–14. Gerlach also describes the audience in his diary: Stephan Gerlach, *Tage-Buch* (Frankfurt, 1674), 363a–b.

12. UBT Mh 466, vol. 1, fol. 4.

13. UBT Mh 466, vol. 1, fol. 15.

14. UBT Mh 466, vol. 1, fol. 7.

15. UBT Mh 466, vol. 1, fol. 149–150.

16. For an insightful case study of a European ambassador's work in the Ottoman capital, see John-Paul Ghobrial, *The Whispers of Cities: Information Flows in Istanbul, London, and Paris in the Age of William Trumbull* (Oxford: Oxford University Press, 2013). For forms of sociability in other parts of the Ottoman Empire, see Helen Pfeifer, *Empire of Salons: Conquest and Community in Early Modern Ottoman Lands* (Princeton, NJ: Princeton University Press, 2022). For the English chaplains in Aleppo, see Simon Mills, *A Commerce of Knowledge: Trade, Religion, and Scholarship between England and the Ottoman Empire, c. 1600–1760* (Oxford: Oxford University Press, 2020).

17. UBT Mh 466, vol. 1, fol. 635, and Gerlach, *Tage-buch*, 159a, 170a, 493b, 385a, 137a, and 155.

18. Gerlach, *Tage-buch*, 115b.

19. Gerlach, *Tage-buch*, 116, 200.

20. *Acta*, 1.

21. *Acta*, 3.

22. *Acta*, 56.

23. *Acta*, 142.

24. *Acta*, 3.

25. UBT Mh 466, vol. 1, fol. 260.

26. UBT Mh 466, vol. 1, fol. 332–334.

27. UBT Mh 466, vol. 1, fol. 499.

28. UBT Mh 466, vol. 1, fol. 83.

29. UBT Mh 466, vol. 1, fol. 448.

30. On the duke and his Church politics, see Wendebourg, *Reformation und Orthodoxie*, 108–111.

31. On clocks as diplomatic gifts in this context, see Otto Kurz, *European Clocks and Watches in the Near East* (London: Warburg Institute, University of London, 1975). Kurz does not mention these ones.

32. Wendebourg, *Reformation und Orthodoxie*, 110–111.

33. Wendebourg, *Reformation und Orthodoxie*, 111–112.

34. UBT Mh 466, vol. 1, fol. 554.

35. UBT Mh 466, vol. 1, fol. 556.

36. UBT Mh 466, vol. 1, fol. 565–566.

37. UBT Mh 466, vol. 1, fol. 597. See also UBT Mh 466, vol. 1, fol. 629 and 605, and Wendebourg, *Reformation und Orthodoxie*, 115.

38. UBT Mh 466, vol. 1, fol. 598, 629.

39. UBT Mh 466, vol. 1, fol. 598.

40. UBT Mh 466, vol. 1, fol. 631.

41. UBT Mh 466, vol. 1, fol. 612–613.

42. UBT Mh 466, vol. 1, fol. 641, 480.

43. UBT Mh 466, vol. 1, fol. 672–677.

44. UBT Mh 466, vol. 2, fol. 73–74.

45. *Concordia ... Christliche Widerholete einmütige Bekentnüs nachbenanter Churfürsten, Fürsten vnd Stende Augspurgischer Confession vnd derselben Theologen Lere vnd Glaubens* (Dresden: Matthes Stöckel & Gimel Bergen, 1580), 229ʳ.

46. UBT Mh 466, vol. 2, fol. 39–43.

47. UBT Mh 466, vol. 2, fol. 142–143. Earlier invitations from the Lutherans for clarifications on their views on the status of scripture had not had the desired effect; see UBT Mh 466, vol. 2, fol. 117, 124–125, and 126.

48. *Acta*, 261.

49. Wendebourg, *Reformation und Orthodoxie*, 131.

50. By comparison, in the almost four years that Gerlach spent in the Ottoman capital, he had sent almost fifty letters to Tübingen. See Wendebourg, *Reformation und Orthodoxie*, 117, 121–122.

51. UBT Mh 466, vol. 2, fol. 392. For a more detailed description of the situation, see Wendebourg, *Reformation und Orthodoxie*, 133.

52. *Acta*, 261–262.

53. *Acta*, 348.

54. *Acta*, 350.

55. *Acta*, 369.

56. *Acta*, 369.

57. *Acta*, 370.

58. UBT Mh 466, vol. 2, fol. 487, 537.

59. UBT Mh 466, vol. 2, fol. 513.

60. UBT Mh 466, vol. 3, fol. 5.

61. UBT Mh 466, vol. 3, fol. 10–11.

62. UBT Mh 466, vol. 3, fol. 12–13.

63. For the episode, as well as the failed attempt to send Weigenmaier to Fez, see Hermann Ehmer, "Die Reise des Tübinger Magisters Valentin Cless nach Nordafrika 1583—Plan oder Wirklichkeit? Zugleich ein Beitrag zu den Anfängen der Arabistik in Deutschland," *Blätter für württembergische Kirchengeschichte* 107 (2007): 139–168.

64. Daniel Benga, *David Chytraeus (1530–1600) als Erforscher und Wiederentdecker der Ostkirchen: Seine Beziehungen zu orthodoxen Theologen, seine Erforschungen der Ostkirche und seine ostkirchlichen Kenntnisse* (Giessen: VVB Laufersweiler Verlag, 2012), 159–162.

65. Martin Luther, *Il catechismo: Translato della lingua todesca in la lingua italiana per Sal. Sveigger, Allamagno Wirt., predicatore del evangelio in Constantinopoli* (Tübingen: Georg Gruppenbach, 1585). On the catechism, see Valdo Vinay, "Die italienischen Übersetzungen von Luthers Kleinem Katechismus," in *Vierhundertfünfzig Jahre lutherische Reformation 1517–1967: Festschrift für Franz Lau zum 60. Geburtstag* (Göttingen, 1967), 384–394, at 387–388; and Luigi Santini, "A proposito di una traduzione italiana del Piccolo Catechismo di M. Lutero," *Nuova Rivista Storica* 49, nos. 5–6 (1965): 627–635. For catechisms and proselytization in the Catholic context, see the articles collected in Antje Flüchter and Rouben Wirbser, eds., *Translating Catechisms, Translating Cultures: The Expansion of Catholicism in the Early Modern World* (Leiden: Brill, 2017).

66. UBT Mh 466, vol. 1, fol. 410–411; UBT Mh 466, vol. 2, fol. 392, 573; and Gerlach, *Tagebuch*, 205. See also Wendebourg, *Reformation und Orthodoxie*, 99, 107, 116.

67. For this revisionist historiography, see Johnson, *Cultural Hierarchy*; Christine R. Johnson, *The German Discovery of the World: Renaissance Encounters with the Strange and Marvelous* (Charlottesville: University of Virginia Press, 2008); Renate Dürr, Ronnie Po-Chia Hsia, Carina L. Johnson, Ulrike Strasser, and Merry Wiesner-Hanks, "Forum: Globalizing Early Modern German History," *German History* 31, no. 3 (2013): 366–382; Renate Dürr, "The World in the German Hinterlands: Early Modern German History Entangled," *Sixteenth Century Journal* 50, no. 1 (2019): 148–155; Stephanie Leitch, *Mapping Ethnography in Early Modern Germany: New Worlds in Print Culture* (Basingstoke: Palgrave Macmillan, 2010); Ulinka Rublack, ed., *Protestant Empires: Globalizing the Reformations* (Cambridge: Cambridge University Press, 2020); Brad Gregory, Ute Lotz-Heumann, and Randall Zachman, "The Global Impact of the Reformations: Longterm Influences and Contemporary Ramifications," *Archiv für Reformationsgeschichte* 108 (2017): 7–11; Philip Benedict, "Global? Has Reformation History Even Gotten Transnational Yet?" *Archiv für Reformationsgeschichte* 108 (2017): 52–62; Richard Calis, "The Impossible Reformation: Protestant Europe and Greek Orthodox Church," *Past & Present* 259, no. 1 (2023): 43–76.

68. Charles H. Parker, "The Reformation in Global Perspective," *History Compass* 12, no. 12 (2014): 924–934.

69. Anthony Grafton, "Comparisons Compared: A Study in the Early Modern Roots of Cultural History," in *Regimes of Comparatism: Frameworks of Comparison in History, Religion and Anthropology*, ed. Renaud Gagné, Simon Goldhill, and Geoffrey Lloyd (Leiden: Brill, 2018), 18–48, at 23.

70. Nicholas Terpstra, "Reframing Reformation: Framing, Mobilizing, and Transcending Religious Difference in Early Modern Europe," in *Reframing Reformation: Understanding Religious Difference in Early Modern Europe*, ed. Nicholas Terpstra (Toronto: Centre for Reformation and Renaissance Studies, 2020), 17–28, at 17.

71. *Acta*, 3.

2. A Lutheran Philhellene

1. Lyndal Roper, *Martin Luther: Renegade and Prophet* (London: Bodley Head, 2016), 9; Arnoud Visser, "Erasmus, Luther, and the Margins of Biblical Misunderstanding" in *For the Sake of Learning: Essays in Honor of Anthony Grafton*, ed. Ann Blair and Anja-Silvia Goeing (Leiden:

Brill, 2016): 2:232–250; and Arnoud Visser, "Irreverent Reading: Martin Luther as Annotator of Erasmus," *Sixteenth Century Journal* 48, no. 1 (2017): 87–109.

2. Guy Stroumsa, *A New Science: The Discovery of Religion in the Age of Reason* (Cambridge, MA: Harvard University Press, 2010); Claudia Brosseder, *The Power of Huacas: Change and Resistance in the Andean World of Colonial Peru* (Austin: University of Texas Press, 2014), 267.

3. Mary Laven, *Mission to China: Matteo Ricci and the Jesuit Encounter with the East* (London: Faber and Faber, 2011), 67 and 21, respectively.

4. UBT Mh 466, vol. 1, fol. 656. The passage is contextualized in Dorothea Wendebourg, "»Alles Griechische macht mir Freude wie Spielzeug den Kindern«. Martin Crusius und der Übergang des Humanismus zur griechischen Landeskunde," in *Graeca recentiora in Germania. Deutsch-griechische Kulturbeziehungen vom 15. bis 19. Jahrhundert*, ed. Hans Eideneier (Wiesbaden: Harrassowitz, 1994), 113–121.

5. Crusius, *Turcograeciae*, 426. Translation in Andreas Rhoby, "The Friendship between Crusius and Zygomalas: A Study of Their Correspondence," *Medioevo Greco: Rivista di storia e filologia bizantina* 5 (2005): 250–267, at 267. See also UBT Mh 466, vol. 2, fol. 292–293. Throughout this book I use "vernacular" and "contemporary" Greek as a shorthand for what Crusius called "barbarograeca," even though linguists nowadays differentiate between different forms of Byzantine, vernacular/colloquial, and modern Greek. For the study of ancient Greek in this particular context, see Walther Ludwig, *Hellas in Deutschland. Darstellungen der Gräzistik im deutschsprachigen Raum aus dem 16. Und 17. Jahrhundert: Vorgelegt in der Sitzung vom 30. Januar 1998* (Hamburg: Joachim Jungius-Gesellschaft der Wissenschaften, 1998), 28–82; and Ben-Tov, *Lutheran Humanists and Greek Antiquity: Melanchthonian Scholarship between Universal History and Pedagogy* (Leiden and Boston: Brill, 2009).

6. UBT Mb 35, fol. 520.

7. He later made a neat copy of these marginalia in another notebook and highlighted which parts contained which bits of information about Greek Orthodox religious practices; see UBT Mb 37, fol. 49ʳ–65ᵛ.

8. UBT Mb 10, third pagination, fol. 181. Parts of this manuscript, as Crusius noted while copying the texts, had been brought to Basel by the Croatian Dominican theologian John of Ragusa, when he presided over the Church Council of Basel. The manuscript is now at Basel University Library, Cod. Basiliensis F. VIII. 4; see Thomas Wilhelmi, "Martin Crusius als Benützer griechischer Handschriften der Universitätsbibliothek Basel," *Codices Manuscripti* 6 (1980): 25–40.

9. UBT Mb 10, third pagination, fol. 187. The reference is to Isaiah 63:3.

10. UBT Mb 10, third pagination, fol. 187.

11. UBT Mb 10, third pagination, fol. 190. Crusius nevertheless remained unaware of the exact history of this piece of writing, which was no ordinary chant, but the so-called *akathist* hymn in honor of Mary the Theotokos, written in the seventh century, according to Byzantine tradition, after Constantinople was saved from invaders through the mediation of Mary.

12. Ὡρολόγιον (Venice: Kunadis, 1584), UBT Gb 580, unpaginated index.

13. Bridget Heal, *The Cult of the Virgin Mary in Early Modern Germany: Protestant and Catholic Piety, 1500–1648* (Cambridge: Cambridge University Press, 2007). No such forms of Marian devotion existed, to the best of my knowledge, in Crusius's Tübingen.

14. Markos Depharanas, Ἱστορία τῆς Σωσάννης (Venice; Giacomo Leoncini, 1569), Dk I 10, second untitled treatise, fol. 5ᵛ.

15. UBT Mc 62, fol. 395. See also UBT Mb 12, second pagination, fol. 242; UBT Mb 12, fol. A-XI^v; and UBT Mb 12, second pagination, fol. 242.

16. UBT Mb 12, first pagination, fol. 46; and UBT Mb 12, first pagination, fol. 87.

17. UBT Mb 12, first pagination, fol. 38.

18. UBT Mb 12, third pagination, fol. 189. See also UBT Mb 12, first pagination, fol. 46, 87, 110, and third pagination, fol. 5, 13, 21, 83, 113, 120, 128, 188.

19. Pietro Martyre Vermigli, *Una semplice dichiaratione sopra gli 12 articoli della fede Christiana* (Basel, 1544); UBT Gf 638, 127, 128. On Vermigli's treatise, see Frank A. James, *Peter Martyr Vermigli and Predestination: The Augustinian Inheritance of an Italian Reformer* (New York: Oxford University Press, 1998), 44–45.

20. Jonathan Sheehan, "Sacred and Profane: Idolatry, Antiquarianism, and the Polemics of Distinction in the Seventeenth Century," *Past & Present* 192, no. 1 (2006): 37–66.

21. David Chytraeus, *Oratio . . . In Qva, De Statv Ecclesiarum hoc tempore in Graecia, Asia, Vngaria, Boëmia etc. narrationes cognitu non inutiles, nec iniucundae, exponuntur* (Wittenberg: Johann Crato, 1575), 14. On Chytraeus and his oration, see Benga, *David Chytraeus (1530–1600) als Erforscher und Wiederentdecker der Ostkirchen*, 76, 114.

22. For Schweigger and Gerlach, see Salomon Schweigger, *Ein newe Reiss Beschreibung auss Teutschland nach Constantinopel und Jerusalem* (Nuremberg: Johann Lantzenberger, 1608), 213; and Gerlach, *Tage-Buch*, 473.

23. Sergiusz Michalski, *Reformation and the Visual Art: The Protestant Image Question in Western and Eastern Europe* (London and New York: Routledge, 1993), 133.

24. Robert Kolb, *For All the Saints: Changing Perceptions of Martyrdom and Sainthood in the Lutheran Reformation* (Macon, GA: Mercer University Press, 1987).

25. Scott H. Hendrix, "Deparentifying the Fathers: The Reformers and Patristic Authority," in *Auctoritas patrum: Zur Rezeption der Kirchenväter im 15. und 16. Contributions on the Reception of the Church Fathers in the 15th and 16th Century*, ed. Leif Grane, Alfred Schindler, and Markus Wreidt (Mainz: Phillipp von Zabern, 1993), 55–68, at 57–58.

26. UBT Mb 12, A-XI^v and B-II^r.

27. UBT Mb 33, fol. 129^r–140^v.

28. UBT Mb 12, second pagination, fol. 242; and UBT Mb 12, B-II^r.

29. UBT Mb 10, fol. 68. For a similar assessment of Philostratus's *vita*, see Noel L. Brann, *Trithemius and Magical Theology: A Chapter in the Controversy over Occult Studies in Early Modern Europe* (Albany: State University of New York Press, 1999), 62–63.

30. John Chrysostom, *Divi Ioannis Chrysostomi, Qvod multae quidem dignitatis, sed difficile sit episcopum agere: dialogi sex* (Tübingen: Morhardus, 1548); UBT Gb 98, blank flyleaf in the back.

31. UBT Mb 12, second pagination, fol. 242: "Chrysostomi vita, plus caeteris me delectavit"; and UBT Mb 12, B-II^r: "Ist schon, und nütz."

32. Martin Crusius, *Poematum Graecorum libri duo . . . Orationum liber unus* (Basel: Johannes Oporinus, 1566), 39.

33. Matthias Flacius Illyricus, *Catalogus testium Veritatis* (Basel: Johannes Oporinus, 1566), A3^{r-v}.

34. Differences in emphasis existed, of course, among different confessions and parties. See Quantin, *Church of England and Christian Antiquity*, passim. Luther himself, for instance, also did not believe that there had been an original time of perfection in the history of the church, though he certainly believed that Christianity had deteriorated over time. See John Headley, *Luther's View of Church History* (New Haven, CT: Yale University Press, 1963).

35. Crusius's copy of Flacius's *Catalogus testium Veritatis* has to my knowledge not survived, but he referenced the work in his annotations to Anna Comnena's *Alexiad*; see Dieter Roderich Reinsch, "Die Editio Princeps eines Auszugs aus der Alexias Anna Komnenes aus dem Jahr 1562; ein unabhängiger Überlieferungsträger," *Byzantinische Zeitschrift* 84/85 (1991/92): 12–16, at 14.

36. Flacius, *Catalogus testium Veritatis*, 33. For an analysis and contextualization of this passage and Flacius's work as a whole, see Irene Backus, *Historical Method and Confessional Identity in the Era of the Reformation (1378–1615)* (Leiden and Boston: Brill, 2003), 343–350.

37. Quantin, *Church of England*.

38. Arnoud Visser, *Reading Augustine in the Reformation: The Flexibility of Intellectual Authority in Europe, 1500–1620* (New York: Oxford University Press, 2011), 4–5.

39. Visser, *Reading Augustine in the Reformation*, 42.

40. Nicholas Naquin, *'On the Shoulders of Hercules': Erasmus, the Froben Press and the 1516 Jerome Edition in Context* (PhD diss., Princeton University, 2013), esp. 61–88.

41. Backus, *Historical Method and Confessional Identity*, 196–252.

42. Paul Eber, *Calendarium historicum: conscriptum . . . et recens . . . auctum. Calendarium Romanum vetus* (Wittenberg: heirs of Georg Rhau, 1559), UBT Fb 18.

43. On Eber's *Calendarium* and its position within the longer tradition of organizing time, see Daniel Rosenberg and Anthony Grafton, *Cartographies of Time: A History of the Timeline* (New York: Princeton Architectural Press, 2010), 74. On the interplay between the Reformation and ordering time, see Robin B. Barnes, "Reforming Time," in *The Oxford Handbook of the Protestant Reformations*, ed. Ulinka Rublack (Oxford and New York: Oxford University Press, 2017), 64–82, esp. 65–69.

44. Philip M. Soergel, *Miracles and the Protestant Imagination: The Evangelical Wonder Book in Reformation Germany* (New York: Oxford University Press, 2012), 101.

45. Virginia Reinburg, *French Books of Hours: Making an Archive of Prayer, c. 1400–1600* (Cambridge: Cambridge University Press, 2012).

46. UBT Mc 223, fol. 12^v, 68^v–71^r. On contemporary interests in the Greek calendar, see Paul Botley, "Renaissance Scholarship and the Athenian Calendar," *Greek, Roman, and Byzantine Studies* 46 (2006): 395–431.

47. Eber, *Calendarium Historicum*; UBT Fb 18, 1 and 49.

48. Stanislav Socolovius, *Censura Orientalis Ecclesiae* (Cracow: Johann Mayer, 1582), ij^v–iij^r.

49. The *Censura Orientalis Ecclesiae* was reprinted in 1583, 1584, and 1591 (the latter as part of Socolovius's *Opera Omnia*).

50. UBT Mh 466, vol. 1, fol. 394. See also Wendebourg, *Reformation und Orthodoxie*, 94, 347.

51. Johann Baptist Fickler, *Censur Oder Urtheil der Orientalischen Kirchen und ihres Patriarchen zu Constantinopel uber die Augspurgische Confession* (Ingolstadt: David Sartorius, 1583). It was reprinted at least once in 1585.

52. Willem Lindanus, *Concordia discors sive querimonia catholicae Christi Jesu Ecclesiae* (Cologne: Arnold Birckmann, 1583).

53. Georg Scherer, *Gewisse und warhaffte Newe Zeytung aus Constantinopel vom Hieremia jetzigen Patriarchen daselbsten, was sein und aller griechischen und orientalischen Kirchen Urtheil und Meynung sey von allen Articuln Augspurgerischer Confession* (Ingolstadt: Wolfgang Eder, 1583); Scherer, *Catholische Glossa oder Erleutterung . . . auff ein Epistel oder Sendschreiben der Ubiquentlerischen Predicanten und Professoren zu Tübingen an Griechische Patriarchen zu Constantinopel* (Ingolstadt: David Sartorius, 1584); Scherer, *Drey Tractaetle . . . von alten erdichteten Maehrlein und gewissen*

warhafften Newzeitungen vom Hieremia Constantinopolitanischen Patriarchen unnd Sendschreiben der Professoren zu Tübingen (Mainz: Caspar Behem, 1585).

54. Jacob Heerbrand, *Ableinung unnd Abfertigung der newen Zeittung auß Constantinopel, so diss 83. Jars zu Wien von einem Jesuiter, wider die Christliche Augspurgische Confession außgesprengt* (Tübingen: Georg Gruppenbach, 1583); and Lucas Osiander, *Warhafftiger Bericht auff die unverschembten Luegen, mutwillige Verkerungen, hoenisch Gespoett und greuliche Lesterungen Georgii Scherers* (Tübingen: Georg Gruppenbach, 1584).

55. *Acta*, ij^r.

56. *Acta*, ij^r.

57. *Acta*, iiij^v, vi^r.

58. Johann Baptist Fickler, *Spongia . . . Schwammen oder Abwischung, etlicher angesprengten Lügen vnnd Lästerung, der jhenigen Wirtenbergischen Predicanten, welche vor etlichen Jaren, dem Patriarchen zu Constantinopel, die Augspurgische Confession, vmb sein Vrtheyl vnd Gutachten, zugeschickt* (Munich: Berg, 1589), 244. Cited in Josef Steinruck, *Johann Baptist Fickler, ein Laie im Dienste der Gegenreformation* (Munster: Aschendorff, 1965), 240. Fickler's own annotated copy of the *Spongia* is Bayerische Staatsbibliothek Munchen, Polem 985. For the translations of the second and third letter, see Johann Baptist Fickler, *Anderer und dritter Theil der Censur und Urtheils dess Patriarchen zu Constantinopel* (Ingelstadt: David Sartorius, 1585). Fickler's own copy of the *Acta* is Bayerische Staatsbibliothek Munchen, Codex Latinus monacensis 731.

59. Thomas Sunobig, *Sententia definitiva Jeremiae Patriarchae Constantinopolitani, de doctrina et religione Wirtembergensium Theologorum* (Trier: widow of Edmond Hatot, 1586); UBT L XIII 24.

60. Jacob Gorski, *Animadversio sive Crusius in theologos Wirtembergenses, sua acta . . . apud Patriarcham Constaninopolitanum iactantes* (Cologne: Maternus Cholinus, 1586); UBT L XIII 24.

61. UBT L XIII 24; Sunobig, preface, 3–4.

62. UBT L XIII 24; Sunobig, preface, 13.

63. UBT L XIII 24; Sunobig, preface, 13.

64. UBT L XIII 24; Socolovius, *Antidotum*, title page.

65. UBT L XIII 24; Socolovius, *Antidotum*, 10.

66. UBT L XIII 24; Socolovius, *Antidotum*, 14.

67. UBT L XIII 24; Socolovius, *Antidotum*, 14, 15, 17, 18, 20, 22, 74.

68. Jorgenson, *Augustana Graeca*, 70.

69. UBT L XIII 24; Socolovius, *Antidotum*, 58.

70. UBT L XIII 24; Gorski, *Animadversio*, 1–2.

71. UBT L XIII 24; Gorski, *Animadversio*, 60.

72. UBT L XIII 24; Gorski, *Animadversio*, title page.

73. UBT L XIII 24; Gorski, *Animadversio*, 6.

74. UBT L XIII 24; Gorski, *Animadversio*, 10.

75. UBT L XIII 24; Gorski, *Animadversio*, 287.

76. On the *fidus interpres*, see Sebastian Brock, "Aspects of Translation Technique in Antiquity," *Greek, Roman, and Byzantine Studies* 20, no. 1 (1979): 69–87; and Werner Schwarz, "Die Bedeutung des 'fidus interpres' für die mittelalterliche Übersetzung," in *Schriften zur Bibelübersetzung und mittelalterlichen Übersetzungstheorie*, ed. Werner Schwarz (Hamburg: Friedrich Wittig Verlag, 1985), 54–57.

77. UBT L XIII 24, front pastedown.

78. UBT L XIII 24, blank flyleaves in the back; and UBT L XIII 24, blank flyleaves in the back.

79. Anthony Grafton and Joanna Weinberg, *"I Have Always Loved the Holy Tongue": Isaac Casaubon, the Jews, and a Forgotten Chapter in Renaissance Scholarship* (Cambridge, MA: Belknap Press of Harvard University Press, 2011); Matthias Pohlig, *Zwischen Gelehrsamkeit und konfessioneller Identitätsstiftung. Lutherische Kirchen- und Universalgeschichtsschreibung 1546–1617* (Tübingen: Mohr Siebeck, 2007).

80. UBT L XIII 24; Gorski, *Animadversio*, 346.

81. For an account of Crusius's life and that of his father, see, in addition to Crusius's own family history, UBT Mh 466; and Albert Gaier, "Pfarrer Martin Krauβ," *Blätter für Wüttembergische Kirchengeschichte* 68/69 (1968/1969): 497–521.

82. UBT Mh 443, vol. 1, fol. 7.

83. UBT Mh 443, vol. 1, fol. 10^r.

84. For two recent, though different, accounts of Luther, his character, and his message, see Andrew Pettegree, *Brand Luther* (New York: Penguin Press, 2015); and Roper, *Martin Luther*.

85. Andrew Pettegree, *Reformation and the Culture of Persuasion* (Cambridge: Cambridge University Press, 2005).

86. For the *Turmerlebnis*, see W. D. J. Cargill Thompson, "The Problems of Luther's 'Tower-Experience' and Its Place in His Intellectual Development," *Studies in Church History* 15 (1978): 187–211; and Roper, *Martin Luther*, 99–101.

87. UBT Mh 443, vol. 1, fol. 10^v.

88. Gerald Strauss, *Luther's House of Learning: Indoctrination of the Young in the German Reformation* (Baltimore and London: Johns Hopkins University Press, 1978). For the debate it initiated, see Gerald Strauss, "The Reformation and Its Public in an Age of Orthodoxy," in *The German People and the Reformation*, ed. Ronnie Po-Chia Hsia (Ithaca, NY: Cornell University Press, 1988), 194–214. For another seminal description of how Luther's message spread, see Robert W. Scribner, *For the Sake of Simple Folk: Popular Propaganda for the German Reformation* (Cambridge: Cambridge University Press, 1981).

89. Paul A. MacKenzie, *Caritas Pirckheimer: A Journal of the Reformation Years, 1524–1528* (Cambridge: D. S. Brewer, 2006).

90. Pettegree, *Reformation and the Culture of Persuasion*, 3.

91. UBT Mh 443, vol. 1, fol. 12^r.

92. UBT Mh 443, vol. 1, fol. 15^r.

93. For the duke's effort to reform the duchy, including Tübingen, see Charlotte Methuen, "Securing the Reformation through Education: The Duke's Scholarship System of Sixteenth-Century Wurttemberg," *Sixteenth Century Journal* 25, no. 4 (1994): 841–851; Charlotte Methuen, *Kepler's Tübingen: Stimulus to a Theological Mathematics* (Brookfield, VT: Ashgate, 1998). On the theology faculty of the university, see Richard Leigh Harrison, *The Reformation of the Theological Faculty of the University of Tübingen, 1534–1555* (PhD diss., Vanderbilt University, 1975); Susan Spruell Mobley, *Confessionalizing the Curriculum: The Faculties of Arts and Theology at the Universities of Tübingen and Ingolstadt in the Second Half of the Sixteenth Century* (PhD diss., University of Wisconsin-Madison, 1998); Ulrich Köpf, *Die Universität Tübingen und ihre Theologen: Gesammelte Aufsätze* (Tübingen: Mohr Siebeck, 2020).

94. UBT Mh 433, vol. 1, fol. 16^v.

95. UBT Mh 443, vol. 1, fol. 17^r.

96. UBT Mh 443, vol. 1, fol. 18^v.

97. Anton Schindling, *Humanistische Hochschule und Freie Reichsstadt. Gymnasium und Akademie in Strassburg 1538–1621* (Wiesbaden: Steiner, 1977); Lewis W. Spitz and Barbara Sher Tinsley, *Johann Sturm on Education: The Reformation and Humanist Learning* (Saint Louis, MO: Concordia, 1995); Matthieu Arnold, ed., *Johannes Sturm (1507–1589): Rhetor, Pädagoge und Diplomat* (Tübingen: Mohr Siebeck, 2009).

98. UBT Mh 443, vol. 1, fol. 18^v.

99. Barbara Stollberg-Rilinger, *The Emperor's Old Clothes: Constitutional History and the Symbolic Language of the Holy Roman Empire* (New York: Berghahn Books, 2015). For school orations in general, see Frederick John Stopp, *The Emblems of the Altdorf Academy: Medals and Medal Orations, 1577–1626* (London: Modern Humanities Research Association, 1974). UBT Mh 443, vol. 1, fol. 21^v.

100. In a letter of recommendation, Sturm was equally praiseworthy of Crusius's capabilities; see UBT Mh 443, vol. 1, fol. 27^v.

101. UBT Mh 443, vol. 1, fol. 19^{r-v}.

102. UBT Mh 443, vol. 1, fol. 19^v–20^r.

103. UBT Mh 443, vol. 1, fol. 20^r.

104. UBT Mh 443, vol. 1, fol. 20^{r-v}.

105. UBT Mh 443, vol. 1, fol. 20^{r-v}.

106. UBT Mh 443, vol. 1, fol. 20^v–21^r.

107. UBT Mh 443, vol. 1, fol. 21^r.

108. UBT Mh 443, vol. 1, fol. 28^v; and UBT Mc 221, fol. 3.

109. UBT Mh 443, vol. 1, fol. 20^v.

110. UBT Mh 443, vol. 1, fol. 14^r. On the Lutheran emphasis on domestic instruction, see Strauss, *Luther's House of Learning,* especially 108–131.

111. Thomas Naogeorgus, *Tragoedia alia nova Mercator seu iudicium, in qua in conspectum ponuntur Apostolica et papistica doctrina* (Ingolstadt, 1540), UBT DK II 132a, title page.

112. Martin Luther, *Jhesus. Das New Testament Deutsch* (Strasbourg: Hans Schotten, 1522–1523), Ga LIII 54-1/2, title page.

113. Martin Luther, *Das Newe Testament* (Wittenberg: Hans Lufft, 1534); UBT Ga LIII 43, title page.

114. UBT Mh 443, vol. 1, 10^v, 12^r, 14^r, 14^v, 15^r, 16^r, 16^v.

115. UBT Mh 443, vol. 1, fol. 10^v, 12^r, 14^r, 16^r. For Crusius's father's reading and note-taking habits, see also *Biblia* (Basel: Froben, 1491), UBT Ga XXXVI 2; and Jerome, *Epistolae* (Basel: Kessler, 1497), UBT Gb 43.2. Crusius adopted various readerly practices of his father: like him, Crusius often recorded how much a book, or the binding of a book, had cost. Both men left lengthy excerpts in the back of their books and turned to the title page to summarize their readings. They also shared an interest in making lists, even recording the names of the men and women who attended their weddings.

116. For preaching in the Lutheran context, see Pettegree, *Reformation and the Culture of Persuasion,* 10–39. For the Catholic context, see Emily Michelson, *The Pulpit and the Press in Reformation Italy* (Cambridge, MA: Harvard University Press, 2013). For preaching in general, John M. Frymire, *The Primacy of the Postils: Catholics, Protestants, and the Dissemination of Ideas in Early Modern Germany* (Leiden and Boston: Brill, 2010).

117. Chrysostom, *Qvod multae quidem dignitatis, sed difficile sit episcopum agere: dialogi sex,* UBT Gb 98, unpaginated blank flyleaf.

118. UBT Mb 19, vol. 6, fol. 11^v. See also Thomas Wilhelmi, *Die griechischen Handschriften der Universitätsbibliothek Tübingen: Sonderband Martin Crusius: Handschriftenverzeichnis und Bibliographie* (Wiesbaden: Harassowitz, 2002), 25–172; and Anthony Grafton, "Martin Crusius Reads His Homer," *Princeton University Library Chronicle* 64, no.1 (2002): 63–86, at 65.

119. Norbert Hofmann, *Die Artistenfakultät an der Universität Tübingen, 1534–1601* (Tübingen: Mohr Siebeck, 1982), 121.

120. Crusius also collected and studied Greek sermons, such as those of Zygomalas and Theophanes the Confessor, to inform himself about various aspects of Greek Orthodox theology.

121. On the *Corona Anni,* see Charlotte Methuen, "Preaching and the Shaping of Public Consciousness in Late Sixteenth-Century Tübingen: Martin Crusius' Corona Anni," *Zeitschrift für Kirchengeschichte* 123 (2012): 173–193.

122. UBT Mh 466, vol. 9, fol. 250. The original letter is Hamburg University Library, 1907.1494,2b.

123. On the sermon as a tool for proselytization, see Emily Michelson, "Conversionary Preaching and the Jews in Early Modern Rome," *Past & Present* 235, no. 1 (2017): 68–104.

124. UBT Mh 466, vol. 9, fol. 483.

125. Wilhelm Göz, "Martin Crusius und das Bücherwesen seiner Zeit," *Zentralblatt für Bibliothekswesen* 50 (1933): 717–737, at 730.

126. UBT Mh 466, vol. 9, fol. 507, 530.

127. Eusebius, *Evangelicae praeparationis libri XV* (Paris: Robert Estienne, 1544), UBT Gb 110.2, title page. See also Crusius's marginal note on page 11. In his summary of Eusebius's *Ecclesiastical History* Crusius made similar claims about the superiority of the Christian religion. See Eusebius, *Ecclesiasticae historiae libri decem* (Paris: Robert Estienne, 1544), UBT Gb 407.2, I.

3. Wandering Greeks

1. UBT Mh 466, vol. 3, fol. 590.

2. UBT Mh 466, vol. 3, fol. 620.

3. See also Natalie Zemon Davis, *Fiction in the Archives: Pardon Tales and Their Tellers in Sixteenth-Century France* (Stanford: Stanford University Press, 1987), 45.

4. Levi, ""On Microhistory", in *New Perspectives on Historical Writing,* ed. Peter Burke (Cambridge, Polity: 1991): 98–99.

5. For a selection of recent studies on this topic, see Nicholas Terpstra, *Religious Refugees in the Early Modern World: An Alternative History of the Reformation* (Cambridge: Cambridge University Press, 2015); Peter Burke, *Exiles and Expatriates in the History of Knowledge, 1500–2000* (Waltham, MA: Brandeis University Press, 2017); Sanjay Subrahmanyam, *Three Ways to Be Alien: Travails and Encounters in the Early Modern World* (Waltham, MA: Brandeis University Press, 2011); Geert H. Janssen, "The Republic of the Refugees: Early Modern Migrations and the Dutch Experience," *Historical Journal* 60, no.1 (2017): 233–252.

6. Bernard Heyberger, "Sécurité et insécurité: les chrétiens de Syrie dans l'espace méditerranéen (XVIIe-XVIIIe siècles)," in *Figures Anonymes, Figures d'Elite: Pour Une Anatomie De l'Homo Ottomanicus,* ed. Meropi Anastassiadou and Bernard Heyberger (Istanbul: Isis, 1999), 147–163;

Bernard Heyberger, "Chrétiens orientaux dans l'Europe catholique (XVIIe–XVIIIe siècles)," in *Hommes de l'entre-deux: parcours individuels et portraits de groupes sur la frontière de la Méditerranée (XVIe–XXe siècle)*, ed. Bernard Heyberger and Chantal Verdeil (Paris: Indes savantes, 2009), 61–93; John-Paul Ghobrial, "The Secret Life of Elias of Babylon and the Uses of Global Microhistory," *Past & Present* 222, no. 1 (2014): 51–93; John-Paul Ghobrial, "Migration from Within and Without: In the Footsteps of Eastern Christian in the Early Modern World," *Transactions of the Royal Historical Society* 27 (2017): 153–173; Hanna Diyab, *D'Alep à Paris: Les pérégrinations d'un jeune Syrien au temps de Louis XIV* ed. and tr. Paule Fahmé-Thiéry, Bernard Heyberger and Jérôme Lentin (Paris: Sindbad, 2015); John Barren, *From Samos to Soho: The Unorthodox Life of Joseph Georgirenes, a Greek Archbishop* (Oxford and Bern: Peter Lang, 2017); Stefano Saracino, "Griechisch-orthodoxe Almosenfahrer im Heiligen Römischen Reich und ihre wissensgeschichtliche Bedeutung (1650–1750)," in *Praktiken frühneuzeitlicher Historiographie*, ed. Markus Friedrich and Jacob Schilling (Berlin and Boston: De Gruyter, 2019), 141–173.

7. Charalampos Chotzakoglu and Christian Gastgeber, "Griechische Mönche in Ungarn. Zwei Dokumente aus dem 17. Jahrhundert über das Sammeln von Almosen und den Einfluß der Unierten am Athos," *Hellenika* 48 (1998): 87–112, at 89. On the *ziteia* more generally, see Eleni Angelomati-Tsoungaraki, "Τὸ φαινόμενο τῆς ζητείας κατὰ τὴ μεταβυζαντινὴ περίοδο," in *Ἰόνιος Λόγος. Τμῆμα Ἱστορίας, Ἰόνιο Πανεπιστήμιο. Ἐπιστημονικὴ περιοδικὴ ἔκδοση. Τόμος Α΄. Τόμος χαριστήριος στὸν Δημήτρη Ζ. Σοφιανό* (Corfu: Kerkyra, 2007), 247–293. On the *fetva* and its effects: Molly Greene, *The Edinburgh History of the Greeks, 1453 to 1774: The Ottoman Empire* (Edinburgh: Edinburgh University Press, 2015), 66.

8. There is one important exception: in a series of articles, José M. Floristán has found evidence of some of Crusius's guests' travels in Italy and Spain; see José M. Floristán, "(Arz) obispos griegos en Roma y España (1596–1602)," *Erytheia* 26 (2005): 187–212; and José M. Floristán, "Basilios ortodoxos y política mediterránea de España," *Erytheia* 28 (2007): 156–157. I would like to thank Cecilia Tarruell for bringing his scholarship to my attention.

9. UBT Mb 37. For a detailed description of this manuscript, see Wilhelm Schmid, *Verzeichnis der griechischen Handschriften der Königlichen Universitätsbibliothek* (Tübingen: G. Schnürlen, 1902), 61–67. Crusius also recorded his interactions with these Greek Orthodox Christians in his diary (UBT Mh 466), albeit in considerably less detail.

10. For the two lists that Crusius made of the Greeks who visited him, see UBT Mb 37, fol. 83ʳ–84ᵛ. In the following I occasionally use "Greeks" as a shorthand to describe these men and women knowing full well that some of them came from Cyprus or other places where local individuals may have identified differently.

11. UBT Mb 37, fol. 85, GH51–52.

12. UBT Mb 37, fol. 85, GH57–76.

13. UBT Mb 37, fol. 85, GH97–99.

14. UBT Mb 37, fol. 85, GH97–99.

15. UBT Mb 37, fol. 85, GH152. See also UBT Mh 466, vol. 3, fol. 286.

16. UBT Mb 37, fol. 85, GH83.

17. UBT Mb 37, fol. 85, GH84.

18. UBT Mb 37, fol. 85, GH84–85.

19. UBT Mb 37, fol. 85, GH85–87.

20. UBT Mb 37, fol. 85, GH9, 11, 14, 19, 88.

21. UBT Mb 37, fol. 85, GH150.

22. Salvatore Bono, *Schiavi: una storia mediterranea (XVI–XIX secolo)* (Bologna: Società editrice Il mulino, 2016), 71–75. See also Daniel Hershenzon, *The Captive Sea: Slavery, Communication, and Commerce in Early Modern Spain and the Mediterranean* (Philadelphia: University of Pennsylvania Press, 2018).

23. UBT Mh 443, vol. 3, fol. 57^v.

24. The literature on this topic is vast. For some perceptive studies, see Linda Colley, *Captives: Britain, Empire and the World, 1600–1850* (London: Jonathan Cape, 2002); Gillian Weiss, *Captives and Corsairs: France and Slavery in the Early Modern Mediterranean* (Stanford, CA: Stanford University Press, 2011); Nabil Matar, *British Captives from the Mediterranean to the Atlantic, 1573–1760* (Leiden: Brill, 2014); and, most recently, Hershenzon, *Captive Sea*.

25. UBT Mb 37, fol. 85, GH159.

26. UBT Mh 466, vol. 2, fol. 366.

27. UBT Mh 466, vol. 3, fol. 462.

28. Greene, *Edinburgh History of the Greeks*. Molly Greene, "Trading Identities: The Sixteenth Century Greek Moment," in *A Faithful Sea: The Religious Cultures of the Mediterranean: 1200–1700*, ed. Adnan A. Husain and K.E. Fleming (Oxford: Oneworld, 2007), 121–148.

29. Colley, *Captives*, 84.

30. UBT Mh 466, vol. 2, fol. 24, 512.

31. UBT Mh 466, vol. 3, fol. 516.

32. UBT Mh 466, vol. 3, fol. 521.

33. UBT Mh 466, vol. 3, fol. 559.

34. UBT Mh 466, vol. 3, fol. 525.

35. UBT Mh 466, vol. 3, fol. 557, 559.

36. UBT Mh 466, vol. 3, fol. 516.

37. *D. Martin Luthers Werke. Kritische Gesamtausgabe. Tischreden 5. Band* (Weimar: H. Böhlaus, 1919), 581.

38. UBT Mh 466, vol. 3, fol. 577–578. On May 13, 1582, a Jew called Solomon was baptized in the *Stiftskirche* (UBT Mh 466, vol. 2, fol. 552). I have not found any other such baptisms among Crusius's records. Nevertheless, throughout the Holy Roman Empire, baptisms of non-Christians were often great spectacles; see Renate Dürr, "Inventing a Lutheran Ritual: Baptisms of Muslims and Africans in Early Modern Germany," in *Protestant Empires: Globalizing the Reformations*, ed. Ulinka Rublack (Cambridge: Cambridge University Press, 2020), 196–227.

39. This kind of apprehension most certainly filled those involved in the efforts to baptize a Jew called Jacob Barnet in Oxford in 1612. For nearly two years this learned rabbi—who was the Hebrew teacher of that other great early modern Hellenist Isaac Casaubon—had received financial support to entice him to embrace Christianity. Yet when the day of his conversion had finally come, he backed out and ran away, much to the dismay of Casaubon and others who felt deceived. See Anthony Grafton and Joanna Weinberg, *"I have always loved the holy tongue": Isaac Casaubon, the Jews, and a Forgotten Chapter in Renaissance Scholarship* (Cambridge, MA: Belknap Press of Harvard University Press, 2011), 253–267.

40. UBT Mh 466, vol. 3, fol. 578.

41. UBT Mh 466, vol. 3, fol. 580. See also UBT Mh 466, vol. 4, fol. 325.

42. UBT Mh 466, vol. 3, fol. 578–587.

43. UBT Mh 466, vol. 1, fol. 719, 724, 728.

44. UBT Mh 466, vol. 3, fol. 298.

45. UBT Mb 37, fol. 85, GH156.

46. UBT Mh 466, vol. 2, fol. 610.

47. Miriam Eliav-Feldon, *Renaissance Impostors and Proofs of Identity* (Basingstoke: Palgrave Macmillan, 2012). Other notable works include Natalie Zemon Davis, *The Return of Martin Guerre* (Cambridge, MA: Harvard University Press, 1983); Natalie Zemon Davis, *Trickster Travels: A Sixteenth-Century Muslim between Worlds* (New York: Hill and Wang, 2006); Miriam Eliav-Feldon and Tamar Herzig, eds., *Dissimulation and Deceit in Early Modern Europe* (Houndmills, Basingstoke, Hampshire: Palgrave Macmillan, 2015). For dissimulation as an agent of secularization, see Jean-Pierre Cavaillé, *Dis/simulations. Jules-César Vanini, François La Mothe Le Vayer, Gabriel Naudé, Louis Machon et Torquato Accetto. Religion, Morale et Politique au XVIIe siècle* (Paris: Honoré Champion, 2002).

48. Jon R. Snyder, *Dissimulation and the Culture of Secrecy in Early Modern Europe* (Berkeley: University of California Press, 2009), xiii.

49. Carlo Ginzburg, *Il Nicodemismo. Simulazione e Dissimulazione Religiosa nell'Europa del' 500* (Turin: Einaudi, 1970); Perez Zagorin, *Ways of Lying: Dissimulation, Persecution, and Conformity in Early Modern Europe* (Cambridge, MA: Harvard University Press, 1990); Eliav-Feldon, *Renaissance Impostors and Proofs of Identity*, 16–67.

50. From the rich historiography on this topic, Lyndal Roper, *Witch Craze: Terror and Fantasy in Baroque Germany* (New Haven, CT: Yale University Press, 2004) remains the best overview. Ulinka Rublack, *The Astronomer & the Witch: Johannes Kepler's Fight for His Mother* (Oxford: Oxford University Press, 2015) offers a particularly perceptive case study of how suspicions of witchcraft could ruin a woman's life, disrupt a town, and break up a family.

51. On travel, credibility, and autopsy, see Percy Adams, *Travelers and Travel Liars, 1660–1800* (Berkeley: University of California Press, 1962); Stephen Greenblatt, *Marvelous Possessions: The Wonder of the New World* (Chicago: University of Chicago Press, 1991); Anthony Pagden, *European Encounters with the New World: From Renaissance to Romanticism* (New Haven, CT: Yale University Press, 1993); Christine R. Johnson, "Buying Stories: Ancient Tales, Renaissance Travelers, and the Market for the Marvelous," *Journal of Early Modern History* 11, no. 6 (2007): 405–446; Surekha Davies, *Renaissance Ethnography and the Invention of the Human: New Worlds, Maps and Monsters* (Cambridge: Cambridge University Press, 2016). On travel as knowledge, see Justin Stagl, *A History of Curiosity: The Theory of Travel, 1550–1800* (Chur: Harwood Academic, 1995).

52. Robert Jütte, *Poverty and Deviance in Early Modern Europe* (Cambridge: Cambridge University Press, 1994).

53. Daniel Jütte, "Entering a City: On a Lost Early Modern Practice," *Urban History* 41, no. 2 (2014): 204–227. For the broader context, see Jason Coy, *Strangers and Misfits: Banishment, Social Control, and Authority in Early Modern Germany* (Leiden: Brill, 2008).

54. UBT Mb 37, fol. 85, GH153.

55. UBT Mb 37, fol. 85, GH52–53, 86.

56. UBT Mb 37, fol. 85, GH158–159.

57. UBT Mb 37, fol. 85, GH154–156.

58. On renegades and conversion to Islam in the early modern Mediterranean, see Davis, *Trickster Travels*; Marc Baer, *Honored by the Glory of Islam* (Oxford: Oxford University Press, 2007); Tijana Krstić, *Contested Conversions to Islam: Narratives of Religious Change in the Early Modern Ottoman Empire* (Stanford: Stanford University Press, 2011); Eric R. Dursteler, *Renegade Women:*

Gender, Identity and Boundaries in the Early Modern Mediterranean (Baltimore, MD: Johns Hopkins University Press, 2011); Tobias P. Graf, *The Sultan's Renegades: Christian-European Converts to Islam and the Making of the Ottoman Elite, 1575–1610* (Oxford: Oxford University Press, 2017).

59. Eric R. Dursteler, "Fearing the 'Turk' and Feeling the Spirit: Emotion and Conversion in the Early Modern Mediterranean," *Journal of Religious History* 39, no. 4 (2015): 484–505.

60. UBT Mh 466, vol. 1, fol. 481.

61. UBT Mb 37, fol. 85, GH9, 89.

62. UBT Mh 466, vol. 3, fol. 363. See also UBT Mb 37, fol. 84^r.

63. UBT Mh 466, vol. 3, fol. 374.

64. Steven Shapin, *A Social History of Truth: Civility and Science in Seventeenth-Century England* (Chicago: University of Chicago Press, 1994); Brendan Dooley, *The Social History of Skepticism: Experience and Doubt in Early Modern Culture* (Baltimore, MD: Johns Hopkins University Press, 1999); Carlo Ginzburg, *History, Rhetoric and Proof* (Hanover, NH: University Press of New England, 1999); Richard Serjeantson, "Testimony and Proof in Early-Modern England," *Studies in History and Philosophy of Science* 30, no. 2 (1999): 195–236; Richard Serjeantson, "Proof and Persuasion," in *The Cambridge History of Science: Volume 3, Early Modern Science*, ed. Katherine Park and Lorraine Daston (Cambridge: Cambridge University Press, 2006), 132–175; Barbara Shapiro, *A Culture of Fact: England, 1550–1720* (Ithaca, NY: Cornell University Press, 2000); Andrea Frisch, *The Invention of the Eyewitness: Witnessing and Testimony in Early Modern France* (Chapel Hill: University of North Carolina Press, 2004); David Randall, *Credibility in Elizabethan and Early Stuart Military News* (London: Pickering and Chatto, 2008); Nicholas Popper, "An Ocean of Lies: The Problem of Historical Evidence in the Sixteenth Century," *Huntington Library Quarterly* 74, no. 3 (2011): 375–400.

65. Simon Ditchfield, *Liturgy, Sanctity, and History in Tridentine Italy: Pietro Maria Campi and the Preservation of the Particular* (Cambridge: Cambridge University Press, 1995), esp. 273–327; Katherine van Liere, Simon Ditchfield, and Howard Louthan, eds., *Sacred History: Uses of the Christian Past in the Renaissance World* (Oxford: Oxford University Press, 2012), 164–230.

66. Rhetorica Ad Herennium 3.10–15; Cicero, De Inventione 26.37–28.43; Quintilian, *Institutio Oratoria* 5.10.23–52. See also Peter Mack, *A History of Renaissance Rhetoric, 1380–1620* (Oxford: Oxford University Press, 2011); and Serjeantson, "Proof and Persuasion," 147–149.

67. Panagiotis Toufexis, *Das Alphabetum vulgaris linguae graecae des deutschen Humanisten Martin Crusius (1526–1607): Ein Beitrag zur Erforschung der gesprochenen griechischen Sprache im 16. Jh.* (Cologne: Romiosini, 2005), 186–187.

68. UBT, Mb 37, fol. 85, GH62.

69. UBT, Mb 37, fol. 85, GH52.

70. UBT Mb 37, fol. 85, GH108–109.

71. Valentin Groebner, *Who Are You? Identification, Deception, and Surveillance in Early Modern Europe*, trans. Mark Kyburz and John Peck (New York: Zone, 2007).

72. Ulinka Rublack, *Dressing Up: Cultural Identity in Renaissance Europe* (Oxford: Oxford University Press, 2010). See also Ann Rosalind Jones and Peter Stallybrass, *Renaissance Clothing and the Materials of Memory* (Cambridge: Cambridge University Press, 2000).

73. On Oporinus, see Martin Steinmann, *Johannes Oporinus. Ein Basler Buchdrucker um die Mitte des 16. Jahrhunderts* (Basel: Helbing and Lichtenhahn, 1967).

74. Crusius, *Germanograecia*, 118.

75. UBT Mh 466, vol. 3, fol. 589.

76. On letters of recommendation, see Antoni Maczak, *Travel in Early Modern Europe*, trans. Ursula Phillips (Cambridge: Polity, 1995), 112; and Heyberger, "Chrétiens orientaux dans l'Europe catholique."

77. UBT Mh 466, vol. 3, fol. 675.

78. UBT Mh 466, vol. 7, fol. 305.

79. UBT Mh 466, vol. 7, fol. 296.

80. Otto Kresten, "Ein Empfehlungsschreiben des Erzbischofs Gabriel von Achrida für Leontios Eustratios Philoponos an Martin Crusius (Vind. suppl. gr. 142)," *Rivista di Studi bizantini e neoellenici* 6–7 (1969–70): 93–125; Hans Gerstinger, "Martin Crusius' Briefwechsel mit den Wiener Gelehrten Hugo Blotius und Johannes Sambucus (1581–1599)," *Byzantinische Zeitschrift* 30 (1929): 202–211.

81. Francesca Trivellato, *The Familiarity of Strangers: The Sephardic Diaspora, Livorno, and Cross-Cultural Trade in the Early Modern Period* (New Haven, CT: Yale University Press, 2009), 177–193, at 181.

82. On the various uses of credit in the early modern period, see Craig Muldrew, *The Economy of Obligation: The Culture of Credit and Social Relations in Early Modern England* (London: Palgrave MacMillan, 1998).

83. Shapin, *Social History of Truth*, xxxv. For a substantial critique of Shapin's model, see Mordechai Feingold, "When Facts Matter," *Isis* 87, no. 1 (1996): 131–139.

84. UBT Mh 466, vol. 7, fol. 298.

85. UBT Mh 466, vol. 7, fol. 305.

86. UBT Mh 466, vol. 8, fol. 211–212.

87. UBT Mb 37, fol. 184.

88. Ghobrial, "Migration from Within and Without," 159. See also Julia Chatzipanagioti-Sangmeister, *Graecia mendax: das Bild der Griechen in der französischen Reiseliteratur des 18. Jahrhunderts* (Vienna: WUV-Universitätsverlag, 2002), for emerging stereotypes of lying Greeks.

4. Household Conversations

1. Lorraine Daston, "The Sciences of the Archive," *Osiris* 27, no. 1 (2012): 156–187.

2. Deborah Harkness, "Managing an Experimental Household: The Dees of Mortlake and the Practice of Natural Philosophy," *Isis* 88, no. 2 (1997): 247–262; Alix Cooper, "Homes and Households," in *The Cambridge History of Science, vol. 3, Early Modern Science*, ed. Katharine Park and Lorraine Daston (Cambridge: Cambridge University Press, 2006), 224–237; Elaine Leong, *Recipes and Everyday Knowledge Medicine, Science, and the Household in Early Modern England* (Chicago: Chicago University Press, 2018).

3. On Monardes, see Daniela Bleichmar, "Books, Bodies, and Fields: Sixteenth-Century Transatlantic Encounters with New World *Materia Medica*," in *Colonial Botany: Science, Commerce, and Politics*, ed. Londa Schiebinger and Claudia Swan (Philadelphia: University of Pennsylvania Press, 2005), 83–99.

4. James de Lorenzi, "Red Sea Travelers in Mediterranean Lands: Ethiopian Scholars and Early Modern Orientalism, ca. 1500–1668," in *World-Building in the Early Modern Imagination*, ed. Allison B. Kavey (Basingstoke: Palgrave Macmillan, 2010), 173–200; Samantha Kelly, *Trans-

lating Faith: Ethiopian Pilgrims in Renaissance Rome (Cambridge, MA: Harvard University Press, 2024).

5. Ronnie Po-Chia Hsia, "Christian Ethnographies of Jews in Early Modern Germany," in *The Expulsion of the Jews: 1492 and After,* ed. Raymond B. Waddington and Arthur H. Williamson (New York: Garland, 1994), 223–236; Ronnie Po-Chia Hsia, "Witchcraft, Magic, and the Jews in Late Medieval and Early Modern Germany," in *From Witness to Witchcraft: Jews and Judaism in Medieval Christian Thought,* ed. Jeremy Cohen (Wiesbaden: Harrassowitz, 1996), 419–434; Mark R. Cohen, "Leone da Modena's Riti: A Seventeenth-Century Plea for Social Toleration of Jews," *Jewish Social Studies* 34, no. 4 (1972): 287–321; Eva Johanna Holmberg, *British Encounters with Ottoman Minorities in the Early Seventeenth Century: "Slaves" of the Sultan* (Basingstoke: Palgrave Macmillan, 2022); Yaacov Deutsch, *Judaism in Christian Eyes: Ethnographic Descriptions of Jews and Judaism in Early Modern Europe* (Oxford: Oxford University Press, 2012).

6. See also Natalie Rothman, "Afterword: Intermediaries, Mediation, and Cross-Confessional Diplomacy in the Early Modern Mediterranean," *Journal of Early Modern History* 19, nos. 2/3 (2015): 245–259, at 247.

7. For these (and other) sites of knowledge making, see the articles collected in Katharine Park and Lorraine Daston, eds., *The Cambridge History of Science, vol. 3, Early Modern Science* (Cambridge: Cambridge University Press, 2006).

8. Peter Burke, *Art of Conversation* (Ithaca, NY: Cornell University Press, 1993).

9. My emphasis on hearing differs slightly from earlier work on orality that focused on the ubiquity of the spoken word and from recent work on aurality and the early modern soundscape that has focused, predominantly, on the sounds and types of music that early modern individuals heard rather than the act of hearing in and of itself. See, for instance, Tess Knighton and Ascensión Mazuela-Anguita, *Hearing the City in Early Modern Europe* (Turnhout: Brepols, 2018); Niall Atkinson, *The Noisy Renaissance: Sound, Architecture, and Florentine Urban Life* (University Park: Pennsylvania State University Press, 2016); and Philip Hahn, "The Reformation of the Soundscape: Bell-Ringing in Early Modern Lutheran Germany," *German History* 33, no. 4 (2015): 525–545.

10. Olga Weijers, *In Search of the Truth: A History of Disputation Techniques from Antiquity to Early Modern Times* (Turnhout: Brepols, 2013).

11. Hyun-Ah Kim, *Music and Religious Education in Early Modern Europe: The Musical Edification of the Church* (Leiden: Brill, 2023).

12. Arnold Hunt, *The Art of Hearing: English Preachers and Their Audiences, 1590–1640* (Cambridge: Cambridge University Press, 2010).

13. Georg Reichert, "Martin Crusius und die Musik in Tübingen um 1590," *Archiv für Musikwissenschaft* 10, no. 3 (1953): 185–212.

14. UBT Mb 37, fol. 12^r. Music was also a common interest of early modern travelers and ethnographers. Peiresc, for instance, talked about the Holy Sepulchre as a place where chants can be compared; see Peter Miller, *Peiresc's Mediterranean World* (Cambridge, MA: Harvard University Press, 2015).

15. Charlotte Methuen, "Securing the Reformation through Education: The Duke's Scholarship System of Sixteenth-Century Württemberg," *Sixteenth Century Journal* 25, no. 4 (1994): 841–851.

16. Carlo Ginzburg, "The Inquisitor as Anthropologist," in Carlo Ginzburg, *Clues, Myths, and the Historical Method,* trans. John and Anne C. Tedeschi (Baltimore, MD: Johns Hopkins

University Press, 1989), 156–164, at 160. Ginzburg's focus is, admittedly, on deepening our understanding of the methods of inquistors by comparing them to anthropologists rather than vice versa. But the comparison works the other way around as well.

17. Mary Louise Pratt, *Imperial Eyes: Travel Writing and Transculturation* (London and New York: Routledge, 1992), 4.

18. Ulrich Moennig, "On Martinus Crusius's Collection of Greek Vernacular and Religious Books," *Byzantine and Modern Greek Studies* 21 (1997): 40–78.

19. UBT Mh 466, vol. 1, fol. 76, 293, 314, 711; UBT Mh 466, vol. 2, fol. 27–28, 292–293, 527. See also Moennig, "On Martinus Crusius's Collection," 47; and Panagiotis Toufexis, *Das Alphabetum vulgaris linguae graecae des deutschen Humanisten Martin Crusius (1526–1607): Ein Beitrag zur Erforschung der gesprochenen griechischen Sprache im 16. Jh.* (Cologne: Romiosini, 2005), 77–86, 101n19. On Severus, see Dimitris G. Apostolopulos, *Gavriil Seviros, arcivescovo di Filadelfia a Venezia, e la sua epoca: atti della giornata di studio dedicata alla memoria di Manussos Manussacas (Venezia, 26 settembre 2003)* (Venice: Istituto ellenico di studi bizantini e postbizantini di Venezia, 2004), with references to earlier literature.

20. UBT Mb 37, fol. 85, GH9. See also UBT Mh 466, vol. 3, fol. 23.

21. For bibliographical details of these works, see Evro Layton, *The Sixteenth Century Greek Book in Italy: Printers and Publishers for the Greek World* (Venice: Istituto ellenico di studi bizantini e postbizantini di Venezia, 1994), 179–183, 183–184, 191–193, 202–203, 226, 231, 241; and Toufexis, *Das Alphabetum*, 324–326, 327–329, 333–334, 346–347. Tübingen's University Library still has three of these four books: the *Flower of Virtue* and the *Apolonios* are bound together with two other Greek texts in UBT DK I 6.4° (1) and the paraphrase of the *Iliad* is UBT Cd 6055 4°.

22. Toufexis, *Das Alphabetum*, 192, 204.

23. Moennig, "On Martinus Crusius's Collection," 67–69.

24. UBT Mh 466, vol. 3, fol. 674.

25. Andreas Kunades, Ἄνθος τῶν Χαρίτων (Venice: Nicolini da Sabbio, 1546), UBT DK I 6 4°, 10.

26. UBT Mb 37, fol. 85, GH51.

27. UBT Mb 37, fol. 85, GH68.

28. UBT Mb 37, fol. 85, GH61 and 160.

29. UBT Mb 37, fol. 85, GH49.

30. The manuscripts in question are UBT Mh 466 and UBT Mb 37, respectively. For the lists, see Aldus Manutius, *Thesaurus cornu copiae* (Venice: Aldus Manutius, 1496). Crusius's copy is currently in the Beinecke Library: BEIN Zi + 5551, copy 3.

31. Toufexis, *Das Alphabetum*, 107ff. For the broader context, see John Considine, *Small Dictionaries and Curiosity: Lexicography and Fieldwork in Post-Medieval Europe* (Oxford: Oxford University Press, 2017).

32. UBT Mb 37, fol. 85, GH10, 88.

33. UBT Mb 37, fol. 85, GH10 and GH18.

34. Crusius, *Turcograecia*, 209. See also UBT Mb 37, fol. 85, GH13.

35. UBT Mb 37, fol. 85, GH10.

36. On Bodin, see Marie-Dominique Couzinet, *Sub specie hominis: Études sur le savoir humain au XVIe siècle* (Paris: Librairie Philosophique J. Vrin, 2007).

37. For the broader context, see John Gallagher, "'To Heare It by Mouth': Speech & Accent in Early Modern Language-Learning," *Huntington Library Quarterly* 82, no. 1 (2019): 63–86.

38. Eric Dursteler, "Speaking in Tongues: Multilingualism and Multicultural Communication in the Early Modern Mediterranean," *Past & Present* 217, no. 1 (2012): 47–77, at 76.

39. John Gallagher, *Learning Languages in Early Modern England* (Oxford: Oxford University Press, 2019).

40. Liam Matthew Brockey, *Journey to the East: The Jesuit Mission to China, 1579–1724* (Cambridge, MA: Harvard University Press, 2007), 244, 246.

41. Miguel León-Portilla, *Bernardino de Sahagún, first anthropologist*, trans. Mauricio J. Mixco (Norman: University of Oklahoma Press, 2002). See also Daniel I. Wasserman-Soler, "Language and Communication in the Spanish Conquest of America," *History Compass* 8 (2010): 491–502.

42. Gerard Wiegers, "A Life between Europe and the Maghrib: The Writings and Travels of Ahmad b. Qâsim al Hajarî al-Andalusî," in *The Middle East and Europe: Encounters and Exchanges*, ed. Geert Jan van Gelder and Ed de Moor (Amsterdam: Rodopi, 1992), 87–115; and Oumelbanine Nina Zhiri, *Beyond Orientalism: Ahmad ibn Qasim al-Hajari between Europe and North Africa* (Oakland: University of California Press, 2023). For the role of moriscos in teaching Arabic beyond the Iberian Peninsula, see Gerard Wiegers, "Moriscos and Arabic Studies in Europe," *Al-Qantara* 31 (2010): 587–610. For the comparable case of the Moroccan diplomat 'Abd al-'Azīz b. Muhammad, who for four months instructed the Dutch professor of Hebrew Jan Theunisz in Arabic, see Dorrit van Dalen, "Johannes Theunisz and Abd Al-Azīz: A Friendship in Arabic Studies in Amsterdam, 1609–1610," *LIAS* 43, no. 1 (2016): 161–189.

43. Martin Crusius, *De Imperatore Romano Friderico Ahenobarbo Vel Barbarossa Oratio* (Tübingen: Georg Gruppenbach, 1593), unpaginated appendix. I would like to thank Janika Päll for bringing this book to my attention.

44. UBT Mb 37, fol. 85, GH19. For other Greek musicians in the Holy Roman Empire, see Nikos Panajotakis, "Griechische Musiker in Deutschland des 16. Jahrhunderts," in *Graeca recentiora in Germania: deutschgriechische Kulturbeziehungen vom 15. bis 19. Jahrhundert*, ed. Hans Eideneier (Wiesbaden: Harrassowitz, 1994), 137–148.

45. Crusius, *Germanograecia*, 237.

46. Πορτολάνος (Venice, 1573), UBT Fa 16a.

47. UBT Mh 466, vol. 2, fol. 334.

48. UBT Mh 466, vol. 3, fol. 527.

49. Πορτολάνος, UBT Fa 16a, 1^b, 1^c, 1^g, 2, and 89.

50. Πορτολάνος, UBT Fa 16a, 55.

51. Πορτολάνος, UBT Fa 16a, 139.

52. Πορτολάνος, UBT Fa 16a, 16^b, 19^v, and 105^e.

53. Πορτολάνος, UBT Fa 16a, 1. The Greek μπούσουλο comes from the Italian *"bussola,"* compass.

54. Πορτολάνος, UBT Fa 16a, final unpaginated page.

55. UBT Mb 37, fol. 85, GH9.

56. UBT Mb 37, fol. 85, GH17.

57. UBT Mb 37, fol. 85, GH63–65. The information is reproduced in Crusius, *Turcograecia*, 207.

58. UBT Mb 37, fol. 85, GH64.

59. UBT Mb 37, fol. 85, GH65.

60. UBT Mb 37, fol. 85, GH90.

61. UBT Mb 37, fol. 85, GH118.

62. UBT Mb 37, fol. 85, GH 90.

63. UBT Mb 37, fol. 85, GH135–136.

64. UBT Mh 466, vol. 3, fol. 369–370.

65. UBT Mh 466, vol. 3, fol. 592.

66. On Buondelmonti, see Benedetta Bessi, "Cristoforo Buondelmonti: Greek Antiquities in Florentine Humanism," *Historical Review/La Revue Historique* 9 (2012): 63–76. For a recent facsimile and translation, see Evelyn Edson, *Cristoforo Buondelmonti. Description of the Aegean and Other Islands, Copied, with Supplemental Material, by Henricus Martellus Germanus: A Facsimile of the Manuscript at the James Ford Bell Library, University of Minnesota* (New York: Italica, 2018). On Fra Mauro, see Piero Flachetta, *Fra' Mauro's World Map: A History* (Rimini: Imago, 2013). On Peiresc, see Peter Miller, *Peiresc's Mediterranean World* (Cambridge, MA: Harvard University Press, 2015).

67. Chorography is a relatively understudied scholarly method. For a preliminary study, see Darrell J. Rohl, "Chorography: History, Theory and Potential for Archaeological Research," in *TRAC 2011: Proceedings of the Twenty First Annual Theoretical Roman Archaeology Conference, Newcastle 2011*, ed. M. Duggan, F. McIntosh, and D. J. Rohl (Oxford: Oxbow, 2012), 19–32.

68. Steven Shapin, "Pump and Circumstance: Robert Boyle's Literary Technology," *Social Studies of Science* 14, no. 4 (1984): 481–520.

69. UBT Mb 37, fol. 85, GH147, 159.

70. For the use of *depingere* and *pingere* in this context, see Mary Carruthers, *The Craft of Thought: Meditation, Rhetoric, and the Making of Images, 400–1200* (Cambridge and New York: Cambridge University Press, 1998), 133.

71. UBT Mb 37, fol. 85, GH163.

72. UBT Mb 37, fol. 85, GH161.

73. UBT Mh 466, vol. 3, fol. 299–301.

74. UBT Mh 466, vol. 3, fol. 299. Eisen was pro-chancellor in Ansbach, a town not too far from Nuremberg, and also the son-in-law of Jacob Heerbrand.

75. For the case of Rome, a city that stimulated such cartographical and antiquarian work like no other, see Ian Verstegen and Allan Ceen, eds., *Giambattista Nolli and Rome: Mapping the City before and after the Pianta Grande* (Rome: Studium Urbis, 2014); Jessica Maier, *Rome Measured and Imagined: Early Modern Maps of the Eternal City* (Chicago: University of Chicago Press, 2015); Pamela O. Long, *Engineering the Eternal City: Infrastructure, Topography, and the Culture of Knowledge in Late Sixteenth-Century Rome* (Chicago: University of Chicago Press, 2018), 113–162.

76. For mapmaking and missionary work, see Mary Laven, *Mission to China: Matteo Ricci and the Jesuit Encounter with the East* (London: Faber and Faber, 2011), 22–28; and Florin-Stefan Morar, "The Westerner: Matteo Ricci's World Map and the Quandaries of European Identity in the Late Ming Dynasty," *Journal of Jesuit Studies* 6 (2019): 14–30.

77. Crusius, *Turcograecia*, 188.

78. Crusius, *Turcograecia*, 188.

79. Ulrike Ilg, "The Cultural Significance of Costume Books in Sixteenth-Century Europe," in *Clothing Culture, 1350–1650*, ed. Catharine Richardson (Aldershot and Burlington, VT: Ashgate 2004), 29–47. In addition to the materials Gerlach provided, Crusius also owned at least one (sadly unannotated) costume book: Jacobus Sluperius, *Omnium Fere Gentium, nostraeque aetatis Nationum, Habitus & Effigies* (Antwerp: Johannes Bellerus, 1572), UBT Fq 99.

80. For some perceptive case studies, see Eva Johanna Holmberg, *Jews in the Early Modern English Imagination: A Scattered Nation* (Farnham: Ashgate, 2011); Chandra Mukerji, "Costume and Character in the Ottoman Empire: Dress as Social Agent in Nicolay's *Navigations*," in *Early*

Modern Things: Objects and Their Histories, 1500–1800, ed. Paula Findlen (London: Routledge, 2013), 151–169; and Robyn Dora Radway, *Paper Portraits of Empire: Habsburg Albums from the German House in Constantinople* (Bloomington: Indiana University Press, 2023).

81. UBT Mb 37, fol. 85, GH10, GH12, and GH13.
82. UBT Mb 37, fol. 85, GH142.
83. UBT Mb 37, fol. 84^v.
84. UBT Mb 37, fol. 85, GH140.
85. UBT Mb 37, fol. 85, GH51.
86. UBT Mb 37, fol. 85, GH100, 120.
87. Toufexis, *Das Alphabetum*, 239.
88. UBT Mb 37, fol. 85, GH75.
89. UBT Mb 37, fol. 85, GH12.
90. UBT Mb 37, fol. 85, GH149.
91. Gabriele Jancke, *Gastfreundschaft in der frühneuzeitlichen Gesellschaft: Praktiken, Normen und Perspektiven von Gelehrten* (Göttingen: V & R Unipress, 2013), esp. 339–345.
92. Steven Shapin, "The Philosopher and the Chicken: On the Dietetics of Disembodied Knowledge," in *Science Incarnate: Historical Embodiments of Natural Knowledge*, ed. Christopher Lawrence and Steven Shapin (Chicago: University of Chicago Press, 1998), 21–50; Steven Shapin, "'You Are What You Eat': Historical Changes in Ideas about Food and Identity," *Historical Research* 87, no. 237 (2014): 377–392; Gadi Algazi, "Food for Thought: Hieronymus Wolf Grapples with the Scholarly Habitus," in *Egodocuments and History: Autobiographical Writing in Its Social Context since the Middle Ages*, ed. Rudolf Dekker (Hilversum: Verloren, 2002), 21–43.
93. Algazi, "Food for Thought," 25. For the ideals of the republic of letters, see Kathy Eden, *Friends Hold All Things in Common: Tradition, Intellectual Property and the "Adages" of Erasmus* (New Haven, CT: Yale University Press, 2001).
94. Gadi Algazi, "Scholars in Households: Refiguring the Learned Habitus, 1480–1550," *Science in Context* 16, nos. 1–2 (2003): 9–42.
95. Charlotte Methuen, "Securing the Reformation through Education: The Duke's Scholarship System of Sixteenth-Century Württemberg," *Sixteenth Century Journal* 25, no. 4 (1994): 841–885, at 844. On the Collegium, see Rudolf von Roth, *Urkunden zur Geschichte der Universität Tübingen aus den Jahren 1476 bis 1550* (Tübingen: Laupp, 1877), 179; Eugen von Schneider, *Das Tübinger Collegium illustre* (Stuttgart: Kohlhammer, 1898); August Willburger, *Das Collegium illustre zu Tübingen* (Tübingen: Verlag des Bürgervereins, 1912); Gerhard Rauscher, *Das Collegium Illustre zu Tübingen und die Anfänge des Unterrichts in den neueren Fremdsprachen: unter besonderer Berücksichtigung des Englischen 1610–1817* (PhD diss., University of Tübingen, 1957).
96. Gadi Algazi, "Scholars in Households," 18.
97. UBT Mh 443, vol. 1, fol. 49^{r-v}. She died on August 16, 1561. The last boarder lived with Crusius until October 1562.
98. UBT Mh 443, vol. 1, fol. 59^v.
99. UBT Mh 443, vol. 1, fol. 61^v.
100. Veit Müller, *Oratio de vita et obitu . . . Martini Crusii* (Tübingen: Philipp Gruppenbach, 1608), 21. Crusius also mentioned in his diary that he was very lonely after the death of his third wife: UBT Mh 466, volume 7, fol. 495.
101. On marrying locally, see Algazi, "Scholars in Households," 20. On the families of Catharina Vogler and Catharina Vetscher, see UBT Mh 443, vol. 1, fol. 51^v and fol. 61^v, respectively.

Esslingen was a town with which Tübingen maintained close ties: the university moved there twice when the plague had erupted in Tübingen.

102. Felicity Heal, *Hospitality in Early Modern England* (Oxford: Clarendon, 1990), 391.

103. A case in point is the home of John and Jane Dee, one of the few early modern scholarly households that has been studied in some considerable depth. In their case, natural philosophy moved into the home and prompted a rearrangement of the domestic space, in which Jane Dee had to guarantee that her husband had his own private quarters to engage in his experiments and angelic conversations with the scryer Edward Kelley, while making sure that these activities remained hidden from the public gaze; see Harkness, "Managing an Experimental Household."

104. These conversations in the Lutherhaus came to be known as Luther's *Table Talk* (*Tischreden*). For an excellent selection from the *Tischreden*, see Susan C. Karant-Nunn and Merry E. Wiesner-Hanks, *Luther on Women: A Sourcebook* (Cambridge: Cambridge University Press, 2003). For the records of these and similar conversations as a genre, see Francine Wild, *Naissance du genre des Ana* (1574–1712) (Paris: Champion, 2001).

105. UBT Mh 466, vol. 6, fol. 751, 821, 826; and vol. 7, fol. 477, 495. His wife also managed parts of the household's finances; see UBT Mh 466, vol. 5, fol. 683.

106. UBT Mb 37, fol. 85, GH67.

107. Barbara Hagelloch, the maid who called Crusius back from the Österberg to welcome the archbishop of Ohrid, is the only servant whom I have been able to identify by name. For the fame that Crusius and his hospitality enjoyed in contemporary Greece, see UBT Mb 37, fol. 85, GH130; UBT Mh 466, vol. 3, fol. 512; and UBT Mb, 37 fol. 85, GH164.

108. Harkness, "Managing an Experimental Household," 251.

109. Sarah Gwyneth Ross, *The Birth of Feminism: Woman as Intellect in Renaissance Italy and England* (Cambridge, MA: Harvard University Press, 2009).

110. Leong, *Recipes and Everyday Knowledge*. For a similar study of Enlightenment scholars and their families, see Meghan K. Roberts, *Sentimental Savants: Philosophical Families in Enlightenment France* (Chicago: University of Chicago Press, 2016).

111. For Protestant reading households, see Femke Molekamp, *Women and the Bible in Early Modern England: Religious Reading and Writing* (Oxford: Oxford University Press, 2013). For madrigal singing, see Susan Hammond, *Editing Music in Early Modern Germany* (Aldershot: Ashgate, 2007).

112. Lyndal Roper, *The Holy Household: Women and Morals in Reformation Augsburg* (Oxford: Clarendon, 1989), 1.

113. UBT Mh 466, vol. 3, fol. 589.

114. UBT Mh 466, vol. 6, fol. 326.

115. UBT Mb 37, fol. 85, GH53 and GH142.

116. Jason Scott-Warren, *Sir John Harington and the Book as Gift* (Oxford: Oxford University Press, 2001). For the broader context, see Natalie Zemon Davis, *The Gift in Sixteenth-Century France* (Madison: University of Wisconsin Press, 2000).

117. UBT Mb 37, fol. 85, GH141. For the *Civitas Coelestis*, also known by its Greek title Πολίτευμα οὐράνιον, see Martin Crusius, *Πολίτευμα οὐράνιον . . . Civitas Coelestis, seu Catecheticae conciones* (Tübingen: Georg Gruppenbach, 1587).

118. UBT Mh 466, vol. 3, fol. 420.

119. UBT Mh 466, vol. 3, fol. 527.

120. UBT Mh 466, vol. 3, fol. 418.

121. UBT Mb 37, fol. 85, GH63.

122. UBT Mb 37, fol. 85, GH147.

123. Donatus received this portrait in 1579; Andreas and Lukas Argyrus in 1581. Mauricius also received a portrait, a Greek epithalamium on the marriage of Duke Ludwig III, and some money. See, respectively, UBT Mb 37, fol. 85, GH53, 67 and GH159. I have found the same portrait in the following books and manuscripts: UBT Mb 12; UBT Mb 13; UBT Mb 14; UBT Mb 18; UBT Mb 20; UBT Mb 35; UBT Mc 62; UBT Mh 466 (vol. 1); and UBT Cd 855 ½ 2.2.

124. Andrea von Hülsen-Esch, *Gelehrte im Bild: Repräsentation, Darstellung und Wahrnehmung einer sozialen Gruppe im Mittelalter* (Göttingen: Vandenhoeck & Ruprecht, 2006); Ulinka Rublack, *Dressing Up: Cultural Identity in Renaissance Europe* (Oxford: Oxford University Press, 2010), 99–101.

125. The inscription reads: "Μαρτῖνος Κρούσιος ἐν Τυβιγγῃ Διδάσκ. ἔτει ἡλικ. ΝΒ΄ 1578." On the importance of beards, see Will Fisher, "The Renaissance Beard: Masculinity in Early Modern England," *Renaissance Quarterly* 54, no.1 (2001): 155–187.

126. UBT Mb 37, fol. 85, GH53, GH67. Crusius often used quotations from this psalm when his visitors left. See UBT, Mb 37, fol. 85, GH53 and GH142.

127. UBT Mb 37, fol. 85, GH89–90.

128. UBT Mb 37, fol. 85, GH53 and GH67.

129. UBT Mb 37, fol. 85, GH150.

130. UBT Mb 37, fol. 85, GH119.

131. UBT Mh 466, vol. 2, fol. 289.

132. Werner Wilhelm Schnabel, *Das Stammbuch. Konstitution und Geschichte einer textsortenbezogenen Sammelform bis ins erste Drittel des 18. Jahrhunderts* (Tübingen: Niemeyer, 2003). For a beautiful analysis of the themes of intimacy and friendship in such *alba amicorum*, see Marisa Anne Bass, *Insect Artifice: Nature and Art in the Dutch Revolt* (Princeton, NJ: Princeton University Press, 2019), ch. 4.

133. UBT Mh 466, vol. 3, fol. 422. In 1585 Crusius left a note of recommendation in Johannes Tholoitis's notebook; see UBT Mb 37, fol. 85, GH151. Crusius also exchanged *alba* with his colleagues and acquaintances and signed them. See UBT, Mh 466, vol. 2, fol. 633–634.

134. B. A. Mystakides, "Notes sur Martin Crusius: ses livres, ses ouvrages et ses manuscrits," *Revue des Études Grecques* 11 (1898): 279–306, at 294.

135. Gadi Algazi, "Introduction: Doing Things with Gifts," in *Negotiating the Gift: Pre-Modern Figurations of Exchange*, ed. Gadi Algazi, Valentin Groebner, and Bernhard Jussen (Göttingen: Vandenhoeck & Ruprecht, 2003), 9–27.

136. UBT Mh 466, vol. 3, fol. 674–675; UBT Mh 466, vol. 4, fol. 636; UBT Mb 37 fol. 85, GH88.

137. See, for instance, UBT Mb 37, fol. 85, GH142.

138. UBT Mh 466, vol. 7, fol. 303–304.

139. See also UBT Mh 466, vol. 2, fol. 556.

140. Daniel Jütte, *The Age of Secrecy: Jews, Christians, and the Economy of Secrets, 1400–1800*, trans. from German by Jeremiah Riemer (New Haven, CT, and London: Yale University Press, 2015), 207.

141. Eusebius, *Ecclesiasticae historiae libri decem*, UBT Gb 407, 13^v.

142. For Crusius's study of Hebrew, see the scant notes in Manfred Faust, "Die Mehrsprachigkeit des Humanisten Martin Crusius," in *Homenaje a Antonio Tovar* (Madrid: Gredos, 1972), 137–149.

His (lack of) progress is evident from the marginal notes that he left in his Hebrew grammars. For the murder trials, see Ronnie Po-chia Hsia, *The Myth of Ritual Murder: Jews and Magic in Reformation Germany* (New Haven, CT: Yale University Press, 1988).

5. Communities of Experts

1. For a similar argument about sixteenth-century physicians, see Nancy G. Siraisi, *Communities of Learned Experience: Epistolary Medicine in the Renaissance* (Baltimore, MD: Johns Hopkins University Press, 2013). For the history of expertise as well as debates about the application of this idea to the early modern world, see Eric H. Ash, "By Any Other Name: Early Modern Expertise and the Problem of Anachronism," *History and Technology: An International Journal* 35 (2019): 3–30; and Eric H. Ash, "Introduction: Expertise and the Early Modern State," *Osiris* 25 (2010): 1–24. For the use of anachronism in history, Nick Jardine, "Uses and Abuses of Anachronism in the History of the Sciences," *History of Science* 38 (2000): 251–270.

2. The literature is vast. For an overview of these changes, see Matthias Asche and Stefan Gerber, "Neuzeitliche Universitätsgeschichte in Deutschland—Entwicklungslinien und Forschungsfelder," *Archiv für Kulturgeschichte* 90 (2008): 159–201; Stefan Ehrenpreis, "Frühneuzeitliche Universitätsgeschichte—Leistungen und Defizite der Deutschen Forschung seit 1990," *Jahrbuch für Universitätsgeschichte* 6 (2003): 262–266; Helga Robinson-Hammerstein, "Recent Research on the History of Universities in the Early Modern Period," *Bulletin of the German Historical Institute London* 20, no. 2 (1998): 5–31. For some perceptive case studies, see Anton Schindling, *Humanistische Hochschule und freie Reichsstadt—Gymnasium und Akademie in Straßburg 1538 bis 1621* (Wiesbaden: Franz Steiner, 1977); Anthony Grafton and Lisa Jardine, *From Humanism to the Humanities: Education and the Liberal Arts in Fifteenth- and Sixteenth-Century Europe* (London: Duckworth, 1986); Gadi Algazi, "Scholars in Households: Refiguring the Learned Habitus, 1480–1550," *Science in Context* 16, nos. 1–2 (2003); Richard Kirwan, ed., *Scholarly Self-Fashioning and Community in the Early Modern University* (Farnham, Surrey, and Burlington, VT: Ashgate, 2013).

3. Mack Walker, *German Home Towns: Community, State, and General Estate, 1648–1871* (Ithaca, NY: Cornell University Press, 1971). See also Erving Goffman, *The Presentation of Self in Everyday Life* (Woodstock, NY: Overlook, 1973).

4. For the history of the University of Tübingen, see Hansmartin Decker-Hauff, Gerhard Fichtner, and Klaus Schreiner, *Beiträge zur Geschichte der Universität Tübingen: 1477–1977* (Tübingen: Attempto-Verlag, 1977); Walter Jens, *Eine deutsche Universität: 500 Jahre Tübinger Gelehrtenrepublik* (München: Kindler, 1977); Waldemar Teufel, *Universitas Studii Tuwingensis: Die Tübinger Universitätsverfassung in vorreformatorischer Zeit (1477–1534)* (Tübingen: Mohr, 1977). For the UNESCO bid, see W. T. M. Frijhoff, *University Town of Tübingen. Report on the application of Tübingen for the UNESCO World heritage list / Universitätsstadt Tübingen. Gutachten zur Bewerbung Tübingens um Aufnahme in die Unesco Welterbeliste* (Tübingen: Magistrat der Universitätsstadt, 2013).

5. UBT Mh 466, vol. 7, fol. 56, 328, 355.

6. UBT Mh 466, vol. 9, fol. 71.

7. UBT Mh 466, vol. 5, fol. 707.

8. UBT Mh 466, vol. 8, fol. 417, 505; and UBT Mh 466, vol. 9, fol. 347, 449, 456.

9. Gudrun Emberger, *Ain ewig Stipendium. Das Collegium Sanctorum Georgii et Martini— Eine Tübinger Studienstiftung des 16. Jahrhunderts* (Göttingen: V&R Unipress, 2013); and Gudrun

Emberger, "Kehrwoche und Festschmaus. Gemeinschaftsleben im Tübinger Stipendium Martinianum im 16. Jahrhundert," in *Gastlichkeit und Geselligkeit im akademischen Milieu in der Frühen Neuzeit,* ed. Kirsten Bernhardt, Barbara Krug-Richter, and Ruth-E. Mohrmann (Münster and New York: Waxmann, 2013).

10. UBT Mh 466, vol. 5, fol. 679; UBT Mh 466, vol. 8, fol. 182, 208, 238, 250, 259, 262, 270, 280, 287, 324, 589; UBT Mh 466, vol. 9, fol. 68, 74, 85, 118, 307, 439; and UBT Mh 198, fol. 93, 103.

11. UBT Mh 466, vol. 9, fol. 74.

12. UBT Mh 466, vol. 3, fol. 517–518.

13. UBT Mh 160, fol. 14. See also Wilhelm Schmid, "Eine Fußwanderung des Martin Crusius von Tübingen auf den Hohenstaufen Pfingsten 1588," *Württembergische Vierteljahreshefte für Landesgeschichte* 27 (1918): 14–33; Alfons Nitsch, "Martin Crusius: Eine Fußwanderung von Tübingen auf den Hohenstaufen und nach Lorch vor 371 Jahren," *Gmünder Heimatblätter* 20, no. 6 (1959): 46–47; and Wilhelm Schmid, "Martin Crusius: Eine Fußwanderung von Tübingen auf den Hohenstaufen und nach Lorch vor 371 Jahren," *Gmünder Heimatblätter* 20, no. 7 (1959): 49–51.

14. Filippo de Vivo, "Walking in Sixteenth-Century Venice: Mobilizing the Early Modern City," *I Tatti Studies in the Italian Renaissance* 19 (2016): 115–141, at 116.

15. UBT Mh 466, vol. 8, fol. 280.

16. Crusius frequently notes in his diary how he returned from such meals sober; see, for instance, UBT Mh 466, vol. 9, fol. 237.

17. Charlotte Methuen, *Kepler's Tübingen: Stimulus to a Theological Mathematics* (Brookfield, VT: Ashgate, 1998); Richard Leigh Harrison, *The Reformation of the Theological Faculty of the University of Tübingen, 1534–1555* (PhD diss., Vanderbilt University, 1975); Susan Spruell Mobley, *Confessionalizing the Curriculum: The Faculties of Arts and Theology at the Universities of Tübingen and Ingolstadt in the Second Half of the Sixteenth Century* (PhD diss., University of Wisconsin-Madison, 1998); and Ulrich Köpf, *Die Universität Tübingen und ihre Theologen: Gesammelte Aufsätze* (Tübingen: Mohr Siebeck, 2020).

18. UBT Mh 466, vol. 2, fol. 558.

19. For European encounters with the Mesoamerican codex, see Daniela Bleichmar, "Translation, Mobility, and Mediation: The Case of the Codex Mendoza," in *Sites of Mediation: Connected Histories of Places, Processes, and Objects in Europe and Beyond, 1450–1650*, ed. Susanna Burghartz, Lucas Burkart, Christine Göttler (Leiden: Brill, 2016), 240–269. For Europeans making sense of Egyptian hieroglyphs, see Anthony Grafton, "Kircher's Chronology," in *Athanasius Kircher: The Last Man Who Knew Everything*, ed. Paula Findlen (New York: Routledge, 2004), 171–187. On responses to Chinese documentary records, see Edwin J. Van Kley, "Europe's 'Discovery' of China and the Writing of World History," *American Historical Review* 76, no. 2 (1971): 358–385 and Alexander Statman, *A Global Enlightenment: Western Progress and Chinese Science* (Chicago: Chicago University Press, 2023).

20. UBT Mh 466, vol. 1, fol. 591.

21. Ἀπολλώνιος (Venice, 1564), UBT Dk I 6.4, title page.

22. UBT Mb 10, third pagination, fol. 192. The original is Basel University Library, Cod. Bas. F VIII 4. For a similar description, see UBT Mb 12, third pagination, fol. 1.

23. Ioannikios Kartaros, Ἡ Παλαιά τε καὶ Νέα Διαθήκη (Venice, 1536); UBT Ge 1179; and Damascenus Studites, Βιβλίον ὀνομαζόμενον Θυσαυρός (Venice, 1570); UBT Gi 288.4. In actuality, only the latter has a Greek style binding. I would like to thank Anna Gialdini for pointing this out to me.

24. UBT Mb 37, fol. 6ᵛ; and UBT Mb 13, fol. 520.
25. UBT Mb 12, second pagination, fol. 242.
26. UBT Mb 12, B-IIʳ.
27. UBT Mb 37, fol. 149, pencil pagination 34ᵛ.
28. Silvia Rizzo, *Il lessico filologico degli umanisti* (Rome: Edizioni di storia e letteratura, 1973).
29. UBT Mb 14, fol. 362. Crusius's copy of that other manuscript is UBT Mb 34.
30. UBT Mb 12, first pagination, fol. 292.
31. Thucydides, *Histories*, 6.54.6. I would like to thank Mathieu de Bakker for bringing this passage to my attention.
32. UBT Mb 37, fol. 149, pencil pagination 42ʳ.
33. UBT Mc 62, fol. 382.
34. UBT Mb 10, third pagination, fol. 1; and UBT Mb 13, fol. 520. See also UBT Mb 37, fol. 141ᵛ.
35. For Valla and Poliziano, see Anthony Grafton, "On the Scholarship of Politian and Its Context," *Journal of the Warburg and Courtauld Institutes* 40 (1977): 150–188 and Sebastiano Timpanaro, *La genesi del metodo del Lachmann* (Turin: UTET Università, 2010), 15–21. For the broader context, see Carlotta Dionisotti, "From Stephanus to Du Cange: Glossary Stories," *Revue d'histoire des textes* 14–15 (1984–85): 303–336.
36. UBT Mb 12, B-IIʳ; and UBT Mc 62, second pagination, fol. 16. See also UBT Mb 12, first pagination, fol. 185; UBT Mb 12, second pagination, fol. 12, 153; UBT Mb 12, third pagination, fol. 261.
37. UBT Mc 62, first pagination, fol. 153.
38. For similar detective work by modern scholars, see Kathryn M. Rudy, *Piety in Pieces: How Medieval Readers Customized Their Manuscripts* (Cambridge: Open Book, 2016).
39. Bayerische Staatsbibliothek Munich, Cod. Graec. 141, rear pastedown. It was a detail so important that he even included it in the *Turcograecia*; see Crusius, *Turcograecia*, 190. For Gerlach's response, see UBT Mh 466, vol. 1, fol. 600.
40. UBT Mh 466, vol. 1, fol. 52, 470.
41. UBT Mb 37, fol. 149, pencil pagination, 27ᵛ.
42. UBT Mh 466, vol. 2, fol. 505. The original document was reproduced in the travelogue that Schweigger published in 1608. See Schweigger, *Ein newe Reiss Beschreibung*, 233. At various moments in his life, Crusius confessed he was incapable of reading similar documents in Arabic and Syriac. See, for instances, the notes and sketches that he left in UBT Mb 37, fol. 149, pencil pagination, 70ʳ.
43. UBT Ma VI 214, fol. Iʳ.
44. UBT Ma VI 214, fol. 55ʳ.
45. UBT Ma VI 214, fol. 1ᵛ. For a description of the manuscript (which also contains Arabic and Turkish prayers), see Max Weisweiler, *Verzeichnis der Arabischen Handschriften II* (Leipzig: Verlag von Otto Harrassowitz, 1930), 139–140.
46. Béatrice Fraenkel, *La signature: genèse d'un signe* (Paris: Gallimard, 1992).
47. UBT Mh 466, vol. 1, fol. 464.
48. UBT Mh 466, vol. 1, fol. 396.
49. UBT Mb 37, fol. 149, pencil pagination, 67ᵛ, 69ʳ. The word order of one transcription is incorrect. I would like to thank Feras Krimsti for transcribing and explaining the Arabic to me.
50. UBT Mb 37, fol. 11ᵛ; UBT Mb 30, fol. 89; UBT Mb 35, fol. V; UBT Mb 36, fol. 339.

51. Jason Scott-Warren, "Reading Graffiti in the Early Modern Book," *Huntington Library Quarterly* 73 (2010): 363–381, at 371. See also Ann Blair, "Early Modern Attitudes toward the Delegation of Copying and Note-taking," in *Forgetting Machines: Knowledge Management in Early Modern Europe*, ed. Alberto Cevolini (Leiden and Boston: Brill, 2016), 265–285.

52. For humanist experiments with latinized and hellenized names, and with adding toponyms to their signatures, see Reinhard Bodenmann, "L'auteur et son nom de plume. Autopsie d'un choix. Le cas des pays francophones et germanophones du XVIe siècle," in *L'auteur à la Renaissance: l'altro que è in noi Turnhout*, ed. Rosanna Gorris Camos and Alexandre Vanautgaerden (Brepols: Turnhout, 2009), 19–63.

53. UBT Mc 181, front pastedown: "Martinus Craus. Me possidet. 1546"; and UBT Mc 223, fol. 1^r: "Martinus Kraus me possidet," respectively.

54. Crusius, *Turcograecia*, 441.

55. James Daybell, *The Material Letter in Early Modern England: Manuscript Letters and the Culture and Practices of Letter-writing, 1512–1635* (Houndmills: Palgrave Macmillan, 2012).

56. Ulinka Rublack, "Grapho-Relics: Lutheranism and the Materialization of the Word," *Past & Present* 206, no. 5 (2010): 144–166.

57. UBT Mh 466, vol. 8, fol. 212–213. See also UBT Mh 466, vol. 8, fol. 606. Mentioned in Andreas Rhoby, "The Friendship between Crusius and Zygomalas: A Study of Their Correspondence," *Medioevo Greco: Rivista di storia e filologia bizantina* 5 (2005): 264.

58. UBT Mb 13, fol. 520; and UBT Mb 34, fol. 264.

59. Gadi Algazi, "At the Study: Notes on the Production of the Scholarly Self," in *Space and Self in Early Modern European Cultures*, ed. David Warren Sabean and Malina Stefanovska (Toronto: University of Toronto Press, 2012), 17–50.

60. UBT Mb 37, fol. 149, pencil pagination 52^r.

61. On Isaac Casaubon's denial of his body, see Anthony Grafton, *Worlds Made by Words: Scholarship and Community in the Modern West* (Cambridge, MA: Harvard University Press, 2009), 216–231; and Anthony Grafton and Joanna Weinberg, *"I have always loved the holy tongue": Isaac Casaubon, the Jews, and a Forgotten Chapter in Renaissance Scholarship* (Cambridge, MA: Belknap Press of Harvard University Press, 2011), 11. On the persona of the scholar, see Gadi Algazi, "Exemplum and Wundertier: Three Concepts of the Scholarly Persona," *Low Countries Historical Review* 131, no. 4 (2016): 8–32.

62. For Maier's copying activities, see UBT Mh 466, vol. 2, fol. 80–94, 159; vol. 3, fol. 1–8, 10–14, 16–24, 28–34; and UBT Mb 37, fol. 149, pencil pagination 55–63. Crusius calls Maier his "θεράπων"; see UBT Mb 37, fol. 149, pencil pagination, 20^r.

63. UBT Mh 466, vol. 2, fol. 21–53, 61–73, 74, 98–111.

64. UBT Mh 466, vol. 2, fol. 622–626. These letters are copied by Johan Springer, from Vienna, who matriculated on July 18, 1582. See Heinrich Hermelink, *Die Matrikeln der Universität Tübingen* (Stuttgart: W. Kohlhammer, 1906–1953), 605.

65. UBT Mb 11, fol. C-II; and UBT Mb 11, third pagination, fol. 421. For the students involved in this work, see Wilhelm Schmid, *Verzeichnis der griechischen Handschriften der Königlichen Universitätsbibliothek* (Tübingen: G. Schnürlen, 1902), 27.

66. Anthony Grafton, *The Culture of Correction in Renaissance Europe* (London: British Library, 2011).

67. UBT Mb 10, fol. 190.

68. UBT Mb 11, first pagination, fol. 18ᵃ, 131.

69. UBT Mb 11, second pagination, fol. 172.

70. Ann Blair, *Too Much to Know: Managing Scholarly Information before the Modern Age* (New Haven, CT: Yale University Press, 2010), 108–112; Ann Blair, "Early Modern Attitudes toward the Delegation of Copying and Note-taking."

71. UBT Mh 466, vol. 1, fol. 711.

72. For Crusius as a reader of Byzantine materials, see Richard Calis, "Martin Crusius's Lost Byzantine Legacy," in *The Invention of Byzantium in Early Modern Europe*, ed. Nathanael Aschenbrenner and Jake Ransohoff (Cambridge, MA: Harvard University Press, 2021), 105–142.

73. On the delegation of tasks to amanuenses, see Ann Blair, "New Knowledge-Makers," in *New Horizons for Early Modern Europe*, ed. Ann Blair and Nick Popper (Baltimore, MD: Johns Hopkins University Press, 2021), 167–182; and Blair, "Early Modern Attitudes toward the Delegation of Copying and Note-taking."

74. Blair, *Too Much to Know*, 102–112.

75. Richard J. Oosterhoff, "Apprenticeship in the Renaissance University: Student Authorship and Craft Knowledge," *Science in Context* 32 (2019): 119–136.

76. Kristine Haugen, "Academic Charisma and the Old Regime," *History of Universities* 22, no. 1 (2007): 199–228.

77. UBT Mh 466, vol. 1, fol. 642–643. On Heinrich Schweigger as a painter, see UBT Mh 466, vol. 2, fol. 12.

78. UBT Mh 466, vol. 1, fol. 641–642.

79. UBT Mh 466, vol. 2, fol. 23–25.

80. Andreas Rhoby, "The Letter Network of Ioannes and Theodosios Zygomalas," in *Ιωάννης και Θεοδόσιος Ζυγομαλάς. Πατριαρχείο-θεσμοί-χειρόγραφα. Ioannes et Theodosios Zygomalas. Patriarchatus–institutions–codices*, ed. Stavros Perentides and Georgos Steires (Athens: Daidalos, 2009), 125–152, at 135.

81. Martin Crusius, *Hodoeporicon sive Itinerarium D. Solomonis Sweigkeri Sultzensis* (Leipzig, 1586). Crusius later included the coin in the list of things "brought to him from Byzantium"; see UBT Mb 37, new pagination, fol. 175.

82. UBT Mh 466, vol. 2, fol. 11–12. See also Dorothea Wendebourg, *Reformation und Orthodoxie: Der ökumenische Briefwechsel zwischen der Leitung der Württembergischen Kirche und Patriarch Jeremias II von Konstantinopel in den Jahren 1573–1581* (Göttingen: Vandenhoeck & Ruprecht, 1986), 122.

83. UBT Mh 466, vol. 1, fol. 10.

84. UBT Mh 466, vol. 1, fol. 321, 327, 373, 374, 375.

85. UBT Mh 466, vol. 1, fol. 717–718.

86. Crusius, *Hodoeporicon*, unpaginated.

87. UBT Mh 466, vol. 1, fol. 712.

88. UBT Mh 466, vol. 1, fol. 704.

89. UBT Mh 466, vol. 2, fol. 11–12. See also Crusius, *Germanograecia*, 231.

90. Crusius, *Germanograecia*, fol. 231. See also UBT Mh 466, vol. 2, fol. 17.

91. UBT Mh 466, vol. 1, fol. 529.

92. UBT Mh 466, vol. 1, fol. 203. Crusius's transcription of the letter is UBT Mh 466, vol. 1, fol. 194–203. It was also translated and printed in the *Turcograecia*: Crusius, *Turcograecia*, 435–440. See also Rhoby, "Letter Network of Ioannes and Theodosios Zygomalas," 143.

93. UBT Mb 37, 19ʳ–26ᵛ.

94. UBT Mh 466, vol. 3, fol. 528–529.

95. UBT Mh 466, vol. 1, fol. 40. See also Ulrich Moennig, "On Martinus Crusius's Collection of Greek Vernacular and Religious Books," *Byzantine and Modern Greek Studies* 21 (1997): 45n35, 47, 51, 67, and 71.

96. UBT Mh 466, vol. 1, fol. 156. See also UBT Mh 466, vol. 1, fol. 17; and UBT Mh 466, vol. 1, fol. 718. See also Moennig, "On Martinus Crusius's Collection," *passim* for a detailed examination of how Crusius acquired his vernacular Greek chapbooks.

97. UBT Mh 466, vol. 1, fol. 603.

98. UBT Mh 466, vol. 1, fol. 604.

99. Stephan Gerlach, *Tage-Buch* (Frankfurt: Johann David Zunner, 1674), 279b.

100. Moennig, "On Martinus Crusius's Collection," 46. Toufexis, *Das Alphabetum,* 323, 331.

101. For the matriculation dates of Vischer, Seng, and Haug, see Lucia Rossetti, *Matricula Nationis Germanicae Artistarum in Gymnasio Patavino, 1553–1721* (Padua: Antenore, 1986), 46, 63. On the *Natio Germanica,* see Loris Premuda, "Die Natio Germanica an der Universität Padua: Zur Forschungslage," *Sudhoffs Archiv für Geschichte der Medizin und der Naturwissenschaften* 47, no. 2 (1963): 97–105. For Vischer, see Moennig, "On Martinus Crusius's Collection," 55–57, 64–65. For Seng, who upon his return would be interviewed by Crusius about seeing the Turkish fleet in Venice, see UBT Mh 466, vol. 2, fol. 181, 199, 489. Seng matriculated at the University of Tübingen on March 5, 1571, and again on October 25, 1581; see Hermelink, *Die Matrikeln der Universität Tübingen,* 510, 599. He would later defend a disputation with the Tübingen professor of medicine Johann Vischer (the father of Hieronymus Vischer) and become a physician in Rothenburg; see Jeremias Seng, *Dispvtatio De Arthritidis Ac Podagrae Cavsis atque curatione* (Tübingen: Georg Gruppenbach, 1581); and Johann Neser, *Christliche Predigt. Bey Leichbestattung / Weylandt deß Ghrens vesten unnd hochgelehrten Herren Ieremiae Sengen / der Artzney Doctorn vnnd Bestelten Physici der Stadt Rotenburg vff der Tauber* (Rotenburg: Hieronymus Körnlein, 1618). Crusius sent Seng and Hieronymus Vischer a congratulatory note upon obtaining their degrees in Padua; see Martin Crusius, *Ad D. Hieronymum Viscerum Vemdingensem, et D. Hieremiam Sengium Nördlingensem, Medicinae Doctores in Academia Tubingensi creatos, gratulatio* (Tübingen: Georg Gruppenbach, 1582). On Haug, who hailed from Augsburg, see UBT Mh 466, vol. 4, fol. 37–39. Haug was also an acquaintance of Georg Remus, a man who would regularly send letters from Crusius to Venice and other places. On Remus, see UBT Mh 466, vol. 3, fol. 396.

102. UBT Mh 466, vol. 1, fol. 590; and UBT Mh 466, vol. 2, fol. 196–197.

103. On Pietro Longo, see Angela Nuovo, *The Book Trade in the Italian Renaissance* (Leiden and Boston: Brill, 2013), 287ff.

104. UBT Mh 466, vol. 2, fol. 322–323.

105. UBT Mh 466, vol. 2, fol. 610.

106. UBT Mh 466, vol. 3, fol. 205.

107. UBT Mh 466, vol. 1, fol. 572.

108. UBT Mh 466, vol. 2, fol. 439; and UBT Mh 466, vol. 2, fol. 441.

109. UBT Mh 466, vol. 1, fol. 40.

110. Margaret Meserve, *Empires of Islam in Renaissance Historical Thought* (Cambridge, MA: Harvard University Press 2008), 2.

111. Calis, "Martin Crusius's Lost Byzantine Legacy."

112. Martin Luther, *Cronica . . . Deudsch* (Wittenberg: Hans Lufft, 1551), UBT Ce 1094. For Luther's method of reckoning the years, see James Barr, "Luther and Biblical Chronology," *Bulletin of the John Rylands Library* 72, no. 1 (1990): 51–68.

113. Wolfgang Drechsler, *De Saracenis et Turcis Chronicon: item de origine et progressu et fine Machometi* (Strasbourg, 1550), UBT Gi 128, 235.

114. Drechsler, *De Saracenis et Turcis Chronicon*, UBT Gi 128, 235.

115. Thomas Gloning, "«Nova Wellingiana»—Nachrichten-Exzerpte in den Tagebüchern von Martin Crusius (1526–1607). Ein Beitrag zur Frühgeschichte der Presse und der Zeitungssprache," in *Bausteine zur Tübinger Universitätsgeschichte. Bd. 5*, ed. Volker Schäfer (Tübingen: Attempto-Verlag, 1991), 13–52.

116. UBT Mh 466, vol. 5, fol. 591, 645, 655, 701–702, 714–715, 720–721; UBT Mh 466, vol. 6, fol. 11, 17, 53–54, 61–62, 83, 105, 137, 313, 341, 525, 534, 581.

117. UBT Mh 466, vol. 8, fol. 218.

118. Gloning, "«Nova Wellingiana»," 22.

119. Stahlecker, "Das Tagebuch von Martin Crusius," 30, discussed in Gloning, "«Nova Wellingiana»."

120. UBT Mh 466, vol. 5, fol. 673–674.

121. Jakob Horst, *De aureo dente maxillari pueri Silesii* (Leipzig: Valentin Vögelin, 1595). Crusius owned a copy of the German translation that was published a year later: Jakob Horst, *Zwey Bücher: eins von dem güldenen Zahn, so einem Knaben in Schlesien gewachsen; das ander von den Nachtwanderern, welche im Schlaff umgehen usw* (Leipzig: Valentin Vögelin, 1596). For the general context, see Robert Jütte, *Ein Wunder wie Der Goldene Zahn: Eine 'unerhörte' Begebenheit aus dem Jahre 1593 macht Geschichte(n)* (Ostfildern: Thorbecke, 2004).

122. UBT Mh 466, vol. 5, fol. 717. See also UBT Mh 466, vol. 5, fol. 723–728.

123. UBT Mh 466, vol. 6, fol. 6.

124. UBT Mh 466, vol. 5, fol. 733–734.

125. UBT Mh 466, vol. 6, fol. 17. This victory was confirmed in a later report; see UBT Mh 466, vol. 6, fol. 43.

126. UBT Mh 466, vol. 5, fol. 722–723. Crusius also wrote to Johannes Spon and Oswald Croll, an alchemist and professor of medicine. See UBT Mh 466, vol. 6, fol. 49; and Jütte, *Ein Wunder wie Der Goldene Zahn*.

127. UBT Mh 466, vol. 5, fol. 723–728.

128. UBT Mh 466, vol. 6, fol. 8–9. See also UBT Mh 466, vol. 6, fol. 11–12.

129. At the time, Kepler supplemented his meager income by compiling *prognostica* and drawing up horoscopes; the accuracy of some of these even brought him some renown. On Kepler and astrology, see Owen Gingerich, "Kepler on Astrology," *Journal for the History of Astronomy* 45, no. 1 (2014): 137–139; and Aviva Rothman, *The Pursuit of Harmony: Kepler on Cosmos, Confession, and Community* (Chicago: Chicago University Press, 2017).

130. UBT Mh 466, vol. 6, fol. 14–15.

131. Claudia Brosseder, "The Writing in the Wittenberg Sky: Astrology in 16th-Century Germany," *Journal of the History of Ideas* 66 (2005): 557–576, at 558 and 570; and Claudia Brosseder, *Im Bann der Sterne. Caspar Peucer, Philipp Melanchthon und andere Wittenberger Astrologen* (Berlin: Akademie Verlag, 2004). For the history of astrology and the Reformation, see Robin B. Barnes, *Astrology and Reformation* (Oxford: Oxford University Press, 2016).

132. Aristotle, *Opera. . . . omnia*, UBT Cd 855 ½ 2.2, 266; UBT Mb 10, fol. 227; UBT Mh 443, vol. 1, fol. 93ʳ.

133. UBT Mh 443, vol. 1, fol. 71ᵛ; and UBT Mh 443, vol. 1, 79ʳ. On the early modern study of this comet, see Clarisse Doris Hellman, *The Comet of 1577: Its Place in the History of Astronomy* (New York: Columbia University Press, 1944).

134. UBT Mh 466, vol. 6, fol. 11–12; Aristotle, *Opera. . . . omnia*, UBT Cd 855 ½ 2.2, 470.

135. On Maestlin, see Richard A. Jarrell, *The Life and Scientific Work of the Tübingen Astronomer Michael Mästlin 1550–1631* (PhD diss., University of Toronto, 1970); Anthony Grafton, "Michael Maestlin's Account of Copernican Planetary Theory," *Proceedings of the American Philosophical Society* 117 (1973): 523–550; Charlotte Methuen, "Maestlin's Teaching of Copernicus: The Evidence of His University Textbook and Disputations," *Isis* 87, no. 2 (1996): 230–247; Gerhard Betsch, "Südwestdeutsche Mathematici aus dem Kreis um Michael Mästlin," in *Der 'mathematicus': Zur Entwicklung und Bedeutung einer neuen Berufsgruppe in der Zeit Gerhard Mercators*, ed. Irmgard Hantsche (Bochum: Brockmeyer, 1996), 121–150.

136. UBT Mh 466, vol. 6, fol. 17.

137. UBT Mh 466, vol. 6, fol. 468. Cited in Asaph Ben-Tov, "*Turco-Graecia*: German Humanists and the End of Antiquity—Cultural Exchange and Misunderstanding," in *The Renaissance and the Ottoman World*, ed. Anna Contadini and Claire Norton (Farnham and Burlington, VT: Ashgate, 2013), 181–195, at 181. Translation my own.

138. UBT Mh 466, vol. 7, fol. 5.

139. Martin Crusius, *Commentariolum in primam Demosthenis Olynthiacam Sturmianum* (Strasbourg: Blasius Fabricius Chemnicensis, 1554), A2ʳ.

6. Travel in the Mind's Eye

1. For earlier descriptions of the *Turcograecia*, see Émile Legrand, *Bibliographie hellénique: ou description raissonnée des ouvreages publiés par des Grecs aus XVe et XVIe siècles*, vol. 4 (Paris: Ernest Leroux, 1903): 272–274; and Carlo de Clercq, "Des jumeaux typographiques: La Turcograecia et la Germanograecia de Martin Crusius," *Gutenberg-Jahrbuch* (1967): 144–155.

2. Crusius, *Turcograecia*, title page.

3. Crusius, *Turcograecia*, dedicatory epistle, 3ʳ.

4. UBT Mh 466, vol. 1, fol. 704. The original manuscript is UBT Mb 18. On Malaxos, see Giuseppe De Gregorio, *Il copista greco Manouel Malaxos: studio biografico e paleografico-codicologico* (Vatican City: Scuola vaticana di paleografia, diplomatica e archivistica, 1991). On the chronicle, see Marios Philippides, "Patriarchal Chronicles of the Sixteenth Century," *Greek, Roman and Byzantine Studies* 25 (1984): 87–94.

5. Crusius, *Turcograecia*, 190, 202.

6. Crusius, *Turcograecia*, dedicatory epistle, 3ʳ.

7. Crusius, *Turcograecia*, dedicatory epistle, 3ʳ.

8. Crusius, *Turcograecia*, dedicatory epistle, 3ʳ.

9. Crusius, *Turcograecia*, dedicatory epistle, 3ʳ.

10. Crusius, *Turcograecia*, 64, 239, 498, 507, 193, 65, 48, 189–190, 197, 198, 203, 205, respectively.

11. Crusius, *Turcograecia*, 51, 207, 222, 336.

12. Hieronymus Wolf, *Nicetae Acominati Choniatae . . . LXXXVI annorum historia: uidelicet ab anno restitutae Salutis circiter MCXVII, in quo Zonaras desinit, usque ad annum MCCIII, libris XIX descripta* (Basel: Johannes Oporinus, 1557), UBT Cd 4980.

13. Crusius, *Turcograecia*, 527–529.

14. Crusius, *Turcograecia*, 485.

15. On pilgrimage to the Holy Land in this context, see Sundar Henny and Zur Shalev, "Jerusalem Reformed: Rethinking Early Modern Pilgrimage," *Renaissance Quarterly* 75, no. 3 (2022): 796–848; Zur Shalev, *Sacred Words and Worlds: Geography, Religion, and Scholarship, 1550–1700* (Leiden: Brill, 2012), 73–139.

16. Crusius, *Turcograecia*, 231–236.

17. Crusius, *Turcograecia*, 485. This information was taken almost verbatim from one of Gerlach's letters; see UBT Mh 466, vol. 1, fol. 10.

18. Crusius, *Turcograecia*, 315. The observation is based on Pierre Belon, *Les observations de plusieurs singularitez et choses memorables, trouvées en Grèce, Asie, Indée, Egypte, Arabie, et autres pays estranges* (Antwerp: Plantin, 1555), UBT Fc 33.4, 149.

19. Crusius, *Turcograecia*, 64, 99, 210, 218, 219.

20. Crusius, *Turcograecia*, 218.

21. Crusius, *Turcograecia*, 227.

22. Crusius, *Turcograecia*, 219.

23. Crusius, *Turcograecia*, dedicatory epistle, 3^r.

24. In the 1593 *Antiquitatum judaicarum libri IX*, Benito Arias Montano would make a similar point about maps, arguing that they could serve as a replacement for pilgrimage. See Shalev, *Sacred Words and Worlds*, 57.

25. Crusius, *Turcograecia*, dedicatory epistle, 3^v.

26. UBT Mh 466, vol. 1, fol. 722–723.

27. Crusius, *Turcograecia*, 189–190. Crusius's manuscript draft can be found in UBT Mh 466, vol. 1, fol. 721–722.

28. Crusius, *Turcograecia*, 188.

29. UBT Mb 18, fol. 98.

30. The original manuscript of the chronicle, annotated by Crusius, is Bibliothèque Nationale de France, Supplément Grec 1152.

31. On travel, credibility, and autopsy, see Stephen Greenblatt, *Marvelous Possessions: The Wonder of the New World* (Chicago: University of Chicago Press, 1991); Anthony Pagden, *European Encounters with the New World: From Renaissance to Romanticism* (New Haven, CT: Yale University Press, 1993); Christine Johnson, "Buying Stories: Ancient Tales, Renaissance Travelers, and the Market for the Marvelous," *Journal of Early Modern History* 11, no. 6 (2007): 405–446; Surekha Davies, *Renaissance Ethnography and the Invention of the Human: New Worlds, Maps and Monsters* (Cambridge: Cambridge University Press, 2016). On travel as knowledge, see Justin Stagl, *A History of Curiosity: The Theory of Travel, 1550–1800* (Chur: Harwood Academic, 1995).

32. Anthony Grafton, *What Was History? The Art of History in Early Modern Europe* (Cambridge: Cambridge University Press, 2007).

33. Arnaldo Momigliano, *The Classical Foundations of Modern Historiography* (Berkeley: University of California Press, 1990), 150; and Arnaldo Momigliano, "Pagan and Christian Histo-

riography in the Fourth Century AD," in *The Conflict between Paganism and Christianity in the Fourth Century*, ed. Arnaldo Momigliano (Oxford: Clarendon, 1963), 77–99.

34. Grafton, *What Was History?*

35. Crusius, *Poematum Graecorum libri duo . . . Orationum Liber unus* (Basel: Johannes Oporinus, 1566).

36. Anthony Grafton, *The Footnote: A Curious History* (Cambridge, MA: Harvard University Press, 1997), 153; and Arnaldo Momigliano, "Ancient History and the Antiquarian," *Journal of the Warburg and Courtauld Institutes* 13, nos. 3–4 (1950): 285–315. For history writing in this period more generally, see Grafton, *What Was History?*

37. Christopher Wood, "Notation of Visual Information in the Earliest Archeological Scholarship," *Word & Image* 17, nos. 1–2 (2001): 94–118; William Stenhouse, "Panvinio and Renditions of History and Antiquity in the Late Renaissance," *Papers of the British School at Rome* 80 (2012): 233–256; Shalev, *Sacred Words and Worlds*, 33–43.

38. Ian Maclean, *Scholarship, Commerce, Religion: The Learned Book in the Age of Confessions, 1560–1630* (Cambridge, MA: Harvard University Press, 2012).

39. UBT Mh 466, vol. 2, fol. 601, 610, 621.

40. UBT Mh 466, vol. 2, fol. 370.

41. UBT Mh 466, vol. 2, fol. 441, 547.

42. UBT Mh 466, vol. 2, fol. 667, 689.

43. UBT Mh 466, vol. 2, fol. 601.

44. UBT Mh 466, vol. 2, fol. 549.

45. UBT Mh 466, vol. 2, fol. 697–698. On Greek books not selling well, see Maclean, *Scholarship, Commerce, Religion*, 54–55. Crusius's own posthumously printed commentary on Homer's *Iliad* was a commercial failure as well: 1,057 copies of the original print run remained unsold. See Maclean, *Scholarship, Commerce, Religion*, 96.

46. Crusius, *Hodoeporicon*.

47. UBT Mh 466, vol. 2, fol. 441.

48. UBT Mh 466, vol. 2, fol. 591.

49. UBT Mh 466, vol. 2, fol. 614.

50. UBT Mh 466, vol. 2, fol. 699.

51. UBT Mh 466, vol. 2, fol. 443, 558.

52. UBT Mh 466, vol. 2, fol. 444, 547.

53. UBT Mh 466, vol. 2, fol. 538, 550.

54. UBT Mh 466, vol. 2, 611.

55. UBT Mh 466, vol. 2, fol. 580, 582, 588, 611.

56. UBT Mh 466, vol. 2, fol. 589.

57. Crusius did not to my knowledge own any works by Petrarch. Yet the parallels between this dream and the Italian humanist's ascent of Mont Ventoux are striking. Keeping in mind that Petrarch's letter is now often read not as an account of an actual hike but as an allegory about his lack of spiritual progress or as investigation of the self, one wonders what to make of Crusius's dream. For interpretations of Petrarch's letter, see Jill Robbins, "Petrarch Reading Augustine: 'The Ascent of Mont Ventoux,'" *Philological Quarterly* 64 (1985): 533–553; and Carol Everhart Quillen, *Rereading the Renaissance: Petrarch, Augustine, and the Language of Humanism* (Ann Arbor: University of Michigan Press, 1998).

58. UBT Mh 466, vol. 2, fol. 659. In the letters that he subsequently sent to his contacts, he nevertheless seemed less certain; see UBT Mh 466, vol. 2, fol. 662, 663, 664, 665. It was only on September 24, 1583, that Crusius received the final confirmation via Gruppenbach. See UBT Mh 466, vol. 1, fol. 679. For other dreams, see UBT Mh 466, vol. 3, fol. 73.

59. UBT Mh 466, vol. 3, fol. 65, 73.

60. UBT Mh 466, vol. 2, fol. 537.

61. UBT Mh 466, vol. 2, fol. 551.

62. UBT Mh 466, vol. 2, fol. 602–603. For their earlier letter, see UBT Mh 466, vol. 2, fol. 558. The *Germanograecia* raised similar problems; see UBT Mh 466, vol. 3, fol. 104.

63. Maclean, *Scholarship, Commerce, Religion*, 77.

64. E.g., UBT Mh 466, vol. 2, fol. 614.

65. UBT Mh 466, vol. 2, fol. 486, 506, 507, 522.

66. Ann Goldgar, *Impolite Learning: Conduct and Community in the Republic of Letters, 1680–1750* (New Haven, CT, and London: Yale University Press, 1995), 36.

67. UBT Mh 466, vol. 2, fol. 346, 440.

68. UBT Mh 466, vol. 2, fol. 620.

69. UBT Mh 466, vol. 3, fol. 77.

70. UBT Mh 466, vol. 3, fol. 104.

71. UBT Mh 466, vol. 3, fol. 67, 69, 70, 76. See also UBT Mh 466, vol. 2, fol. 699.

72. UBT Mh 466, vol. 3, fol. 71. Later on Crusius sent a copy of the *Germanograecia* to Wechel; see UBT Mh 466, vol. 3, fol. 72–73, 80.

73. UBT Mh 466, vol. 3, fol. 76.

74. UBT Mh 466, vol. 3, fol. 81, 88, 89.

75. UBT Mh 466, vol. 4, fol. 575.

7. Visions of Ottoman Greece

1. Crusius, *Turcograecia*, dedicatory epistle, 2^v.

2. Crusius, *Turcograecia*, dedicatory epistle, 3^v–4^r.

3. Terence Spencer, *Fair Greece! Sad Relic: Literary Philhellenism from Shakespeare to Byron* (London: Weidenfeld and Nicolson, 1954), 1.

4. Eliza Mariam Butler, *The Tyranny of Greece over Germany: A Study of the Influence Exercised by Greek Art and Poetry over the Great German Writers of the Eighteenth, Nineteenth and Twentieth Centuries* (New York: Macmillan Company; and Cambridge: University Press, 1935). See also Constanze Güthenke, *Placing Modern Greece: The Dynamics of Romantic Hellenism, 1770–1840* (Oxford: Oxford University Press, 2008); Suzanne L. Marchand, *Down from Olympus: Archaeology and Philhellenism in Germany, 1750–1790* (Princeton, NJ: Princeton University Press, 1996); Glenn W. Most, "On the Use and Abuse of Ancient Greece for Life," *Cultura Tedesca* 20 (2002): 31–53.

5. John-Paul Ghobrial, *The Whispers of Cities: Information Flows in Istanbul, London, and Paris in the Age of William Trumbull* (Oxford: Oxford University Press, 2013); Alexander Bevilacqua, *The Republic of Arabic Letters: Islam and the European Enlightenment* (Cambridge, MA: Belknap Press of Harvard University Press, 2018); Simon Mills, *A Commerce of Knowledge: Trade, Religion, and Scholarship between England and the Ottoman Empire, c. 1600–1760* (Oxford: Oxford University Press, 2020); Paul Babinski, *World Literature in Practice: The Orientalist's Manuscript between*

the Ottoman Empire and Germany (PhD diss., Princeton University, 2020); Natalie Rothman, *The Dragoman Renaissance: Diplomatic Interpreters and the Routes of Orientalism* (Ithaca, NY: Cornell University Press, 2021). For brokering across the Ottoman–European border, see Paula Sutter Fichtner, *Terror and Toleration: The Habsburg Empire Confronts Islam 1526–1850* (London: Reaktion, 2008).

6. Gerald Strauss, *Sixteenth-Century Germany: Its Topography and Topographers* (Madison: University of Wisconsin Press, 1959), vii. On chorography, which still lacks its historian, see Darell J. Rohl, "Chorography: History, Theory and Potential for Archaeological Research" in *TRAC 2011: Proceedings of the Twenty First Annual Theoretical Roman Archaeology Conference, Newcastle 2011*, ed. M. Duggan, F. McIntosh, and Darell J. Rohl (Oxford: Oxbow, 2012), 19–32. On Biondo and his methods, see Ottavio Clavuot, *Biondos "Italia illustrata": Summa oder Neuschöpfung?: über die Arbeitsmethoden eines Humanisten* (Tübingen: M. Niemeyer, 1990); and Riccardo Fubini, *Storiografia dell'umanesimo in Italia da Leonardo Bruni ad Annio da Viterbo* (Rome: Edizioni di storia e letteratura, 2003): 54–89.

7. Crusius, *Turcograecia*, dedicatory epistle, 4^v.

8. Crusius, *Turcograecia*, dedicatory epistle, 3^v.

9. Crusius, *Turcograecia*, dedicatory epistle, 4^v.

10. Crusius, *Germanograecia*, 7.

11. Frederic Clark, *Dividing Time: The Making of Historical Periodization in Early Modern Europe* (PhD diss., Princeton University, 2014).

12. Crusius, *Turcograecia*, dedicatory epistle, 3^v–4^r.

13. Crusius, *Turcograecia*, 107–212.

14. For a full analysis of this material, and of Crusius as a reader of Byzantine materials, see Richard Calis, "Martin Crusius's Lost Byzantine Legacy," in *The Invention of Byzantium in Early Modern Europe*, ed. Nathanael Aschenbrenner and Jake Ransohoff (Cambridge, MA: Harvard University Press, 2021), 105–142.

15. Lucy Pollard, *The Quest for Classical Greece: Early Modern Travel to the Greek World* (London: I. B. Tauris, 2015), 151–187; Hélène Pignot, *Christians under the Ottoman Turks: French and English Travellers in Greece and Anatolia (1615–1694)* (Piscataway, NJ: Gorgias, 2009), 1–14; Gerhard Pfeiffer, *Studien zur Frühphase des europäischen Philhellenismus (1453–1750)* (PhD diss., University of Erlangen-Nürnberg, 1968), 87–88, 98. See also Richard Stoneman, *Land of Lost Gods: The Search for Classical Greece* (Norman: University of Oklahoma Press, 1987); David Constantine, *In the Footsteps of the Gods: Travellers to Greece and the Quest for the Hellenic Ideal* (London: Tauris Parke, 2011); Olga Augustinos, *French Odysseys: Greece in French Travel Literature from the Renaissance to the Romantic Era* (Baltimore, MD: Johns Hopkins University Press, 1994).

16. Cited in Eva Johanna Holmberg, *British Encounters with Ottoman Minorities in the Early Seventeenth Century: "Slaves" of the Sultan* (Basingstoke: Palgrave Macmillan, 2022), 44.

17. Pierre Belon, *Travels in the Levant*, trans. James Hogarth (London: Hardinge Simpole, 2012), 19–20, 90. Holmberg, *British Encounters with Ottoman Minorities*, 38, 45–46; Pollard, *Quest for Classical Greece*, 158–159.

18. Belon, *Travels in the Levant*, 21, 55–56. See also Pfeiffer *Studien zur Frühphase des europäischen Philhellenismus*, 82, 99.

19. Holmberg, *British Encounters with Ottoman Minorities*, 47–48; Pfeiffer, *Studien zur Frühphase des europäischen Philhellenismus (1453–1750)*, 85.

20. Holmberg, *British Encounters with Ottoman Minorities*, 47–48.

21. Pollard, *Quest for Classical Greece*, 163. For the pervasiveness of cultural scripts and classical models in this context, see now Holmberg, *British Encounters with Ottoman Minorities*, 34. For a different context, see Sabine MacCormack, *Religion in the Andes: Vision and Imagination in Early Colonial Peru* (Princeton, NJ: Princeton University Press, 1991); and David A. Lupher, *Romans in a New World: Classical Models in Sixteenth-Century Spanish America. History, Languages, and Cultures of the Spanish and Portuguese Worlds* (Ann Arbor: University of Michigan Press, 2003).

22. Paul Rycaut, *The Present State of the Greek and Armenian Churches, anno 1678* (London: John Starkey, 1679), 7–8 ("factious temper"); and Thomas Smith, *An Account of the Greek Church as to Its Doctrine and Rites of Worship* (London: Miles Flesher, 1680), A4^v ("mixture of odd opinions and fancies"), A6^v ("errours and defects"). For the broader context, see Hélène Pignot, "A Trip to the Origins of Christianity: Sir Paul Rycaut's and Rev. Thomas Smith's Accounts of the Greek Church in the Seventeenth Century," *Studies in Travel Writing* 13, no. 3 (2009): 193–205. On Smith, see also the excellent discussion in Thomas Roebuck, "Antiquarianism in the Near East: Thomas Smith (1638–1710) and His Journey to the Seven Churches of Asia," in *Beyond Greece and Rome: Reading the Ancient Near East in Early Modern Europe*, ed. Jane Grogan (Oxford: Oxford University Press 2020), 132–162.

23. Johann Michael Heineccius, *Eigentliche und wahrhafftige Abbildung der alten und neuen Griechischen Kirche, nach ihrer Historie, Glaubens-Lehren und Kirchen-Gebräuchen* (Leipzig: Johann Friedrich Gleditsch and Son, 1711), 24.

24. Heineccius, *Eigentliche und wahrhafftige Abbildung*, 51–52.

25. Helen Roche, "The Peculiarities of German Philhellenism," *Historical Journal* 61, no. 2 (2018): 541–560, at 545.

26. Christopher Meid, *Griechenland-Imaginationen: Reiseberichte im 20. Jahrhundert von Gerhart Hauptmann bis Wolfgang Koeppen* (Berlin: de Gruyter, 2012).

27. Güthenke, *Placing Modern Greece*, 242. For a similar argument about modern English travelers to Greece, see Efterpi Mitsi, *Greece in Early English Travel Writing, 1596–1682* (Cham, Switzerland: Palgrave Macmillan, 2017).

28. Friedrich Wilhelm Thiersch, *Ueber die Sprache der Zakonen* (Munich, 1835), 569; and Leopold von Ranke, *Die Osmanen und die spanische Monarchie im 16. und 17. Jahrhundert* (Leipzig, 1877), 16.

29. Crusius, *Turcograecia*, 64, 476, 487, 501, 503, 504.

30. Crusius, *Turcograecia*, 298. On the poverty of the Greeks, see also Crusius, *Turcograecia*, 449.

31. UBT Mh 466, vol. 2, fol. 706.

32. Crusius, *Turcograecia*, 200.

33. Crusius, *Turcograecia*, 45, 47. The draft versions are in UBT Mb 11, fol. B-III and C-III, respectively.

34. Volker Bauer, *Wurzel, Stamm, Krone: Fürstliche Genealogie in frühneuzeitlichen Druckwerken* (Wiesbaden: Harrassowitz in Kommission, 2013); and Markus Friedrich, "Genealogy as Archive-Driven Research Enterprise in Early Modern Europe," *Osiris* 32, no. 1 (2017): 65–84.

35. Cited in Anthony Grafton, *What Was History? The Art of History in Early Modern Europe* (Cambridge: Cambridge University Press, 2007), 147.

36. Crusius, *Germanograecia*, 221. See also Crusius, *Turcograecia*, 61, where Crusius incorporated Giovanni Antonio Campano's assessment on the "cruelty of the Turks."

37. Crusius, *Germanograecia*, 195.

38. Crusius, *Germanograecia*, 221.

39. Crusius, *Germanograecia*, 33. See also Zachariades, *Tübingen und Konstantinopel*, 57.

40. Asaph Ben-Tov, *Lutheran Humanists and Greek Antiquity: Melanchthonian Scholarship between Universal History and Pedagogy* (Leiden and Boston: Brill, 2009), 197.

41. Crusius, *Turcograecia*, 96.

42. Crusius, *Turcograecia*, 57. See also UBT Mh 466, vol. 3, fol. 604.

43. Crusius, *Turcograecia*, 246, 437, 485.

44. Crusius, *Turcograecia*, 216.

45. Crusius, *Turcograecia*, 246.

46. Crusius, *Turcograecia*, dedicatory epistle, 4^v.

47. Theodor Zwinger, *Methodus apodemica in eorum gratiam, qui cum fructu in quocunque tandem vitae genere peregrinari cupiunt* (Basel, 1577). For the broader context, see Justin Stagl, *A History of Curiosity: The Theory of Travel, 1550–1800* (Chur: Harwood Academic, 1995); and, more recently, Karl A. E. Enenkel and Jan de Jong, eds., *Artes Apodemicae and Early Modern Travel Culture, 1550–1700* (Brill: Leiden, 2019).

48. Crusius, *Turcograecia*, 461.

49. Crusius, *Turcograecia*, 430–431.

50. UBT Mb 10, fol. 1; and UBT Mc 62, fol. 382.

51. Crusius, *Turcograecia*, 224. See also Crusius, *Turcograecia*, 298.

52. Crusius, *Turcograecia*, 489.

53. Heineccius, *Eigentliche und wahrhafftige Abbildung*, 112, 117–118.

54. Michael Neander, *Chronicon sive Synopsis Historiarum* (Leipzig: Georg Deffner, 1586), 162^r. Cited in Ben-Tov, *Lutheran Humanists and Greek Antiquity*, 127.

55. Johannes Meursius, *Glossarium graeco-barbarum* (Leiden: Elzevier, 1614).

56. Johannes Tribbechovius, *Brevia linguae ρωμαϊκῆς sive graecae vulgaris elementa* (Jena: Johann Bielcke, 1705).

57. Johannes Michael Langius, *Philologia barbaro-Graeca*, 2 vols. (Nuremberg and Altdorf: Jobst Wilhelm Kohles, 1708).

58. Langius, *Philologia barbaro-Graeca*, vol. 2, 1. For the broader context, see Hans Eideneier, "Martinus Crusius Neograecus und die Folgen," in *Graeca recentiora in Germania: deutschgriechische Kulturbeziehungen vom 15. bis 19. Jahrhundert*, ed. Hans Eideneier (Wiesbaden: Harrassowitz, 1994), 123–136.

59. Crusius, *Turcograecia*, 185.

60. Universitaire Bibliotheken Leiden, Special Collections (KL) 766 A11, 55, 61, 63, 67, 499.

61. Universitaire Bibliotheken Leiden, Special Collections (KL) 766 A11, 178, 198, 208, 317.

62. Universitaire Bibliotheken Leiden, Special Collections (KL) 766 A11, 3, 46, 48, 102, 194, 329, 493.

63. Universitaire Bibliotheken Leiden, Special Collections (KL) 766 A11, 91, 99, 131, 140, 141, 149, 150, 151, 155, 163.

64. Crusius, *Turcograecia*, 106.

65. Joseph Justus Scaliger, *De emendatione temporum* (Leiden: Plantin, 1598), 494, 720. For Crusius's response, see UBT Mh 466, vol. 6, fol. 735.

66. Archivio della Congregazione per la Dottrina della Fede, *Protocolli Congregationis Indicis*, vol. M, fol. 342. I would like to thank Cornel Zwierlein for bringing this source to my attention.

67. Archivio della Congregazione per la Dottrina della Fede, Index IX, fol. 153. I would like to thank Hannah Marcus for this reference.

68. UBT Mh 466, vol. 7, fol. 299.

69. British Library, Harley 6943, 91^v–92^v. I would like to thank Cornel Zwierlein for bringing this source to my attention.

70. UBT Mh 466, vol. 7, fol. 397.

71. UBT Mh 466, vol. 7, fol. 397, 545; and UBT Mh 466, vol. 5, fol. 498.

72. UBT Mh 466, vol. 7, 546–547.

73. Edward Gibbon, *The History of the Decline and Fall of the Roman Empire*, 6th vol. (London: Andrew Strahan and Thomas Cadell, 1788), 510.

74. Gibbon, *History of the Decline and Fall of the Roman Empire*, 510n83.

75. Gibbon, *History of the Decline and Fall of the Roman Empire*, 508, 510n84.

Conclusion

1. UBT Mh 443, vol. 1, fol. 2^r–3^v. For the creation of this presentation copy and its circulation, see UBT Mh 466, vol. 5, fol. 75, 78, 80, 156, 168, 193.

2. Natalie Rothman, *The Dragoman Renaissance: Diplomatic Interpreters and the Routes of Orientalism* (Ithaca, NY: Cornell University Press, 2021), 11.

3. Johanna Hanink, *The Classical Debt: Greek Antiquity in an Era of Austerity* (Cambridge, MA: Harvard University Press, 2017).

4. Ludwig Zoepf, "Aus der Geschichte der Tübinger Universitätsbibliothek (1477–1607)," *Zentralblatt für Bibliothekswesen* 52 (1935): 471–483. Norbert Hofmann, *Die Artistenfakultät an der Universität Tübingen, 1534–1601* (Tübingen: Mohr Siebeck, 1982), 91–96.

5. Gerd Brinkhus and Arno Mentzel-Reuters, *Die lateinischen Handschriften der Universitätsbibliothek Tübingen: Teil 2: Signaturen Mc 151 bis Mc 379 sowie die lateinischen Handschriften bis 1600 aus den Signaturengruppen Mh, Mk und aus dem Druckschriftenbestand* (Wiesbaden: Harrassowitz, 2001).

6. UBT Mh 466, vol. 8, fol. 576.

7. Ferdinand Friedrich Faber, *Die Württembergischen Familien-Stiftungen: nebst genealogischen Nachrichten über die zu denselben berechtigten Familien. Eilftes Heft* (Stuttgart: Franz Kohler, 1855), 81–83. See also Max Baumgart, *Die Stipendien und Stiftungen zu Gunsten der Studierenden an allen Universitäten des deutschen Reichs* (Berlin: R.v. Decker's Verlag, 1885), 625–626; and UBT Mh 198, fol. 64.

8. Brinkhus and Mentzel-Reuters, *Die lateinischen Handschriften*, 25.

9. Ernst Gottlieb Mayer-Crusianus, *Dissertatio Juridica, De Hereditatis & Bonorum Possessionis Differentiis Primariis* (Tübingen, 1674). For Mayer-Crusianus's BA degree, see UBT L XV 10 b.2, 49. For his life, see Johann Jacob Moser, *Erläutertes Württemberg* (Tübingen, 1729), 250–260; and Christoph Weidlich, *Biographische Nachrichten von den jetzlebenden Rechts-Gelehrten in Teutschland. Dritter Theil* (Halle: Hemmerdeische Buchhandlung, 1783), b4^v–b5^r.

10. On the *Tübinger Professorengalerie*, see Erhard Cellius, *Imagines professorum Tubingensium* (Tübingen: Cellius, 1596); and Reinhold Scholl, *Die Bildnissammlung der Universität Tübingen, 1477 bis 1927* (Stuttgart: Müller, 1927).

11. Hauptstaatsarchiv Stuttgart, J1 79. See Michael Klein, *Die Handschriften der Staatsarchive in Baden-Württemberg. Die Handschriften der Sammlung J 1 im Hauptstaatsarchiv Stuttgart* (Wiesbaden: Otto Harrassowitz, 1980), 147.

12. Johann Jacob Moser, *Martin Crusii,... Schwäbische Chronick... aus dem lateinischen erstmals übersetzt und mit einer Continuation vom Jahr 1596 biss 1733 auch einem vollständigen Register versehen* (Frankfurt: Metzler and Erhard, 1733).

13. Emmanuel Schelstrate, *Acta Orientalis Ecclesiae Contra Lutheri Haeresim* (Rome: Giuseppe Collini, 1739).

14. These are, respectively, as follows: Martin Crusius, *Annales Suevici siue Chronica rervm gestarvm antiqvissimae et inclytae Svevicae gentis* (Frankfurt: Nicolaus Basseus, 1596), UBT 22 C 49; Jacob Micyllus and Joachim Camerarius, *Opus utrumque Homeri Iliados et Odysseae* (Basel: Johann Herwagen, 1541), Princeton University Library PA4018.A31 M52 1541q; Martin Crusius, *Annales Suevici siue Chronica rervm gestarvm antiqvissimae et inclytae Svevicae gentis* (Frankfurt: Nicolaus Basseus, 1596), Princeton University Library Q-000543.

15. Karl Pfaff, *Wirtenbergischer Plutarch: Lebensbeschreibungen berühmter Wirtenberger. Zweiter Theil* (Esslingen: Seeger, 1832), 22, 24.

16. For Reuss's *Catalogus manuscriptum Bibliothecae academicae universitatis Tubingensis* of 1782, see UBT Mh 546. On Reuss, see Regine Benker, *Die Universitätsbibliothek Tübingen in der 2. Hälfte des 18. Jahrhunderts unter besonderer Berücksichtigung des Wirkens von Jeremias David Reuß* (Cologne: Fachhochschule für Bibliotheks- und Dokumentationswesen, 1990).

17. B. A. Mystakides, "Notes sur Martin Crusius, ses livres, ses ouvrages et ses manuscrits," *Revue des Études Grecques* 11 (1898): 279–280. On Mystakides, see Christos Patrinelis, "Ἀναγραφή δημοσιευμάτων Β. Α. Μυστακίδου (1859–1933)," *Ἐπετηρὶς Ἑταιρείας Βυζαντινῶν Σπουδῶν* 33 (1964): 124–139.

Acknowledgments

I could never have written this book without the encouragement and support of friends, family, colleagues, mentors, archivists, librarians, and everyone at HUP. It is a pleasure to express my gratitude to all of them here, but especially to the institutions that I have been fortunate enough to call home: Amsterdam, Princeton, Trinity College, Cambridge, and now Utrecht.

This book started at Princeton. Ann Blair, Molly Greene, Yair Mintzker, and Francesca Trivellato offered incredibly valuable advice on early incarnations of my research, and their tireless encouragement kept me afloat when writing was slow. I hope that the preceding pages reflect the erudition with which they helped me develop my ideas. This book would not exist without Anthony Grafton. His supervision and scholarly generosity are unparalleled: Tony commented on drafts of every part of this book, improved my prose, took my research into directions I could not have imagined, read papers I presented at conferences, encouraged fellowship applications, introduced me to (senior) scholars in the field, wrote countless letters of recommendation, offered crucial advice and much-needed encouragement when I thought none of this made sense, and, most important, showed me how fun researching all of this can be. It means the world to me that he and Louise welcomed me into their home for their Thanksgiving meals and on countless other occasions. I hope I offer my students the kind of scholarly generosity and supervision that I received from Tony.

Several institutions have generously supported my research. I would like to thank the Social Science Research Council, the Andrew W. Mellon Foundation, the Bibliographical Society of America, the DAAD, the University of Notre Dame, the Renaissance Society of America, the Josephine de Karman Fellowship Trust, the Descartes Centre for the History and Philosophy of the Sciences and the Humanities at Utrecht University, the Department of History and Art History at Utrecht University, the Department of Byzantine and Modern Greek Studies at the University of Vienna, the Forschungszentrum Gotha of the University of Erfurt, Dumbarton Oaks and the Trustees of Harvard University, and Trinity College, Cambridge. At Princeton, I received support from the Department of History, the Seeger Center for Hellenic Studies, the Committee for the Study of Late Antiquity, the Center for the Study of Religion, and the Program in the Ancient World. Travel grants from the American Historical Association, the German Historical Institute in Washington, Princeton's Dean's Fund for Scholarly Travel, and Trinity College, Cambridge made it possible to present my work at various venues. I was fortunate enough to have had occasion to present parts of my research in seminars in Tübingen, Oxford, Hamburg, Princeton, Cambridge, Cyprus, Beijing, Vienna, London, Amsterdam, Washington, and Utrecht. I am immensely grateful to the organizers of these events for invitations to speak, and to audiences there and elsewhere for their feedback. Public speaking has been one of the most important ways in which my ideas took shape, and I hope my audiences will see just how much their questions and observations have shaped the project.

Many friends and colleagues made writing this book a joy. I am particularly grateful to Gadi Algazi, Asaph Ben-Tov, Alexander Bevilacqua, Lorenzo Bondioli, Melissa Calaresu, Frederic Clark, Virginia Cox, Lillian Datchev, Jan van Doren, Theodor Dunkelgrün, Christian Flow, Markus Friedrich, Maartje van Gelder, Yonathan Glazer-Eytan, Tobias Graf, Philip Hahn, Heather Hyde Minor, Carina Johnson, Sachiko Kusukawa, Mary Laven, Ian Maclean, Hannah Marcus, Jan Machielsen, Judith Pollmann, Ulinka Rublack, Joan-Pau Rubiés, Hester Schadee, Richard Serjeantson, Jeremy Schneider, Cecilia Tarruell, Will Theiss, Alexandra Walsham, Joanna Weinberg, Elizabeth Yale, and Luca Zenobi for conversation and astute and insightful feedback. Robyn Radway offered her invaluable advice as well as her working notes on more than one occasion. Adam Beaver taught me more about my research than I realized at the time. At Cambridge, the community and companionship of other "Title A" fellows kept me sane, as did dinners and drinks with friends.

My colleagues and students in Utrecht offered further inspiration, and much-needed intellectual nourishment, as I completed this book. In Amsterdam, the "leesclub" and the "ravioliclub" were always a welcome distraction from work. Madeline McMahon and Tom Tölle have helped in ways I cannot express in words: thanks for joining me on this crazy ride and for making me an infinitely better historian. I am truly blessed to have Daan Welle and Gijs Doorn in my life: your friendship has sustained me throughout this project and will hopefully support me for many more years to come.

Several communities at Princeton made this book possible. Princeton's Center for Hellenic Studies became my home away from home when I moved to the United States for my graduate studies. I want to thank Carol, Chris, Eleni, and Monique for all their help and support throughout the years. I owe an enormous debt to Dimitri Gondicas, who enabled this project in countless ways and who helped me believe in the project. Three visits to the Monastery of St. John the Baptist on Mount Menoikeion in northern Greece changed my life. I am beyond grateful to the Sisters of the monastery for their unconditional hospitality, kindness, love, and generosity. Many thanks to Judy Hanson, Lee Horinko, Kristy Novak, and Jackie Wasneski from the Department of History for always helping me out when I had yet another silly question. One community made my time in Princeton truly special: many thanks to my Winthrop family—Christian, Frederic, Jenny, Maddy, and Tony—for all the crazy adventures we shared.

Since starting my studies, I have benefited immensely from the intellectual generosity and mentorship of my teachers and colleagues. I am indebted to Arnoud Visser for introducing me to the history of reading many years ago and for his continuous support ever since. I have incurred many debts to Renate Dürr, who not only welcomed me into her Tübingen home on various occasions but also offered feedback on my work that completely changed the way I looked at Crusius and sixteenth-century Lutheranism. Many thanks to Constanze Güthenke for facilitating four months of writing in the bliss of Corpus Christi's college library and to Lyndal Roper for including me in her *privatissimum* during my time at Oxford. John-Paul Ghobrial has been a constant source of support and advice, for which I am beyond grateful. Guy Geltner did more than anyone to turn me into a historian: thank you so much for all that you've done since I first sat down in your class on medieval monasticism.

Numerous librarians and archivists helped me along the way. I wish to thank Steve Ferguson, Eric White, and the staff of Princeton's Special Collections for their help. Alain St. Pierre offered support when I could not access important materials at a crucial stage of the project. None did more to guide me through the thicket of *Crusiana* than the librarians in Tübingen. I wish to thank them, and Frau Mehringer and Herr Lager in particular, for their support, kindness, efficiency, and knowledge of the intricacies of Crusius's *Nachlass*. Their expertise has enriched this book more than I can describe. I am also grateful for the scans they made in the final stage of the project. It has been a true pleasure spending my summers in Tübingen's *Handschriftenlesesaal*, and I look forward to bringing a copy of this book to Tübingen.

Everyone at Harvard University Press has been fantastic throughout the production process. I wish to thank Emily Silk in particular for believing in the project and for helping me clarify my arguments. Her sharp observations and enormous enthusiasm made finishing this book an absolute joy and allowed me to clarify some of the larger structural arguments of the book.

My family is everything to me. Stefan showed me levels of kindness and caring that I will never be able to approximate. None of this would have been possible without the love and care of my parents, Paul and Tilly. Thank you for always encouraging me to pursue my dreams. Thank you for making sure I always had a home to come back to. And thank you for believing in me no matter what. Your support means everything to me. Aniek has brought me joy and comfort every day of the last fifteen years. I am so happy to have you in my life and so grateful that I got to take this crazy journey with you at my side. I cannot wait to embark on new adventures together with our beautiful daughter, Emma.

Index

Acta et scripta theologorum Wirtembergensium, 55–62, 196, 207, 226, 227. *See also* correspondence, between Jeremias II and Lutheran Tübingen
adiaphora, 25
alba amicorum, 136–138
al-Ḥajarī, Aḥmad ibn Qāsim, 117
alms collecting, 80–97, 99, 138; as a practice in Greek Orthodoxy, 80–81, 216; in Tübingen, 77, 104, 127, 130; suspicions about, 92, 97
amanuenses, 141–142, 158–159, 162, 238. *See also* sociability
Americas, early modern European contact with, 8, 12, 14, 40, 107, 148, 230
Anabaptism, 48, 89
Andreae, Jacob, 24–27, 30, 33, 34, 36, 39–41, 56, 182
Anghiera, Pietro Martire d', 107, 191
Anglicanism, 15, 52, 212
Annales Suevici, 6, 199, 239–240
annotations. *See* reading
antiquarianism, 122, 192
Antonia, Greek visitor, 82, 117
Apian, Peter, 173
Apian, Philipp, 173–174, 184
Apollonius of Tyana, 50
apostasy. *See* conversion
apostles. *See* Early Church

Arabic: Crusius's inability to read, 154, 155; documents written in, 8, 39, 103, 154, 203; European study of, 9, 39, 117, 189, 203, 225
Argyropoulos, Joannes, 219
Argyrus, Andreas, 83, 127, 133; alms collected by, 86; gifts from, 136; as information agent, 87, 98, 112, 114, 121, 128
Argyrus, Lukas, 83, 98, 121, 127, 128, 133, 136
Aristotle, 185, 221
armchair ethnography, 13–14, 107, 126
astrology, 172–173
Athens, 210, 211, 236, 240; ancient, 51, 53, 205; Ottoman, 78, 121–125, 160, 186, 221, 224
Athos, 121, 123, 124–125, 164, 183
Augsburg, 56, 78, 83, 85, 121–122, 159, 164, 166
Augsburg Confession, 24, 56; Catholic reaction to, 58, 226; history of, 25–26; Greek Orthodox reaction to, 30–35, 56; Greek version of, 22, 40, 58
Augsburg Interim, 4
Augustine, 52, 64
aural literacy, 108–109
autographs, 157
autopsy, 10, 14, 94, 106, 127

Bamberg, 3, 63
Baronio, Cesare, 62
Basel, 99–100, 103, 177, 193–199, 221
Basil the Great, 15, 51–52, 124, 151–152
Báthory, Sigismund, 171–174
Báthory, Stephen, 55
Battle of Lepanto, 84, 86, 111, 119
Bebenhausen, 34, 37, 145
Belon, Pierre, 199, 210, 211, 214
Biondo, Flavio, 204–205
Blossius, Sebastian, 146
Bodin, Jean, 115, 200
Book of Concord, 26, 56, 90. *See also* Formula of Concord
books, as agents of religious reform, 41, 71–72, 90
books and manuscripts, as material texts, 148–159
Books of Hours, 47, 53
Buondelmonti, Cristoforo, 122
Byron, Lord, 6
Byzantine history, early modern interests in, 167–168, 208–209, 216–219, 220
Byzantium, name for Ottoman Greece, 160, 189

Cabasylas, Symeon, 182, 221
calligraphy, Ottoman, 103, 152–154
Calonas, Gabriel, 81, 87, 92, 128, 136, 166; as an informant, 112, 121, 195; biography of, 83; prosopography of, 99
Calvinism, 15, 26, 197
Cantacuzenus, Michael, 35
captivity narratives, 81–89, 92, 103, 105, 117, 216, 219
Casaubon, Isaac, 20, 62, 90n39
catechism, 41, 89–90, 109, 135–136, 138
Catholicism: interests in Greek Orthodoxy, 15–17; knowledge of the *Turcograecia*, 226; missionary efforts, 40, 124; response to the Lutheran exchange with Jeremias II, 55–62
Censura Orientalis Ecclesiae, 55–57
Chalkokondyles, 158, 208, 218
Charles V, 66, 68

China, 8, 45, 116
chorography, 122n67, 204–209
Christoph, Duke of Württemberg, 5
Chrysostom, John, 15, 50, 70, 71
Church History. *See* ecclesiastical scholarship
Chytraeus, David, 48–49, 56, 92, 197
Cicero, 4, 86, 98, 191
coins, 5, 162, 163, 183, 192
Collegiate Church, 5, 7, 71, 85, 89, 90, 142, 144–148, 171
Collegium Illustre, 5, 130, 145–146, 238
comparison, as a scholarly practice, 151, 167, 201–202, 204–211
Compendium Theologiae, 33–35, 58
Constantine XI, Byzantine Emperor, 217, 220
Constantinople. *See* Istanbul
conversation, 78, 141, 170; and material culture, 135–138; and the household, 130–135, 163; opportunity to learn Greek, 110–117, 224; way to visualize, 117–127; knowledge making, 13–14, 106–108, 108–110, 138, 143, 147, 170; embodied nature of, 127–130
conversion, 63–64, 88–91, 93, 95–96
Corona Anni, 7, 71–73
correspondence, between Jeremias II and Lutheran Tübingen, 16, 22–24, 29–39, 42–43, 55–62, 196, 207, 226
Costume books, 126, 186
Council of Ferrara-Florence, 16, 28
Covel, John, 227
Credibility, 78–80, 87, 91–104, 190
Crusius, Martin: biography of, 3–8; children of, 5, 133, 134, 146, 238; *Civitas Coelestis*, 135, 138; commentary of Homer, 7, 194n45; death of, 7; descendants of, 237–239; diary of, 2, 7, 18, 240–241; dreams of, 72, 174–175, 196–197; eating a Cypriot dish, 128; education and upbringing of, 3–4, 44–45, 62–72, 109–110; Greek grammars by, 4, 7, 100, 191–192; household of, 5, 130–135, 141–142, 145–146, 158–159; library of, 2,

5, 18, 237–238; *Nachlass*, 237–242; name and signature of, 155–157; philhellenism of, 5, 46; portrait of, 136–138, 163, 239; teaching by, 5, 34, 86, 127, 150, 176; *Panhaeresium*, 73; parents of, 62–72, 231–233; travel by, 6, 99–100; wives of, 99, 100, 130–135, 146, 170
cultural bias, 9–11, 202–204, 229–230

deceit, suspicions of, 89, 90–91, 91–97. *See also* credibility
decline, narratives of, 3, 10–11, 15, 111, 201, 204–224, 228–230
descriptive geography. *See* chorography
devşirme, 95, 183
dictionaries, 111, 203, 224
diplomacy, European-Ottoman, 24–29, 203
discovery, as a category of historical analysis, 14–15
doctrine of justification, 31, 36, 47, 48, 63
Donatus, Stamatius, 91, 96, 127, 128; alms collecting by, 85–86, 94, 99; as an informant, 111–115, 121, 124–126, 128, 186–187, 189, 224, 226; background of, 81, 96; gifts exchanged with, 135–136; biography of, 82
Dondis, Joannes, 88–91, 118–121, 135
Dositheos II, Patriarch of Constantinople, 227
Dousa, George, 210
dress, as identity marker, 98–99, 186–187

Early Church, 22–23, 28, 31, 32, 38, 48, 52, 183
Eastern Christianity, 9, 15–16, 39–42, 79–81, 105, 236. *See also* Greek Orthodox Church
Eber, Paul, 53–55
Ecclesiastical scholarship, 32, 57, 62, 97, 179, 189–193
Egypt, 51, 162–163, 182, 184
Eisen, Simon, 124
encounter, histories of cultural, 11–15
energeia, 123
Enzlin, Matthaeus, 145

Epictetus, 136
Erasmus, 52–53
Esslingen, 99–100, 131, 240
Ethiopian Church, 39, 107
ethnography, hybrid nature of, 11–15
eucharist, 25–31
Eusebius of Caesarea, 15, 49–52, 74, 140, 193, 208
evangelization. *See* proselytization
eyewitnessing. *See* autopsy

Fickler, Johann Baptist, 56–58
Filioque, controversy, 28
Flacius Illyricus, Matthias, 26, 51–52, 62, 193
food, 128–130, 147–148
Formula of Concord, 26, 33, 34, 36, 42, 148. *See also* Book of Concord
Fra Mauro, 122
friendship, 176. *See also* sociability

Gabriel I, archbishop of Ohrid, 76–78, 82, 103, 122, 127, 130
gender. *See* households
genealogy, 98, 216–219, 231–233
Georgievicz, Bartholomaeus, 216
Gerlach, Stephan, 40, 49, 91–92, 94, 101, 128, 166, 182; and the *Turcograecia*, 197, 199; appointment as chaplain, 25; as an information agent, 111, 118, 142, 151, 154–155, 159–167, 171–174, 185, 186–189, 211–213, 218, 220; documents brought home by, 124, 158, 165, 166, 179; on Greek women, 162, 184; on spoken Greek, 223; on the Ottoman Turks, 219; role in the exchange with Jeremias II, 27–29, 30–42
Germanograecia, 6, 182, 199, 227; argument of, 207–208, 219; evidence collected in, 222, 229; printing of, 195, 198
Gibbon, Edward, 2, 6, 228–229
gift giving, 135–138
Gilles, Pierre, 161, 183
global history, 3, 17–18, 235
Gnesio-Lutherans, 26
good works, 25, 31, 36, 47, 48, 90, 139

Gorski, Jacob, 58–61
Grebern, 3, 70
Greece: Crusius's vision of, 179–182, 185–186, 201–209; in the European imagination, 8–11, 14–15, 177–179, 209–215, 236–237
Greek, ancient: interest in, 9, 28, 46, 111; teaching of, 4–5, 7; as a yardstick to measure decline, 206–207
Greek, vernacular: books written in, 110–118, 165–166; classifications of, 46n5, 110–111, 182; difficulty to read, 118, 149; interests in, 46, 81, 110–118, 123, 128–129, 185, 222–225
Greek Orthodox Church: alms collecting practices in, 80–81; antiquity of, 15–16; correspondence with Lutheran Tübingen, 29–39; depictions of, 186–189; European interests in, 11–12, 15–16, 22–24, 42, 46–55, 151, 161, 208; experiences under Ottoman rule, 10, 80–88; ideas about Lutheranism, 28–29, 31–39; opinion about the *Turcograecia*, 226–228; object of proselytization, 25, 32–33, 41, 71–72, 237
Greek War of Independence, 7, 209, 214
Gregory XIII, Pope, 16, 40, 56, 57, 78, 82
Gruppenbach, Georg, 7, 194, 197–198
Grynaeus, Johann Jacob, 197

Halbritter, Johan, 145–146
Hamberger, Georg, 145
Haug, Johann Jakob, 165–166
Haus, Bernard, 158
Hebrew, 4, 8, 37, 38, 39, 140
Heerbrand, Jacob, 34–36, 57, 58, 90, 91, 145–146, 171
Heineccius, Johann Michael, 210, 212–215
Henricpetri, Sebastian, 179, 194, 195, 198, 199, 200
historical topography. *See* chorography
history writing, 178, 190–191
Hitzler, Georg, 145
Hochmann, Johann, 145
Hoeschel, David, 166

Holy Roman Empire, global dimensions of, 16–17, 40–42
Homer, 7, 135, 162, 181, 182, 205, 206, 239; *Batrachomyomachia*, 181, 225; *Iliad*, 7, 112, 135; *Odyssey*, 182; teaching of, 5, 74, 163, 239
Horologion, 47, 49, 54
Horst, Jacob, 171
household: gendered nature of, 130–135; site of knowledge making, 106–107, 114, 127–130, 141–142, 163

Identification, processes of, 97–104
idolatry, 48–49, 50, 93
images, knowledge making through, 119–121, 123–127, 152–157, 186–189
Ingolstadt, 56–57
Islam: conversion to, 40, 93, 95, 183, 213; European study of, 9, 168, 203, 213, 235
Istanbul, 22, 35, 40–41, 92, 122, 161, 223, 240–241; and Tübingen, 29–39; captives in, 82, 84, 97; descriptions of, 122; diplomatic hub, 24–29, 159–165, 203; Greek books in, 164–166, 179; map of, 183–184; monuments in, 163, 183; news about, 170. *See also* patriarchate of Constantinople

Jeremias II, Patriarch of Constantinople, 87, 95, 101, 161, 163; audience with, 27–28; Lutheran correspondence with, 22–24, 29–39, 55, 215
Jesuits, 12, 40, 41, 45, 56, 116, 195–196
Josephus, 232
Judaism, 8, 14, 140
Julius Caesar, 232

Kepler, Johannes, 5, 172–174
Koran, 58, 154
Kraus, Martin, 3–4, 62–72, 231–233

Langius, Johann Michael, 224–225
letters of recommendation, 39, 80–82, 85, 101–104, 184
lexicography, 111–117, 224, 225

Lindanus, Willem, 56–57
Livy, 190
Louis III, Duke of Württemberg, 25
Luther, Martin, 20, 32, 43, 49, 70, 73, 140, 196; and Johann Eck, 57; Bible translation by, 68–69; death of, 67; fascination with the Early Church, 183; household of, 133; portrait of, 36; preaching by, 4, 63–64; translations of, 40; writings by, 90, 167–169
Lutheranism: calendar, 53–55; Catholic attacks on, 41, 55–62; encounter with Greek Orthodoxy, 15–16, 22–24, 29–39, 42–43; faith in book, 41, 71; factionalism in, 25–27, 56; global dimension of, 15–17, 39–42; Greek views on, 28–29; interests in signatures, 157; in Tübingen, 5, 24, 65, 147–148; missionary efforts, 17, 25, 32–33, 39–42, 71–72, 88–91, 235–236, 237

Maestlin, Michael, 172–174
Magdeburg Centuries, 193
Maier, Jakob, 158, 238
Manasses, Constantine, 46, 158, 208
manuscripts, 18; Greek preference for, 164; scholarly interests in, 111, 148–159, 241–242
Manutius, Aldus, 115
marginalia. *See* reading
Margunius, Maximus, 227
Martyrologium Romanum, 53
materiality, of documents, 103, 142, 148–159, 192
Mauricius, Philippus, 92, 94–96, 101–102, 112, 123
Maximilian II, Holy Roman Emperor, 25
mediation, cultural, 9–11, 106–108, 202–204
Mediterranean, history of, 9–11
Megisser, Hieronymus, 158
Melanchthon, Philip, 4, 20, 26, 70, 144
Memmingen, 4, 48, 176
Metrophanes III, Patriarch of Constantinople, 35, 37

Meursius, Johannes, 224
Milander, Engelbert, 165
missionary work. *See* proselytization
Monardes, Nicolás, 107
monokondylon. *See* signatures
moriscos, 93, 117
Moryson, Fynes, 211
Moser, Johann Jacob, 239
Mystakides, Basileos Athanasiou, 240–241
Müller, Veit, 7, 238, 240
music, 82, 109–110, 114, 117, 147, 161, 185

Nauclerus, Johannes, 193
Nazianzus, Gregory of, 233
Neander, Michael, 166, 224
news, 5, 93, 147, 167–174, 175–176, 203, 228
Nicodemism. *See* deceit, suspicions of

observation. *See* autopsy
Oesterlin, Michael, 158
Oporinus, Johannes, 100, 103, 192, 200, 208
orality, 70, 107–110, 109n9, 110–127, 186–189
orientalism, 3, 203–204, 235, 237
Orthodoxy. *See* Greek Orthodox Christianity
orthography, 119, 150–151, 222, 223
Osiander, Lucas, 34–36, 39, 47, 59, 96, 148, 162, 166
Ostein, Leonard, 179, 198, 199
Ottoman Turks: European fears about, 5–6; news about, 167–170

Pachymeres, George, 157, 208
Padua, 85, 165, 166, 167, 221
Palaeologus, Daniel, 82, 123–125, 127
Palaeologus, Thomas, 91
Papadatos, Cosmas, 88–91, 119
Paraskeva, Joannes Constantinus, 84, 87, 127
patriarchate of Constantinople, European study of, 186–189, 207, 213. *See also* Greek Orthodox Church
Peasants' War, 147
Peiresc, Nicholas-Claude Fabri de, 122

penmanship, 18, 142, 152, 155–157, 159, 175
Pfaff, Karl, 240
philhellenism, 2, 3, 6, 46, 202, 214, 236, 237
Philippists, 26
Pietism, 17, 41, 235
Plato, 150, 205, 206, 221
Poland, 82–84, 101
Poliziano, Angelo, 150
Polybius, 190
Pomponius Mela, 204
portents. *See* astrology
Portolanos, 118–120
prejudice. *See* cultural bias
primary sources, 57, 177–178, 179–182, 190–191, 199
prognostications. *See* astrology
proselytization: Catholic, 12, 16–17, 40; Lutheran, 14, 16–17, 25, 32–33, 39–42, 71–72, 235–236, 237
Ptolemy, 122, 204
publishing, 6–7, 193–198

Quintilian, 98

Ranke, Leopold von, 214
reading: as a collaborative endeavor, 110–117; as an occasion to travel, 185–186; as a religious practice, 46–55; as a tool for learning languages, 110–117; in religious disputes, 55–62
record keeping, practices of, 5, 12, 18, 234
Reformation, global dimensions of, 15–17
Republic of Letters, 20, 108, 143, 166
Reuchlin, Johannes, 4, 219
Reuss, Jeremias David, 240
Rhoner, Sybilla, 130–132, 135
Rhoner, Wolfgang, 170, 172
Ricci, Matteo, 20, 45–46, 116
Ritter, Matthaeus, 194, 198
Rudolph II, Holy Roman Emperor, 171
Ruggieri, Michele, 116
Rycaut, Paul, 212, 214

Sahagún, Bernadino de, 20, 116
Salzburg, 56, 83, 85

Sandys, George, 210
Scaliger, Joseph Justus, 6, 200, 225–226
Scherer, Georg, 57–58
Scheurlin, Johan, 166
Schmalkaldic War, 4, 44, 66–68, 70, 72
scholarly persona, 136–137, 143, 155–158
Schweigger, Salomon, 30, 41, 166, 184, 212; as an information agent, 36–37, 49, 111, 118, 142, 152, 155, 159–164; catechism by, 40, 135–136, 138
scripture. *See* tradition and scripture, relationship between
seals, 99, 152–54, 155
Seidel, Bruno, 92, 166
Selim II, Sultan, 80, 168, 228
Seng, Jeremias, 165–166
sermons, as evidence of faith, 27, 30, 70–72, 73, 135
Severus, Gabriel, 111, 112, 182, 227–228
signatures, study of, 136–138, 149, 152–153, 154–157, 164, 194
sincerity. *See* deceit, suspicions of
Sinzendorf, Johann Joachim von, 40
Smith, Thomas, 212, 214
sociability: and food, 128–130, 163, 170; in the household, 129, 130–135, 146, 163; in the university town, 141–142, 145–148, 163, 170; Ottoman-European, 29
Socolovius, Stanislav, 55–60
stereotypes, creation of, 10, 79, 105, 230
Stetter, Eusebius, 145, 147
Stift, 5, 25, 65, 131, 146, 147, 172, 240
Stiftskirche. *See* Collegiate Church
Strabo, 122, 204
Strasbourg, 4, 65, 66, 68, 83
streets, as conduits for learning, 147
Sturm, Johannes, 4, 65
Stuttgart, 1, 25, 39, 64–65, 140, 162, 239, 240; archives in, 239, 240; authorities in, 89; court of the duke in, 25, 39, 140, 159; as a destination to collect alms, 94, 95
Suda lexicon, 50, 51
Suleiman the Magnificent, Sultan, 168
superstition, 35, 43, 73, 93, 210, 212
Synod of Jerusalem, 227

INDEX

Taritzius, Jonas, 127
Thalius, Johannes, 39
Tholoitis, Joannes, 81, 86, 112, 123, 127
Thucydides, 150, 163, 206
Tourkokratia, 10, 211
tradition and scripture, relationship between, 36–39, 52
translation, 27, 34–35, 56–61, 181–182, 185, 191; difficulties with, 148; *fidus interpres*, 60–61; of images, 124; of the *Annales Suevici*, 239; oral nature of, 110–117, 128; as a tool for proselytization, 40–41
Travel writing, 190, 192, 211, 214
Tribbechovius, Johannes, 224
Trucello, Alexandro, 81, 84–86, 87, 94, 96
Trummer, Maria Magdalena, 3, 63, 233, 238
trust, 78–80, 91–92, 102–104. *See also* credibility
Tübingen, history of, 142–148. *See also* University of Tübingen
Turcograecia, 2, 6; argument of, 10, 201–204; comparisons in, 205–209; content and composition of, 12, 178–189, 199; evidence collected in, 216–224; models for, 189–193; origins of, 179; publishing history of, 193–198; reception of, 224–228, 239; sales of, 199–200
Turkish, Ottoman, 103, 115, 152–154, 189, 203, 225

Ulm, 4, 65, 66–68, 78, 85, 170
Ulrich, Duke of Württemberg, 4, 65, 131
Ungnad, David, 24–25, 27
University of Tübingen: centennial jubilee of, 109–110, 144; graduates of, 165, 166, 167, 172, 239; history of, 65, 143–148, 145n4; library of, 189, 237–238, 239, 241; Lutheran stronghold, 5, 24–25, 65, 148; learned sociability at, 142–148, 158–159, 163, 170, 171–172, 174, 175, 234
university town, as a category of analysis, 142–148, 175–176, 234
unleavened bread, 28, 31

Valla, Lorenzo, 150
Venice, Republic of, 82, 166, 170, 175, 184; as a destination for itinerant Greeks, 78, 83, 85, 95; Greeks living in, 5, 111, 182, 227–228; as a market for Greek books and manuscripts, 87, 149, 164–166, 176
Vermigli, Pietro Martyre, 48
Vetscher, Catherina, 76, 100, 131, 133, 134–135, 146
Vienna, 25, 170, 198
virtual witnessing. *See* visualization
Vischer, Hieronymus, 118, 165, 166
visualization, 117–127, 185–186
Vogler, Catharina, 99, 130, 131, 135
Vossius, Gerard, 225

walking, as a form of scholarly sociability, 147
Weigenmaier, Georg, 39–40, 147, 154, 172
Welling, Heinrich, 170
Wittenberg, 4, 5, 26, 57, 63, 65, 194–196, 197
Württemberg, 4, 25, 40, 41, 65, 71, 72, 240

ziteia. *See* alms collecting
Zonaras, Joannes, 51, 208
Zygomalas, Joannes, 27, 29, 161, 162, 165
Zygomalas, Theodosius, 35, 37, 40, 49, 87, 161–165, 213; as an informant, 111, 164, 213, 220; letters by, 158, 163, 164, 181, 185, 220–222, 223–224
Zwinger, Theodor, 197, 221
Zwinglianism, 25, 195, 197